John Owen, Richard Baxter and the Formation of Nonconformity

TIM COOPER
University of Otago, New Zealand

ASHGATE

© Tim Cooper 2011

Published by
Ashgate Publishing Limited
Wey Court East
Union Road
Farnham
Surrey, GU9 7PT
England

Ashgate Publishing Company
Suite 420
101 Cherry Street
Burlington
VT 05401-4405
USA

www.ashgate.com

British Library Cataloguing in Publication Data
Cooper, Tim, 1970-
    John Owen, Richard Baxter and the Formation of Nonconformity.
    1. Owen, John, 1616-1683. 2. Owen, John, 1616–1683 – Political and social views.
    3. Baxter, Richard, 1615-1691. 4. Baxter, Richard, 1615–1691 – Political and social
    views. 5. Dissenters, Religious – England – History – 17th century. 6. Protestant
    churches – Doctrines – History – 17th century. 7. Religion and politics – England –
    History – 17th century. 8. Great Britain – History – Civil War, 1642–1649 –
    Influence. 9. England – Church history – 17th century. I. Title
    280.4'0942'09032–dc22

Library of Congress Cataloging-in-Publication Data
Cooper, Tim, 1970-
    John Owen, Richard Baxter, and the Formation of Nonconformity / Tim Cooper.
       p.   cm.
    Includes bibliographical references (p.   ) and index.
    1. Owen, John, 1616–1683. 2. Baxter, Richard, 1615-1691. 3. Dissenters, Religious –
    England. 4. Great Britain – Church history – 17th century. I. Title.
    BX5207.O88C66 2012
    285'.9092'242 – dc23   2011027837

ISBN   9780754663614 (hbk)
ISBN   9781409439769 (ebk)

Printed and bound in Great Britain by the
MPG Books Group, UK

University of Plymouth
Charles Seale Hayne Library
Subject to status this item may be renewed
via your Voyager account

http://voyager.plymouth.ac.uk
Tel: (01752) 232323

JOHN OWEN, RICHARD BAXTER AND THE FORMATION OF NONCONFORMITY

dedicated to

William M. Lamont

with deep respect and great fondness

Contents

Acknowledgements

Any list of my debts – and there are many – must begin with my family. I am so very grateful to my wife, Kate, and to my four sons – Michael, Jonathan, James and Samuel – for their patience and generosity. They were especially forbearing during my annual research trips to Britain and they graciously put up with me as my focus on 'the book' became increasingly concentrated over the final few months. I thank them for the freedom they gave me to complete this work.

I must also acknowledge the generosity and support of my colleagues within the Department of Theology and Religion at the University of Otago, particularly Professor Paul Trebilco and Professor Murray Rae, both of whom served as Head of Department during the course of the project; and my former colleague, Professor Ivor Davidson, who lent valuable encouragement, interest and advice as the book took shape. In addition, Mary Griffiths and Sandra Lindsay provided extremely able administrative support to make my research and travel so much simpler.

I am also grateful to the University of Otago for allowing me a period of study leave in 2008; and for the award of a Humanities Research Grant in 2007 and a University of Otago Research Grant in 2008. The travel funded by those grants helped me to overcome the tyranny of distance. The staff at the University of Otago Library has been unfailingly helpful, patient, innovative and supportive. So too has John Timmons, the Librarian of Hewitson Library, Knox College, Dunedin, who went out of his way to supply me with so many books I needed along the way. My colleagues in the University of Otago Early Modern Thought Research Cluster have been consistently constructive and encouraging.

There are numerous other locals who have helped me out in numerous ways. Gerard Ellis supplied me with Latin translations. Rev. Dr. Damian Wynn-Williams, Parish Priest of St Bernadette's, graciously offered me working space above his church in Caversham, Dunedin, during my study leave in 2008. Lynlea Forbes made that practically possible; and Jo St Baker – the most gifted artist I have ever met – proved a very hospitable neighbour.

My research frequently led me to Britain, where my debts continued to accumulate. I record my thanks to the consistently professional staff at the Bodleian Library, Oxford, and in London the National Archives, the British Library and especially the Dr Williams' Library. I recall with gratitude many helpful conversations with other scholars, notably Professor Conal Condren, Martin Foord, Paul Chang-Ha Lim, Susan Hardman Moore, Kelly Kapic, Brian

Kay, Alison Searle, Elliot Vernon and Professor Blair Worden. I cannot fully convey how grateful I am to Professor Neil Keeble, Professor John Spurr, Joel Halcomb and Hunter Powell for reading draft chapters. I am especially indebted to Crawford Gribben for providing feedback on an early draft of the whole book; and to Professor John Coffey who read a final draft and continued to offer timely advice to the very end. Any remaining mistakes and misunderstandings are entirely my own, but there are surely fewer of those than there would have been without the generosity of all these partners in scholarship.

As ever, I acknowledge Professor Glenn Burgess, who got me started on this journey; and Professor John Morrill, who has been consistently interested and encouraging. He offered the initial suggestion to take a look at Owen; this book is the end result. I hope it does something of what he had in mind.

It seemed only appropriate to me to dedicate this book to William M. Lamont. I first met Willie on a research trip to Britain late in 1995 during the course of my PhD on Richard Baxter, and I have been fortunate enough to meet with him again on a number of occasions during my recent journeys. I acknowledge his hospitality and generosity on those visits, but also the significance of his scholarship over many years. His work has been extremely helpful to me, especially with its cognizance of the 'darker side' of Richard Baxter. It gave me cover for developing my own interpretation of the man. Meanwhile one of Lamont's earlier books, *Godly Rule*, published in 1969, touches on many of the same themes and issues addressed in this one. I hope it will be seen as a worthy tribute to a very fine historian.

Even then, the debts are not at an end, and I fear I have forgotten others that I should have included. Early on, Justin Taylor showed himself to be heroically generous by sending me copies of most of the recent books on Owen, together with some old ones. I will not forget his investment. I am grateful to the editors of the *Journal of Ecclesiastical History* for allowing me in Chapter 1 to rework material that appeared in an article in their journal in 2010. I also appreciate the willingness of an old friend, Don Grant, to proofread the manuscript of this book; and the readiness of Kirsten Weissenberg, my desk editor at Ashgate, to work with me again in seeing it through to publication.

Finally, I note the hospitality of The Very Reverend Dr John Hall, Dean of Westminster, for allowing me to visit the Jerusalem Chamber at Westminster Abbey. This is the room in which John Owen and Richard Baxter met for the first time; it was a very special, moving moment to have travelled all the way from New Zealand several centuries later to stand in that space. It is a beautiful and elegant chamber, but it is not large. One wonders how the divines of the Westminster Assembly possibly managed to fit into it during the 1640s. And there, in November 1654, Owen and Baxter faced each other at last. What an awkward moment it must have been, for reasons we are about to uncover.

Abbreviations

CCRB	*Calendar of the Correspondence of Richard Baxter*, ed. N.H. Keeble and Geoffrey F. Nuttall. 2 vols. Oxford: Oxford University Press, 1991.
CJ	*Journals of the House of Commons*
CJO	*The Correspondence of John Owen (1616–1683) with an Account of his Life and Work*, ed. Peter Toon. Cambridge: James Clarke and Co, 1970.
DWL MS *BC*	Dr Williams' Library, London: Manuscript: *Baxter Correspondence*
DWL MS *BT*	Dr Williams' Library, London: Manuscript: *Baxter Treatises*
Practical Works	*The Practical Works of Richard Baxter with a Preface Giving Some Account of the Author, and of this Edition of his Practical Works: An Essay on his Genius, Works and Times; and a Portrait.* 4 vols. Ligonier, PA: Soli Deo Gloria reprint, 1990–1.
Rel. Bax.	Richard Baxter. *Reliquiae Baxterianae, or, Mr. Richard Baxter's narrative of the most memorable passages of his life and times*, ed. Matthew Sylvester. 1696.
SP	State Papers
Thomason Tracts	*Catalogue of the Pamphlets, Books, Newspapers, and Manuscripts Relating to the Civil War, the Commonwealth, and Restoration, Collected by George Thomason, 1640–1661.* 2 vols. London: William Clowes and Sons, 1908.
Works	*The Works of John Owen*, ed. William H. Goold, 16 vols. Edinburgh: Banner of Truth reprint, 1983.

A Note on Quotations and References

Several principles have been observed in the quotation of primary sources. Dates have been modernized. Original spelling has been maintained, but obvious printer's errors have been silently corrected. All contractions, abbreviations and ampersands have been silently extended. The only significant alteration is in the use of square brackets, which have been silently replaced. Where they served as speech or quotation marks, these have been used. Where they functioned as rounded brackets, these also have been used. Thus all square brackets now signal additions to the quoted text.

Each reference to Richard Baxter's correspondence includes the names of sender and recipient, and the date of each letter. These dates have been extracted from N.H. Keeble and Geoffrey F. Nuttall's *Calendar of the Correspondence of Richard Baxter*. All quotations from the correspondence have been referenced in the following way: DWL [Dr. Williams' Library] MS [Manuscript] *BC* [Baxter Correspondence] [volume] vi. [folio] 120r (*CCRB* [letter] #54). The same format is used for the treatises, except that *BT* replaces *BC*, and the item number is added. For example, DWL MS *BT* vii.1r, item #218 (*CCRB* #1150). This is consistent with Hans Boersma's referencing system in *A Hot Pepper Corn* and with my first book on Baxter, *Fear and Polemic in Seventeenth-Century England*. A similar pattern is used in references to Owen's correspondence.

When I have expanded on biblical verses or allusions in the footnotes I have used *The New Revised Standard Version* (Nashville, TN: Thomas Nelson, 1990). Where I have discussed verses in the text I have used the form of words quoted by the author concerned.

In all references to primary sources the place of publication is London unless otherwise stated.

Introduction

Owen as a man, as a human being, still remains an elusive character. After reading the *Reliquiae* or Dr Nuttall's biography one feels that one knows Owen's contemporary, Richard Baxter, as a real, living person, but the same cannot be said of Owen.

Peter Toon[1]

This book is about a relationship both fraught and consequential. It seeks to answer two very specific questions: why did John Owen and Richard Baxter not like each other; and what effect did their strained relationship have on the development of English nonconformity?

To place the two men briefly in perspective, John Owen (1616–83) came to prominence in the 1640s first as an author then as a preacher to Parliament. During the Interregnum he served as a chaplain to Oliver Cromwell in his Irish and Scottish campaigns, and then as Dean of Christ Church and Vice-Chancellor of Oxford University. He quickly emerged as a leading figure within the English Congregationalist movement, joining the Dissenting Brethren in pursuing a policy of ecclesiastical freedom from imposed conformity and of liberty of conscience. He remained close to politically powerful Congregationalist figures and after the Restoration he continued to guide the movement through difficult political waters until his death in 1683. Over the course of his life he was the author of around 80 books: some of them extremely long, all of them weighty, and many of them seeking to shore up the shrinking fortunes of Reformed Protestantism.

Richard Baxter (1615–91) was one of only a few authors to exceed Owen's tally, writing around 140 books. Unlike Owen, he also left behind a massive pile of private papers and manuscripts, well over one thousand items of correspondence and a sprawling autobiography. He came to national prominence during the 1650s through his early published works both polemical and devotional, and through his successful demonstration at Kidderminster of what pastoral and parish discipline could look like within the unsettled landscape of Interregnum England. The Restoration put an end to those efforts, but Baxter continued to work towards an effective national church structure and the comprehension of

---

[1]   Peter Toon, *God's Statesman: The Life and Work of John Owen* (Grand Rapids, MI: Zondervan, 1971), 176.

tolerable dissenters. He could never be ignored as a leader within the Presbyterian stream of nonconformity, though his standing declined in the years leading to his death in 1691, at the age of 76.

Focus and Proportion

I need to be precise at the outset about the parameters and the proportions of this book, since the two men most in view were such imposing figures. Their careers were, as even a brief summary has indicated, long, complex and significant. That reality signals the challenge involved in bringing Owen and Baxter together in a book of any manageable size. Combined, they might easily swamp the project, and sink it. Therefore, I wish to be clear that the focus of this book is not Owen and Baxter – it is the *relationship* between Owen and Baxter. This is a subtle distinction with important implications. This book is not about their lives, as such. Rather, I have selected certain aspects of their careers only as they have explanatory value in, say, accounting for the strain in their relationship. Even then, I have not said all that might be said about those dimensions under discussion. For example, in Chapter 4 I consider Owen's work as Vice-Chancellor, but only in enough depth to demonstrate that he possessed a quality of political skill that stands in contrast to that of Baxter and to identify a strand within Owen's temperament that would make Baxter's missteps particularly grating on Owen. A complete investigation of Owen's service at Oxford still needs to be written and I have felt no compulsion to write it here. Nor have I gone so far as to detail every point of difference or similarity between the two men. I have certainly dealt with the main ones, which is enough to answer the questions I have set for myself; it would be tedious and unnecessary to supply an exhaustive list of contrasts. Finally, I am aware of dimensions of this project that might have been further enriched. For instance, the wider geographical interconnections with Ireland, New England and the Continent, and the nature of the broader networks – both overlapping and distinct – to which Owen and Baxter belonged, deserve more attention than I have given them here.[2] As far

---

[2]   For an indication of how fruitful this might be for Owen, see Francis J. Bremer, *Increase Mather's Friends: The Trans-Atlantic Congregational Network of the Seventeenth Century* (Worcester, MA: American Antiquarian Society, 1984). Carl Trueman, who does so much to locate Owen in a broad intellectual context, says that theological projects such as his were 'first and foremost European events in terms of their sources, content, dialogue partners and means of expression, as well as their authors' self-understanding as being part of a European-wide movement for the reformation of the church'. Carl Trueman, 'Puritan Theology as Historical Event: A Linguistic Approach to the Ecumenical Context', in *Reformation and Scholasticism:*

as possible I have tried to keep a light touch, but not too light; to say enough to account for their relationship without getting bogged down in unnecessary detail. Only the reader can say if I have been successful.

As a further challenge, the contrast in the autobiographical styles of Owen and Baxter has had a significant effect on their historiographies. It is decades now since F.J. Powicke laid his hand on the shoulder of the young Geoffrey Nuttall with this encouragement: 'Read Baxter; read Baxter; read Baxter. He touches on every point at issue in the seventeenth century, and you will never regret the time spent on him. He has a flowing easy style which makes him pleasant to read, and you will find he grows upon you, until you come to know him and to love him.'[3] And that was exactly Nuttall's experience: 'there is something about Baxter's writing which I find peculiarly affecting: the style, the self-expression, is so direct, penetrating, sure, yet so sincerely modest, almost ingenuous, and produces a strange feeling that the man is personally present, at least that he wrote this only yesterday and wrote it to *you*.'[4] The point is that no one has ever said the same thing of Owen. It is unlikely that anyone ever will.

This is not to say that Owen is without admirers, but what they find compelling are his ideas rather than the man himself. Kelly Kapic, one of Owen's capable current expositors, candidly admits that 'as much as I have learned from John Owen, it is hard for me to imagine hanging out with him at the local pub'.[5] The touch of warm and lively personal affection in those reflections on Baxter is incongruous with a typical appreciation of Owen, for his writing style was curiously impersonal. This is the man who suffered the premature death of all 11 of his children and the loss of his first wife,[6] and who makes not one single,

---

An Ecumenical Enterprise, ed. Willem J. van Asselt and Eef Dekker (Grand Rapids, MI: Baker Academic, 2001), 260. Sebastian Rehnman points out the 'almost complete absence of references to English theologians' in Owen's works, testament to his profound Continental intellectual heritage, in *Divine Discourse: The Theological Methodology of John Owen* (Grand Rapids, MI: Baker Academic, 2002), 21–4. Also, for the Irish context, see especially Crawford Gribben, *God's Irishmen: Theological Debates in Cromwellian Ireland* (Oxford: Oxford University Press, 2007).

[3]   Geoffrey F. Nuttall, 'The Personality of Richard Baxter', in *The Puritan Spirit: Essays and Addresses*, ed. Geoffrey F. Nuttall (London: Epworth Press, 1967), 104.

[4]   Ibid.

[5]   Kelly Kapic, 'John Owen Unleashed: Almost. Response to Tim Cooper', *Conversations in Religion and Theology* 6 (2008): 250.

[6]   One of Owen's children survived into adulthood, but she predeceased him. [Anon.], *A Vindication of the Late Reverend and Learned John Owen D.D.* (1684), 38; [Anon.], 'The Life of the Late Reverend and Learned John Owen D.D.', in *Seventeen Sermons Preach'd by the Late Reverend and Learned John Owen* (London: William and Joseph Marshall, 1720), xxxiv.

explicit reference to his loss in all of his writings.[7] Compare that to Baxter's *Breviate of the Life of Margaret*, which he wrote 'under the power of melting grief' shortly after the death of his wife in 1683.[8] We are told that Owen's experience of grief coloured his mature spirituality,[9] but we have to take that on trust. Likewise, Kapic's conclusion that if Owen's 'logic sometimes appears cold and crisp, its goal is warm and human'.[10] In contrast, Baxter's writing of any stamp was capable of warmth and humanity; he was invariably personal. He 'could never write for long without inserting some autobiographical reminiscence, some reference to his own experience'.[11] He presented something of himself on nearly every page, while Owen did his best to reveal nothing at all. Baxter's compulsion to lay it all out in sometimes embarrassing detail was mirrored in the totality with which Owen kept himself to himself. Owen consciously contrasted himself with Baxter's tendency to talk about himself – 'how I go, and walk, and look'.[12] 'Neither do I conceive it wisdom, in these quarrelsome days', he explained elsewhere, 'to intrust more of a man's self with others than is very necessary. The heart of man is deceitful; some that have smooth tongues have sharp teeth'.[13] And so, writing in this protective, defensive mould, he gave little of himself away. 'Owen never trusts himself to his readers. There is very little of the confidential or communicative about his mind. He was intensely self-reliant. He learned from few living men, and leaned on none. He had no close friend. Hence his private life and feelings remain for the most part a mystery still.'[14] Peter Toon, Owen's most recent biographer, says that 'Owen as a man, as a human being, still remains an elusive character. After reading the *Reliquiae* or Dr Nuttall's biography one feels that one knows Owen's contemporary, Richard

---

[7]   Godfrey Noel Vose also notes this 'enigma' in 'Profile of a Puritan: John Owen (1616–1683)', PhD Thesis, State University of Iowa, 1963, 30–31.

[8]   Richard Baxter, *A Breviate of the Life of Margaret...Wife of Richard Baxter* (1681), epistle to the reader.

[9]   John Piper, *Contending For Our All: Defending Truth and Treasuring Christ in the Lives of Athanasius, John Owen and J. Gresham Machen* (Wheaton, IL: Crossway Books, 2006), 87.

[10]   Kelly Kapic, *Communion with God: The Divine and the Human in the Theology of John Owen* (Grand Rapids, MI: Baker Academic, 2007), 235.

[11]   Geoffrey Nuttall, 'The MS. of Reliquiae Baxterianae (1696)', *Journal of Ecclesiastical History* 6 (1955): 73.

[12]   Owen, *Of the Death of Christ and of Justification* (1655): *Works*, xii.594.

[13]   Owen, *A Short Defensative About Church Government* (1646): *Works*, viii.44.

[14]   James Moffatt, *The Golden Book of John Owen: Passages from the Writing of the Rev. John Owen, M.A., D.D., Sometime Vice-Chancellor of the University of Oxford and Dean of Christ Church: Chosen and Edited with a Study of his Life and Age* (London: Hodder and Stoughton, 1904), 19–20.

Baxter, as a real, living person, but the same cannot be said of Owen'.[15] Baxter is readily accessible; Owen is not. He did not think the world was interested in his personal affairs.[16] No doubt there was genuine humility and admirable reticence in such a posture, but it is possible to feel Owen's deliberate hiddenness as a calculated rejection of the reader.

More than that, Owen wrote in such a cumbersome manner as to frustrate even his most sympathetic admirers. His nineteenth-century biographer, William Orme, for instance, conceded that the 'chief deficiency is to be found in [Owen's] style. His sentences are frequently long, perplexed, and encumbered with adjectives, often carelessly selected'.[17] Owen himself professed 'a fixed and absolute disregard for all elegance and ornaments of speech' when he wrote any of his works.[18] Thus he made few concessions to his readers. And then there is the content of Owen's theology. His staunch commitment to the fixed Calvinism of Reformed Protestantism has potentially rendered him a reactionary figure whose views on toleration seem progressive and welcome, but whose soteriology may seem to some to be harsh and uninviting.

Accompanying Owen's daunting writing style is the relative paucity of factual material when it comes to his life and career. It is difficult to resist the suspicion that this, too, was a deliberate strategy on Owen's part. We know that his younger Presbyterian contemporary, John Howe, ordered from his deathbed that his private papers be destroyed,[19] and perhaps Owen arranged the same end for his. Whatever the means or intent, we have little to go on. It was impossible for him to tidy everything away, of course, and there are in enough places obvious evidence of his having passed through. But these are stepping stones across a broad and deep-flowing river. It is difficult to pierce through the surface of things. Thus Owen's biographers have been engaged essentially in an exercise of recycling much the same set of facts. The first biographies were extremely compact, reflecting the reality of how little there was to draw on.[20] In later

---

[15]   Toon, *God's Statesman*, 176.

[16]   Owen, *Death of Christ and of Justification* (1655): *Works*, xii.612.

[17]   William Orme, 'Memoirs of the Life and Writings of Dr. Owen', in *The Works of John Owen D.D.*, ed. Thomas Russell (London: Richard Baynes, 1826), i.356.

[18]   Owen, *A Dissertation on Divine Justice* (1653): *Works*, x.494.

[19]   Martin Sutherland, *Peace, Toleration and Decay: The Ecclesiology of Later Stuart Dissent* (Carlisle: Paternoster Press, 2003), 31.

[20]   [Anon.], 'Life of John Owen'; John Asty, 'Memoirs of the Life of John Owen', in *A Complete Collection of the Sermons of the Reverend and Learned John Owen...And to the Whole are Prefixed Memoirs of His Life*, ed. John Asty (London: John Clark, 1721), i–xxxviii.

centuries a small number of biographers (especially William Orme)[21] corrected the errors in those first attempts and considerably expanded the pool of available material, but even Peter Toon, for all his additions, assembled essentially the same elements of the story. A recent MPhil thesis very ably considers a precise aspect of Owen's career, his relationship with Oliver Cromwell.[22] There was still not much in the way of new information, and plenty of broad gaps and open speculation remains. That is no fault of the student; it is testament to Owen's success in hiding his trail.[23] Again, the contrast is striking. If Baxter is impossible to avoid, Owen is nearly as difficult to find. We are faced with the effusive Baxter, the elusive Owen.

So it is no surprise to find that there has been almost no historical work done on Owen over the four decades since Toon published his biography. Perhaps we should not expect historians to wade through 24 laborious volumes of published works knowing full well that their author will throw out only the most meagre of biographical scraps and affirm a blend of theology that hardly finds favour within the modern academy. Whatever the reason, Owen is in desperate need of historical examination. I hope this book will make a contribution to the task of understanding Owen in light of the massive historiographical shifts that have occurred since the last biography so many years ago.

Fortunately, there has been regular interest in Owen from theologians and a significant resurgence of such scholarship over the last 15 years. It is impossible not to connect this resurgence with the work of Richard Muller, whose *Post-Reformation Reformed Dogmatics* did so much to redeem Protestant Scholasticism in general from the kinds of caricatures that had been similarly applied to Owen.[24] Carl Trueman has been a key figure in the Owen renaissance. He is a Reformation scholar of considerable reach whose first book on Owen examined his Trinitarian theology, particularly his doctrines of God, of the person of Christ and of the nature of satisfaction.[25] In addition, Randall Gleason

---

[21]   William Orme's first biography of Owen was *Memoirs of the Life, Writings and Religious Connexions of John Owen, D.D. Vice-Chancellor of Oxford and Dean of Christ Church, During the Commonwealth* (London: T. Hamilton, 1820). He expanded on this in 'Memoirs of Dr. Owen'.

[22]   Selwyn Leggett, 'John Owen as Religious Advisor to Oliver Cromwell 1649–1659', MPhil Thesis, Cambridge University, 2006.

[23]   I might say that this limited pool of material and published historiography has required me to rely in places on unpublished theses. Fortunately, there are some reliable and useful theses to work from.

[24]   Richard Muller, *Post-Reformation Reformed Dogmatics: The Rise and Development of Reformed Orthodoxy, ca. 1520 to ca. 1725*, 4 vols (Grand Rapids, MI: Baker Academic, 2003).

[25]   Carl R. Trueman, *The Claims of Truth: John Owen's Trinitarian Theology* (Carlisle: Paternoster Press, 1998). The quote comes from page 1.

compared the views of John Calvin and Owen on mortification; Richard Daniels examined Owen's Christology; and Sebastian Rehnman charted the rich breadth of Owen's theological and philosophical heritage.[26] Remarkably, four books on Owen's theology were published in 2007. Carl Trueman presents a general review of the major aspects of Owen's thought within its rich intellectual heritage and context.[27] Kelly Kapic and Brian Kay draw out in different ways the pastoral and devotional potential that is not always obvious within Owen's work, while Alan Spence explores Owen's efforts to grapple with Christology.[28] Together these books offer a considerable advance in Owen scholarship.[29] But the fact remains that these are works of Theology rather than History. Their appearance has made it all the more urgent to pursue the kind of comprehensive historical treatment of Owen that will complement this burst of theological research and ground Owen's theology within its proper historical context.

In contrast to Owen, Baxter has continued to generate a great deal of historiography. Following on from the earlier work of Powicke and Nuttall, William Lamont and Neil Keeble have done much to build up a comprehensive understanding of Baxter in his context.[30] And in recent years several PhD dissertations have made their way into print. My own earlier book discusses Baxter's career from the vantage point of his antipathy towards, and even obsession with, Antinomian doctrine.[31] Paul Chang-Ha Lim offers a very helpful examination of the driving concerns within Baxter's ecclesiology.[32] Bill Black describes in detail (if not always very convincingly) the origins and nature

---

[26]   Randall C. Gleason, *John Calvin and John Owen on Mortification: A Comparative Study in Reformed Spirituality* (New York: Peter Lang, 1995); Richard Daniels, *The Christology of John Owen* (Grand Rapids, MI: Reformation Heritage Books, 2004); Rehnman, *Divine Discourse*.

[27]   Carl R. Trueman, *John Owen: Reformed Catholic, Renaissance Man* (Aldershot: Ashgate, 2007).

[28]   Kapic, *Communion with God*; Brian Kay, *Trinitarian Spirituality: John Owen and the Doctrine of God in Western Devotion* (Carlisle: Paternoster, 2007); and Alan Spence, *Incarnation and Inspiration: John Owen and the Coherence of Christology* (London: T&T Clark, 2007).

[29]   For my assessment of these four books, see Tim Cooper, 'John Owen Unleashed: Almost', *Conversations in Religion and Theology* 6 (2008): 226–42.

[30]   In particular, see William M. Lamont, *Richard Baxter and the Millennium: Protestant Imperialism and the English Revolution* (London: Croom Helm, 1979) and N.H. Keeble, *Richard Baxter: Puritan Man of Letters* (Oxford: Clarendon Press, 1982).

[31]   Tim Cooper, *Fear and Polemic in Seventeenth-Century England: Richard Baxter and Antinomianism* (Aldershot: Ashgate, 2001).

[32]   Paul Chang-Ha Lim, *In Pursuit of Purity, Unity, and Liberty: Richard Baxter's Ecclesiology in Its Seventeenth-Century Context* (Leiden: Brill, 2004).

of Baxter's preferred model of parish discipline and practice.[33] On the subject of Baxter's soteriology, Hans Boersma published *A Hot Pepper Corn*, while J.I. Packer finally published his 1954 D.Phil dissertation.[34] In addition, and in a more popular, pastoral vein, Murray Capill examines Baxter's preaching; Timothy Beougher, his understanding of conversion.[35] Together all these books have added much to our understanding of Baxter, and there seems no danger of his fading away from the historiography.

I accept that I may be too starkly distinguishing Theology from History and there is a fair amount of the former in these works on Baxter. The point I wish to make, though, is that where we can identify at least seven historical treatments of Baxter over the last several decades, we cannot list even one for Owen. Therefore, placing Baxter next to Owen serves a very useful purpose. If we have relatively little to go on in the project of recovering the elusive Owen, the proximity of Baxter makes better use of what we do have. This approach to Owen prevents us from simply going over the same set of facts. It opens up the options of what we can say and the questions we can ask, and it makes for a much richer use of Owen's writings. Passages that, on their own, seem of little significance, take on new levels of meaning when placed alongside Baxter. By way of illustration, it is some time now since I was struck by one of those rare moments of scholarly inspiration. I was reading Owen's 1646 sermon to Parliament in which he applauded the liberation of England from Laudian bondage and urged Parliament to ignore those who looked about them and saw only sects, errors and heresy, only the weeds among the corn.[36] It occurred to me then that he was describing Baxter in perfect detail, even though the two had never met. That moment was the genesis of this book. It set me thinking on a long course of contrasts between Owen and Baxter and it prompted me to consider in much more detail a passage that I

---

[33]   J. William Black, *Reformation Pastors: Richard Baxter and the Ideal of the Reformed Pastor* (Bletchley: Paternoster, 2004). Black is determined to argue that Baxter gained his vision for parish discipline from Martin Bucer (see, for instance, p. 168). His book is haunted by the lack of explicit evidence for that connection. It seems highly implausible that Baxter had something to say and chose not to say it, especially when he was prepared to make links with Bucer on other issues (p. 101). I join John Morrill (foreword, p. xiv) in wishing that Black had maintained only a consonance between Baxter's views and Bucer's.

[34]   Hans Boersma, *A Hot Pepper Corn: Richard Baxter's Doctrine of Justification in Its Seventeenth-Century Context of Controversy* (Zoetmeer: Uitgeverij Boekencentrum, 1993). J.I. Packer, *The Redemption and Restoration of Man in the Thought of Richard Baxter* (Carlisle: Paternoster Press, 2003).

[35]   Murray A. Capill, *Preaching With Spiritual Vigour: Including Lessons from the Life and Practice of Richard Baxter* (Fearn: Mentor, 2003); Timothy Beougher, *Richard Baxter and Conversion: A Study of the Puritan Concept of Becoming a Christian* (Fearn: Mentor, 2007).

[36]   Owen, *Vision of Free Mercy* (1646): *Works*, viii.27–8.

might otherwise have glossed over entirely. Therefore, in this book Baxter is also acting as a foil for Owen – I hope that he will be seen in a new light. And not just Owen. I have been surprised by the extent to which Baxter is further illuminated by this juxtaposition. In particular, Baxter's vitiated view of Owen should cause us to read his post-Restoration actions vis-à-vis his Congregationalist fellow travellers in a more nuanced, cautious and critical way. The story in this book makes Owen more of a human figure and, though it is less necessary in his case, it does the same for Baxter.

On the First Question

Why did Owen and Baxter dislike each other? Even after more than three centuries of scholarly attention on the two men this question has not yet been answered.[37] Their mutual animosity has been a feature of the historiography from the very beginning – it could hardly be otherwise – but, in the main, historians have tended to point to their theological differences and assume this was a sufficient explanation for the divergence between them.[38] That is not an unreasonable assumption, since the two men certainly differed over ecclesiology and soteriology. But it does not adequately account for the animosity between them. There are two main reasons for saying this. First, Baxter was entirely capable of warm relations with people who shared precisely the same disagreements with him as he had with Owen. Second, both men began the 1640s in much the same theological territory. Both were close to Antinomian in their Calvinism and both were Presbyterians.[39] So we need to identify the factors that served to drive them apart.

This first question, therefore, helps to account for much of the shape of the book. Chapter 1 draws out their contrasting experiences of the first civil war. I argue that these profoundly shaping experiences had the effect of placing

---

[37]   Three of the more obvious places where Owen and Baxter have been juxtaposed are Ely Bates, 'Baxter and Owen', *The National Review* 15 (1862): 95–120; Alan C. Clifford, *Atonement and Justification: English Evangelical Theology 1640–1790 – An Evaluation* (Oxford: Clarendon Press, 1990); and Trueman, *Claims of Truth*, Appendix 2, 241–5. There is also Gavin McGrath's PhD thesis, 'Puritans and the Human Will: Voluntarism Within Mid-Seventeenth Century English Puritanism as Seen in the Works of Richard Baxter and John Owen', Durham, 1989. The focus in all this is largely on their theological differences.

[38]   For detailed evidence for this claim, see Tim Cooper, 'Why Did Richard Baxter and John Owen Diverge? The Impact of the First Civil War', *Journal of Ecclesiastical History* 61 (2010): 497–500.

[39]   Again, for further detail, see ibid., 500–502.

them in different worlds before they had even met. There were, one might say, supralapsarian forces at work, establishing consequences before their first falling out. In particular, they were propelled out of the first civil war pursuing contrasting soteriological agendas, which I seek to uncover in Chapter 2. Owen sought to preserve the gains that the godly forces had achieved in the Laudian defeat by preventing any sort of reversion to any doctrine (like Arminianism or Socinianism) that put human free will in the driving seat of personal salvation. Baxter, on the other hand, still recovering from his traumatic war experience, advertised his own homemade blend of soteriology that guarded any inclination to make God alone the engineer of salvation without any conceptual space for human activity and responsibility. In Chapter 3 we examine the first point of contact between the two men. It was not as inevitable as it at first may seem, and there is more than a touch of the accidental about it. Here we will begin to assess the question of blame and complicity. Despite Baxter's well-earned reputation for starting and sustaining controversy, he may be rather more innocent in the beginning of things than we have been led to believe. From there we move into the question of personality – this was in large measure a clash of personality, and it is possible to distil the precise factors provoking that clash. In Chapters 5 and 6 we consider the competing positions and agendas revealed in the contributions of Owen and Baxter towards a permanent religious settlement and godly unity in Interregnum England. Chapter 7 returns to the question of soteriology by examining the renewed dispute between them in 1655. Chapter 8 assesses the fateful events of 1659: the downfall of Richard Cromwell and Owen's alleged part in it. I suggest that we need to see 1659 – not 1660 – as the decisive turning point in Baxter's career and the moment at which his already-strained relationship with Owen passed the point of no return. The implications of this are drawn out in the final chapter, which briefly surveys the relationship between Owen and Baxter during the Restoration period.

My intention is to maintain some sort of chronological flow at the same time as distinguishing the different strata in their disagreements. By considering experience, agenda, personality and theological differences over salvation and the Church we begin to glimpse the complex, underlying, shifting forces that combined to produce the cracks on the surface. For this reason I have been careful to track their relationship in 'real time'. We cannot take the pronouncements of any person from different phases of their life and expect them always to cohere, ignoring the pressures of change and circumstance. So also I have resisted the urge to pluck evidence for the strain in this relationship from different periods. For instance, what Baxter said about Owen in, say, 1654 – the year in which they first met – emerged out of his sense of their relationship at that time, and that sense may well be different (either better or worse, or better or worse in different ways) than in, say, 1659 or, more to the point, 1664, when he began to write his autobiography. For this reason I have tried to observe the data on the relationship in their exact context with only minimal reliance on Baxter's autobiography, the *Reliquiae Baxterianae*.

All this is to uncover the reasons for the differences between the two men, but the very real commonalities between Owen and Baxter must also be kept in mind,[40] again for two reasons. First, even though Baxter observed in 1670 that 'all our business with each other had been contradiction',[41] it would misread their relationship to see only the differences and disagreements or to convey that there could be no co-operation between them. Second, it was the commonalities that made the differences so important and potentially damaging. The disagreement between Owen and Baxter was so strong only because they shared so much. For example, despite the labels they were inclined to throw around, both men shared a common Calvinist heritage and there was much common ground in their theology of salvation. In fact, both men said at different times that the differences between them, at least in the issues under debate, were slight. This made them allies of a sort, though each found the other unreliable and obstructive. They provide a specific instance of a common pattern within the history of Christianity: those who are closest to each other often have the most violent disputes. Ann Hughes saw this at work in mid-1640s intra-Puritan controversy: 'the heretic "other" is someone you know; the error is something you have worried about'.[42] Judith Maltby puts that a little more colourfully. 'It is worth remembering', she says, 'that most violence is precisely domestic violence'.[43] Thus the central question of this book is essentially the same question that William Haller asks of the Puritan movement as a whole: 'how and why did they come to differ'? 'What was there in their common religious experience which led them, the more earnestly they strove after understanding and agreement, deeper and deeper into disagreement and confusion?'[44] For this reason, the contest between Owen and Baxter will look a lot like sibling rivalry. Such rivalry is especially

---

[40] I would like to acknowledge one of the anonymous readers of my original book proposal who rightly made the point that, for all the contrasts, the similarities between Owen and Baxter should not be overlooked.

[41] *Rel. Bax.*, iii.61.

[42] Ann Hughes, *Gangraena and the Struggle for the English Revolution* (Oxford: Oxford University Press, 2004), 78. See also, pp. 80 and 81.

[43] Judith Maltby, 'Suffering and Surviving: The Civil Wars, the Commonwealth and the Formation of "Anglicanism", 1642–60', in *Religion in Revolutionary England*, ed. Christopher Durston and Judith Maltby (Manchester: Manchester University Press, 2006), 167.

[44] William Haller, 'The Word of God in the Westminster Assembly', *Church History* 18 (1949): 200.

intense because there is a vying for attention from the same set of authorities. And the faults seen in a friend or acquaintance are not nearly so grating as the same faults in one who shares the same house and genes. Just so, in accounting for the strain in the relationship between Owen and Baxter the commonalities are, strangely enough, nearly as important as the differences. Eventually, Baxter wondered aloud at the bitterness with which Owen claimed to believe exactly the same things.

On the Second Question

All of this is a truly fascinating story in itself, one that reveals much that is new about the two men, but the import extends far beyond just them. So the second question seeks to measure the effect of the strain in their relationship on the development of nonconformity. In other words, why did it matter?

It mattered for two main reasons. First, Owen and Baxter were both extremely influential leading figures within the two central streams of orthodox nonconformity. J.I. Packer is possibly the most ambitious when he sums up Owen as a 'Puritan colossus and perhaps the best theologian England ever produced'.[45] With noticeably cooler detachment, R.A. Beddard calls Owen one of the two 'ayatollahs of Independency';[46] a contemporary critic, George Vernon, picked him for the '*Atlas* of *Independency*' and 'the *Prince*, the *Oracle*, the *Metropolitan* of *Independency*, the *Achitophel* of *Oliver Cromwell*.[47] Blair Worden describes Owen as 'the architect of the Cromwellian Church', 'politically the most influential clergyman of the 1650s' and almost certainly

---

[45]   See Packer's foreword to Kay, *Trinitarian Spirituality*, xiii. Stephen P. Westcott repeats this claim in the introduction to his recent translation of Owen's Latin work, *Biblical Theology: The History of Theology from Adam to Christ* (Grand Rapids, MI: Soli Deo Gloria Publications, 2009), xvii.

[46]   R.A. Beddard, 'Restoration Oxford and the Remaking of the Protestant Establishment', in *The History of the University of Oxford*, vol. 4, ed. Nicholas Tyacke (Oxford: Clarendon Press, 1997), 812.

[47]   [George Vernon], *A Letter to a Friend Concerning some of Dr. Owen's Principles and Practices* (1670), 36, 58. Achitophel was the adviser to Absalom during Absalom's revolt against his father King David (2 Samuel 15–19). According to the biblical narrative his advice was received as if it came from God. He lost a debate, however, with Hushai the Archite, who was David's 'mole' in Absalom's court during the rebellion, and subsequently killed himself in shame. Anthony Wood quoted Vernon in *Athenae Oxonienses: An Exact History of all the Writers and Bishops who have had their Education in the...University of Oxford from...1500 to the Author's Death in 1695*, 2nd edn (London: Knaplock, Midwinter and Tonson, 1721), ii.740.

'Cromwell's mouthpiece'.[48] Ruth Spalding sees him as 'the presiding genius of the Cromwellian church'.[49] It may well be that Philip Nye's enduring leadership has been overshadowed in these comments, not to mention the likes of Thomas Goodwin, but there is no disputing Owen's influence, especially after the Restoration when he became the leading figure among the Congregationalists. Baxter, we will find, was rather too idiosyncratic to be acclaimed *the* leader of any movement, let alone the Presbyterians; and his autobiography, his literary output and his surviving correspondence may have served to exaggerate his importance in the historiography. Even so, again there can be no doubting his influence. From the mid-1650s on he was an essential player in any negotiations over church settlement up to the Glorious Revolution. In May 1654 his friend and fellow minister, John Humfrey, was concerned by what he thought was undue adulation, 'seeing wee are so ready to make an Idoll of you'.[50] After the Restoration one of his critics, Thomas Delaune, labelled him 'the *Goliah* of your party'.[51] For John Coffey, Baxter 'became the epitome of moderate Puritanism'.[52]

---

[48]   Blair Worden, 'Toleration and the Cromwellian Protectorate', in *Persecution and Toleration: Papers Read at the Twenty-Second Summer Meeting and the Twenty-Third Winter Meeting of the Ecclesiastical Historical Society*, ed. W.J. Sheils, Studies in Church History Series, vol. 21 (Oxford: Basil Blackwell, 1984), 205, 207; and *The Rump Parliament 1648–1653* (Cambridge: Cambridge University Press, 1974), 69. For similar claims, see J.C. Davis, 'Cromwell's Religion', in *Oliver Cromwell and the English Revolution*, ed. John Morrill (London: Longman, 1990), 206; Andrew R. Murphy, *Conscience and Community: Revisiting Toleration and Religious Dissent in Early Modern England and America* (University Park, PA: Pennsylvania State University Press, 2001), 120; Jeffrey R. Collins, *The Allegiance of Thomas Hobbes* (Oxford: Oxford University Press, 2005), 231; and Nigel Smith, '"And if God was One of Us": Paul Best, John Biddle, and Anti-Trinitarian Heresy in Seventeenth-Century England', in *Heresy, Literature and Politics in Early Modern English Culture*, ed. David Loewenstein and John Marshall (Cambridge: Cambridge University Press, 2006), 172. Vivian de Sola Pinto lists Owen among 'the group of Independent divines who really became the leaders of the Church under the Protectorate', in *Peter Sterry: Platonist and Puritan* (Cambridge: Cambridge University Press, 1934), 20.

[49]   Ruth Spalding, ed., *The Diary of Bulstrode Whitelocke 1605–1675* (Oxford: Oxford University Press, 1990), 227, note 1.

[50]   John Humfrey to Baxter, 11 May 1654: DWL MS *BC* i.193v (*CCRB* #179).

[51]   Thomas Delaune, *Truth Defended: Or, a Triple Answer to the Late Triumvirates Opposition on their Three Pamphlets, viz. Mr. Baxter's Review, Mr. Wills his Censure, Mr Whiston's Postscript to his Essay* (1677), 4. The image was hardly flattering. Goliath was the Philistine giant defeated by David (see 1 Samuel 17).

[52]   John Coffey, 'A Ticklish Business: Defining Heresy and Orthodoxy in the Puritan Revolution', in *Heresy, Literature and Politics in Early Modern English Culture*, ed. David Loewenstein and John Marshall (Cambridge: Cambridge University Press, 2006), 125. Neil Keeble also says that after 1660 'Baxter emerges as the pre-eminent champion not only of the nonconformists, but of the Puritan tradition', in *Richard Baxter*, 18.

For Mark Goldie, he was 'the undisputed doyen of Restoration Presbyterianism' and 'the figure who towered over Restoration Puritanism'.[53] Therefore, both Owen and Baxter were clearly very significant leadership figures. Theirs is possibly the most important relationship within seventeenth-century English nonconformity.[54] If it was strained beyond repair, that matters. At the very least, it hindered any capacity to develop compromise and agreement between the two main Puritan parties. Moreover, their influence did not end with their deaths; it continued to affect nonconformity and later Evangelicalism, even to the present day. And if that is true, the differences between them (and between their respective admirers) continue to matter.

The second reason why their relationship matters is that it illustrates in elaborate detail the kinds of strains and tensions that were at work also within the broader movement, since the same issues that divided Owen and Baxter also worked to complicate the relationship between the Presbyterians and Congregationalists more generally. That is why I have given so much space to elucidating in detail the steady deterioration of their relationship and the reasons for it; and that is why the focus falls so heavily on just these two figures. If we can develop a fully rounded appreciation of why they fell out we will then be much better placed to understand why the distinct parties within Restoration nonconformity ended up being 'at one another's throats'.[55] This may well be putting the situation too harshly,[56] but there is no denying that broad divisions existed within nonconformity that proved in the end to be permanent. The same was true of Owen and Baxter. Their failure to see eye to eye, despite their proximity, was mirrored in this much broader failure. Understand one and we will better understand the other.

I will return to this point shortly, but first I would like to locate this project in the space between two not-unrelated recent historiographical trajectories. First, I would like to follow the lead set by Ann Hughes in her study of the mid-1640s

[53]   Mark Goldie, gen. ed., *The Entring Book of Roger Morrice 1677–1691*, vol. 1, *Roger Morrice and the Puritan Whigs* (Woodbridge: The Boydell Press, 2007), 251, 225. Roger Thomas also points to 'the fact that the Presbyterians found in Baxter their acknowledged leader', in 'The Rise of the Reconcilers', in *The English Presbyterians: From Elizabethan Puritanism to Modern Unitarianism*, ed. C. Gordon Bolam et al. (London: George Allen and Unwin Ltd, 1968), 71.

[54]   For recognition of this possibility, see Carl Trueman, 'Lewis Bayly (d.1631) and Richard Baxter (1615–1691)', in *The Pietest Theologians: An Introduction to Theology in the Seventeenth and Eighteenth Centuries*, ed. Carter Lindberg (Malden, MA: Blackwell Publishing, 2005), 55.

[55]   John Spurr, 'From Puritanism to Dissent', in *The Culture of English Puritanism, 1560–1700*, ed. Christopher Durston and Jacqueline Eales (Houndmills: Macmillan Press, 1996), 256.

[56]   More recently John Spurr has emphasised the unity alongside the disagreement within the movement, in 'Religion in Restoration England', in *A Companion to Stuart Britain*, ed. Barry Coward (Malden, MA: Blackwell Publishing, 2003), 421, 425, 427.

conflict between the Presbyterians and the Congregationalists. Her focus is on Thomas Edwards and his notorious *Gangraena* but both are set within a broader context that is sketched with subtlety and generosity. She explicitly departs from the main patterns within the prevailing historiography since the 1960s, which are 'based on boxes, linear developments, or factions'. There has been 'a drive to fit people into hard and fast categories'. Or there has been 'a search for a clearly defined turning point, the time when once and for all religious and political divisions emerged, party alignments were fixed, or adversary politics sprang into life'. Or the third alternative 'is to see politics in terms of shifting factions, based on practical matters such as patronage connections or regional interests'. Such simplifications will not do. Adequately comprehending complex events in such momentous times as the mid-1640s 'requires a more sophisticated understanding of political identities, both individual and collective, as more fragmentary, contradictory, and contingent than dominant modes of analysis imply'.[57] Indeed it does. To use other language, after all the lumping it is time for some splitting.[58] That is, I would like to move past the casual use of opposing labels and to open up space to observe the endlessly nuanced complexities of what were many different shifting and overlapping positions within the Puritan movement. We need to pay due attention to the varieties of difference and proximity; to see that ideas never exist in an impersonal and abstract vacuum, divorced from mundane factors as personality and circumstance; and to register that positions and former realities can shift over time, for better or worse. I hope this book does justice to these imperatives.

The second historiographical trajectory relates to the Restoration period. Mark Goldie led the editorial team that produced a critical edition, in seven volumes, of the *Entring Book of Roger Morrice*. The first volume, written by Goldie himself, is a superb introduction to the Restoration context particularly as it relates to Roger Morrice and his chronicle of events covering the years from 1677 and 1691. Goldie demonstrates a similar subtlety and sympathy to Hughes, if in a different context. In other words, he avoids the 'boxes' and the 'linear developments'. He does not see the eventual outcome of toleration and denominationalism as fixed or inevitable. He discerns just how close the Presbyterians were to the Church from which they had been forced to depart: the differences between them 'were sometimes scarcely perceptible', while their

---

[57]   Hughes, *Gangraena*, 330. See also, Avihu Zakai, 'Religious Toleration and Its Enemies: The Independent Divines and the Issue of Toleration During the English Civil War', *Albion* 21 (1989): 5–7; Davis, 'Cromwell's Religion', 184; and J.C. Davis, 'Religion and the Struggle for Freedom in the English Revolution', *Historical Journal* 35 (1992): 511–12, 530.

[58]   See J.H. Hexter, *On Historians: Reappraisals of Some of the Makers of Modern History* (London: Collins, 1979), 242–3.

affinities with the tolerationist Congregationalists may have been overstated.[59] Furthermore, he is inclined to accept that a narrow band of churchmen and parliamentarians maintained their dominance in the Church of England to the detriment of those moderates.[60] And he is acutely aware of the Restoration period's essential continuity with the pre-Restoration past.[61]

> Puritan politics was continuous in the sense that religious and political convictions formed in the reign of Charles I and hardened in the Civil War continued to structure ways of thinking and acting. They were convictions that revolved around conceiving of politics as a godly calling and as the practical means of achieving 'further reformation'. It was continuous also in the sense that the personnel remained largely the same. The Puritan Whigs of the 1680s were in good measure still the men and women of the Civil War era: they shared a common experience and memory, and by and large took the same stands in every climacteric from the 1640s onwards.[62]

The 'bonds of piety and personal friendship', he concludes, 'remained strong'. So too did the animosities. Again to use different language, Goldie's approach is 'horizontal' rather than 'vertical'.[63] Notwithstanding the different 'personnel' in view, I hope a similar perspective will be evident in this book.

The Interregnum is positioned between these two trajectories – the period of 'godly rule'. The verdict of historians has been generally negative. In a collection of essays focused on the development of nonconformity, Anne Whiteman puts it bluntly: 'the birth of Dissent must also be regarded as the direct consequence

---

[59]   Goldie, *Entring Book of Roger Morrice*, i.225–8. I do not want to suggest that Goldie is alone in this view. John Spurr, for one, also presents a similar perspective, especially in 'From Puritanism to Dissent', 234–65.

[60]   See also, Mark Goldie, 'The Theory of Religious Intolerance in Restoration England', in *From Persecution to Toleration: The Glorious Revolution and Religion in England*, ed. O.P. Grell, J.I. Israel and N. Tyacke (Oxford: Clarendon Press, 1991), 331–68.

[61]   Again, this is not a unique view. Tim Harris, for example, questions whether there was a 'fundamental watershed' at the Restoration, in 'Introduction: Revising the Restoration', in *The Politics of Religion in Restoration England*, ed. Tim Harris, Paul Seaward and Mark Goldie (Oxford: Basil Blackwell, 1990), 2, 6. Neil Keeble also emphasizes continuity, in *The Literary Culture of Nonconformity in Later Seventeenth-Century England* (Athens, GA: University of Georgia Press, 1987), 39–40.

[62]   Goldie, *Entring Book of Roger Morrice*, i.149.

[63]   See ibid., i.278; and, behind that, Patrick Collinson, 'The Early Dissenting Tradition', in *Godly People: Essays on English Protestantism and Puritanism*, ed. Patrick Collinson (London: The Hambledon Press, 1983), 527.

of the "Puritan Revolution", a revolution which failed'.[64] Christopher Durston similarly concludes that the Puritan agenda to reform the Church calendar, religious rites and social morals was, despite some isolated and limited instances of success, a 'dismal failure'. Both local officials and the populace, he argues, resented the changes and impositions.[65] In the same vein, Derek Hirst concludes that the 'signs of parochial involvement in the work of reformation are lacking'.[66] John Morrill contends that the official efforts to implement this 'negative, sterile' agenda 'have been shown largely to have failed'.[67] But this view appears to be changing. More recently, Morrill offered a far more positive assessment than his earlier one. Oliver Cromwell, he says, 'had reason to be proud of the church he established, a radically Erastian church, a partnership of his providentially validated civil authority and the aspirations of the godly in each local community'. '[I]t is a major achievement.'[68] Other historians have also qualified this earlier verdict of failure. Elliot Vernon explicitly modifies Hirst's view by emphasizing the evidence for some success in the Presbyterian concern to reform parish structures so as to bring parishioners to a lively faith, especially through catechizing.[69] Bernard Capp offers a case study of the county of Middlesex to show 'the energy and drive of the Puritan Reformers, sustained throughout the Interregnum, and the co-operation they secured from many ordinary citizens'. Those citizens might have had their own quite different reasons for co-operation, and there was considerable popular hostility, but there is no

---

[64]   Anne Whiteman, 'The Restoration of the Church of England', in *From Uniformity to Unity 1662–1962*, ed. Geoffrey F. Nuttall and Owen Chadwick (London: SPCK, 1962), 22.

[65]   See Christopher Durston, 'Puritan Rule and the Failure of Cultural Revolution', in *The Culture of English Puritanism, 1560–1700*, ed. Christopher Durston and Jacqueline Eales (Houndmills: Macmillan Press, 1996), 210–33.

[66]   Derek Hirst, 'The Failure of Godly Rule in the English Republic', *Past and Present* 132 (1991): 46.

[67]   John Morrill, 'The Church in England 1642–1649', in *Reactions to the English Civil War 1642–1649*, ed. John Morrill (London: Macmillan Press Ltd, 1982), 113, 114. This essay was republished in *The Nature of the English Revolution: Essays by John Morrill*, ed. John Morrill (London: Longman, 1993), 148–75.

[68]   John Morrill, 'The Puritan Revolution', in *The Cambridge Companion to Puritanism*, ed. John Coffey and Paul C.H. Lim (Cambridge: Cambridge University Press, 2008), 82–3. Claire Cross says a similar thing in 'The Church in England 1646–1660', in *The Interregnum: The Quest for Settlement 1646–1660*, ed. G.E. Aylmer (London: Macmillan Press, 1972), 99.

[69]   Elliot Vernon, 'A Ministry of the Gospel: The Presbyterians During the English Revolution', in *Religion in Revolutionary England*, ed. Christopher Durston and Judith Maltby (Manchester: Manchester University Press, 2006), 115–36.

ignoring the impact of the campaign.[70] Jeffrey Collins contends that the system of triers and ejectors established during the 1650s was very effective. 'In truth, the church settlement of 1654 was implemented pervasively, and it probably ranks as the greatest administrative achievement of Oliver Cromwell's centralizing regimes.'[71] To return to Ann Hughes: 'The orthodox godly are too often seen simply as disappointed failures, whose hopes for overall reform were destroyed by aggressive sectaries or sabotaged by stubborn traditionalists.' She does not wish to say that the Presbyterian agenda was 'straightforwardly attractive to a majority', but they 'could rally large strategic minorities in the 1640s' and 'the cause of orthodox reformation and city independence was attractive to many beyond the city governors'.[72] She also points out the success of the triers and ejectors, and she suggests that an overall failure to establish a Presbyterian model in principle (or in legislation) was 'balanced by real opportunities in practice'.[73]

This forms important background, but it is not my purpose in this book to establish the success or otherwise of godly reform on the ground during the Interregnum. Yet I am very interested in the question of failure in other terms. For all the success of the ejectors and triers, and for all the scope for local action in phenomena such as the association movement, the search for a permanent religious settlement in England was, indeed, largely a failure.[74] The particular failure was to agree on a list of 'fundamentals': those beliefs that marked off the orthodox, that provided the parameters for a relative toleration, and without which a person could not be saved. John Morrill's point is well made: 'In religion, as in politics, the Parliamentarians knew what they would not have, but not what

---

[70]   Bernard Capp, 'Republican Reformation: Family, Community and the State in Interregnum Middlesex, 1649–60', in *The Family in Early Modern England*, ed. Helen Berry and Elizabeth Foyster (Cambridge: Cambridge University Press, 2007), 63–6.

[71]   Jeffrey R. Collins, 'The Church Settlement of Oliver Cromwell', *History* 87 (2002): 29. See also, Collins, *Allegiance of Thomas Hobbes*, 167–71.

[72]   Hughes, *Gangraena*, 18, 21. See also, Ann Hughes, 'The Frustrations of the Godly', in *Revolution and Restoration: England in the 1650s*, ed. John Morrill (London: Collins and Brown, 1992), 76–7; and 'The Meanings of Religious Polemic', in *Puritanism: Transatlantic Perspectives on Seventeenth-Century Anglo-American Faith*, ed. Francis J. Bremer (Boston, MA: Massachusetts Historical Society, 1993), esp. 205.

[73]   Ann Hughes, '"The Public Profession of these Nations": The National Church in Interregnum England', in *Religion in Revolutionary England*, ed. Christopher Durston and Judith Maltby (Manchester: Manchester University Press, 2006), 98, 104. See also, Ann Hughes, '"Popular" Presbyterianism in the 1640s and 1650s: The Cases of Thomas Edwards and Thomas Hall', in *England's Long Reformation 1500–1800*, ed. Nicholas Tyacke (London: UCL Press, 1998), 235–59.

[74]   Hughes, 'Frustrations of the Godly', 78, 86, 90.

they would have.'[75] The same held true for the orthodox godly throughout the 1650s. It was very easy to agree on what was wrong with the Laudian status quo, but apparently impossible to agree on what to put in its place, and this among a group of believers with a shared Puritan, Calvinist heritage and agenda. Why did this group – braced with so much in common and with seemingly every political advantage – fail to come to agreement?

This is where the story of the relationship between Owen and Baxter has so much significance. Tracking their progress also illuminates the progress (or lack of it) towards agreement in these terms. It clarifies the sticking points and obstacles. And it shows how personality and memory got in the way. There is, then, a much larger question in view: how do we account for the 'fragmentation of later Dissent'? In some ways, the question is a misnomer. Nonconformity, or its earlier manifestations, had always been fragmented. David Como and Peter Lake, for example, have shown us just what sort of divisions and tensions existed among the Puritan community in the pre-Civil War period.[76] And the pressure valve of New England emigration during the Laudian ascendency is in its own way testament to variations in ecclesiology. Precisely those sorts of tensions played themselves out in the search for settlement during the 1650s and were ruthlessly exposed under the pressure of shared nonconformity in the Restoration period. If there was any period of relative equanimity and agreement, it obtained in the early 1640s. But that was disrupted by the very visible disturbances in the alliance as the Westminster Assembly did its work in the mid-1640s. There was a distinct failure to see eye to eye. This book uncovers the slow process by which that failure worked itself out by examining the relationship between Owen and Baxter in its broader context.

I wish, then, to relate that story in a way that avoids the simple categories and judgements of some past historiography and that emulates the generous approach of both Ann Hughes and Mark Goldie. In doing so I hope to advance what I believe is an important task: to revisit the nature and activities of the orthodox godly. On the one hand, some earlier scholarship (though excellent and enduring) was written at the height of the Ecumenical movement and was deliberately tied in to the desire for contemporary Church unity.[77] In this

---

75   Morrill, 'Church in England', 148.

76   In particular, see David Como, *Blown by the Spirit: Puritanism and the Emergence of an Antinomian Underground in Pre-Civil-War England* (Stanford: Stanford University Press, 2004); and Peter Lake, *The Boxmaker's Revenge: 'Orthodoxy', 'Heterodoxy', and the Politics of the Parish in Early Stuart London* (Stanford: Stanford University Press, 2001).

77   For instance, *From Uniformity to Unity*, edited by Geoffrey F. Nuttall and Owen Chadwick and published in 1962, traces an arc from mid-seventeenth-century disputes to the modern Ecumenical movement. And the final chapter of A. Harold Wood's work on Baxter and

setting, the seventeenth-century failure to agree was lamentable. Perhaps this is betrayed most clearly in the observation of Roger Thomas that the Presbyterians and Congregationalists 'were aware of some common ground between them and sometimes had the grace to be ashamed of their quarrels'.[78] Goldie notes that in the context of modern ecumenism (and secular indifference) we find 'narratives of intramural intolerance among English Protestants less interesting, even embarrassing'.[79] I feel no such embarrassment and I prefer to allow these actors their differences; to respect and understand them. For groups with so much in common to retain their principled disagreement must mean that the issues at stake were important indeed. On the other hand, historians have been especially dazzled and distracted by the existence of the 'radicals', whose numbers and influence (except, perhaps, for the Quakers) was always small. Ann Hughes notes that the 'godly have rarely been the direct concern of historians who have been more excited by sectaries who took Calvinist ideas to radical conclusions or who rejected them altogether'.[80] There is a pressing need for new scholarship on the Congregationalists and for more work that will build on recent scholarly attention on the Presbyterians. I hope this book will make a contribution towards that end. With that in mind, some definitions are now in order.

Presbyterians and Congregationalists

It should be apparent by now that my focus is principally on the orthodox godly – generally speaking, those English Christians who were marked out by shared Puritan concerns – but I admit that I have not been precise about the parameters of that label. To offer some clarification, I will use rather loosely the labels of 'Puritan movement' and 'nonconformist movement' to describe successive phases in the fortunes of the orthodox godly. I am following convention here by ceasing to use the word Puritan at the Restoration and replacing it with the word nonconformist, but I do not want to imply by this any disjunction of nature or personnel in 1660. I will use the label of nonconformist where

---

comprehension is entitled 'Can there be Unity without Uniformity Today?'. See A. Harold Wood, *Church Unity Without Uniformity: A Study of Seventeenth-Century Church Movements and of Richard Baxter's Proposals for a Comprehensive Church* (London: Epworth Press, 1963). See also, A. Morgan Derham, 'Richard Baxter and the Oecumenical Movement'. *Evangelical Quarterly* 23 (1951): 96–115.

[78]   Roger Thomas, 'The Break-Up of Nonconformity', in *The Beginnings of Nonconformity*, ed. Geoffrey F. Nuttall et al. (London: James Clarke and Co, 1964), 34.

[79]   Goldie, *Entring Book of Roger Morrice*, i.19.

[80]   Hughes, 'Frustrations of the Godly', 76.

other scholars use that of dissent, but I see no great difference between them. I appreciate that even this does little to define precisely what I mean by 'Puritan' or 'nonconformist' or 'movement'. Perhaps the ambiguity can be mitigated by a very specific examination of the two labels deployed most often to describe the divisions among the orthodox godly.

Historians of seventeenth-century England have generally used the ecclesiastical labels of Presbyterian and Independent (mostly preferring this label to that of Congregationalist) without defining what they mean.[81] This has several unfortunate results. Those looking for definitions will have a hard time finding them and be forced to resort to older scholarship. The absence of explicit definitions implies that they should be self-evident; that the differences between the Presbyterians and Congregationalists were fixed, without any kind of adjustment over time; and that the gap between the two parties was wide. In fact, none of that is the case. Relative positions could change over time. Those figures who have been collected together under a generic label did not all agree on the same positions in the same way. The gap between the two groups on the main issues was minute: 'In terms of theology and even of church practice the Independents of the Assembly and their colleagues in New England stood very close to the Presbyterians.'[82] It is crucial to appreciate this. And yet at the same time the differences between them presented an unbridgeable gulf. Part of the purpose of this book is to help work out why that was. Here we can say that there was far more complexity than the carefree use of these labels implies. For this reason, I would like to offer some definitions in a way that also serves to mark out the initial historical context for the book.

On 1 July 1643 the House of Commons on its own authority brought into being the Westminster Assembly and commissioned it with the task of advising the Commons on a religious settlement for England.[83] 'Thus, to the extent that

---

[81]   A particularly egregious example of this is Noel Henning Mayfield, *Puritans and Regicide: Presbyterian-Independent Differences over the Trial and Execution of Charles (I) Stuart* (Lanham, MD: University of America Press, 1988). Despite the subtitle, the book does not define either Presbyterian or Independent. This introduces a fatal circularity into the argument: those who supported the regicide were Independents, and the Independents were those who supported the regicide. John Spurr is an exception to this general rule. He consistently defines what he means by the terms. See, for example, 'From Puritanism to Dissent', 238–44; *English Puritanism 1603–1689* (Houndmills: Macmillan Press, 1998), 104–7; *The Post-Reformation: Religion, Politics and Society in Britain, 1603–1714* (Harlow: Pearson Longman, 2006), 103–5.

[82]   Robert S. Paul, *The Assembly of the Lord: Politics and Religion in the Westminster Assembly and the 'Grand Debate'* (Edinburgh: T&T Clark, 1985), 122.

[83]   For a full description of the forming of the Assembly, see Paul, *Assembly of the Lord*, chapter 2. See also, J.T. Cliffe, *Puritans in Conflict: The Puritan Gentry During and After the Civil Wars* (London: Routledge, 1988), chapter 8.

religion was a cause of the Civil War, the Assembly at Westminster was supposed to be a solution.'[84] On 25 September the Commons took the Solemn League and Covenant: in return for a military alliance with the Scots, the English would endeavour 'the reformation of religion in the kingdoms of England and Ireland, in doctrine, worship, discipline and government, according to the Word of God and the example of the best reformed Churches'.[85] Three months later a group of 21 ministers among the Assembly put their names to a document entitled *Certaine Considerations to Dis-swade Men from Further Gathering of Churches in this Present Juncture of Times*. The list of names included four of the five who, less than one week later, would present themselves as the Dissenting Brethren.[86] But here they all spoke with one voice and in a way that would have given those proto-Dissenting Brethren nothing to fear. The purpose of the document was to declare a moratorium on the formation of gathered church congregations, a practice 'judged to be lawfull [but] unseasonable'. It recognized the role of the magistrate as a partner in reformation and it assured the reader that the Assembly would 'concurre to preserve whatever shall appear to be the rights of particular Congregations, according to the Word; and to bear with such whose Consciences cannot in all things conforme to the publicke Rule, so farre as the Word of God would have them borne withall'. The tone was hopeful, open and generous. 'Nothing can be more destructive to the friends of the cause of Religion, then to be divided amongst themselves.'[87] It is curious that the *Apologeticall Narration* followed so closely on the heels of this conciliatory document, but this may only be because the *Narration* has been taken by historians to be a declaration of independence by the Dissenting Brethren that provoked dissonance after harmony.[88] In fact, further research may reveal that

---

[84]   Chad B. van Dixhoorn, 'New Taxonomies of the Westminster Assembly (1643–52): The Creedal Controversy as Case Study', *Reformation and Renaissance Review* 6 (2004): 84.

[85]   Samuel Rawson Gardiner, ed., *The Constitutional Documents of the Puritan Revolution 1625–1660*, 3rd edn (Oxford: Clarendon Press, 1906), 268.

[86]   Rosemary Bradley, 'The Failure of Accommodation: Religious Conflicts between Presbyterians and Independents in the Westminster Assembly 1643–1646', *Journal of Religious History* 12 (1982): 34. The Dissenting Brethren were Thomas Goodwin, Philip Nye, Sidrach Simpson, Jeremiah Burroughes and William Bridge.

[87]   William Twisse et al., *Certaine Considerations to Dis-swade Men from Further Gathering of Churches in this Present Juncture of Times* (1643), 3, 5.

[88]   For description and reception of the *Apologeticall Narration*, see Robert S. Paul, ed., *An Apologeticall Narration* (Philadelphia, PA: United Church Press, 1963); Paul, *Assembly of the Lord*, 124–7; George Yule, *Puritans in Politics: The Religious Legislation of the Long Parliament 1640–1647* (Appleford: Sutton Courtenay Press, 1981), 124–5 and chapter 6.

the document was predictable and mundane, consistent with earlier platforms and therefore not all that surprising or threatening.[89]

But this is not to deny that important differences of opinion existed among the Westminster divines,[90] and the involvement of the Scots made a Presbyterian settlement much more likely.[91] Presbyterianism envisaged a national Church complete in itself: it possessed full rights to self-government vis-à-vis the magistrate with every freedom to appoint its own officers; and with interlocking layers of authority within its internal structures, so that no individual parish church could act in isolation from all the others. 'Its primary watchword and essential feature is this – Every preaching Presbyter or Pastor of a flock is a true Bishop in the Scripture sense of the term, with no higher order of Bishops or Prelates by divine right or apostolic institution.'[92] Government in the local congregation was by elders (or presbyters) and there were two types: the preaching elder (the pastor or minister) and the ruling elders. Together, these elders possessed the power of the keys (church discipline, admonishment and excommunication) and the power of ordination.[93] Indeed, the Presbyterians believed that a minister could be ordained only with the involvement of those who had also been ordained, to preserve apostolic succession. But these bodies of local elders were not free to act independently. Each individual presbytery (or church or congregation) was part of a classis (or classical presbytery). Representatives of each classis met regularly in a regional synod, which in turn sent representatives to a national synod.[94] Thus important decisions affecting the local congregation – such as ordination or the appointment of a particular minister to a particular congregation – had to be ratified at a higher level.[95] There was a great deal of difference among the

---

[89]   In this connection I will be very interested to read the Cambridge PhD dissertation of Hunter Powell when it is completed, as I am confident it will deliver important correctives and reappraisals.

[90]   For a summary of the debates and divisions within the Westminster Assembly, see W.M. Hetherington, *History of the Westminster Assembly of Divines* (Edinburgh: James Gemmell, 1890), Period III, chapters 3–5; Bradley, 'Failure of Accommodation', 23–47; and Francis J. Bremer, *Congregational Communion: Clerical Friendship in the Anglo-American Puritan Community, 1610–1692* (Boston: Northeastern University Press, 1994), 133ff.

[91]   Paul, *An Apologeticall Narration*, 69–73.

[92]   A.H. Drysdale, *History of the Presbyterians in England: Their Rise, Decline, and Revival* (London: Publication Committee of the Presbyterian Church of England, 1889), 6.

[93]   Though there was disagreement among Presbyterians on this point. See Bradley, 'Failure of Accommodation', 35, 38.

[94]   Rosemary Bradley sees the issue of binding, authoritative synods as 'essential to any definition of a Presbyterian', in 'Failure of Accommodation', 26.

[95]   For further description of Presbyterian ecclesiology see Drysdale, *Presbyterians in England*, 3–8; Ann Hughes, 'Public Profession of these Nations', 94–5; Vernon, 'Ministry of the

Presbyterians on many of these questions,[96] but this description captures what might be called a generic Presbyterianism.

It was in some ways a very clerical system.[97] Predictably, it ran afoul of Parliament's Erastian determination to keep control of ministerial appointments.[98] The Commons kept a tight leash on the Assembly's powers and processes – it was always only ever an advisory body.[99] Parliament never supported the idea of a national synod, nor were provincial assemblies or classical presbyteries given coercive powers.[100] Thus 'the structure of English Presbyterianism was developed in an unsatisfactory and ramshackle fashion through various acts and ordinances that came into force between 1645 and 1648'.[101] They were implemented half-heartedly, and even then only in a very small number of localities, particularly London and Lancashire.[102]

It should also be acknowledged that the label of Presbyterian is a slightly misleading catchall for garden-variety Puritan members of the Church of England. They 'were more open-minded on details of church government' than Presbyterians proper, 'but supported a national church [that was] Calvinist in doctrine, with an effective well-maintained preaching ministry and a rigorous disciplinary structure'.[103] This broader group would include Richard Baxter.[104] Roger Thomas suggests, with some merit, that they might be called 'Parish Puritans', since they held on to the parish system in a national Church.

Gospel', 116–17.

[96]   Thomas, 'Rise of the Reconcilers', 47.

[97]   The *Directory for the Publike Worship of God Throughout the Three Kingdoms of Scotland, England, and Ireland*, issued in 1645 to replace the Book of Common Prayer, illustrates this. Maltby, 'Suffering and Surviving', 160–162.

[98]   Drysdale, *Presbyterians in England*, 301–2, 345.

[99]   Bradley, 'Failure of Accommodation', 28.

[100]   Tai Liu, *Puritan London: A Study of Religion and Society in the City Parishes* (Newark, DE: University of Delaware Press, 1986), 53–4.

[101]   Vernon, 'Ministry of the Gospel', 116.

[102]   Thomas M'Crie, *Annals of English Presbytery* (London: James Nisbet and Co, 1872), 192; Hughes, 'Public Profession of these Nations', 95; Vernon, 'Ministry of the Gospel', 116–17; Morrill, 'Church in England', 156–7; Michael Mahony, 'Presbyterianism in the City of London, 1645–1647', *Historical Journal* 22 (1979): 114.

[103]   Hughes, '"Popular" Presbyterianism in the 1640s and 1650s', 235–6. See also, Bradley, 'Failure of Accommodation', 26.

[104]   *Rel. Bax.*, ii.146. For an assessment of Baxter's position vis-à-vis Presbyterianism, see Thomas, 'Rise of the Reconcilers', 48–9; and Geoffrey F. Nuttall, 'The First Nonconformists', in *From Uniformity to Unity 1662–1962*, ed. Geoffrey F. Nuttall and Owen Chadwick (London: SPCK, 1962), 182–3.

For until the luckless and generally unwanted experiment of Parliamentary Presbyterianism, English Presbyterianism had never had any clear definition, for the good and sufficient reason that until the Civil War it had never had the semblance of any sort of formulated system as the established practice of any church in England ... It would be quite improper to distinguish between Presbyterians and Anglicans at this period, for Presbyterians *were* Anglicans and few of them would have been opposed to moderate episcopacy.[105]

They criticized the national Church to which they belonged, but they had no wish to depart from it.

The Congregationalists position was subtly but powerfully different.[106] Here, the individual congregation was complete in itself. The Dissenting Brethren explained how they had, during their time in exile in the Netherlands, retained

the government of our severall congregations for matter of discipline within themselves, to be exercised by their own Elders ... yet not claiming to ourselves an *independent power* in every congregation, to give account or to be subject to none others, but only a ful and entire power compleat within our selves, until we should be challenged to err grossly.[107]

In 1645 they publicly objected to the Assembly's resolution that 'Scripture holds forth, that many particular congregations may be under one Presbyteriall Governement'.[108] Instead, they insisted that the local congregation was complete in itself.[109] The same point can be illustrated by William Bartlet's *A Model of the Primitive Congregational Way*, published in 1647. A Congregationalist minister

---

[105]   Thomas, 'Rise of the Reconcilers', 47.

[106]   For further description of Congregationalism, see Henry W. Clark, *History of English Nonconformity: From Wyclif to the Close of the Nineteenth Century*, vol. 1, *From Wyclif to the Restoration* (New York: Russell and Russell, 1965), 336–8; Hetherington, *History of the Westminster Assembly*, esp. 189–93; Paul, *Apologeticall Narration*, chapter 5; Roger Thomas, 'Parties in Nonconformity', in *The English Presbyterians: From Elizabethan Puritanism to Modern Unitarianism*, ed. C. Gordon Bolam *et al.* (London: George Allen and Unwin Ltd, 1968), 93–4; and Spurr, 'From Puritanism to Dissent', 238–44.

[107]   Thomas Goodwin et al., *An Apologeticall Narration, Humbly Submitted to the Honourable Houses of Parliament* (1644), 14.

[108]   Thomas Goodwin et al., *The Reasons of the Dissenting Brethren Against the Third Proposition Concerning Presbyteriall Government* (1645), 3.

[109]   R.W. Dale, *History of English Congregationalism* (London: Hodder and Stoughton, 1907), 273–4.

at Wapping in Middlesex,[110] Bartlet argued that the local congregation must be 'a communion of visible Saints, embodied and knit together by a voluntary consent, to worship God, according to his Word, making up one ordinary congregation, with power of Government within it selfe onely'.[111] Arguably the most influential voice on this was heard from afar, in New England's John Cotton. His *Keyes of the Kingdom of Heaven* was first published in 1642 with reprinting in 1643 and 1644. In the form of a short catechism, it described a visible Church as 'a mysticall body whereof Christ is the Head, the Members be saints, called out of the world and united together into one Congregation by a holy Covenant to worship the Lord, and to edifie one another, in all his holy Ordinances'. Such a Church 'hath power from Christ to choose and call her own Officers and Members'. 'No Church hath power of Government over another, but each of them hath chief power within it selfe, and all of them equall power with another, every Church hath received alike the power of binding and loosing, opening and shutting the Kingdome of heaven.'[112]

This had important consequences. For a start, as Bartlet identified, this position raised the stakes of church membership. The congregation was in some ways like the individual believer, responsible directly to God. For the analogy to hold true each congregation had to be made up only of believers.[113] In practical terms, this meant that membership of the congregation was voluntary – a person could not be born into it, as in the parish church.[114] Each person needed to demonstrate as far as possible that his or her faith was genuine. The main evidence here was a profession of how the believer had come to faith (conversion) backed by a reputation for godly, moral living.[115] Also, each congregation had the power of the keys to administer communion and this power rested in both the elders of the church and the members of the congregation.[116] In a similar way, the congregation had the right to ordain and call ministers, and to appoint elders,

---

[110]   Geoffrey F. Nuttall, *Visible Saints: The Congregational Way 1640–1660* (Oxford: Basil Blackwell, 1957), 75.

[111]   William Bartlet, *A Model of the Primitive Congregational Way...Together with the Maine Points in Controversie, Touching the Right Visible Church-state Christ hath Instituted under the Gospel* (1647), 30.

[112]   John Cotton, *The Doctrine of the Church to which are Committed the Keyes of the Kingdom of Heaven* (1643), 1, 9, 11.

[113]   Dale, *History of English Congregationalism*, 274.

[114]   Thomas, 'Rise of the Reconcilers', 54–5.

[115]   Dale, *History of English Congregationalism*, 275–6; Nuttall, *Visible Saints*, 107–15.

[116]   Bartlet, *Model*, 37.

without those decisions having to be ratified by any other external body.[117] For this reason, a congregation 'might ordain its own minister without the concurrence of any pastor who had been previously ordained'.[118] Taken to its extreme, 'there is little ground for a National, Diocesan, and Provinciall Church'.[119] This did not, however, mean that each congregation was free to go its own way, blithely ignoring other congregations within the same movement. There would be times when representatives of congregations met together in mutual conference, but such synods were not binding on the participant congregations.[120] Also, a different congregation might well challenge the actions of another, but again that intervention was not binding. The most that could happen was for that congregation to refuse fellowship with the offending congregation.[121] As Geoffrey Nuttall explains, even without binding synods there was ample scope for communion and mutual influence between congregations.[122] This is why the Congregationalists detested the label of Independent, and resisted it as far as they could.[123]

They were also capable of internal variety. The place of the parish is a useful example of this. Bartlet was quick to dismiss the parish structure as 'no other than an humane constitution' since 'experience tels us, that Parish Churches for the generall consist of loose, profane, scandalous lives'.[124] But the Dissenting Brethren were not so dismissive. Initially they

> accepted the principle of a national church settlement, based on the existing parishes, and the four offices, of pastor, teacher, elder and deacon, central to Presbyterian government. But they made four demands. The congregation must agree before its officers imposed a sentence of excommunication; ordination of ministers could be performed by the congregation in default of elders; synods were to be purely advisory;

---

[117] Goodwin et al., *Reasons*, 10–11; Drysdale, *Presbyterians in England*, 298–300; Nuttall, *Visible Saints*, 87–95.

[118] Dale, *History of English Congregationalism*, 275.

[119] Bartlet, *Model*, 51.

[120] Ibid., 52; Goodwin et al., *Reasons*, 30. See also, Zakai, 'Religious Toleration and Its Enemies', 9–10.

[121] Goodwin et al., *Apologeticall Narration*, 17; Dale, *History of English Congregationalism*, 282.

[122] Nuttall, *Visible Saints*, 94.

[123] Goodwin et al., *Apologeticall Narration*, 23; Bartlet, *Model*, 27; Joel Halcomb, 'A Social History of Congregational Religious Practice During the Puritan Revolution', PhD Thesis, Cambridge University, 2009, 8.

[124] Bartlet, *Model*, 56.

and the parish boundaries should not restrict church membership – 'members may be taken out of other churches' if the parish minister agreed.[125]

This position also opened up scope for communion with parish congregations.[126] Some Congregationalists might continue to operate as parish ministers whilst also gathering out of their parish a congregation of visible saints who would meet together for worship and edification at a different time, even taking communion together. Even the Presbyterians confronted the essential pastoral problem.[127] Their response was to deny communion to those who were visibly unworthy or, to put that slightly differently, to offer communion only to those who could give evidence of a godly life.[128] This served to uphold standards while also retaining the parish structure which, as Bartlet observed, could present contrasting shades of visible godliness to say the least. Indeed, this is the nub of the difference between the two groups. A steadfast commitment to the 'conception of a national Church containing both saints and sinners, and their belief that they should labour to preach the gospel to a mixed body of Christians, and not just the visible saints, was at the root of the Presbyterian project'.[129] To varying degrees the Congregationalists diluted and even dissolved that conception, but they did so through wrestling with an issue that everyone faced. Thus we see shadings of positions along a spectrum not just between groups but within them.

As the influence of John Cotton demonstrates, the English Congregationalists could look across the Atlantic Ocean for inspiration. There, the unique political environment and the demands of establishing new settlements almost necessitated and certainly cultivated the 'New England Way'.[130] Susan Hardman Moore shows how these settlements took shape around covenants – agreements between settlers as to their rights and responsibilities.[131] The population was,

---

[125]   Spurr, *English Puritanism*, 105. Spurr is drawing here on Bradley, 'Failure of Accommodation', 40.

[126]   Halcomb, 'Social History of Congregational Religious Practice', 7–9.

[127]   Nuttall, *Visible Saints*, 137.

[128]   Vernon, 'Ministry of the Gospel', esp. 126–7.

[129]   Ibid., 119.

[130]   There is a massive body of scholarship on early New England. To select from among the most relevant works, see also James F. Cooper, *Tenacious of Their Liberties* (Oxford: Oxford University Press, 1999); Bremer, *Congregational Communion*; and Francis J. Bremer, 'The Puritan Experiment in New England, 1630–1660', in *The Cambridge Companion to Puritanism*, ed. John Coffey and Paul C.H. Lim (Cambridge: Cambridge University Press, 2008), 127–42.

[131]   Susan Hardman Moore, *Pilgrims: New World Settlers and the Call of Home* (New Haven, CT: Yale University Press, 2007), chapter 2. See also, Paul, *Apologeticall Narration*, 43–56; and Philip Benedict, *Christ's Churches Purely Reformed: A Social History of Calvinism* (New Haven, CT: Yale University Press, 2002), 389–92.

therefore, generally self-selecting. It also meant that certain traditions within English religion were extracted out in concentrated form to flourish in the new environment. The very act of leaving England for the north American seaboard was an act of separation. Thus Presbyterians back home looked with some suspicion on what seemed to them a vaguely separatist endeavour.[132]

> Advocates of the New England Way made a distinctive claim: Christ's visible Church on earth existed only in local gatherings of 'saints' ... The result – the local autonomy of individual churches in New England – broke the mould in an age where national churches with a strong clerical hierarchy were the norm. The most striking innovation of all was the decision to ask people who wanted to join the church to give a testimony of religious experience.[133]

Understandably, Congregationalists drew nourishment from the rich connections that served to bind communities on both sides of the ocean together.

All of this should give a basic sense of what the labels mean, but one other dimension complicates the matter further. These groups I have been describing were concerned with religious issues, especially church government. But the same labels applied in the political sphere.[134] The political Presbyterians were a grouping of MPs who sought to settle with King Charles I upon terms. The political Independents, in contrast, had little interest in a negotiated settlement to the Civil War and preferred to fight on towards a total victory over the King. Clearly different issues were at stake and there was no neat and tidy overlap between the parallel groups in each sphere. For this reason, I will use the label of Independent to describe the political grouping and the label of Congregationalist to describe the religious grouping (I prefer the label of Congregationalist because it seems to me to be fairer to their ecclesiological concerns).[135] But if there is a correlation between religious Congregationalists and political Independents it lies in their

---

[132]   Bremer, *Congregational Communion*, 115–16.

[133]   Hardman Moore, *Pilgrims*, 41.

[134]   For some discussion of this, see J.H. Hexter, 'The Problem of the Presbyterian Independents', *American Historical Review* 44 (1938): 29–49; George Yule, *The Independents in the English Civil War* (Cambridge: Cambridge University Press, 1958); and David Scott, *Politics and War in the Three Stuart Kingdoms, 1637–49* (Houndmills: Palgrave Macmillan, 2004), 89–91. In May 1970 a debate was held among several historians in volume 47 of *Past and Present* in response to Stephen Foster's article, 'The Presbyterian Independents Exorcized: A Ghost Story for Historians', *Past and Present* 44 (1969): 52–75. For a much more recent discussion, see Halcomb, 'Social History of Congregational Religious Practice', 8–9.

[135]   For the opposite – a defence of the continued use of 'Independent' – see Michael R. Watts, *The Dissenters: From the Reformation to the French Revolution* (Oxford: Clarendon Press, 1978), 94–9.

view of the magistrate. The Presbyterians sought a national Church with full self-government – the freedom to make its own appointments without the sanction of civil authority; the Congregationalists allowed a central place for the magistrate in promoting reformation.[136] The Dissenting Brethren acknowledged that they gave more to 'the Magistrate's power' than the Presbyterians did.[137] Indeed, as events developed, given their small minority, they would need the magistrate's power to advance their own agenda.[138]

It is intriguing to observe the change in tone and posture in the succeeding publications of the Dissenting Brethren. By 1647 they were distinctly aggrieved at their treatment by the Presbyterians and the 'sense of so much remedilesse prejudice' against them.[139] But they had also changed their aims and tactics along the way, which served to escalate the issues.[140] The initial unity was long gone and, as Ann Hughes explains in detail, 1646 was a decisive year and the utterly Presbyterian Thomas Edwards a decisive player. Through *Gangraena*, published in three parts during 1646, he did most to stir up panic about the Congregationalists. He linked them with the issue of toleration, which he argued would give free rein to every sect and error then seemingly running out of control throughout England. There was, indeed, a link to be made.[141] That initial promise of 1643 'to beare with such whose Consciences cannot in all things conforme to the publicke Rule, so farre as the word of God would have them borne withall' intimated a necessary generosity towards those who in different ways placed themselves outside of the usual parish structure.[142] But

---

[136] For a general discussion of the Congregationalist view of the state, see Dale, *History of English Congregationalism*, 284–6; D. Nobbs, 'Philip Nye on Church and State', *Cambridge Historical Journal* 5 (1935): 58–9; and Nuttall, *Visible Saints*, 142–3.

[137] Goodwin et al., *Apologeticall Narration*, 21.

[138] See Sarah Gibbard Cook, 'The Congregational Independents and the Cromwellian Constitutions', *Church History* 46 (1977): 335–57

[139] Thomas Goodwin et al., *The Independents Declaration Delivered in to the Assembly... Declaring their Grounds and Full Resolutions Concerning Church-Government* (1647), 6.

[140] Bradley, 'Failure of Accommodation', 29.

[141] For broader reading on the subject of the development of religious toleration, see especially W.K. Jordan, *The Development of Religious Toleration in England*, vol. 4, *From the Convention of the Long Parliament to the Restoration, 1640–1660: The Revolutionary Experiments and Dominant Religious Thought* (London: George Allen and Unwin Ltd, 1938); John Coffey, *Persecution and Toleration in Protestant England 1558–1689* (Harlow: Longman Pearson, 2000); Murphy, *Conscience and Community*; Perez Zagorin, *How the Idea of Religious Toleration Came to the West* (Princeton, NJ: Princeton University Press, 2003); and Alexandra Walsham, *Charitable Hatred: Tolerance and Intolerance in England, 1500–1700* (Manchester: Manchester University Press, 2006).

[142] Twisse et al., *Certaine Considerations*, 3.

there was no such generosity in Edwards: if orthodox Congregationalists were to be tolerated, where would it end?[143] He managed to forge a direct link between the Congregationalists, unlimited toleration and theological error. They were as orthodox as the Presbyterians, but they would find the reputation for heresy, particularly Antinomian heresy, difficult to shake. Edwards' campaign offered 'an all too plausible sectarian-Independent "other" against which "Presbyterians" could unite. It thus helped to create clear-cut polarities out of a muddled "reality"'. It had the effect of a self-fulfilling prophecy, creating divisions that were neither necessary nor inevitable. At a crucial moment 'Edwards's fatal simplifications sabotaged rival possibilities for alliance among the orthodox godly'.[144] If so, his campaign was self-defeating. The Presbyterians lost control of events during 1646, first to a fundamentally Erastian Parliament and second to the Independents, who rose steadily in influence on the back of the New Model Army's success in winning the first civil war.[145] Indeed, that is not a bad year in which to locate a beginning to this story. The rise of the Independents was revealed in the choice of ministers chosen to preach before Parliament in its monthly fasts. In April 1646 a new name joined the list, a young clergyman from Essex. Here we find John Owen acting on the national stage for the very first time. What he said is revealing indeed.

---

[143]   Dale, *History of English Congregationalism*, 277–8; Haller, 'Word of God', 212–13; Bradley, 'Failure of Accommodation', 30.

[144]   Hughes, *Gangraena*, 331–2.

[145]   See ibid., 333–401.

Chapter 1

Different Wars/Different Worlds

From the beginning of these troubles ... you have held forth religion and the gospel, as whose preservation and restoration was principally in your aims.

John Owen (1646)[1]

In a word, I never yet saw the work of the gospel go on well in wars.

Richard Baxter (1647)[2]

John Owen and Richard Baxter were born within a year of each other. Their careers spanned much the same period, even if Baxter outlived Owen by eight years; they lived through the same events. And yet their experience of some of those events, and how they interpreted them, could hardly provide a greater contrast. This is especially true of the first civil war. It is the foundational difference of experience that gave rise to all those that followed. Before we can begin to understand the complexities of their relationship and the reasons for the strain that it bore, we must understand how their contrasting experiences of the war left them living worlds apart. Owen sailed through the war years largely unscathed; he saw in those events the hand of God rescuing the gospel in England from its Arminian bondage. But for Baxter the war was a personal disaster that brought extended disruption and transiency; he felt he saw the gospel in England slipping irreparably into Antinomian abuse. These contrasting perspectives profoundly reinforced or shaped their soteriological agendas, which we will explore in Chapter 2. In this way Owen and Baxter illustrate a dynamic that was true for England as a whole: the implications of this mid-century upheaval could last a lifetime, and long after the fighting had finished England's inhabitants carried the memory with them, shaping them still and exerting a lingering influence on the country decades after the event. This, then, is how so much of later seventeenth-century English history begins, in a conflict that most just wanted to end.

---

[1]   Owen, *Vision of Free Mercy* (1646): *Works*, viii.33.

[2]   Baxter, *Saints' Everlasting Rest* (1650): *Practical Works*, iii.238. While the book was not published until 1650, Baxter began to write it in 1647.

John Owen: 'A Vision of Free Mercy'

King Charles I slipped out of Oxford disguised as a servant in the early hours of 27 April 1646.[3] For nearly four years the city had been the headquarters for his military operations against the forces of the English Parliament. This inglorious departure offered a tacit acknowledgement that his cause was lost.[4] After nine days of wandering that initially took him within sight of London he surrendered himself to the Scottish forces some 90 miles to the north of Oxford in Nottinghamshire, and the first civil war came to a close.

On 29 April 1646, just two days after Charles had abandoned Oxford, John Owen preached his first sermon to the House of Commons. Four years earlier, Parliament had instituted regular days of 'public humiliation' and fasting in which sermons were preached and published that affirmed the work of God on Parliament's behalf in the struggle underway.[5] But the choice of Owen was part of a significant change of affairs within the Parliamentarian cause.[6] 'The old regulars ... and many others who will soon abandon the revolution, are joined by their future supplanters.'[7] Presbyterian influence was losing ground and at that point Owen was an emerging Congregationalist. This lent some distinctive touches to his sermon, but even so 'these new preachers had to be discreet'[8] and their essential task remained unchanged – to renew national vigour in a time of war.

Owen's sermon neatly fitted the mould. He called it 'A Vision of Unchangeable, Free Mercy, in Sending the Means of Grace to Undeserving Sinners', and he

---

[3]   The story is related in several places. For a recent account, see Trevor Royle, *The British Civil War: The War of Three Kingdoms 1638–1660* (New York: Palgrave Macmillan, 2004), 384; or Austin Woolrych, *Britain in Revolution 1625–1660* (Oxford: Oxford University Press, 2002), 329.

[4]   Barry Coward, *The Stuart Age: A History of England 1603–1714* (London: Longman, 1980), 191.

[5]   For background on this parliamentary preaching programme, see H.R. Trevor-Roper, 'The Fast Sermons of the Long Parliament', in *Religion, the Reformation and Social Change and Other Essays*, ed. H.R. Trevor-Roper (London: Macmillan, 1967), 294–344; John F. Wilson, *Pulpit in Parliament: Puritanism During the English Civil Wars 1640–1648* (Princeton, NJ: Princeton University Press, 1969); Christopher Durston, '"For the Better Humiliation of the People": Public Days of Fasting and Thanksgiving During the English Revolution', *The Seventeenth Century* 7 (1992): 129–49; and J.C. Davis, 'Living with the Living God: Radical Religion and the English Revolution', in *Religion in Revolutionary England*, ed. Christopher Durston and Judith Maltby (Manchester: Manchester University Press, 2006), 25–8.

[6]   See Wilson, *Pulpit in Parliament*, 86–92, for further description of these changes.

[7]   Trevor-Roper, 'Fast Sermons', 323.

[8]   Ibid., 325.

chose Acts 16:9 for his text. In its context, the Apostle Paul was prevented by the Holy Spirit from taking the gospel into the province of Asia. Instead, this verse describes Paul's vision of a man calling him to go to Macedonia. Owen used this passage to demonstrate in classically Calvinist fashion that God chose some, but not others, to salvation.[9] Yet his choice of text made it possible for him to read 'this discriminating counsel of God from eternity' not just in the experience of individuals, but in the history of entire countries and in England's present troubles. 'Amongst other nations, this is the day of England's visitation ... a man of England hath prevailed for assistance, and the free grace of God hath wrought us help by the gospel.' Thus Owen discerned 'the mighty working of Providence' in England's civil war.[10] His purpose was 'to discover how the great variety which we see in the dispensation of the means of grace, proceedeth from, and is regulated by, some eternal purpose of God, unfolded in his word', understanding that '[a]ll things below in their events are but the *wax*, whereon the eternal *seal* of God's purposes hath left its own impression; and they every way answer to it'.[11] Framed in such a way, Owen's sermon identified the hand of God in the nation's history. Going all the way back to the fifth century, Owen showed how the country had twice been blessed with the gospel and twice had allowed it to be lost to corruption, first at the hand of the Saxons, then at the hands of the 'Roman harlot', the Catholic Church.[12] More recently, and much more urgently, the gospel had again been endangered, this time by the Laudians who had risen to such dominance in the Church of England.

It is some time now since Nicholas Tyacke laid out his influential thesis that the English Church carried a Calvinist consensus into the seventeenth century.[13] That consensus began to break down late in the reign of King James I. At an official level at least it disintegrated during the reign of Charles, whose preferment of Archbishop William Laud and his apparent Arminianism served to marginalize the Calvinists. Admittedly, Tyacke's thesis has not been accepted without question,[14] but Kevin Sharpe's well-made point remains obvious: 'Whatever

---

[9]   Owen, *Vision of Free Mercy* (1646): *Works*, viii.15, 21–2.

[10]   Ibid., 6.

[11]   Ibid., 11, 10. See also p. 19.

[12]   Ibid., 26–7, 31–2.

[13]   See Nicholas Tyacke, *Anti-Calvinists: The Rise of English Arminianism c.1590–1640* (Oxford: Oxford University Press, 1987).

[14]   Peter White argues that a Calvinist/Arminian disjunction is too simplistic and that there never was a Calvinist consensus around the litmus test of predestination. Instead, there was a range of views about how prominent predestination should be in the theology and preaching of the Church. Peter White, *Predestination, Policy and Polemic: Conflict and Consensus in the English Church from the Reformation to the Civil War* (Cambridge: Cambridge University Press, 1992),

the historical reality, or the uncritical dependence of Tyacke, Russell and others on Laud's detractors, it remains the case that significant contemporaries did perceive Laud to be the spawn of a papist and an Arminian threat and did fear dangerous innovations in the Caroline church.'[15]

Owen's sermon tied into these fears and suspicions. The Arminians had wanted nothing less than to deliver England up to the Pope:

> In worship, their paintings, crossings, crucifixes, bowings, cringings, altars, tapers, wafers, organs, anthems, litany, rails, images, copes, vestments – what were they but Roman varnish, an Italian dress for our devotion, to draw on conformity with that enemy of the Lord Jesus? In doctrine, the divinity of Episcopacy, auricular confession, free-will, predestination on faith, yea, works foreseen, 'limbus patrum,' justification by works, falling from grace, authority of a church, which none knew what it was, canonical obedience, holiness of churches, and the like innumerable, – what were they but helps to Sancta Clara, to make all our articles of religion to speak good Roman Catholic?[16]

The Arminians had brought England to the brink of corrupting the gospel for a third time in its history, a betrayal that would surely bring in its train God's wrath and judgement. But the providence of God had gloriously intervened. 'O Lord, how was England of late, by thy mercy, delivered from this snare! ... O how hath thy grace fought against our backsliding!'[17] The first civil war had

---

x–xiii. For the debate between Tyacke and White, see Peter White, 'The Rise of Arminianism Reconsidered', *Past and Present* 101 (1983): 34–54; Nicholas Tyacke, 'The Rise of Arminianism Reconsidered', *Past and Present* 115 (1987): 201–16; and Peter White, 'A Rejoinder', *Past and Present* 115 (1987): 217–29. Julian Davies readily accepts that Charles was no Calvinist and deeply suspicious of the Puritans, but he questions whether Charles possessed any Arminian inclinations. He contends that Charles held to an idiosyncratic 'Carolinism' that emphasized deference and order. Julian Davies, *The Caroline Captivity of the Church: Charles I and the Remoulding of Anglicanism* (Oxford: Oxford University Press, 1992), 12–14. And Charles Prior suggests that the focus on soteriology has been misplaced and myopic, missing the larger issues of church government. Charles W.A. Prior, *Defining the Jacobean Church: The Politics of Religious Controversy, 1603–1625* (Cambridge: Cambridge University Press, 2005), 8. Prior 'suggests that critics of Tyacke's thesis have not yet provided the definitive case against it, particularly as it applies to the Jacobean Church' (p. 10).

[15]   Kevin Sharpe, 'Religion, Rhetoric, and Revolution in Seventeenth-Century England', *Huntingdon Library Quarterly* 57 (1994): 263. John Coffey makes a similar point, in *Politics, Religion and the British Revolutions: The Mind of Samuel Rutherford* (Cambridge: Cambridge University Press, 1997), 141.

[16]   Owen, *Vision of Free Mercy* (1646): *Works*, viii.28.

[17]   Ibid., 25. See also p. 30.

been England's redemption. Looking back, it was clear to Owen that England had come to the brink of repudiating the gospel for the last time. Had that occurred, the nation's lamp-stand might have been removed.[18] But disaster had been averted by the free grace of God whose greatest concern was the gospel itself. Owen brought his hearers back to the sovereign purposes of God, 'by discovering that all revolutions here below – especially every thing that concerns the dispensation of the Gospel and kingdom of the Lord Jesus – are carried along according to the eternally fixed purpose of God'.[19] Seen in this light, the war had been a vindication of God's unchanging purposes. The gospel had been rescued, preserved, secured. The hazards and hardships that England had so recently navigated were necessary sacrifices in a great cause that had the backing of God himself.

But such a view dismissed too quickly the pain involved in such sacrifices. At one point in his sermon, Owen compared the nation's travails to mere seasickness. 'If there had been no difficulties, there had been no deliverances. And did we never find our hearts so enlarged towards God upon such advantages as to say, Well, this day's temper of spirit was cheaply purchased by yesterday's anguish and fear; – *that* was but a being sick at sea?'[20] It is difficult to think how anyone who had lost a loved one in the fighting or in the attendant disease and devastation could have thought that England's relief in April 1646 was 'cheaply purchased'. True, Owen's task was to preach a sermon that would boost morale in a time of national crisis.[21] He might not have been so casual or optimistic in other contexts. And yet there can be no doubt that Owen had cultivated an extremely positive view of the war. Such a perspective was possible only because he had emerged from the upheaval remarkably unscathed.

Any map showing the major battles of the wars in England will show that they took place in nearly every corner of the country, from Corbridge in the north, to Winceby in the east, to Cheriton and Lostwithiel in the south, and to Montgomery (in Wales) in the west.[22] The most sustained and intense fighting

---

[18]   Ibid., 31.

[19]   Ibid., 7.

[20]   Ibid., 18.

[21]   Owen was effectively serving as an army chaplain on a national scale. Barbara Donagan has shown how the battle sermons of army chaplains 'were of course designed to spur troops to action, but they also served to connect men in the field to the larger, national purposes of the war, for ministers were spokesmen for parliament as well as for God'. Barbara Donagan, 'Did Ministers Matter? War and Religion in England, 1642–1649', *Journal of British Studies* 33 (1994): 126.

[22]   For example, see Woolrych, *Britain in Revolution*, 798.

occurred in the Midlands, 'the scene of continual warfare and bloodshed'.[23] '[T]his region saw the most vicious small-scale conflict.'[24] Shropshire, in particular, was 'much fought over'.[25] By contrast, there was only one region in England that was spared from conflict: the southeast. The fighting stopped at a line that might be drawn from King's Lynn through Cambridge and London and on down to Arundel. East of that line, a region of strong parliamentarian control, there was settled calm during the first civil war.[26] Of the 563 known incidents in that phase of the fighting, only one took place in Essex.[27] And that is precisely where Owen spent most of the war.

Owen was born in 1616, the second of at least five children.[28] His father, Henry, was a Puritan minister who, about the time of John's birth, took up a living at Stadham (now Stadhampton), a small village some five miles from Oxford. In a rare biographical moment, John explained that 'I was bred up from my infancy under the care of my father, who was a Nonconformist all his days and a painful labourer in the vineyard of the Lord'.[29] The village already had a Puritan tradition and Henry's nonconformity would have been supported and protected by John D'Oyley, who owned the nearby manor and the gift of the living. Around the age of 10, John and his older brother William were sent to a small grammar school in the parish of All Saints, Oxford. Their fees were paid by Henry's brother (or brother-in-law) who lived in Wales. At 12 years of age he entered Queen's College, Oxford, just as the anti-Puritan inclinations of William Laud were about to be felt. In June 1632 he graduated with a Bachelor of Arts and moved on to the Master of Arts, graduating in April 1635. By then, Laud's influence as Archbishop of Canterbury and Chancellor of Oxford University was unmistakeable and unavoidable. Two years later, Owen left Queen's College for good.

Owen's pastoral career began as a chaplain and tutor three miles from Stadham in the household of Sir Robert Dormer in the hamlet of Ascot.[30] The private

---

[23]   Roy Sherwood, *The Civil War in the Midlands 1642–1651* (Gloucester: Allan Sutton Publishing, 1992), 83. See also Stephen Porter, *Destruction in the English Civil Wars* (Gloucester: Allan Sutton Publishing, 1994), 68; and Charles Carlton, *Going to the Wars: The Experience of the British Civil Wars 1638–1651* (London: Routledge, 1992), 116.

[24]   Carlton, *Going to the Wars*, 206.

[25]   Porter, *Destruction in the English Civil Wars*, 66.

[26]   Ibid., 67–8.

[27]   Carlton, *Going to the Wars*, 204, 206.

[28]   The details in this paragraph are drawn from Toon, *God's Statesman*, 1–10; and *CJO*, 3–8.

[29]   Owen, *A Review of the True Nature of Schism* (1657): *Works*, xiii.224.

[30]   The details here are drawn from Toon, *God's Statesman*, 10–26; and *CJO*, 8–18.

situation allowed him to lie low in his nonconformity, but not for long. He soon moved to Hurley,[31] 20 miles closer to London, to be chaplain in the home of John, Lord Lovelace, another well-placed protector who had no great love for Laud. Despite that dislike, Lovelace declared for King Charles when war broke out in 1642. As the fighting developed into a sustained encounter Owen decided to move to London to stay with relatives. His time there included two visits to Ashford, Kent (as the guest of Sir Edward Scott, in December 1642 and July 1643) when the war impinged on his experience: 'Twice, by God's providence, have I been with you when your country [county] hath been in great danger to be ruined, – once by the horrid insurrection of a rude, godless multitude, and again by the invasion of a potent enemy in the prevailing country.'[32] Owen himself does not seem to have been personally threatened or involved. In 1643 he published his first book, *A Display of Arminianism*, and dedicated it to the 'Lords and Gentlemen of the Committee for Religion' in the House of Lords.[33] In the same year that committee offered him the living at Fordham, a village five miles from Colchester in the county of Essex.

Owen began his work there in July 1643. In 1645 he published two catechisms that he had developed for his Fordham parishioners. In the introduction he explained 'how I have been amongst you, and in what manner, for these few years past, and how I have kept back nothing (to the utmost of the dispensation to me committed) that was profitable for you; but have showed you and taught you publicly from house to house, testifying to all repentance towards God, and faith towards our Lord Jesus Christ'.[34] He also emphasized the supreme importance of preaching in his ministry along with catechizing, which may have taken place in regular visits into people's homes. Thus the central elements in his ministry at Fordham speak of continuity and stability: this was a period of consistent, fruitful ministry. It came to an end only with his removal, again around April 1646, to the parish of Coggeshall, a small town again not far from Colchester.[35] Owen followed in a long line of Puritan preachers in the town. His immediate predecessor was Obadiah Sedgwick, a member of the Westminster Assembly who had been presented to the position by Robert Rich, the second

---

[31] The reasons for the move are obscure. Dormer may have come under pressure since he was not strictly allowed his own chaplain, or Owen may have wanted to remain close to his father who had recently moved to Harpsden, just five miles from Hurley. See Toon, *God's Statesman*, 10; and *CJO*, 9.

[32] Owen, *Duty of Pastors and People Distinguished* (1643): *Works*, xiii.3.

[33] See Owen, *Display of Arminianism* (1643): *Works*, x.5.

[34] Owen, *Two Short Catechisms* (1645): *Works*, i.465. The quote has obvious allusions to Paul's last words to the Ephesian elders in Acts 20:20–21, 27.

[35] Toon, *God's Statesman*, 25.

Earl of Warwick and a known opponent of William Laud. Thus Owen would have found a welcoming environment for his preaching and anti-Arminian inclinations. Around 2,000 souls gathered every Sunday to hear him preach.[36]

The civil war years were, then, ones of virtually uninterrupted ministry for Owen, conducted under the eye of some well-placed patrons. In this he demonstrated a happy ability to nurture contacts among those of influence, a capacity that would serve him well on many future occasions. A small testament to this is the invitation to preach his sermon to Parliament in April 1646, organized by a friend, Thomas Westrow, by then a Member of Parliament. Westrow held that Owen's 'judgement to discern the differences of these times, and his valour in prosecuting what he is resolved to be just and lawful, place him among the number of those very few to whom it is given to know aright the causes of things and vigorously to execute holy and laudable designs'.[37] On this occasion Owen certainly demonstrated that perspicacity in a way that could only have pleased Westrow and his likeminded colleagues.

Thus Owen stood before Parliament to preach, wholeheartedly supportive of its cause and determined that all the gains should not now be lost. The Arminian trek back to Egypt had been halted only by the grace of God, but England remained in the wilderness and should now press on to the promised land.[38] As Owen urged England's leaders to forge ahead he did so as an insider (referring to 'our armies' and 'our councils')[39] confident that those to whom he spoke shared his concern. 'From the beginning of these troubles', he reminded them, 'you have held forth religion and the gospel, as whose preservation and restoration was principally in your aims'.[40] Now that the battles were over, it was time for Parliament to fulfil its promise of 'reforming [God's] churches and settling the gospel'.[41] This 'is our day, wherein we must mend or end'.[42] Owen urged Parliament to give every effort to preserving and preaching the gospel in every corner of the land. If it did not, judgement would follow. But if it did, bright days lay ahead: 'the Reformation of England shall be more glorious than of any nation in the world.'[43]

---

[36]   Ibid., 25–6.

[37]   Quoted without citation in Toon, *God's Statesman*, 15–16.

[38]   Owen, *Vision of Free Mercy* (1646): *Works*, viii.25, 40.

[39]   Ibid., 17.

[40]   Ibid., 33.

[41]   Ibid., 18.

[42]   Ibid., 26.

[43]   Ibid., 27.

Yet while much had already been gained,[44] no small number of obstacles stood in the way.[45] In particular, Owen identified 'two sorts of men' who were too quick to dismiss the danger that England had been in and who were therefore reluctant to pursue any sort of costly pilgrimage towards Owen's promised land. The first sort were those who had been 'industriously instrumental' in England's apostasy, 'whose suffrages had been loud for the choice of a captain to return to Egypt'. This sort would have been obvious enough, but the second type were more subtle, those who

> are disturbed in their optics, or have gotten false glasses, representing all things unto them in dubious colours. Which way soever they look, they can see nothing but errors – errors of all sizes, sorts, sects and sexes – errors and heresies from the beginning to the end; which have deceived some men, not of the worst, and made them think that all before was nothing, in comparison of the present confusion. A great sign they felt it not, or were not troubled at it; as if men should come into a field, and seeing some red weeds and cockle among the corn, should instantly affirm there is no corn there, but all weeds, and that it were much better the hedges were down, and the whole field laid open to the boars of the forest: but the harvest will one day show the truth of these things.[46]

The is no doubting that Owen had in mind a figure like Thomas Edwards whose *Gangraena* – then in the very moment of its appearing – was nothing if not a compendium of 'errors of all sizes, sorts, sects and sexes'. The ongoing struggle between Presbyterians and Congregationalists was at the forefront of his mind. But Owen was also, even if only inadvertently, describing with astonishing precision a man that he had never met. Just as he was preaching this sermon in late April 1646, looking out over a field full of corn, Richard Baxter was preaching to soldiers, seeing nothing but weeds wherever he turned.

Richard Baxter: 'Nothing Appears To Our Sight But Ruin'

Unlike Owen, Richard Baxter was an only child.[47] He was born in 1615 in the village of Eaton-Constantine, five miles from the town of Shrewsbury in the

---

44 Ibid., 40.

45 Ibid., 16–17, 18.

46 Ibid., 27–8.

47 For a much more comprehensive account of Baxter's childhood and pre-civil war experience, see Geoffrey F. Nuttall, *Richard Baxter* (London: Thomas Nelson and Sons, 1965), chapter 1.

county of Shropshire. His father, a small estate-holder, had been redeemed from a life of gambling (and its debts) by the bare reading of the Scriptures, in which he instructed his son from an early age. As he grew, the young man faced a stark choice between reading the Bible at home with his parents or dancing with the neighbours around the maypole. 'But when I heard them call my Father *Puritan*, it did much to cure me and alienate me from them: for I consider'd that my Father's Exercise of Reading the Scripture, was better than theirs, and would surely be better thought on by all men at the last.'[48] Baxter could see that his father did not exactly merit 'the odious Name of a *Puritane*',[49] since he had no objections to the Book of Common Prayer or ceremonies or Episcopacy; he simply prayed and read from the Bible on the Lord's Day (instead of dancing) and occasionally ventured to reprove the local drunkards or offer a verse of Scripture. These efforts were hardly appreciated. Richard Baxter senior was regularly abused 'in the common talk of the Vulgar Rabble of all about us'.[50] Therefore, though his wider surroundings were less than supportive – Baxter's Shropshire was, unlike Essex, no Puritan stronghold – he took his father's convictions with him as he ventured into adulthood.

It took some time for Baxter to settle on his career. At the age of 16 he was diverted in his desire to go to university by the advice of his schoolmaster, who recommended him to a position under the ineffectual tutelage of Richard Wickstead, a chaplain to the council at Ludlow. Wickstead had no fondness for Puritans, but Baxter found the necessary time and books for study, and strong encouragement in the Puritan way from an unnamed friend.[51] After 18 months Baxter returned to his father's home to act as the local schoolmaster for the space of three months, the incumbent being gravely ill.[52] At the age of 18 Baxter investigated the common way of preferment by visiting the Court at London, on the advice of Wickstead and the urging of Baxter's parents who 'had no great inclination to my being a Minister'.[53] He discovered much the same anti-Puritan sentiment he had seen in the 'vulgar Rabble' of his village, though more finely dressed, and he left the city after only a month. Baxter then served once again as a schoolmaster, this time in the town of Dudley. There he was ordained in December 1638 and began to preach in the parish church and in the neighbouring villages.[54] After nine months he was 'invited to *Bridgnorth*, the

---

[48]   *Rel. Bax.*, i.2.
[49]   Ibid., 2.
[50]   Ibid., 3.
[51]   Ibid., 4.
[52]   Ibid., 5.
[53]   Ibid., 11.
[54]   Ibid., 13.

second Town of *Shropshire*, to preach there as Assistant to the worthy Pastor of that place'.[55] The results were disappointing: 'the people proved a very ignorant, dead-hearted People.'[56] So in April 1641 Baxter moved on to Kidderminster, the scene of his most memorable pastoral achievements. Certainly, his labours in the town began in a promising fashion. 'Whilst I continued at *Kederminster*, it pleased God to give me much Encouragement by the Success of my weak but hearty Labours.'[57] But these early efforts came to an abrupt end with the arrival of the civil war.

Indeed, Baxter's close engagement in the first civil war stands in stark contrast to Owen's relative isolation from England's upheaval. In large part this was simply a trick of geography. Owen happened to reside in the one region of the country that, as we have seen, would not experience any of the fighting. Baxter lived in the Midlands, the region that experienced the most sustained fighting. As the war began, this is where the royalist forces were most closely concentrated.[58] So it was relatively easy for Owen to evade the effects of the war; Baxter could scarcely avoid them.

The proximity of Baxter to many of the main engagements in the conflict is remarkable. The first physical skirmish of the war occurred late in the afternoon of 23 September 1642 when a band of horsemen from each side made contact at Powick Bridge, just south of Worcester. Prince Rupert responded quickly to the parliamentarian force led by Colonel John Brown, who was unaware of the other's presence and led his men into a quickly laid trap. Parliament's force was routed,[59] and Baxter, who happened to be staying nearby at Inkborough, was there to see it. He had heard that the parliamentarian force was camping in a meadow near the village of Powick: 'I had a great mind to go see them, having never seen any part of an Army.'[60] Baxter seems to have been aware of the deliberations that prompted the force to cross Powick Bridge and thus spring the ambush and he certainly witnessed the rout. 'The Sight quickly told me the Vanity of Armies; and how little Confidence is to be placed in them.'[61]

Baxter was also on hand to see for himself the mournful after-effects of the first full battle of the war, fought at Edgehill precisely one month later. Being a Sunday, Baxter was preaching at Alcester within earshot of the fighting.

---

[55]   Ibid., 14.

[56]   Ibid., 15.

[57]   Ibid., 21.

[58]   Royle, *British Civil War*, 186.

[59]   For a fuller description of the episode, see Royle, *British Civil War*, 186–8.

[60]   *Rel. Bax.*, i.42.

[61]   Ibid.,

As I was preaching the People heard the Cannon play, and perceived that the Armies were engaged; when Sermon was done (in the Afternoon) the report was more audible, which made us all long to hear of the success ... The next Morning being willing to see the Field where they had fought, I went to *Edghill*, and found the Earl of *Essex* with the remaining part of his Army keeping the ground, and the King's Army facing them upon the Hill, a mile off; and about a Thousand dead Bodies in the Field between them (and I suppose many more buried before).[62]

Baxter offered no comment on the grisly sight, but it must have been a harrowing scene. It is impossible to recover the full horror of what such sites (and sights) would have represented to those who looked on, particularly those for whom the trauma of war was an unprecedented experience. The night had been bitterly cold.[63] 'As the frost took its lethal toll of bodies, a terrible moaning prevailed across that Golgotha: it was a low rumbling sound, almost a bass humming that slowly died away into an awful silence. Dumb with horror and mute with relief the living could do nothing.'[64] The next day, explained one onlooker, 'the field was covered with the dead, yet no one could tell to what party they belonged'.[65] Edward Benlowes, poet and army captain, mused on the carnage: 'Edgehill, with graves looked white / With blood looked red / Maz'd at the numbers of the dead.'[66]

And Richard Baxter was there to see it for himself. Edgehill is, of course, quite some distance from Kidderminster but by then the war had brought about Baxter's ejection from the town, leading to a new phase of itinerancy. Even before formal hostilities began, Baxter bore the brunt of living in royalist territory. In June 1642 Charles presented his Commissions of Array, which appointed his own local army commanders, in response to the Militia Ordinance that passed control of the militia from the King to Parliament.[67] As the commission was being read in the streets of Kidderminster 'the Reader (a violent Country Gentleman) seeing me pass in the Streets, stopt and said, *There goeth a Traitor*, without ever giving a syllable of Reason for it'.[68] The outburst did not bode well for Baxter. Routine attacks on those 'that had short Hair and a Civil Habit' – the Roundheads – prompted him to retreat to the relative safety of Gloucester.[69] After a month some friends from Kidderminster encouraged him to come

62   Ibid., 43.
63   Carlton, *Going to the Wars*, 146.
64   Ibid., 118.
65   Ibid., 146.
66   Ibid., 118.
67   Royle, *British Civil War*, 165.
68   *Rel. Bax.*, 40.
69   Ibid., 40–41.

home, since his absence was all too easily interpreted as a sign of guilt or support for Parliament, but his return to the town was a brief one. By then Charles was urgently gathering his forces among the Midland counties and the 'Fury of the Rabble was so hot at home, that I was fain to withdraw again'.[70] This is what took him to Powick Bridge and to Edgehill, though he finally settled in Coventry. Like many other Puritan ministers he 'fled there for Safety from Soldiers and Popular Fury'.[71] In Baxter's case he was driven 'by the insurrection of a rabble that with clubs sought to kill me'.[72]

Thus England descended into civil war and people were forced to choose sides, if only for their survival. Alarmed by the Irish rebellion of 1641 and the accompanying rumours of widespread slaughter and royal approval,[73] and sharing little in common with the 'debauched rabble through the land' that, in Baxter's view, flocked to support the King,[74] his natural drift would always be towards Parliament's side. It is easy to believe that Baxter was describing his own position when he summarized the predicament of many of the English people:

> Thousands had no mind to meddle with the Wars, but greatly desired to live peaceably at home, when the Rage of Soldiers and Drunkards would not suffer them: some stayed till they had been imprisoned; some till they had been plundered, perhaps twice or thrice over, and nothing left them; some were quite tired out with the abuse of all Comers that quartered on them; and some by the insolency of their Neighbours; but most were afraid of their Lives; and so they sought refuge in Parliaments Garrisons.[75]

All they could do was to wish for a quick end to the fighting but such hopes evaporated as the conflict dragged on. The war came nowhere close to a decisive conclusion during 1643, though 'the king was the winner on points'.[76] The Scots entered the conflict in the following year and the New Model Army coalesced: both events steadily turned the course of the war against Charles, but the fatal blow was not struck until mid-1645. Baxter observed these developments from the safety of Coventry, where he preached to the soldiers twice a week and to the people on Sundays. He came as close as he could to being an army chaplain without taking a commission, for which he received food, accommodation and

---

[70]   Ibid., 42.

[71]   Ibid., 44.

[72]   Baxter to [Stephen?] L[obb?] 9 and 16 June 1684: DWL MS *BC* ii.93r (*CCRB* #1139).

[73]   For the very strong impression the Irish Rebellion made on Baxter, see Lamont, *Millennium*, chapter 2.

[74]   *Rel. Bax.*, i.44.

[75]   Ibid.

[76]   Carlton, *Going to the Wars*, 119.

protection.[77] Yet even if Baxter was sheltered from the worst of the violence buffeting the Midlands there was no escaping the tension of waking up every morning and wondering what the latest news would be: who had won, who had lost, '[s]o miserable were those bloody Days, in which he was the most honourable, that could kill most of his Enemies'.[78]

The battle of Naseby in June 1645 was a turning point both for Baxter and for the war. The fight itself was 'the mother of all battles' and the military climax of the first civil war.[79] Once again, Baxter witnessed the aftermath:

> *Naseby* being not far from *Coventry* where I was, and the Noise of the Victory being loudly in our Ears, and I having two or three that of old had been my intimate Friends in *Cromwell's* Army, whom I had not seen of above two Years, I was desirous to go see whether they were dead or alive, and so to *Naseby* Field I went two days after the fight.[80]

This time the shock of his visit was doctrinal, not physical. Previously, Baxter had heard rumours of bad theology percolating through the New Model Army but had disbelieved them. His Naseby visit convinced him otherwise, and he was stunned by what he saw: 'I found a new face of things which I never dreamt of ... Independency and Anabaptistry were most prevalent: Antinomianism and Arminianism were equally distributed.'[81] Regretting the reluctance of godly ministers to serve as army chaplains – a situation that, in Baxter's mind, had led to the current prevalence of heresy within the army – he enlisted as a chaplain in Colonel Edward Whalley's regiment.[82]

Thus began a second phase of much more gruelling itinerancy in which Baxter accompanied Whalley's regiment as it travelled the breadth of England during the last year of the first civil war. His journeys began with a march into the southwest where he witnessed firsthand the battle of Langport on 10 July 1645.[83] In his autobiography he offered a detailed account of how that fight unfolded.[84] From there Baxter's regiment took part in a succession of sieges.

---

[77]   *Rel. Bax.*, i.43–4.

[78]   Ibid., 46.

[79]   Carlton, *Going to the Wars*, 123.

[80]   *Rel. Bax.*, i.50.

[81]   Ibid. I have argued elsewhere that the practical outworking of antinomian doctrine among his friends and in the army was Baxter's greatest concern at this time. See Cooper, *Fear and Polemic*, 90.

[82]   *Rel. Bax.*, i.51–2.

[83]   Royle, *British Civil War*, 335; Woolrych, *Britain in Revolution*, 321.

[84]   *Rel. Bax.*, i.54.

They began with Bristol in August then moved on to other sieges of Sherborne Castle, Winchester Castle and Exeter before ending up in Cornwall.[85] As the country emerged from the heart of winter and as the war entered its final phases Baxter was present at the sieges of Banbury Castle, Worcester and finally Oxford itself, the headquarters of the King and the city from which he escaped in late April 1646.[86] It is easy to assume that sieges inflicted much less suffering than the battles themselves but Charles Carlton ably demonstrates how appalling and barbaric they could be, at least for the besieged. They were 'the most brutal and prolonged experience of the British civil wars'; they accounted for a third of all deaths in military actions and a quarter of the total war dead; and 'even during quiet times sieges could have been bloody affairs'.[87] Baxter offered no description of the intense viciousness that sieges could engender, but these experiences as much as the battles themselves must have served to darken his perspective on the war itself.

It was common enough for army chaplains to be involved in rallying the soldiers before a battle, boosting morale, preaching, praying and exhorting the men even while bullets flew all around,[88] but Baxter's main preoccupations seem to have been of another sort entirely. During his two years in Whalley's regiment

> I set my self from day to day to find out the Corruptions of the Soldiers; and to discourse and dispute them out of their mistakes, both Religious and Political: My Life among them was a daily contending against Seducers, and gently arguing with the more Tractable, and another kind of Militia I had than theirs ... So that I was almost always, when I had opportunity, disputing with one or other of them; sometimes for our Civil Government, and sometimes for Church Order and Government; sometimes for Infant Baptism, and oft against Antinomianism and the contrary Extream.[89]

Though Baxter gave this work his every energy the results were dismal. He had little doubt that the weight of the army leadership were against his endeavours. From his perspective, Oliver Cromwell was Antinomian in theology and separatist in practice, and whenever a position of influence opened up he filled it with one of his own kind.[90] So while the majority of the soldiers were respectable or at least tractable, the influential few were well placed to exert their will and

---

[85] Ibid., 54–5.
[86] Ibid., 55.
[87] Carlton, *Going to the Wars*, 154–5, 156.
[88] Ibid., 127.
[89] *Rel. Bax.*, i.53.
[90] Ibid., 57.

Baxter felt he was fighting a losing battle. He later conceded to a friend that in all these debates he could 'prevaile with none to purpose'.[91]

In the end it was his own body that defeated him. Baxter had stayed in Whalley's regiment through into early 1647, being quartered first at Rous Lench in Worcestershire and then at Ashby de la Zouch in Leicestershire. Just as the winter reached its coldest point Baxter's nose started to bleed. In the medical wisdom of the day this was taken to represent a surfeit of blood in the body so Baxter opened four veins, followed by another more substantial purge. The drastic loss of blood very nearly killed him.[92] It certainly brought his army career to a close, and he had little doubt as to what had brought on his near-death experience. In 1650 he offered proof of his support for Parliament's cause:

> you must thinke that a man will not be very prone to oppose that partye, with whom he
> hath so zealously joyned in their greatest adversity, & endured so many cold stormes,
> & unseasonable marches, & lain out of doores so many raining nights together, & bin
> in so many bloody fights, as I have bin in the space of 4 yeares & a halfe; & contracted
> so many sicknesses to my body, & at last even death it selfe; which is to me even at the
> doore in all probability, occasioned by these distemperings of my body.[93]

This quote does something to convey the intensity of Baxter's experience while he served as chaplain in the army. It involved no little amount of physical and psychological trauma. As he later divulged in a letter to Whalley, 'the remembrance of those years is so little delightfull to me, that I look back upon them as the saddest of my life'.[94] Baxter's nosebleed at the time might be taken as 'a sign of intense psychological strain'.[95] It is true that we find few signs of that strain in this section of Baxter's autobiography, but it was written in a much more detached fashion almost two decades after the event. To catch a glimpse of Baxter's experience and perspective during the events we must turn

---

[91]   Baxter to Richard Vines, 24 July 1650: DWL MS *BC* ii.24r (*CCRB* #46).

[92]   *Rel. Bax.*, i.58.

[93]   Baxter to Friends in the Army [c.June 1650]: DWL MS *BC* ii.269v (*CCRB* #41). After the Restoration, this explanation vanished. Baxter replaced it with another more sanitized and spiritual version in which he attributed his many bodily ailments to the gluttonous eating of apples and pears in his youth. See Tim Cooper, 'Richard Baxter and his Physicians', *Social History of Medicine* 20 (March 2007): 1–19.

[94]   Baxter to Edward Whalley, 8 March 1653: in Baxter, *Rich. Baxters Apology Against the Modest Exceptions of Mr T. Blake. And the Digression of Mr G. Kendall. Whereunto is Added Animadversions on a late Dissertation of Ludiomaeus Colvinus, alias, Ludovicus Molinaeus, M. Dr Oxon. And an Admonition of Mr W. Eyre of Salisbury. With Mr Crandon's Anatomy for Satisfaction of Mr Caryl* (1654), p.*2v (*CCRB* #169).

[95]   Carlton, *Going to the Wars*, 225.

to his immediate writings, and a book first penned just as Baxter began his long recuperation.

The *Saints' Everlasting Rest* was initially intended as Baxter's funeral sermon, but (not for the last time) the text ran away on him. Still in print today, the book has been something of a devotional classic.[96] Though not without its controversial and polemical touches, the work is an impassioned invitation to contemplate the eternal rest that awaits the believer. But it does so firmly embedded in, and in contrast to, the miserable realities of life in this world. During the first civil war, of course, those miseries had become ever more obvious and immediate. 'Look on England's four years' blood', Baxter lamented, 'a flourishing land almost made ruinate'.[97] Indeed, ruin was all around. These were the 'days of common sufferings, when nothing appears to our sight but ruin; families ruined, congregations ruined; sumptuous structures ruined; cities ruined; country [county] ruined; court ruined, kingdoms ruined'.[98] Clearly all those stark images of brutal sieges, heavy warfare and scattered corpses had stayed in Baxter's mind. 'Oh the sad and heart-piercing spectacles that our eyes have seen in four years' space! In this fight a dear friend is slain; scarce a month, scarce a week, without the sight or noise of blood ... the earth covered with the carcasses of the slain.'[99] These were just some of the 'miseries of the late unhappy war'.[100] And even at war's end there were too many places in which Baxter observed the

> weeping eyes, the bleeding sides, the lacerated members, of [English] churches; the reproached gospel, the disappointed reformation, the hideous doctrines, and unheard-of wickedness, that hath followed them; the contemned ordinances, the reproached, slandered, and ejected ministers; the weak that are scandalized, the professors apostasized, the wicked hardened, and the open enemies of the gospel that now insult.[101]

It should be very apparent from these telling references to the 'reproached gospel' and the 'disappointed reformation' that Baxter viewed the war as a disaster for both the gospel and the reformation. This was no liberation of the gospel, only its subversion, as endless numbers of heresies and errors proliferated. 'It is

---

[96]   For a very interesting discussion of the book's reception, see Keith Condie, 'The Theory, Practice, and Reception of Meditation in the Thought of Richard Baxter', PhD Thesis, University of Sydney, 2010, chapter 4.

[97]   Baxter, *Saints' Everlasting Rest* (1650): *Practical Works*, iii.58.

[98]   Ibid., 57.

[99]   Ibid.

[100]   Ibid., 1.

[101]   Ibid., 4.

natural', he explained, 'for both wars and private contentions to produce errors, schisms, contempt of magistracy, ministry and ordinances, as it is for a dead carrion to breed worms and vermin: believe it from one that hath too many years' experience of both in armies and garrisons'.[102] His perspective was bleak indeed, coloured by sad experience. 'Oh, what abundance of excellent, hopeful fruits of godliness have I seen blown down before they were ripe, by the impetuous winds of war.'[103] No harvest here. 'In a word', he concluded, 'I never yet saw the work of the gospel go on well in wars'.[104]

Of Cornfields and Ponds Rent Asunder

The purpose of all this is straightforward: to contrast the experience of the first civil war for Owen and Baxter. The difference between them could not be more obvious. Owen's life was relatively untouched by the war. He maintained his pastoral ministry throughout the conflict, enjoying the peace and stability of the one region in England that saw none of the fighting. He was detached in a way that Baxter never was. Even before the war started Baxter found himself in troubled waters and he was ejected early on from Kidderminster, a promising season of ministry abruptly truncated. Bring driven out of town by a mob threatening to club him to death would hardly lead Baxter to welcome the coming conflict. It is worth noting how the 'vulgar Rabble' were on several occasions decisive in Baxter's life, intimating threat and violence; whereas powerful benefactors were decisive in Owen's career, bringing privilege and preferment. That difference would have shaped their view of the world and even their view of the war. Baxter knew of its violence and brutality in a way that Owen did not. It is astonishing how many times Baxter showed up on the sidelines at key events during the war, beginning with Powick Bridge. If Edgewater, Marston Moor and Naseby were the three decisive engagements of the war,[105] Baxter was nearby for two of them. He experienced life in a garrison and life on the ground, living among the soldiers. He was too well aware of the pain, loss and devastation inflicted by the war. It is inconceivable that he could have claimed, as Owen did, that the gains from all the fighting had been 'cheaply purchased by yesterday's anguish and fear'. This was no mere seasickness. It is not that Owen was necessarily glib or offhand about the war, but it had not been his firsthand experience as it had for most of his compatriots. This gave him much greater freedom to focus on

---

[102]   Ibid., 235.
[103]   Ibid., 238.
[104]   Ibid.
[105]   Carlton, *Going to the Wars*, 125.

the strategic objectives of the war, as he understood them, without their clarity being muddied by the harsh reality of the carnage it caused. There is little doubt in Owen; Baxter was much less certain about what the war achieved, if anything constructive at all. Owen saw the war as a welcome liberation of the gospel; Baxter saw only its corruption and demise. Owen felt England to be on the brink of a glorious reformation; Baxter felt that it had been jettisoned. Owen testified to the freedom of the gospel, newly rescued from the Arminian snare; Baxter saw only 'the gospel departing'.[106]

It is important to note that this argument is limited to just these two men.[107] While I am sure their experience has something to say about how the English responded to the civil war, I am not suggesting that all individuals would have responded in exactly the same way. For instance, few men would have witnessed the carnage of war in closer proximity than Oliver Cromwell, but that did not prevent him from assuring the father of one soldier killed at Marston Moor that the battle 'had all the evidence of an absolute Victory obtained by the Lord's blessing upon the Godly Party principally'.[108] Here, in the most acute and personal of circumstances, Cromwell presented much the same vision as Owen would offer to Parliament two years later. So detachment from the experience of war was not a necessary prerequisite to holding a supremely positive view of what the fighting was about. Nor was engagement with the battles, even from the sidelines, always going to evoke Baxter's pessimism about the overall purpose and merit of the war. Hugh Peter, a Congregationalist minister and army chaplain, also witnessed much of the war at close hand, yet he was an effective communicator of Parliament's cause, raising support in numerous counties through his sermons.[109] He had preached a parliamentary fast sermon nearly four weeks before Owen preached his and, like Owen, he pointed out God's special providence in the nation's recent past.[110] Moreover, Baxter consistently defended

---

[106]   Baxter, *Saints' Everlasting Rest* (1650): *Practical Works*, iii.58.

[107]   I am particularly indebted to Professor John Coffey for his thoughts and suggestions embedded in this paragraph.

[108]   Oliver Cromwell to Colonel Valentine Walton, 5 July 1644: in *Oliver Cromwell's Letters and Speeches with Elucidations Complete in One Volume*, ed. Thomas Carlyle (New York: William H. Colyer, 1846), i.55.

[109]   Carla Gardina Pestana, 'Peter, Hugh (*bap.* 1598, *d.* 1660)', *Oxford Dictionary of National Biography*, Oxford University Press, 2004 [www.oxforddnb.com/view/article/22024, accessed 19 June 2009].

[110]   Hugh Peter, *Gods Doing and Mans Duty, Opened in a Sermon Preached Before Both Houses of Parliament* (London, 1646). He offered a 'List of some special prints of providence' that extended to 42 specific recent events (pp. 19–24).

the writings of John Goodwin[111] even though he was in some ways similar to Owen: a Congregationalist parish minister detached from the experience of the fighting, who advocated its aims and causes.[112] Goodwin was among the first ministers explicitly to advocate armed resistance to the King: 'the cause ... is just, and holy, and good'.[113] The telling difference is that Goodwin was something of an ally in Baxter's most pressing cause, the fight against Antinomianism.[114] Certainly, one correspondent of Baxter's referred to the helpful ministrations of Goodwin in preserving him from Antinomian error,[115] and if Baxter defended anything in Goodwin, it was the thrust of his soteriology. In this light, Goodwin at least offered some comfort; Owen offered only further disequilibrium.

So the examples of other individuals, either in relationship with Baxter or not, make it impossible to say that this divergence in experience between Baxter and Owen is enough in itself to explain their mutual antipathy. Yet it remains an extremely significant factor in the particularly personal nature of their mutual misunderstanding, if only because the contrasts are so glaring and so numerous. Thus we return to Owen's image of the cornfield. He acknowledged the odd stray weed but was impressed by the corn. Baxter saw only the weeds. He was one of those who, to use Owen's words, '[w]hich way soever they look, they can see nothing but errors – errors of all sizes, sorts, sects and sexes – errors and heresies from the beginning to the end'. It is conceivable that at precisely the moment when Owen was preaching his sermon to Parliament, Baxter was

---

[111]   DWL MS *BC* vi.97r (*CCRB* #22). Baxter was defending Goodwin against George Walker's accusations of Socinianism. Two years later, Baxter stood by his support of Goodwin: 'I see now J[ohn] Goodwin is a flatt Arminian: but that Condemneth not any charitable thoughts of him'. DWL MS *BC* ii.20r (*CCRB* #68). And in 1678 Baxter repeated his defence, though it was not published until 1690. Richard Baxter, *A Breviate of the Doctrine of Justification* (1690), sig. A2r–v.

[112]   Goodwin's commonalities with Owen should not be overstated, since Owen reportedly had at least the intention of writing against Goodwin's soteriology. DWL MS *BC* iv.180r (*CCRB* #77).

[113]   John Goodwin, *Anti-Cavalierisme, or, Truth Pleading as well the Necessity, as the Lawfulness of this Present War* (1642), 5. See John Coffey, *John Goodwin and the Puritan Revolution: Religion and Intellectual Change in Seventeenth-Century England* (Woodbridge: Boydell Press, 2006), 85–91; and Tai Liu, 'Goodwin, John (*c.*1594–1665)', *Oxford Dictionary of National Biography*, Oxford University Press, 2004 [www.oxforddnb.com/view/article/10994, accessed 19 June 2009].

[114]   Coffey, *John Goodwin*, 54–5. This also means that Goodwin and Owen were unlikely to agree on soteriology. Owen wrote *The Doctrine of the Saints' Perseverance* (1654) in response to Goodwin's book, *Redemption Redeemed: Wherein the Most Glorious Work of the Redemption of the World by Jesus Christ is...Vindicated and Asserted* (1651). See Owen, *Doctrine of the Saints' Perseverance* (1654): *Works*, xi.1, 12–13.

[115]   *Rel. Bax.*, Appendix, 98 (*CCRB* #887).

contending with his fellow soldiers, arguing them out of the mistakes, heresies and schisms. Looking down on a field of corn, the weeds would be much less apparent; weeding around the stalks, they become much more obvious and urgent. The field is the same, the perspectives are not. Indeed, Baxter offered his own image from nature to describe the war. England's inhabitants were 'like the pond that should grudge at the banks and dam, and thinks it injurious to be thus restrained of its liberty, and therefore combine with the winds to raise a tempest, and so assault and break down the banks in their rage; and now where is that peaceable association of waters?'[116] This is a much more disturbing image. A body of water is a massive, uncontrollable thing, and once the damage is done it cannot be repaired. One is powerless in the face of it; mere weeds, however rampant, can at least be pared back.

Both Owen and Baxter looked for the hand of God in contemporary events, yet they interpreted that hand in starkly different ways. Owen was convinced that

> all things here below, especially such as concern the gospel and Church of Christ, are carried along through innumerable varieties and a world of contingencies, according to the regular motions and goings forth of a free, eternal, unchangeable decree: as all inferior orbs, notwithstanding the eccentricities and irregularities of their own inhabitants, are orderly carried about by the first Mover.[117]

The sense of order here is striking, given the chaos of battles and slaughter and sieges. Owen easily rose above all that to see how God had been moving against the Arminians to defeat them, to frustrate their plans and to rescue the gospel from its captivity. But when Baxter looked for the hand of God he offered a drastically different interpretation. The war was not an expression of God's free grace towards England; it represented, instead, his judgement on the nation. 'I know that you are not such atheists, but you believe it is God that sendeth sickness, and famine, and war; and also that it is only sin that moveth him to this indignation.'[118] In Baxter's view, Christians had been reluctant to reprove their neighbours for their drunkenness, swearing, worldliness and ignorance, so God had acted to speak his own judgement on such behaviour. 'Guns and cannons speak against sin in England, because the inhabitants would not speak.'[119] Thus Owen saw the war as a blessing from God; Baxter, as God's judgement on a sinful people. There is no doubt that Baxter would have thought Owen's

---

116   Baxter, *Saints' Everlasting Rest* (1650): *Practical Works*, iii.236.

117   Owen, *Vision of Free Mercy* (1646): *Works*, viii.6.

118   Baxter, *Saints' Everlasting Rest* (1650): *Practical Works*, iii.226.

119   Ibid.

view mistaken. Even when he wrote the first part of his autobiography in the early 1660s, Baxter critiqued the error. In this case he was referring to a former friend, James Berry, who had turned on him during the war, but he might just as aptly have spoken of Owen himself. Berry had risen to high prominence during the Interregnum and been instrumental, in Baxter's mind, in the downfall of Richard Cromwell. 'And all this was promoted by the misunderstanding of Providence, which he verily thought that God, by their Victories, had so called them to look after the Government of the Land.'[120] The tenor of Owen's sermon to Parliament would have been, then, a similar misunderstanding of providence. His later critic, Anthony Wood, recalled Owen's 'wonderful knack of entitling all the proceedings of his own party, however villainous and inhuman, nay any the least revolutions or turns of affairs, which hapned [*sic*] to be in favour of his own Cause, to an especial Providence, to the peculiar and plainly legible conduct of Heaven, which he zealously preached up'.[121] Baxter would have agreed. He was too closely tied up in the upheaval to see anything else but judgement; Owen easily read into Parliament's victories the blessing of God.

Therefore, Owen and Baxter understood the war in starkly different terms and yet, on the face of it, they fought on the same side. This is further evidence that each side was hardly monolithic and it gives some indication of just how greatly different points of view could vary among those who were supposed to be allies in the same cause. Owen was intimately connected with those in Parliament who could advance his career and opportunities, and it made sense for him consciously to support Parliament against the King. Baxter made no such conscious choice. He drifted into one of Parliament's garrisons only for his personal safety and a lack of empathy with the royalist rabble; he resisted a formal commission; and he took one up only when he felt that the gospel was under threat.[122] His posture towards the cause was markedly different from Owen's. What this means is that even before we come to their diverging theology, we have a divergence of experience and understanding. When Owen and Baxter did eventually meet they were never going to understand each other naturally or easily. It is as if they had served in different wars, so they came from different worlds. In short, their contrasting experiences of the first civil war ensured that their relationship was doomed to struggle before it had even begun.

---

[120]   *Rel. Bax.*, i.57

[121]   Wood, *Athenae Oxonienses*, ii.739. Wood was drawing here on the criticisms of Samuel Parker in *A Defence and Continuation of the Ecclesiastical Politie: By Way of Letter to a Friend in London Together with a Letter from the Author of the Friendly Debate* (1671), 585–97.

[122]   It is possible that my interpretation here has been taken in a little by what Baxter later wanted his reader to believe.

Chapter 2

Opposite Ends

[M]y eye was chiefly on the Socinians.

John Owen[1]

Especially, I confess, mine eye was upon the ... Antinomians.

Richard Baxter[2]

John Owen and Richard Baxter emerged from the first civil war propelled along different trajectories with contrasting agendas. It is not so much that each one represented what the other attacked. Baxter was no Arminian, nor was Owen an Antinomian, though the accusations of each man would come close to alleging that. Rather, it was their commonalities that created such tension between them. To put it simply, each one got in the way of what the other was trying to achieve and each one was seen to give too much ground to what the other feared. Being on the same side strangely magnified the danger each one represented to the other.

In Chapter 3 we will trace the confrontation between them, when it came. In this chapter we will uncover the motivations behind each man's campaign and the different soteriological concerns that made their bitter engagement at least possible. In doing so, the story of their war experience cannot be forgotten, especially for Baxter, since his experience of the war did so much to focus his energies in the aftermath. He deeply feared the spread of Antinomianism. His army service behind him, he turned to the written word to cure England's dreaded disease. The result was the *Aphorismes of Justification* in 1649, his first published work that established his notoriety and brought him into conflict with Owen. Its effect on the fight against Antinomianism was limited, though, if only because – as Baxter eventually conceded – the threat had never been that substantial in the first place.[3] Moving in the opposite direction, Owen's

---

[1]   Owen, *Death of Death in the Death of Christ*, Appendix (1648): *Works*, x.425.

[2]   Richard Baxter, *Rich: Baxter's Confession of his Faith, Especially Concerning the Interest of Repentance and Sincere Obedience to Christ, in our Justification & Salvation* (1655), 2.

[3]   See Cooper, *Fear and Polemic*, 93–4. J.C. Davis also notes that 'in any genuine sense, [the Antinomians] seem to me remarkably few in number', in 'Religion and the Struggle for Freedom', 529.

campaign against the Arminians and, as time went on, the Socinians, took shape in two principal works, *A Display of Arminianism* in 1643 and *The Death of Death in the Death of Christ* in 1648. It is more difficult to assess the impact of these works but there is evidence to indicate that Owen's campaign was also of limited effect.

The point is that we have two men with driving concerns for the gospel in England who saw in each other a theology that gave encouragement to their respective opponents. Identifying their agendas, then, also serves to describe their soteriological convictions and concerns. Owen denied those who gave too much ground to human autonomy; Baxter preserved a central place for human responsibility in the scheme of salvation. Baxter denied those who made salvation entirely God's work, not ours; Owen argued that in his death Christ had paid the exact debt required of each sinner, the sinner contributed nothing at all. Clarifying these contrasting agendas, therefore, is essential to understanding the differences between the two men and offers another reason why Owen and Baxter were worlds apart before they had even met.

Pointing out the respective nature of these agendas inevitably draws us within the orbit of a significant historiographical debate. The issue at stake is the faithfulness of Reformed Orthodoxy to the theology of John Calvin in the century after his death, beginning with his successor at Geneva, Theodore Beza. On one side are those who in different ways and for varying reasons argue for a sharp disjunction between Calvin and the 'Calvinists'.[4] To offer just a couple of examples, Brian Armstrong identifies four defining features of what he labels Protestant scholasticism: it is 'a theological approach which asserts religious truth on the basis of deductive ratiocination … invariably based upon an Aristotelian philosophical commitment'; it gives reason equal standing with faith, 'thus jettisoning some of the authority of revelation'; it comprehends Scripture as 'a unified, rationally comprehensible account' that can be used as a measuring stick for orthodoxy; and it has 'a pronounced interest in metaphysical matters, in abstract, speculative thought'. Armstrong argues that this 'new outlook represents a profound divergence from the humanistically oriented religion of John Calvin and most of the early reformers'.[5] A second example is that of R.T.

---

[4]   For a comprehensive assessment of the variety in this position, see Richard A. Muller, 'Calvin and the "Calvinists": Assessing the Continuities and Discontinuities Between the Reformation and Orthodoxy. Part One', *Calvin Theological Journal* 30 (1995): 345–59. See also Gleason, *John Calvin and John Owen on Mortification*, chapter 1; and Coffey, *Politics, Religion and the British Revolutions*, 116–18.

[5]   Brian G. Armstrong, *Calvinism and the Amyraut Heresy: Protestant Scholasticism and Humanism in Seventeenth-Century France* (Madison, WI: University of Wisconsin Press, 1969), 32.

Kendall, who considers the development of Reformed Orthodoxy mostly in England up until the Westminster Assembly. He also discerns a departure from the theology of John Calvin, particularly on the point of assurance of salvation and in making faith in part an act of the will. His conclusion:

> The architectural mind of Westminster theology ... is Beza. Limiting the death of Christ to the elect robbed reformed theology of the simple idea that Christ alone is the mirror of election, hence the grounds of assurance. Beza, moreover, was the first to use language that virtually made faith a condition that binds God to the promise; the voluntarism of reformed theology centred on this concept, and things were never the same again.[6]

Thus the theology of the mid-seventeenth-century English Puritan establishment was not Calvinist at all, but 'crypto-Arminian' in its voluntaristic view of faith.[7]

On the other side of the debate, this largely prevailing view has come under critique in the last few decades, most notably from Richard Muller.[8] He argues that Reformed Orthodox thinkers such as Beza, Girolamo Zanchi and William Perkins – those particularly singled out for blame – did not make the doctrine of predestination 'the sole or even the primary determinant' of their theology, disconnected from the broad 'exegetical or interpretative tradition of the church'.[9] Moreover, it is mistaken either to expect continuity with Calvin or to criticize discontinuity 'as if Calvin held the patent on particular doctrinal *loci* and was somehow a perpetual norm for Reformed theology to the exclusion of doctrinal development'.[10] John Coffey weighs the debate in his examination of the Scottish Reformed theologian, Samuel Rutherford, and generally agrees with Muller.[11] The example of Rutherford demonstrates that the case for distortion has been exaggerated and over-simplified. It overlooks elements of Calvin's own theology that were indeed consonant with those who came after, particularly his emphasis on God's determinism coupled with a robust moralism. And it ignores crucial absences in his sixteenth-century context, not least a rising tide of sophisticated anti-Augustinianism that required sophisticated intellectual tools in reply.

---

[6]   R.T. Kendall, *Calvin and English Calvinism to 1649* (Oxford: Oxford University Press, 1979), 210.

[7]   Ibid., 212.

[8]   In addition to the essays cited here, see Richard A. Muller, *Post-Reformation Reformed Dogmatics: The Rise and Development of Reformed Orthodoxy, ca. 1520 to ca. 1725*, vol. 4, *The Triunity of God* (Grand Rapids, MI: Baker Academic, 2003), chapter 8.

[9]   Richard A. Muller, 'Calvin and the "Calvinists"', 154.

[10]   Ibid., 158.

[11]   See Coffey, *Politics, Religion and the British Revolutions*, chapter 5.

This debate has had a discernible influence on the historiography of Owen and Baxter, especially as it relates to the concerns in this chapter. Alan Clifford has done most to advance this specific discussion, in *Atonement and Justification*, published in 1990.[12] Clifford asserts that Calvin's scriptural Christology was distorted by Beza and the later Reformed Orthodox who made predestination their governing principle and Aristotelian logic their preferred theological method.[13] Thus 'Calvin was no Calvinist'.[14] Within this framework, Clifford evaluates the theology of Owen, Baxter, John Tillotson and John Wesley. He concludes that Owen – like Beza before him, and too enamoured with Aristotelian logic – offered a corruption of authentic Calvinism.[15] 'Owen became the undoubted champion of the Bezan school; he was inaccurately regarded as "the Calvin of England."' Thus 'the reformers would not recognize Owen's doctrine of the atonement as their own'.[16] In contrast, Baxter in many respects 'emerges as the true advocate of Reformation Calvinism'; he is 'the true heir of Calvin's theology of the atonement'.[17] 'Without pretending that Baxter's overall presentation is flawless ... [his] position may now be seen as a basic reaffirmation of Calvin's soteriology.'[18]

Carl Trueman thinks that much of this is 'nonsense'.[19] 'The simple fact is that both Owen and Baxter made positive, constructive use of Aristotelian causal categories.' Therefore, it is untenable 'to characterize Owen as the scholastic Aristotelian and Baxter the man of simple, biblical faith'.[20] Moreover, there was no fundamental disjunction between Owen and Calvin on the salvific effect of the death of Christ. 'Indeed, for Owen and for Calvin, it is the intercession

---

[12]   But see also, Alan C. Clifford, *Amyraut Affirmed or 'Owenism, A Caricature of Calvinism': A Reply to Ian Hamilton's* Amyrauldianism – Is it a Modified Calvinism? (Norwich: Charenton Reformed Publishing, 2004) and *Spotlight on Scholastics: Clarifying Calvinism: Responses to Carl Trueman, Richard Muller, Paul Helm* (Norwich: Charenton Reformed Publishing, 2005).

[13]   Clifford, *Atonement and Justification*, 70.

[14]   Ibid., 73.

[15]   Ibid., 43, 72.

[16]   Ibid., 82. Because of his relevance to Owen scholarship, I might also add that Peter Toon worked within this view of a disjunction between Calvin and the 'High Calvinists'. He concludes that Owen was distinct from Calvin, but he also believes that although Owen 'was a firm believer in the doctrines of election and particular redemption, he nevertheless believed in the free offer of the Gospel to all and the duty of all to respond to that which the Gospel required, saving faith in Christ'. Peter Toon, *The Emergence of Hyper-Calvinism in English Nonconformity 1689–1765* (London: The Olive Tree, 1967), 136, 144.

[17]   Clifford, *Atonement and Justification*, 82, 105.

[18]   Ibid., 161.

[19]   Trueman, *Claims of Truth*, 222.

[20]   Ibid., 53. See also Trueman, 'Puritan Theology as Historical Event', 261–73.

of Christ set in the whole context of his office of Mediator … that makes this infinite sufficiency efficient for the elect and which provides the unity and continuity between the eternal covenant and the historical economy.'[21] In his most recent book on Owen, Trueman sees little need to 'go over the tired old territory' of the accusations of Clifford and others, but he still makes it very clear throughout that he has little patience for those who continue to argue that Owen represented a corruption of Calvin's true inheritance.[22]

These, then, are the principal issues under debate. In the main, it is a question of who was closer to Calvin: Owen or Baxter. It is a question that has little interest for the purposes of this book, but there is no avoiding the debate and I will offer some brief perspective at the conclusion of the chapter. I should note that while Clifford and Trueman are free to range across the whole corpus of these two men, I am deliberately confined to assessing the contrasts in their soteriological agendas as they appeared only in the 1640s, in the three books I mentioned above. We can now consider each one in its context.

John Owen v. the Arminians and Socinians

No one would have been surprised by the severe anti-Arminianism of Owen's 1646 sermon before Parliament; the same tone had marked his first book, *A Display of Arminianism*, published three years earlier. In recent scholarship the *Display* has generally been compared unfavourably with Owen's later writings. Peter Toon, for instance, considers it 'no masterpiece' and '[l]acking in literary elegance'.[23] Carl Trueman finds Owen's argument 'somewhat overstated and generalized'.[24] Kelly Kapic calls it 'rough at many points'.[25] There are reasonable grounds for all these assessments, yet it would be a mistake to dismiss the book. An author's first published work, in the seventeenth century at least, could have a care and intensity about it that was not so apparent in later works, often written in greater haste and in response to specific polemical provocation. That was

---

[21]   Trueman, *Claims of Truth*, 202–3.

[22]   Trueman, *John Owen*, 8–9. He also acknowledges (p. 1, n. 1) that he had dealt with Clifford sufficiently in *Claims of Truth*.

[23]   Toon, *God's Statesman*, 15.

[24]   Trueman, *Claims of Truth*, 23. See also Trueman, *John Owen*, 86 (and 92): 'Owen was writing as a young theologian at the start of his career, and the work is therefore (as one might expect) somewhat overwrought and full of passages which conflate Arminian and Socinian positions for the sake of a good polemic.'

[25]   Kapic, *Communion with God*, 23.

certainly true of Baxter;[26] and Owen, too, offered in his *Display* an impressive and weighty demolition of his opponents' arguments as he described them.[27] For Owen, it was a remarkably disciplined piece: clearly structured, tightly argued and succinct, without the lengthy and obscure digressions that would be so much a trademark of his other works.

Such clarity was there from the very first page of the book, when Owen summed up the difference between himself and the Arminians in a single head: 'Whether the first and chiefest part, in disposing of things in this world, ought to be ascribed to God or man?'[28] The Arminians tried to do everything possible to preserve ample space for the action and initiative of human free will even if that meant constraining the capacity of God infallibly to achieve his own ends in the lives of his creatures. In short, they substituted God's sovereign will with human free will. To this end they sought, first, to 'exempt themselves from God's jurisdiction' and, second, 'to clear human nature from the heavy imputation of being sinful, corrupted, wise to do evil but unable to do good'.[29] For each of these two aims the Arminians constructed a set of denials. The soteriology Owen laid out in his *Display* was a systematic denial of those Arminian denials.

To begin with, the Arminians constrained the sovereign freedom and predisposing will of God by means of four principal denials. First, they denied 'the eternity and unchangeableness of God's decrees; for these being established, they fear they should be kept within bounds from doing anything but what his counsel hath determined should be done'.[30] In response, Owen affirmed that 'all the decrees of God, as they are internal [to him], so they are eternal, acts of his will; and therefore unchangeable and irrevocable'.[31] God's will could not be separated from his nature so no mutability or temporality could be attributed to his decrees.[32] Therefore, what he willed must infallibly be accomplished.[33] Second, by implication and in consequence the Arminians denied God's foreknowledge of events concerning things free and contingent – involving human choice – because such divine prescience would necessarily overlay infallibility on those

---

[26]   See Cooper, *Fear and Polemic*, 104, 123–4.

[27]   Cook also sees the difference: 'Owen used a tight organization and an abundance of precise footnotes, with a result quite different in tone from his later, more hurried discourses.' Sarah Gibbard Cook, 'A Political Biography of a Religious Independent: John Owen, 1616–1683', PhD Thesis, Harvard University, 1972.

[28]   Owen, *Display of Arminianism* (1643): *Works*, x.11.

[29]   Ibid., 12, 13.

[30]   Ibid., 12.

[31]   Ibid., 14.

[32]   Ibid., 19.

[33]   Ibid., 20.

events: they could unfold only in the manner that God had foreseen.[34] Owen countered this by arguing that God foreknew all actions that were possible, out of which 'God by his decrees freely determineth what [events] shall come to pass'. He arranges cause and effect in such a way as to bring about 'what certainly he will do, or permit to be done'. It is impossible, then, that such events will not fall out in the way that God has decreed and foreseen.[35] Third, the Arminians denied the 'all-governing' and 'energetical, effectual power' of God to rule the thoughts, determine the wills and direct the actions of men and women,[36] thus making all the decrees of God that are dependent on human action uncertain in their execution.[37] Owen would have none of this. Providence 'we may conceive as an ineffable act or work of Almighty God, whereby he cherisheth, sustaineth, and governeth the world, or all things by him created, moving them, agreeably to those natures which he endowed them withal in the beginning, unto the ends which he hath proposed'.[38] In doing so, God does not transgress the free will of human beings.[39] Thus human freedom is preserved, 'but, for all this, let us not presume to deny God's effectual assistance, his particular powerful influence into the wills and actions of his creatures, directing of them to a voluntary performance of what he hath determined'.[40] Finally, the Arminians denied 'the irresistibility and uncontrollable power of God's will', since he is taken by them to will what demonstrably has not been achieved – the salvation of all men and women – and believe that God's will can be resisted.[41] On this point, Owen distinguished the secret and revealed will of God. God's secret will concerns what he will do; his revealed will concerns what we must do if we are to please him. The former cannot fail; the latter is contingent on human action – it is 'metaphorically only called his will' since it concerns his commands and our response. Thus when God is said to will the salvation of all men and women, it should be understood in this sense.[42] The overall thrust of Owen's soteriology should be clear: salvation depends first of all on God's eternal and immutable, efficacious and infallible will to save some.

The reason for that, of course, is that men and women do not have within themselves the resources to save themselves, something the Arminians denied.

---

[34]   Ibid., 12, 22.
[35]   Ibid., 23–4.
[36]   Ibid., 12.
[37]   Ibid., 42.
[38]   Ibid., 31. Italics removed.
[39]   Ibid., 36.
[40]   Ibid., 37.
[41]   Ibid., 12–13, 44.
[42]   Ibid., 45. Owen quoted John 6:40 as an example.

Owen broke down that grand negation into seven discreet denials. Briefly, the Arminians denied predestination; original sin; any difference in men and women from Adam as he was created; the efficacy of Christ's death in fulfilling the conditions and providing merit for the elect; the necessity of Christ's death in salvation; the corruption and constraints of human free will; and, finally, the incapacity of the will to effect the salvation of the individual.[43] In successive chapters of his book Owen countered each denial with affirmations that expressed clearly Calvinist convictions. Several times he presented the human soul as a dead thing incapable of bringing itself to life. 'And what ability, I pray, hath a dead man to prepare himself for his resurrection? Can he collect his scattered dust, or renew his perished senses.'[44] There is not only an impotence in corrupt human nature, there is also an unrelenting enmity towards that which is good.[45] 'There is nothing in ourselves, as ourselves, but sin.'[46] Therefore, the resources for salvation have to flow from God specifically and infallibly towards those particular individuals whom he has decreed to save. Owen's scheme is, then, one of limited atonement: Christ died only for the elect. They alone are purchased, ransomed by his death. It is for those and only those that Christ died and for whom he continually intercedes as they are brought to full salvation.[47] They are enabled infallibly to perform the conditions of salvation by the Holy Spirit who brings about faith in the believer.[48] The will is merely passive in the first act of salvation but is thereafter revived and enabled to co-operate with the irresistible saving grace of God. 'The operation of grace is resisted by no hard heart; because it mollifies the heart itself.'[49] There is co-operation in the revived heart but the work is God's from beginning to end. Where the Arminians enfeebled God in the face of human choice – a frequent refrain throughout the book[50] – Owen acknowledged God's sovereign, irresistible power to accomplish whatever he has willed.

In 1648 Owen followed up this first work with a second, longer discussion of soteriology, *The Death of Death in the Death of Christ*. This book is viewed as

---

43   These are quickly summarized in ibid., 13–14.

44   Ibid., 126. See also, pp. 130, 136–7.

45   Ibid., 127.

46   Ibid.

47   Ibid., 90–92.

48   Ibid., 89, 94.

49   Ibid., 134.

50   The Arminians made God into an 'idle spectator' who hangs around waiting for the individual to use him if he or she chooses. This makes Christ 'as altogether useless as if he were but a fig-tree log', since it is at least conceivable that none would be saved by his death if none chose to accept his grace, and sin would have been punished twice. See ibid., 35, 37, 93, 94, 96, 120.

the superior of the two: his classic work on soteriology and 'the most extensive and thoroughly biblical defence of the high Calvinist doctrine of limited atonement'.[51] Most notably, J.I. Packer declared the book to be the last word on that doctrine. 'One searches his book in vain for the leaps and flights of logic by which Reformed theologians are supposed [by their modern critics] to establish their positions; all that one finds is solid, painstaking exegesis and a careful following through of biblical ways of thinking.' No one, says Packer, can deny the doctrine of limited atonement until he or she 'has refuted Owen's proof that it is part of the uniform biblical presentation of redemption, clearly taught in plain text after plain text. And nobody has done that yet'.[52] It is possible that Packer has done Owen a disservice with such unstinting and, in this case, undeserved praise of this particular book. It is, frankly, not Owen's best work. If Packer's enthusiasm has helped to render *Death of Death* one of Owen's classic texts, and if Packer has done anything to make it the first port of call for an introduction to Owen's theology, then the prospective reader has hardly been helped and neither has Owen's reputation. Ultimately, the book is weak and unconvincing, because it is exactly the opposite of what Packer claims.

Owen structured *Death of Death* in four books, but his argument unfolded in three phases. First, and in a Trinitarian fashion that would be typical of so many of his later writings, Owen discussed the distinct operations of the Father, Son and Holy Spirit in the working of salvation. Second, he explored the means of salvation: the oblation and intercession of Christ. These two discussions were relatively brief, comprising the first of the four books and just over 40 pages in a work of around 270 pages in total.[53] In the third and most substantial phase of his argument, the remainder of the book, Owen presented the ends intended and infallibly achieved by the death of Christ, principally the salvation of the elect. Here he repeated his defence of limited atonement (book two); demolished arguments for universal redemption, the new face of Arminianism[54] (book three); and dealt with those verses that seemed to encourage a view towards universal redemption (book four).

There is much that might be said about such a large and significant book, but I would like to note only two aspects in passing. First, the Socinians were a more prominent target here than in Owen's earlier *Display*. Sarah Mortimer has recently offered a sensitive reconstruction of the reception of Socinian ideas on

[51] Kay, *Trinitarian Spirituality*, 136–7.
[52] J.I. Packer, *Among God's Giants: The Puritan Vision of the Christian Life* (Eastbourne: Kingsway Publications, 1991), 177–8.
[53] The two phases comprise pages 157–179 and 179–200 in the Goold edition.
[54] Owen, *Death of Death in the Death of Christ* (1648): *Works*, x.367. Owen compared 'our new Universalists' with 'our old Arminians'.

the Continent and in England itself.[55] Socinianism takes its name from Faustus Socinus, an Italian jurist who moved from Florence to Basle to Rakow, in 1579, where he came to lead a community of anti-Trinitarians and Anabaptists known as the Polish Brethren. Socinus approached Theology from the perspective of Roman law, thereby significantly reinterpreting Christianity. At its heart, his new formulation sought to sever the connection between religion and natural law. The effect of this was to disrupt the presumed continuity between natural law, the Old Testament and the teachings of Christ. These were taken to be new, superseding the moral law of the Hebrew Scriptures. Men and women were saved by his teaching and moral example, not by his death on the Cross. Like any Roman ruler, God had the right to punish sinners but could choose not to use it, so the Cross of Christ was not the basis of forgiveness and reconciliation. For religion to be praiseworthy it had to be a matter of choice, not of an inner inclination or instinct tied to a universal natural law embedded in all people, much less the result of God's own choice and election. So salvation came by responding to revelation (principally through the New Testament Scriptures), guided by reason and motivated by reward. Clearly all this kicked aside many of the underpinnings of Christian orthodoxy. Socinus denied the eternal pre-existence and deity of Christ; such notions were unsupported by the gospels and unnecessary, since Christ was merely a historical figure who revealed a new way. He therefore rendered irrelevant the metaphysical basis of the Trinity. He dispensed with the doctrine of original sin, arguing that we are just like Adam, not in some fallen state, and capable of making a reasoned choice. He asserted that the Christian could have confidence in revelation because the Scriptures could be (and should be) assessed just like any other historical text and withstand the scrutiny. By removing religion from the domain of natural law Socinus also parted with Calvinist resistance theory and bolstered the pacifist stance of the Polish Brethren.

Thus Socinianism was born, with unmistakeable effect. 'Few religious groups inspired such extreme reactions, or found such careful readers.'[56] One

---

[55]   I have drawn the description in this paragraph largely from Sarah Mortimer, *Reason and Religion in the English Revolution: The Challenge of Socinianism* (Cambridge: Cambridge University Press, 2010), chapter 1. But see also H. John MacLachlan, *Socinianism in Seventeenth-Century England* (Oxford: Oxford University Press, 1951), esp. chapter 1; Muller, *Triunity of God*, 83–120; Philip Dixon, *Nice and Hot Disputes: The Doctrine of the Trinity in the Seventeenth Century* (London: T&T Clark, 2003), chapter 2; Smith, 'And if God was One of Us', 160–184; and, for broader background, Martin Mulsow and Jan Rohls, eds, *Socinianism and Arminianism: Antitrinitarians, Calvinists and Cultural Exchange in Seventeenth-Century Europe* (Leiden: Brill, 2005).

[56]   Mortimer, *Reason and Religion*, 1.

of the strengths of Mortimer's approach is to reveal that 'Socinian theology was never staid nor static'.[57] It continued to evolve among Socinus's followers after his death and, especially in England, thinkers accused of Socinianism rarely if ever adopted his system wholesale. Instead, they selectively reworked the foundations of his thought, appropriating what was useful for their own particular purposes at the time. For this reason, writers accused of Socinianism might also be involved in battles among themselves. Mortimer shows that in the early decades of the seventeenth century, Socinianism barely registered in England (in contrast to parts of the Continent, notably the Dutch territories, where it was the topic of intense debate) partly because 'the theological and political battle-lines were drawn rather differently'.[58] That changed during the 1630s. The 'Great Tew Circle', which (located at the house of Lucius Cary, Second Viscount Falkland, 18 miles from Oxford) lay outside academic and church structures, provided an environment in which Socinian ideas could be openly discussed and even published, notably in William Chillingworth's *The Religion of Protestants* (1638).[59] And in the context of rising Laudian ceremonialism and apparent Arminianism, Socinianism was a safe proxy target because it was still condemned on all sides.[60] During the 1640s Socinianism emerged even further into the open. Some Royalists found it extremely useful to separate natural law and Christian law, since that move undermined the parliamentarian defence of resistance to the King.[61] By the end of the decade the Socinian threat loomed large in the minds of many English divines.[62]

This helps to account for its growing presence in Owen's publications throughout the 1640s. He had been made well aware of the Socinians during his time at Oxford under the tutelage of Thomas Barlow.[63] Barlow had republished a metaphysics textbook for use by his students, 'and this gave him the opportunity to discuss the Socinians and their errors'.[64] Clearly Owen had not forgotten. When he wrote chapters 7–9 of Book III of *Death of Death*, those that dealt with the satisfaction of Christ, his 'eye was chiefly on the Socinians'.[65] Trueman suggests that both Arminians and Socinians existed 'on a sliding scale of heresy, with the difference being one of quantity, rather than quality, of error'. Though

---

[57] Ibid., 38.

[58] Ibid., 40.

[59] Ibid., chapter 3.

[60] Ibid., 53, 55.

[61] Ibid., chapter 4.

[62] Dixon, *Nice and Hot Disputes*, 47–8.

[63] See Toon, *God's Statesman*, 5–6; and Collins, *Allegiance of Thomas Hobbes*, 239–40.

[64] Mortimer, *Reason and Religion*, 57.

[65] Owen, *Death of Death in the Death of Christ*, Appendix (1648): *Works*, x.425.

they derived from different pedigrees, both were 'manifestations of the same heretical tendency towards notions of human autonomy'. The 'connection Owen makes between Arminianism and Socinianism [was] in terms of the relative autonomy each tradition grants to the human agent'. Both effectively made God subject to human action, and men and women into 'creators, gods, with reference to their own actions'.[66] So the Socinians were growing in significance for him. By the mid-1650s they would be critically important.

The second aspect to note is another closely related target in the book: the Dutch theologian, Hugo Grotius. He supported the Remonstrants in the controversy over Arminianism, which inevitably attracted the accusation of Socinianism. Grotius was no Socinian, but his position on the new law of Christ was something of a middle ground between the Socinians and Protestants.[67] More important for Owen, several important lines of argument in Grotius buttressed the Arminian cause, especially the view that Christ died for all, not just for the elect. This is why he critiqued Grotius over the issue of the nature of the debt Christ had paid on the Cross on behalf of sinners. Two views were possible: 'The one being *solution ejusdem*, payment of the same thing that was in the obligation; the other *solution tantidem*, of that which is not the same, nor equivalent unto it, but only in the gracious acceptation of the creditor.'[68] To put this scholastic distinction in plainer terms: when Christ offered himself as a sacrifice for sin, thereby remitting the debt that sinners owed against God, did he pay the exact debt for the precise and particular sins of those individuals – standing specifically in their place and bearing the exact punishment that was theirs – or did he make some general form of recompense that was not, in fact, precisely the same in nature but was graciously taken to be so by God? Owen argued that Christ paid the exact debt for sin. He did this in order to collapse one of the supports undergirding Grotius's argument for universal redemption; to move the grounds of the nature of satisfaction from the general and universal to the particular and individual; to preserve God's justice, which could only be diluted by suggesting he had accepted anything less than what was due to him by the affront of sin; and to underline the full, perfect and eternal remission of sin achieved by Christ for the individual believer. The importance of this point will emerge when we move to consider Baxter's soteriology.

Both Owen's supporters and detractors have latched on to the *Death of Death* as a defence of limited atonement but Trueman argues that this 'is only one aspect of his wider preoccupation with the priesthood of Christ. If one

---

[66]   Trueman, *John Owen*, 26–9.

[67]   Mortimer, *Reason and Religion*, 29.

[68]   Owen, *Death of Death in the Death of Christ* (1648): *Works*, x.267.

wishes to press the point, it is more the effectiveness, not its limitation, which is his real interest and concern'.[69] I agree. Owen's position on the extent of the atonement flowed out of more important presuppositions and was ultimately grounded in his determination to preserve God's sovereign free will. Covenantal thinking (which had developed even in the space between 1643 and 1648)[70] and Owen's Trinitarianism shaped his presentation in much more fundamental ways than a mere fixation with limited atonement. Salvation begins with the covenant of redemption, the agreement between the Father and the Son to appoint the Son as a mediator and as the one whom the Father would punish for the sin of those he has chosen to save.[71] The Son, by taking on human flesh, offering himself as a sacrifice for sin, and making intercession for the elect, has fulfilled his part in the covenant of grace.[72] And the Spirit has enabled this work of Christ by acting in power in his incarnation, death and resurrection.[73] The subsequent covenant of grace is the agreement God has made, in Christ, to save the elect, of whom there is a specific number. This covenant has conditions, but God has determined to fulfil those conditions in the elect.[74] 'From all which we draw this argument: – That which the Father and the Son intended to accomplish in and towards all those for whom Christ died, by his death that is most certainly effected.' The intention of the Father and Son 'to redeem, purge, sanctify, purify, deliver from death, Satan, the curse of the law, to quit of all sin, to make righteousness in Christ, to bring nigh unto God, all those for whom he died', has been perfectly fulfilled. '[T]herefore, Christ died for all and only those in and towards whom all these things recounted are effected.'[75] The magnitude of what had been achieved for the elect could have been attained only by the power and initiative of the triune God. Thus limited atonement was not the driver of Owen's soteriology, it was the consequence.

However, I am in sympathy with Alan Clifford when he suggests that Owen's exegesis was not always faithful to Scripture. To help make this point I would like to assess the effectiveness of Owen's campaign and to suggest that it failed to gain significant ground because it evaded the point that was most heavily pressed by his opponents, a two-pronged argument that exposed the implications of limited atonement. While that doctrine was not the driver of Owen's theology,

---

69   Carl Trueman, 'John Owen Unleashed: Almost. Response to Tim Cooper', *Conversations in Religion and Theology* 6 (2008): 243.

70   Trueman, *John Owen*, 86.

71   Owen, *Death of Death in the Death of Christ* (1648): *Works*, x.163ff.

72   Ibid., 174ff.

73   Ibid., 178–9.

74   Ibid., 223; Trueman, *John Owen*, 79.

75   Owen, *Death of Death in the Death of Christ* (1648): *Works*, x.211.

it should have been much more to the fore in his polemical response. It was the Achilles heel in his argument to which he paid surprisingly little attention. As a result, it is likely his books failed to convince anyone beyond those who already agreed with him.

Owen's political agenda was made clear in *A Display of Arminianism*, which he dedicated to the Committee on Religion in the House of Lords. He presented it as 'a bill of complaint against no small number in this kingdom' who had fought against God for 'thrice ten years' and against whom Owen now urged a 'holy war'.[76] In his dedication he pointed the Committee beyond the domestic threat of the Arminians to their foreign backers and the prospect of forced re-Catholization. He claimed not to know the intention of the Arminians themselves, 'but this I have heard … that the introduction of Arminianism among us was the issue of a Spanish consultation', a clever ploy 'to oppose the Calvinists, and so, by cherishing dissension, reduce the people again to Popery'.[77]

In this light the book was a forceful piece of polemic whose logic and scriptural authority were not to be taken lightly. But it was not without a fatal weakness, a telling absence. It is exposed in what Owen did not say, and is revealed by a consideration not of the generic Arminians he had in mind but by one specific target he held in his sights. In 1633 Samuel Hoard, the Arminian rector of Moreton, Essex, had published *Gods Love to Mankind Manifested by Dis-prooving his Absolute Decree for their Damnation*. The book was republished in 1635, 1656 and 1673. It homed in on the implication of the doctrine of limited atonement: if God had specifically decreed the salvation of an elect few he had also decreed everlasting damnation for the majority of men and women before they were even born. Launching a sustained – if repetitive – attack on that implication, Hoard assembled a number of objections. Calvinist doctrine led men and women into despair if they could not know themselves to be among the elect.[78] It was the death of piety, since it removed the twin incentives of hope and fear.[79] One could have no hope of salvation if one was not among the elect and one would have no fear of damnation if one was.[80] It 'would hereby open a doore to liberty and profaneness'.[81] But worse even than that, the doctrine distorted the character and grace of God. It contradicted his attributes of holiness, mercy,

---

[76]   Owen, *Display of Arminianism* (1643): *Works*, x.5, 38, 7

[77]   Ibid., 7.

[78]   Samuel Hoard, *Gods Love to Mankind Manifested, By Dis-prooving his Absolute Decree for their Damnation* (1633), 100–101.

[79]   Ibid., 91.

[80]   Ibid.

[81]   Ibid., 97.

justice and sincerity.[82] It made God the author of sin, and worse than the devil (who merely tempts and persuades) in forcing sin on the reprobate.[83] For that reason he cannot judge sin, since he himself has decreed it. This doctrine

> chargeth [God] with mens *Eternall torments* in hell, maketh him to be the prime, principall and invincible cause of the damnation of millions of miserable soules: the *prime* cause, because it reporteth him to have appointed them to destruction, of his own voluntary disposition, antecedent to all deserts in them; and the *principall* and *invincible* cause: because it maketh the damnation of Reprobates to be necessary and unavoydable through Gods absolute and uncontrollable Decree: and so necessary.[84]

Hoard could hardly imagine a father marrying and having children only to torture them 'that he may shew what his authority and power is over them'. Could, then, the God of mercy do the same to his own creation?[85] If so, he 'cannot be God; because he should not bee just, nor holy, not the judge of the world, all properties essential to God'.[86]

Hoard's intellectual capacities were no match for Owen's. On one level, Owen's *Display of Arminianism* was an easy rebuttal of *Gods Love to Mankind*. But the victory came at a cost, because at no point did Owen engage with Hoard's central thesis nor did he recognize the emotional and pastoral weight of Hoard's case. The *Display* was simply a determined restating of those convictions that had worried Hoard in the first place. Owen's response was, for that reason, incapable of taking the conversation forward or breaking fresh ground that might have led to some measure of mutual understanding. And, when it came, Owen's re-presentation of Hoard's book was misleading:

> The sum of [the Arminians'] doctrine in this particular is laid down by one of ours in a tract entitled 'God's Love to Mankind,' etc.; a book full of palpable ignorance, gross sophistry, and abominable blasphemy, whose author seems to have proposed nothing unto himself but to rake all the dunghills of a few of the most invective Arminians, and to collect the most filthy scum and pollution of their railings to cast upon the truth of God; and, under I know not what self-coined pretences, to belch out odious blasphemies against his holy name. The sum, saith he, of all these speeches (he cited

---

[82] Ibid., 51–80.
[83] Ibid., 24–5.
[84] Ibid., 14.
[85] Ibid., 15.
[86] Ibid., 25.

to his purpose) is, 'That there is no decree of saving men but what is built on God's foreknowledge of the good actions of men.'[87]

These sentences represent a 'railing' to match anything found in Hoard's book. Rather than engaging with Hoard's thesis, Owen heaped abuse and then distorted it. Hoard's main argument did not concern an obscure point about God's foreknowledge. Instead, as the title made very clear, it was an objection to the idea that God hated most men and women from eternity. Owen would have been well capable of deflecting the criticism but, curiously, he never even tried.

Owen's approach can be contrasted with that of John Davenant, one of the British representatives at the Synod of Dort, Bishop of Salisbury, and the author of *Animadversions...Upon a Treatise Entitled God's Love to Mankind* that appeared in 1641, the year of Davenant's death and two years before Owen's *Display*.[88] Davenant wrote the book to satisfy a friend who had been persuaded by Hoard's attack.[89] It is true that Davenant's *Animadversions* was a lengthy, sustained and specific response to Hoard's book in a way that Owen's *Display* was not. But the difference in approach is obvious even in the first few pages. Davenant immediately acknowledged the issue that most concerned Hoard and, in a nice manoeuvre, agreed with him. If Hoard

> had no other aim, then the overthrowing of such an eternall Decree of Predestination and Preterition as is fondly supposed will save men whether they repent or not repent, believe or not believe, persevere or not persevere; and such an absolute Decree of Reprobation as will damne men though they should repent and believe, or will hinder any man from repenting and believing, or will cause and work any mans impenitency or infidelity; we both wish, and shall endeavour together with him to root such erroneous fansies [*sic*] out of all Christian minds.[90]

Davenant's words simultaneously deflected most of Hoard's simplistic critique of Calvinist belief, rescued God from the charge of unjustly hating his creatures, and accepted that Hoard's concern to preserve God from such a charge had merit. It was of course a polemical move, and an effective one. I appreciate that Davenant's theology, with its hypothetical universalism, was built along different

---

[87]   Owen, *Display of Arminianism* (1643): *Works*, x.61.

[88]   Owen did not refer to Davenant's book in his *Display*.

[89]   John Davenant, *Animadversions...Upon a Treatise Entitled God's Love to Mankind* (Cambridge, 1641), 3. The letter from the friend laying out his concerns and directly quoting *God's Love to Mankind* appeared on pages 21–3. Davenant did not know if he had been successful in winning his friend back to the Calvinist cause (p. 3).

[90]   Davenant, *Animadversions*, 2.

lines from Owen's, but even so he sounded just like Owen when he went on
to assert that 'God is he who according to his absolute and infallible purpose
giveth in time that grace unto his elect which before all time he decreed should
be an effectuall means to bring them unto glory'.[91] Thus Davenant built some
acceptance and understanding of Hoard's concern into the foundation of his
reply, thereby reassuring the reader unsettled by the thrust of Hoard's criticism.
Owen did not. The pastoral implications of Hoard's challenge – the despair over
assurance of salvation, the encouragement to licentiousness, the corruption of
God's mercy and nature – all went unanswered. Owen's *Display* might have been
a proficient statement of his soteriology and he might have won the debate on
points, but the result was a pyrrhic victory in a long, losing war.

The same sort of thing can be said of *The Death of Death in the Death of
Christ*. The book was a direct response to Thomas Moore, who had published
The Universality of God's Free-Grace in Christ to Mankind in 1646, an earnest
assertion of universal redemption over against limited atonement. Like Hoard
before him, Moore criticized those who denied and blasphemed the love of
God 'as if God ever, and from all eternity hated the greatest number of men',
withholding from them the 'meanes of life'.[92] Instead, Moore asserted that Christ
gave himself as a ransom for 'all men', and that his death was effectual for 'all
men'. Those two words were a constant refrain throughout the book: when the
Scriptures use the plain language of all men, in relation to the salvific ambit of
the death of Christ, that was exactly what was meant. Thus these two words
were in italics wherever they appeared in his work, and they appeared often.
Moore constantly referred to the 'plaine sayings of the Gospel' and the 'plaine
terms' of Scripture.[93] 'That which may be proved in and by Scripture, both by
plain Sentences therein, and necessary consequences imported thereby: without
wrestling, wrangling, adding to, taking from, or altering the Sentences, and
words of Scripture, is a truth to be believed.'[94] Moore's writing was replete with
Scripture references, pointing the reader to what he felt were plain statements
not to be twisted in the hands of partisan interpreters. While he accepted that
the same words could certainly mean different things in different contexts,[95] that
was not the case when it came to the death of Christ. Thus he rebuked those
who argued that Christ 'dyed for all his Elect, and onely for those that are elect
to *Sonne-ship*, and eternall Inheritance, and for no other; Not for *all men, every*

---

[91]   Ibid., 3.

[92]   Thomas Moore, *The Universality of God's Free-Grace in Christ to Mankind Proclaimed
and Displayed* (1646), To the Christian Reader, sig. A1.

[93]   Ibid., To the Christian Reader, sig. A1, p. 129.

[94]   Ibid., 131.

[95]   Ibid., 28.

man, any man, but the Elect. This is flat against, and openly contradictory to the affirmation of Scripture, and is that opposed in the whole drift of this Tract'.[96]

Here was another work that, like Hoard's, harped on a single theme and offered a quality of argument that would never stand up to Owen's logic. In the epistle to the reader Owen claimed that 'in the ensuing treatise ... the book of Thomas Moore [is] in all the strength thereof fully met withal and enervated'.[97] He was 'fully resolved that I shall not live to see a solid answer given unto it'.[98] And as we have seen, recent scholars have also declared Owen to be the clear winner. But in asserting that Christ died only for the elect, Owen was confronted with what seemed the plain words of Scripture. For instance, 1 Timothy 4:10 describes God as 'the Saviour of all men, especially of those that believe'. In a lengthy discussion Owen interpreted the word 'Saviour' not in the sense of salvation from sin, but in the sense of God's general providence in protecting people, especially his elect, from mishap and disaster.[99] However plausible Owen found his interpretation of this verse, it required a considerable exercise in reinterpretation to make it cohere with his argument. Likewise, John 3:16 seemed to stand in his way: 'God so loved the world, that he gave his only-begotten Son, that whosoever believeth in him should not perish, but have everlasting life.' Owen spent a whole chapter glossing the words 'loved' and 'world' to show that the love in view was actually 'the special love of God to his elect' and not to 'all and every man in the world'.[100] Again, Owen's arguments made a certain sense, but it was also obvious that a great deal of massaging was required to force the verse to say what Owen thought it should say. Indeed, the final book of around 130 pages was essentially a long exercise in such reinterpretation. Verse after verse that gave such encouragement to the proponents of universal redemption was dismantled by Owen and forced to bend to the strictures of his system. The cumulative effect of this manipulation is to render Owen's arguments unconvincing if it requires so many verses to undergo such rigorous scrutiny in order to allow his system to stand. Certainly, it is difficult to cast the work, as J.I. Packer did, as an appeal to 'plain text after plain text'.[101] Moore's endless refrain that words like 'all' really did mean 'all' was, if anything, only vindicated.

So there were two arguments launched against Owen and the proponents of limited atonement: they made God out to hate most people from eternity; they mangled the plain sense of Scripture. Owen evaded the first and confirmed the

---

[96]   Ibid., 35.
[97]   Owen, *Death of Death in the Death of Christ* (1648): *Works*, x.154.
[98]   Ibid., 156.
[99]   Ibid., 190–192.
[100]   Ibid., 323, 325. Italics removed.
[101]   Packer, *Among God's Giants*, 178.

second. So it would be no surprise to find that Owen's book failed to convince. In 1650 John Horn, rector of All Saints, King's Lynn, published *The Open Door for Mans Approach to God*, an extended, page-by-page unpicking of Owen's *Death of Death*. Horn made his way from one end of Owen's book to the other without making as much as a single concession, gradually rounding his argument into an explicit defence of Moore and presenting a further instalment in the long debate over whether the word 'all' really did mean 'all'. Owen was prepared 'to leap over a hedge and a ditch to his own purposes, not considering how full the Scriptures are against him'.[102] Specifically, he had failed convincingly to rebut the two lines of argument. On the first, and even after two lengthy publications, 'we challenge Mr. *Owen*, or any of them All, to shew us one expression in Scripture contradictory to our Assertion; any that says Christ did not dy for All'.[103] On the second, 'That God hated any from eternity, he [Owen] hath often said, but never yet proved it'.[104] Horn's book makes for depressing reading, in that it reveals the way in which the whole controversy resembles First World War warfare: each side deeply entrenched, small victories proclaimed for the benefit of supporters, and the ground gained or lost measured in metres. In almost two decades of debate the issues had advanced precisely nowhere. It is difficult to see that Owen's books had achieved much at all. Given the polemical environment it could hardly have been otherwise, but it is at least possible that Owen's approach was not as effective as it might have been.

In the last chapter of *The Death of Death* Owen finally came around to a brief discussion of the consolation his soteriological system could offer the believer. Note that where Davenant placed it right at the start, Owen had it right at the end, and even he recognized just how brief it was. Here at last he offered some recognition of the emotional charge latent in the accusations of those who denied his doctrine and he explained why it had been missing thus far: his purpose had not been 'to speak of things in a *practical*, so *atheological* way, having designed this discourse to be purely *polemical*'. Such devotional warmth was 'no more expected in controversies of this nature, than knotty, crabbed, scholastic objections in popular sermons and doctrinal discourses, intended merely for edification'.[105] This helps to account for his failure to respond to the specific challenge of the likes of Hoard, Moore and Horn, but his excuse is unconvincing for several reasons. First, when he penned his Epistle to the Reader, presumably among the last words he wrote, he hoped that 'the weak' might find 'something

---

102   John Horn, *The Open Door for Mans Approach to God* (1650), 58.

103   Ibid., 169.

104   Ibid., 226.

105   Owen, *Death of Death in the Death of Christ* (1648): *Works*, x.421.

for their strengthening and satisfaction'.[106] Second, he directly contradicted himself just three years later when he defended himself against Richard Baxter: 'I was desired and pressed to handle the things of that discourse [*Death of Death*] in the most popular way they were capable of, and in the best accommodation to vulgar capacities, so that it is no wonder if some expressions therein may be found to want some grains of accurateness ... in a scholastical balance.'[107] Third, even if his books were works of polemic the grounds of that polemic had been laid at least in part by Hoard and Moore. So acknowledging their two-pronged attack would have done nothing to prevent his book remaining a polemical exercise. Owen's apparent choice not to respond directly to their main lines of argument was, then, a tactical decision that weakened the force of his response.

Still, that initial comment revealed his intentions in writing books like *A Display of Arminianism* and *The Death of Death in the Death of Christ*: his approach was polemical, not practical. Above all, his intention was to limit human agency and affirm God's sovereign freedom in the process of salvation. His target was not just the Arminians in both tracts but also, especially in the latter, the Socinians. So Owen was in the 1640s a man on a mission. It is revealed in both these books and in his sermons to Parliament. He was determined to do what he could to rescue England from the Arminian threat that had been badly beaten, but had life in it yet. It would not please him, therefore, to find one of his fellow Puritans also on a mission – one that cut across the grain of Owen's intentions and threatened a further revival of something like Arminian doctrine.

Richard Baxter v. the Antinomians

Richard Baxter's fears lay in quite the opposite direction from Owen's. Where Owen detected a Roman Catholic-backed Arminian threat – thwarted for now, but still latent and dangerous – Baxter held no such concern. Instead, the Antinomians fired his efforts as he emerged from the first civil war. They are what kept him in the field for so long, serving as army chaplain two years after the fighting had ended. They are what sparked his first publication. True, he later recalled that Arminianism and Antinomianism were 'equally distributed' throughout the army;[108] and during his army years he would indeed have argued against any soldiers of an Arminian persuasion. At the time, though, one looks

---

106   Ibid., 156.
107   Owen, *Of the Death of Christ* (1650): *Works*, x.435.
108   *Rel. Bax.*, i.50.

in vain among the remnants of Baxter's writings for any indication of significant concern with the Arminians. Instead, the Antinomians had all the running.

In my earlier book I explored Baxter's late-1640s obsession with the bogey of Antinomianism.[109] I sought to demonstrate how the Antinomians served to channel his fears, allowing him to fix blame for the perversion of the first civil war. I also showed how he reversed the dominant emphases in his soteriological position – shifting from something like Antinomianism to something much closer to Arminianism – in the face of a widespread Antinomian threat. I do not intend to replicate that work here, but a general sketch is necessary to place Baxter alongside Owen in order to contrast their principal concerns and agendas.

Strict imputation lay at the very core of Baxter's construction of Antinomian soteriology, the belief that the particular sins of the believer were imputed to Christ at the Cross, and that his righteousness was imputed to them. This was, he said,

> the root, the heart of all Antinomianism, from whence all the rest doth unavoidably follow: and that is the misunderstanding of the nature and use of Christs Death and Obedience, and thinking that *Christ obeyed or satisfied by suffering, or both, as in our Persons, so that the Law takes it, to all ends and uses, as done by our selves.*[110]

This was the fatal mistake of the Antinomians, with a swarm of undesirable consequences. Believers were justified before they were born, at the Cross or even from eternity. They were passive in the process of justification, a one-off event that was simply a matter of having one's eyes opened to a prior justification already completed in Christ. The Antinomians believed the gospel was a promise not a law. In Baxter's eyes, this removed the kingship of Christ – he could be no king if he had no law – and supplied the link he discerned between the supplanting of Christ as king and the removal of Charles as king. Thus the sinner was not required to accept Christ as king or lord, only as priest: a 'false Faith [that] doth not justifie'.[111] The gospel itself lost its power. The Antinomians understood the new covenant to have no conditions requiring fulfilment on the part of the believer, since the matter was settled from eternity. The elect did not

---

[109]   Cooper, *Fear and Polemic.* See also, David P. Field, *Rigide Calvinism in a Softer Dresse: The Moderate Presbyterianism of John Howe, 1630–1705* (Edinburgh: Rutherford House, 2004), 18–29.

[110]   Richard Baxter, *Richard Baxter's Confutation of a Dissertation For the Justification of Infidels: Written by Ludomaeus Colvinus, Alias Ludovicus Molinaeus, Dr. of Physick and History-Professor in Oxford, Against his Brother Cyrus Molinaeus*, 1654, Epistle Dedicatory. In *Rich. Baxters Apology.*

[111]   Richard Baxter, *The Substance of Mr. Cartwright's Exceptions Considered* (1675), 208. In *Treatise of Justifying Righteousness.*

need to repent, believe or obey since Christ had already done that perfectly in their place.

Baxter believed the effect of such errant theology was devastating. It rendered the elect free from sin at any point, removing any need for pardon, and as righteous as Christ from all eternity. Thus men and women were made their own redeemers. On the other hand, Antinomian doctrine transformed Christ into a sinner, making him out to be 'a hater and blasphemer of God and Holiness, and the greatest murderer, adulterer, thief, lyar, perjured Traytor in all the World, the sins of all the Elect being truly His sins'.[112] Once again the professed concern was what the doctrine at hand did to a right understanding of the nature and character of God. The Antinomians delivered up 'a wicked God' by turning Christ into a sinner and making a liar of the Father who was said to declare those righteous who clearly were not.[113] They also produced wicked believers: 'where there is no Law, there can be no obedience'.[114] If Christ perfectly obeyed in the place of the elect, there remained no need for their own obedience and no fear of punishment. Any duties that might be performed were irrelevant, since the end was achieved without recourse to any means that concerned them; repentance and obedience were shunted aside. Antinomian soteriology could bring men and women only to licentiousness. Indeed, that is all the doctrine amounted to.[115] It needs to be said that much of this construction and its alleged effect was a significant misreading of the authors Baxter had in mind, men like Tobias Crisp, John Saltmarsh and William Dell. Baxter unfairly distorted their position and intentions.[116] But that is beside the point. This is what Baxter believed he was seeing. And when he presented the *Aphorismes* to the world he prescribed the perfect antidote to this deadly disease.

The governing design of Baxter's new soteriology was to ward off Antinomianism at every point: 'because the *Antinomians* deny it, let us prove it'.[117] Thus the scheme he laid out in the *Aphorismes* was the mirror image of

---

[112]   Richard Baxter, *A Defence of Christ, And Free Grace: Against the Subverters Commonly Called, Antinomians or Libertines* (1690), 10. In *Scripture Gospel Defended*. See also pp. 3–4; and Richard Baxter, *Richard Baxter's Catholick Theologie: Plain, Pure, Peaceable: For Pacification Of the Dogmatical Word-Warriors* (1675), I.ii.66.

[113]   Baxter, *Defence of Christ, and Free Grace*, 11; Richard Baxter, *A Breviate of the Doctrine of Justification, Delivered in many Books, By Richard Baxter: In many Propositions, and the Solutions of 50 Controversies about it* (1690), prologue. In *Scripture Gospel Defended*.

[114]   Baxter to [John Warren], 22 October 1651: DWL MS *BT* vi.84, item #199 (*CCRB* #74).

[115]   Baxter, *Richard Baxter's Confutation*, 288.

[116]   See Cooper, *Fear and Polemic*, 65–7.

[117]   Joseph Read, ed., *Universal Redemption Of Mankind, By The Lord Jesus Christ: Stated and Cleared by the late Learned Mr. Richard Baxter. Whereunto is Added a Short Account of Special*

Antinomianism as he understood it. His defence began with the distinction between God's will as *Dominus* and God's will as *Rector*.[118] As *Dominus* God brought about his secret and insuperable 'Will of Purpose', which determined events according to his own purpose. Absolute and unconditional, it included the decrees of predestination, election and reprobation. As *Rector*, God exercised his 'Legislative or Preceptive will', which focused on law and duty, and prescribed what was required of men and women in order to be saved. It was revealed, not secret; conditional, not absolute; and it required duty – faith, obedience and perseverance – from the believer.[119] Because of these conditions, some who had been 'conditionally pardoned and justified, may be unpardoned and unjustified again for their non-performance of the conditions, and all the debts so forgiven be required at their hands', though 'in regard to God's Will of Purpose, which determineth eventually, whether they shall fall quite away or not, I do believe, that the justified by Faith never do'.[120] Therefore, those who fulfilled all the conditions under God's Will of Precept were exactly the same as those who were elected under God's Will of Purpose. Even so, the gospel could be rightly offered to all. Baxter did not dwell on the question of universal redemption in the *Aphorismes*, since he intended to deal fully with that subject in a subsequent work.[121]

He also distinguished two types of righteousness, which had the effect of limiting the scope of Christ's work on the Cross and of preserving a central place for human responsibility. The first type was 'Legal Righteousness': perfect conformity to the moral law. This is what Christ achieved and supplied. Only this kind of righteousness was imputed to the believer and only to those who had provided in themselves the second type, 'Evangelical Righteousness'.[122] This comprised a sincere but imperfect fulfilment of the gospel conditions.[123] Thus Christ fulfilled the conditions of the old covenant, the believer fulfilled the condition of the new.[124] Christ could not have fulfilled both, since the offer was universal and, if so, everyone would be saved;[125] and '[t]hese two kinds of

---

Redemption, by the Same Author (1694), 398.

[118]   For thorough assessments of Baxter's soteriology, see Boersma, *Hot Peppercorn* and Packer, *Redemption and Restoration of Man*. On this distinction between *Dominus* and *Rector*, also see Lamont, *Millennium*, 136ff.

[119]   Baxter outlined these distinctions in *Aphorismes*, 1–11.

[120]   Ibid., 196–8.

[121]   Ibid., 197; Postscript; Appendix, 164.

[122]   Ibid., 108–15.

[123]   Ibid., 286.

[124]   Ibid., 109–11.

[125]   Ibid., 112.

Righteousnesse cannot stand together in the same person, in regard to the same Law and Actions'.[126] Nor could the believer supply both, since he or she was incapable of perfectly obeying the law. As a result, strict imputation was denied:

> The Righteousness of the new Covenant then being, the performance of its conditions, and its conditions being obeying the Gospel or believing, it must needs be plain, That on no other terms do we partake of the Legal Righteousness of Christ. To affirm therefore that our new Covenant-Righteousness is in Christ, and not in ourselves, or performed by Christ, and not by ourselves, is such a monstrous piece of Antinomian doctrine, that no man who knows the nature and difference of the Covenants, can possibly entertain, and which every Christian should abhor as unsufferable.[127]

In a similar fashion, Baxter disagreed with '[m]ost of our ordinary Divines' who said that both Christ's passive righteousness and his active righteousness were imputed to the believer.[128] This view of imputation might have been prevalent, but Baxter was not afraid to disagree with his fellow divines, and even insult them. 'The maintainers of it (beside some few able men) are the vulgar sort of Divines, who having not ability or diligence to search deeply into so profound a Controversie, do all hold that opinion which is most common and in credit.'[129]

Among his objections to that common doctrine, this understanding 'maketh Christ to have paid the *Idem*, not the *Tantundum*', which is 'the core of the mistake'.[130] He conceded that the 'resolving of this depends upon the resolving of questions both great and difficult. 1. What it was which the Law did threaten 2. what it was that Christ did suffer?'[131] On the first question, 'exceeding difficult it is to determine, because it hath pleased the Holy Ghost to speake of it so sparingly'. 'It is hard to conclude peremptorily in so obscure a case.'[132] The second question was 'disputable'.[133] Even so, Baxter was firm enough in his own position:

> I conclude then, that in regard of the proper penalty, Christ did suffer a paine and misery of the same sort, and of equall weight with that threatened; but yet because

---

126   Ibid., 99.
127   Ibid., 110–111.
128   Ibid., 45.
129   Ibid., 51.
130   Ibid., 47.
131   Ibid., 27.
132   Ibid., 31.
133   Ibid., 35.

it was not in all respects the same, it was rather satisfaction that the payment of the proper debt, being such a payment as God might have chosen to accept.[134]

This is the basis from which he engaged with Owen. Even though he recognized the complexity of the issue, Baxter was clear that the Antinomians (and Owen) were wrong on this point. The result was devastating: 'almost all Religion is overthrown at a blow'.[135]

Notwithstanding Baxter's conviction that the elect would infallibly come to faith and persevere, his scheme rendered their position tenuous. For one thing, the Old Testament law with all its provisions, threats and curses remained in place so that 'the sins even of the justified are still breaches of that Law, and are threatened and cursed thereby'.[136] For another, justification was progressive; always incomplete and provisional in this life. The punishments of the law were merely suspended for a time:

> an absolute Discharge is granted to none in this life. For even when we perform the Condition, yet still the Discharge remains conditional till we have quite finished our performance. For it is not one instantaneous Act of believing which shall quite discharge us; but a continued Faith. No longer are we discharged, then we are Beleevers. And where the condition is not performed, the Law is still in force, and shall be executed upon the offender himself.[137]

Far from being justified from eternity, the process of justification was completed only in stages. The first stage was constitutive justification, which was achieved when the believer fulfilled the initial gospel conditions of faith and obedience.[138] The two were connected, since faith implied action, like the galley slave who receives release from his slavery, accepting that such release will entail lifelong duty to his new master.[139] Faith involved such duties as repentance, praying for pardon, forgiving others, 'sincere Obedience and Works of Love'.[140] So this first justification was only virtual, not actual, like a suitor who knows the law is fully on his side yet awaits the actual sentence of the judge. This was the second stage,

---

[134] Ibid.

[135] Baxter, *Universal Redemption*, 80. For further detail, see Cooper, *Fear and Polemic*, 60–65.

[136] Baxter, *Aphorismes*, 78.

[137] Ibid., 81–2.

[138] Baxter, *Aphorismes*, 183–5. Baxter would later develop this into a tri-fold justification. See Boersma, *Hot Pepper Corn*, 89–92.

[139] Baxter, *Aphorismes*, 239.

[140] Ibid., 235–6.

declarative justification, which involved the declaration by God the Judge that a person was justified. This justification could occur only after he or she had died, having fulfilled the condition of perseverance – the required duration of faith.[141] Thus salvation was by 'degrees toward our full and perfect Justification at the last Judgment'.[142]

While the believer had 'far less to doe in the work of his Salvation', he or she did not have nothing to do.[143] 'Christ intended not to remove all our misery as soon as he dyed, nor as soon as we believed. I am now to shew, That he doth not justifie by the shedding of his blood immediately, without somewhat of man intervening, to give him a legal title thereto.'[144] Baxter agreed that the believer could perform the conditions only by grace, but he or she still had to perform them; Christ did not fulfil them in his or her place.[145] In this sense the believer was 'said to be personally righteous', a phrase sure to rankle with those 'ignorant wretches' the Antinomians.[146] In another striking image, God was the landlord of a bankrupt tenant. In his generosity he had decided on a new terms of lease, and, yes, payment was required from the tenant: 'but a pepper corn yearly'.[147] However, one could argue (and others certainly did) either that the burden Baxter placed on the believer amounted to much more than that, or that even a single pepper corn was far too much if it gave any ground to human merit and righteousness.

Indeed, the *Aphorismes* provoked no little amount of controversy that helped to establish Baxter's reputation, for better or worse, and that took up many of his subsequent energies and publications. Certainly it left behind a more visible impact than either of Owen's works, in the form of private animadversions and published attacks. Little of it was favourable. It is true that some of Baxter's correspondents felt they had benefitted from his book. John Jackson, a London rector, was one of the most effusive. 'I thinke you have fully answered your own expression in cutting asunder the unobserved sinews of Antinomianisme, with which I confesse I had like to have been entangled, had I not by the goodnes[s] of God met with such cleare beams of truth in your discourse.'[148] And there were other encouragements from a small number of widely scattered admirers,[149]

---

[141]   Ibid., 183–5, 283.
[142]   Ibid., 194.
[143]   Ibid., 77.
[144]   Ibid., 93.
[145]   Ibid., 115.
[146]   Ibid., 118, 123.
[147]   Ibid., 127.
[148]   John Jackson to Baxter, 6 July 1652: DWL MS *BC* ii.264r (*CCRB* #91).
[149]   For a brief summary, see Cooper, *Fear and Polemic*, 102.

including John Horne. He chided Baxter for being too concerned with men's opinions in holding back his thoughts on universal redemption.[150] By then Baxter would have felt that he could not win. Keeping silent brought Horne's rebuke, while speaking out in the *Aphorismes* had evoked only a very loud chorus of disapproval.

The noise had come from every direction. At least seven men sent private animadversions in response to Baxter's request.[151] They included Richard Vines and Anthony Burgess, both respected members of the Westminster Assembly and the two men to whom Baxter had dedicated his book – their critique was hardly an encouraging sign of success. Vines disapproved of some points in Baxter's scheme; while Burgess's vehement dissent blossomed from a day's conference with Baxter into subsequent publications between the two men.[152] John Tombes, a neighbouring minister and old opponent on the issue of infant baptism, weighed in, along with John Warren, the vicar of Hatfield Broad who had lived with Baxter as a schoolboy at Bridgnorth. The extended correspondence between Baxter and Warren supplies further insight into the drivers of Baxter's anti-Antinomianism.[153] George Lawson, Christopher Cartwright and John Wallis were the remaining three animadverters, more sympathetic than the others but even they failed to offer anything like wholehearted support and agreement.

The *Aphorismes* also came in for very public attack.[154] In his assault against John Goodwin in 1653, George Kendall took a detour to disagree with Baxter on several points, thereby implicitly lumping Baxter in with that well-known Arminian figure.[155] William Eyre, curate of St Thomas, Salisbury, also connected Baxter with the Arminians. 'Though Mr. *B.* seems to mince the matter, calling his conditions but a *sine qua non*, and a *pepper corn*, *&c.* he attributes as much, if not more to works, then the Papists, Arminians, and Socinians, have done.'[156]

---

[150]   John Horne to Baxter, 13 August 1655: DWL MS *BC* iv.223r–224v (*CCRB* #263).

[151]   For an excellent summary, see Boersma, *Hot Pepper Corn*, 33–41.

[152]   See Anthony Burgess, *The True Doctrine of Justification Asserted and Vindicated from the Errours of Many* (1654), though Burgess does not name Baxter; and Richard Baxter, *Of Justification: Four Disputations Clearing and Amicably Defending the Truth, Against the Unnecessary Oppositions of Divers Learned and Reverend Brethren* (1658).

[153]   See Cooper, *Fear and Polemic*, 106–12.

[154]   For a fuller summary see Boersma, *Hot Pepper Corn*, 44–57.

[155]   See George Kendall, *Theokratia: Or, A Vindication of the Doctrine Commonly Received in the Reformed Churches* (1653), i.134–45.

[156]   William Eyre, *Vindiciae Justificationis Gratuitae: Justification Without Conditions; Or, The Free Justification of the Sinner* (1654), 190.

And John Crandon, rector of Fawley, Hampshire, launched by far the most savage attack on Baxter.

> I cannot, I dare not use words that might strengthen but rather vilifie the self confidence and arrogance of the man. So when the Wolf comes in sheeps clothing to devour, when under the profession of a Protestant and Presbyterian Divine, he vends his Popish and Arminian [doctrines] under the name of Protestant Tenets, dissembling his confederacy with the enemies thereof.[157]

The main purpose of Crandon's lengthy polemic was to demonstrate that Baxter was a Papist in disguise. His attack was uniquely personal, vindictive and sustained. While it cannot be taken as a reasoned or balanced response to the *Aphorismes*, it does serve to demonstrate just how badly the book had come across. Baxter had written the dedicatory epistle to the *Aphorismes* with all the carefully crafted humility of a man who fully expects the whole world to agree with him. 'I was then', he later explained, 'a stranger to the dispositions of Divines'.[158] Such naivety was quickly and permanently shattered. Far from being enamoured with Baxter's new insights, most of his colleagues were profoundly disturbed and dismissive.

There was no avoiding the fallout. With a judicious employment of hindsight, Baxter claimed to have seen it coming:

> I have voluntarily bin more prodigall of my reputation in putting out that pamphlet of Justification, which I well knew was like to blast my reputation with most divines, as containing that which they judged a more dangerous errour than Antipaedobaptism: and the issue hath answered my expectation: I am now so hissed at by them, that I feele temptation enough to schisme in my discontents.[159]

Baxter felt annoyed that his efforts to thwart the Antinomians had been so badly misunderstood and poorly appreciated, and he lapsed into a sullen disgruntlement.[160] But faced with such a barrage of abuse and disagreement some sort of response was required. Baxter was forced to offer appropriate concessions, but his embarrassed apologies for the book did not amount to

---

[157]   John Crandon, *Mr Baxters Aphorisms Exorized and Anthorized: Or an Examination of and Answer to a Book Written by Mr. Ri: Baxter* (1654), Epistle Dedicatory, n.p.

[158]   Baxter, *Confession of his Faith*, 1.

[159]   Baxter to John Tombes, 11 September [1649]: DWL MS *BC* iii.253r (*CCRB* #21). Baxter made much the same point on the same day to John Warren, DWL MS *BC* vi.96r (*CCRB* #22).

[160]   See Cooper, *Fear and Polemic*, 101–2.

much. He publicly acknowledged the haste with which he had sent it out into the world (even though he had taken the care to send the main body of it to a friend for comment) and the resulting errors in expression. He regretted the many hours it cost him, over too many years, to respond to all of his critics, either in private correspondence or in a significant pile of published works. And despite his public protestations and his eventual denial of the book he never altered in any significant way the main outlines of his system. He could never concede that the core of his book was fundamentally mistaken. The *Aphorismes of Justification* was, then, a flawed and failed effort to pursue his agenda in England. The outcry was just too great ever to allow the thrust of his message and concern to be clearly heard.

Assessing Success

The contrast in the soteriological agendas of Owen and Baxter should now be apparent. We are now in a position to sum up what was at stake for them, and to assess the debate between Alan Clifford and Carl Trueman. To begin with, I repeat my earlier point that the question of each man's faithfulness to John Calvin is of little relevance. For one thing, it is a question they never stopped to ask themselves. Baxter mentioned Calvin only once in the *Aphorismes*.[161] Owen also alluded to Calvin only once in his *Display* and again only once in *Death of Death*.[162] On this admittedly very limited basis, it is difficult to think of an authority they were less interested in. More to the point, the question potentially distracts us from the issues actually at stake for each man in 1640s England.

I do not want to suggest that the complex soteriologies of Owen and Baxter can be reduced to a single, practical concern; the theological heritage of each one was too deep for that. Certainly Owen, with his extensive university training among other shaping factors (such as his upbringing, as far as we can discern it), located his thought within an intellectual stream stretching back through Reformed Protestantism to medieval Catholic thinkers and the early Church Fathers. I think Trueman has done a good job of tracking those sources and influences that made Owen a 'Reformed Catholic' as well as a 'Renaissance man'.[163] And even Baxter, though self-taught, was remarkably well read and conversant in disputes and texts both Continental and domestic, Latin and English. It would be a profound mistake to overlook the heavy weight of the

---

[161]   Baxter, *Aphorismes of Justification*, 53.

[162]   Owen, *Display of Arminianism* (1643): *Works*, x.16; *Death of Death in the Death of Christ* (1648): *Works*, x.275.

[163]   See Trueman, *John Owen* and *Claims of Truth*.

shared intellectual and theological context of both men and to suggest that immediate pragmatic, political and polemical pressures were solely responsible for each one's theology.

And yet, such pressures cannot be omitted or overlooked, either. Theology is not immune to historical drift; it is shaped by the layering of many different socio-political contexts.[164] This is most clearly seen in the case of Baxter, whose theology fundamentally shifted throughout the 1640s. It did so in the face of a very practical reality. It is no surprise to find that Baxter, confronted by the carnage of war and haunted by what seemed so many departures from human decency and morality, should craft for himself a soteriology that would safeguard those very qualities he thought were desperately in danger of being lost. So he promoted a theology that would preserve human moral responsibility. At its simplest level, his argument that faith, repentance and ongoing obedience were prior conditions of salvation embodied his pressing concern to prevent the excesses of human behaviour he had just witnessed.

Owen also argued for conditions, but they were infallibly brought about in the elect by God through the means of their own free volition. Where this was an implication in Baxter's system, it was an overt and oft-repeated assertion in Owen's. This is why there was, in fact, a great deal the two men held in common – the point with which we shall begin the next chapter. The stark differences lay in the prominence and priority of particular elements. What Baxter sought to underline were those aspects that Owen sought to downplay, while not abandoning them. There was, then, moral responsibility in Owen, just as there was God's sovereignty in Baxter. The difference lay in their placement. In contrast to Baxter, Owen's concern was to preserve the sovereignty of God against those who wanted to locate the deciding factor in salvation in human free will. If he had a decisive, shaping experience, it came earlier than Baxter's, in the 1630s as he witnessed the growing encroachment of Laudianism on Oxford University. The situation had grown intolerable by 1637 when Owen left Queen's College to take up a private chaplaincy.[165] We cannot know for sure just how much that experience confirmed his theology. Certainly it seems most likely that Owen's convictions remained what they had been through his childhood in the home of his nonconformist father. Nor is there evidence that the experience was nearly as traumatic for Owen as the 1640s were for Baxter. Even so, Owen's practical

---

[164]   This recognition is exemplified in the work, for example, of Mark A. Noll in *America's God: From Jonathan Edwards to Abraham Lincoln* (Oxford: Oxford University Press, 2002). Noll describes the book as 'a contextual history of Christian theology' pursuing 'what might be called a social history of ideas' in which 'social and political events are enlisted to help explain grand shifts in theological conviction' (pp. 3, 5, 6).

[165]   Toon, *God's Statesman*, 9, 10.

experience of the Laudian regime – what was preached, what was censured, who was preferred – would undoubtedly have fed into his concern to affirm God's sovereignty. That is surely seen in the exuberant tone of his 1646 sermon to Parliament, following the Arminian defeat.

Therefore, to ask whether Baxter or Owen was the more faithful to Calvin seems tangential, to say the least. But the debate is there and something needs to be said. On one side there are dangers in arguing that Owen and his fellow Calvinist Puritans were faithful to Calvin and in close continuity with him. Paul Helm illustrates the danger. He published *Calvin and the Calvinists* in 1982, primarily in response to R.T Kendall. He argues that Kendall's account of Calvin is inaccurate, that his caricature of the Puritans is exaggerated, and therefore that the argument for fundamental discontinuity is flawed.[166] What is fascinating is the persistence of one of the very ideas that proved so difficult to maintain in the 1640s – it seems that 'all', still, does not mean 'all'. 'To say, in Calvin's typical fashion, that "Christ died for us" is certainly compatible with the statement "Christ died for the elect". But as it stands it is also compatible with "Christ died for all men".'[167] As I said above, Owen's handling of certain Scriptures was hardly straightforward; this is not an especially encouraging defence. Trueman has not sought to argue that Owen was in continuity with Calvin, but that he was in continuity with the broad context of the late medieval catholic and Reformed theological inheritance. This is a much safer line of argument.

On the other side, I am not convinced by Clifford's argument: the angles are wrong. To put that another way, Clifford wants to align himself broadly with Kendall: 'the validity of his revisionist approach is not questioned'.[168] But they cannot both be right. The voluntarism that Kendall discerned within the Westminster tradition was not present in the *Display* or in *Death of Death*, but it was present in the *Aphorismes*. It was Baxter, not Owen, who made obedience and perseverance ingredients of faith. If that is the tradition that Kendall blames for distorting Calvin, Baxter is one of the foremost exemplars. Clifford accepts that 'Baxter's neonomian or new law conception of the gospel is a highly ingenious amalgam of gospel theory and seventeenth-century political theory',[169] but he gives this recognition very little force. The language of *Dominus* and *Rector* is no mere metaphor: it is the governing construct of Baxter's soteriology. And it is, surely, even more of a non-scriptural invention than Owen's alleged over-reliance on 'commercial metaphors'.[170] Clifford allows Baxter his metaphors and

---

[166] Paul Helm, *Calvin and the Calvinists* (Edinburgh: Banner of Truth Trust, 1982), 10.
[167] Ibid., 13.
[168] Clifford, *Atonement and Justification*, 241.
[169] Ibid., 192.
[170] Ibid., 126–7.

denies Owen his, but I suggest that Baxter's were far more critical and central to his soteriology. In this light, it seems faintly absurd to argue that for 'Baxter, as for Calvin, the supreme issue for the Reformed theologian was integrity of exegesis'[171] if the purpose is to suggest that Baxter was in some way more faithful at this than Owen.

Was Owen or Baxter closer to Calvin? It seems to me that both men stood within the Calvinist tradition, and both were similar to and different from Calvin, in different ways.[172] My hope is that we can move on from the debate. I have already suggested that we need to do this in the case of Owen,[173] and I now extend that to Baxter. If the question is never posed again, it will not be missed.

To return to the seventeenth century, Owen and Baxter pursued their respective agendas in the same hostile polemical environment that did so much to shut down any sort of mutual understanding. So we should not blame them entirely if their agendas showed few signs of success. The very environment was against them. Beyond that shared obstacle, though, were weaknesses in their approach. When faced with two very potent lines of attack, Owen avoided the first (by tacking on the issue of assurance only at the very end of the second of his two books) and confirmed the second (by contorting the plain words of Scripture). On the other hand, Baxter showed a remarkable and never-to-be-repeated naivety in sending out into the world a system that was so very idiosyncratic. No wonder he was subsequently accused of singularity and novelty.[174] It seems that Baxter entirely missed the irony of his own Epistle to the Reader when he condemned '[e]very ignorant, empty braine (which usually hath the highest esteem of it selfe) [that] hath the liberty of the Presse, whereby (through the common itch that pride exciteth in men, to seeme somebody in the world) the number of bookes is grown so great, that they begin with many to grow contemptible'.[175] While a few were helped by his book, most were offended and unconvinced, and the worst dynamics of seventeenth-century English polemic were brought to bear against him. Owen and Baxter had, then, largely failed in their polemic endeavours. But that did not stop them persevering in their respective stances and agendas. Nor did it stop them from turning their sights on each other, beginning with Baxter, and a regrettable ending to his *Aphorismes*. It is time these two men came into contact.

---

[171]   Ibid., 82.

[172]   Gavin McGrath also came to a similar conclusion, in 'Puritans and the Human Will', 386.

[173]   Cooper, 'John Owen Unleashed. Almost', 238. I should note that Trueman has also advocated a 'new agenda' that moves on from the debate as it has traditionally been cast, in 'Puritan Theology as Historical Event', 255–6.

[174]   Baxter, *Confessions of his Faith*, Preface, sig. b4r.

[175]   Baxter, *Aphorismes of Justification*, Epistle to the Reader, sig. a1r–v.

Chapter 3
An Accidental Animosity

Justice obliges me to state that Baxter was invariably the aggressor; as Owen seems never to have meddled with him but in the way of self-defence.

William Orme (1826)[1]

When a relationship turns sour the question of blame inevitably arises and often that has a lot to do with how the problems first began. For John Owen and Richard Baxter, their relationship was in trouble from the very beginning. Indeed, from all that we have seen so far the chances of them ever meshing smoothly, given their contrasting experience and agendas, were always slim. In this sense, 'Who started it?' is the wrong question to ask. The origins of the strain go back well beyond any one act of provocation. It might also seem a rather childish question. But the two men could at times come across rather like squabbling children; their specific difficulties did have an easily identifiable starting point in Baxter's *Aphorismes of Justification*, or, to be more exact, the Appendix to that book; and the question lingered beyond the seventeenth century. Generally, the blame has fallen on Baxter. 'Justice obliges me to state', decreed William Orme, 'that Baxter was invariably the aggressor; as Owen seems never to have meddled with him but in the way of self-defence'.[2] This is an understandable view and it is not without truth. Baxter quickly and deservedly earned a reputation as an aggressive and insulting attacker of other men. More than that, in several places he identified himself as 'the beginner of the Controversie' with Owen.[3] But the whole story is not so simple. A falling out requires more than an act of provocation from one of the parties; it involves the choice of the other person to be provoked. Both must share responsibility in an ongoing dispute. Baxter's defences, therefore, as well as his confessions and apologies, have merit. Owen's role cannot be ignored or minimized. Indeed, a case can be made that Owen deserves much more critical scrutiny than has so far been allowed, and Baxter

---

[1] Orme, 'Memoirs of Dr Owen', 89.

[2] Ibid.

[3] Richard Baxter, *Rich. Baxter's Admonition to William Eyre of Salisbury; Concerning his Miscarriages in a Book Lately Written for the Justification of Infidels, Against M. Benj. Woodbridge, M. James Cranford and the Author* (1654), 36. In *Rich. Baxters Apology*.

may be less to blame than Orme and others have imagined. On one level, in fact, Baxter's initial stumbling over the tripwire was really quite accidental.

The Sixteenth Query

It should be clear from our summary of Baxter's 1649 soteriology that there was a lot that Owen might choose to disagree with, but there was also a considerable amount of common ground between the two men. For all the accusations of Arminianism, Baxter never abandoned an essentially Calvinist theology, even in the *Aphorismes*.[4] For instance, both Owen and Baxter agreed on such a basic distinction as that between the secret and revealed will of God. Both men talked of a covenant of redemption (though Baxter preferred to call it a decree) between the Father and the Son to save the elect.[5] Both emphasized a willing human response.[6] Both accepted that salvation entailed a lifetime of perseverance and evidence of faith. Both believed that the elect would infallibly persevere. Baxter could sound just like Owen in saying, for example, that God's

> promises of taking the hard heart out of us, and giving us hearts of flesh, one heart, a new heart, and of putting his fear in us, that wee shall not depart from him, &c. are generally taken to be absolute promises (for here is not Condition expressed or intimated) made to all the Elect and only them, as yet not regenerate; and so not to any either named or qualified persons. These are not therefore fulfilled upon condition of our Faith, or made ours by believing, as other promises are.[7]

And both Owen and Baxter agreed that the new covenant came with conditions that were fulfilled by the believer only because Christ enabled the believer to fulfil them.[8]

The point is that such commonalities as these might have prevented Owen and Baxter from ever coming to blows, although two further factors made that possible. First, the 1649 Baxter was one still in the grip of an over-exaggerated fear of Antinomianism.[9] This distorted his soteriology by lending it a determined moralism that was not always so evident in later works. It led

---

[4]   Even if they were in 'two camps', both Owen and Baxter 'remained committed to predestination teachings'. Benedict, *Christ's Churches Purely Reformed*, 323.

[5]   Baxter, *Aphorismes*, 8.

[6]   On this point, see McGrath, 'Puritans and the Human Will', 388.

[7]   Baxter, *Aphorismes*, 8–9.

[8]   Ibid., 307.

[9]   See Cooper, *Fear and Polemic*, 133.

him to labour the necessity of a sustained response on the part of the believer as he systematically closed down every avenue of Antinomian approach. It is no wonder, then, that he was accused of attaching too much importance to human effort. Indeed, in publications written in the later 1650s, when the Antinomians were a fading threat and he could safely trust his audience again, the Calvinist grounding of his scheme was given much greater freedom of expression.[10] It was not that he abandoned the essential soteriology of the *Aphorismes*; he simply shifted his emphasis away from human responsibility and towards a genuine free act of God's grace. Such an emphasis was impossible for him to contemplate in 1649. That profoundly shaped the balance and manner of his presentation – emphasizing human effort and insulting his opponents – which made the attacks on the *Aphorismes* inevitable and an attack from Owen at least possible. The second cause of potential conflict lay in the fact that, despite extensive commonalities, there were areas of significant divergence in the soteriology of the two men. In this chapter we will identify the particular issues that brought them into disagreement.

And yet, even then Baxter and Owen might not have fallen out so publicly and so permanently. It is startling to realize that Baxter had never read any of Owen's works when he wrote the main part of the *Aphorismes*, and he might not have done so for some time yet. To make this point clear we need to understand the chronology of the construction of the book. Baxter began to write it as he recovered from the collapse of his health in February 1647. We do not know how long it took him to write what would become the main body of the *Aphorismes* (335 pages) but at the end of that portion of the book he inserted a tiny postscript, in which he explained that he was writing 'a few pages' on the subject of universal redemption but 'being hindered by continual sickness, and also observing how many lately are set a work on the same subject, (as *Whitfield, Stalham, Howe, Owen*, and some men of note that I hear are now upon it) I shall a while forbear'. His comment suggests an approbation of Owen as a man of note. He did not expect Owen to take a position he would strongly disagree with and he could have held that opinion only if he was unfamiliar with what Owen had actually written. Indeed, there were many authors whom Baxter mentioned by name in the main part of the *Aphorismes* – I count 43 – but he never referred to Owen at all.[11] Of course, *Death of Death* was not published until 1648, probably after Baxter had completed this first and main portion of the *Aphorismes*.

---

10 Ibid., 142–4.

11 The most-cited author was William Pemble, followed by Grotius and John Goodwin, then Anthony Wotton and George Downham. As with Owen, Baxter made no reference to Maccovius, the second author he engaged with in the Appendix.

Having finished that section of the work Baxter sent it to a friend, who responded with a reasonably critical list of 16 questions.[12] The last of them was this: 'I desire some satisfaction in that which [Johannes] *Maccovius*, and Mr *Owen* oppose in the places which I mentioned.'[13] Obviously *Death of Death* had come out by then. Baxter responded to this list with a 188-page appendix, yet Owen did not make an appearance until page 123 when Baxter finally came around to deal with his friend's sixteenth query. Here Baxter's choice of words conveys a prior unfamiliarity with Owen: 'The Authors which you refer me to, are two, D. Maccovius, and Mr. Owen'; 'This [point], you say, Mr. *Owen* confuteth in *Grotius*, in his late Treatise of *Universall Redemption*, lib. 3 cap. 7. p.140'; 'And here you send me to Mr. *Owen*'; 'To these of *Maccovius*, Mr. *Owen* (in the place against *Grotius*) which you referre me to'.[14] Baxter's language in these statements suggests that he had no prior disagreement with Owen and would not have dealt with him at all if not for the direct request of his friend. And when Baxter did engage with *Death of Death*, he referred only to pages 137–43, the chapter in which Owen responded to Grotius, in the section that had the Socinians mainly in mind.[15] So it would seem that Baxter had never read Owen's *Display* nor *Death of Death* before he was sent to the latter book by his friend, and even then he read only a very small portion of it. Baxter and Owen were inevitably going to encounter one another at some point, but the subsequent relationship between the two men might just have played out more positively, or at least in a different fashion, if not for that final, incidental, almost accidental request of this anonymous friend.

Still, the connection had been made and Baxter's entanglement with Owen had begun. It was a reluctant one. He had no desire at all to engage with either Owen or Maccovius: 'the last task you set me, is of all the rest most ungratefull, endlesse, and (in my judgment) unnecessary, *viz*. To answer what other men have written against some doctrines which I have here asserted.'[16] He bluntly informed his friend: 'If mens names did not more take with you then their Arguments, you might have spared me this labour.'[17] And he had three reasons for objecting. First, 'It is a work ungratefull to search into other mens weaknesse and mistakes, to handle the truth that way of correction or to speak a way of derogation of the labours of the learned and godly'. Second, it would be an

---

[12]   Baxter, *Aphorismes*, Appendix, 5–9.

[13]   Ibid., 9. Johannes Maccovius (1588–1644) was 'the Polish high Calvinist at the University of Franeker'. See Boersma, *Hot Pepper Corn*, 113.

[14]   Baxter, *Aphorismes*, Appendix, 124, 125, 137, 151.

[15]   Ibid., 125, 137, 143.

[16]   Ibid., 123–4.

[17]   Ibid., 124.

endless work, piling words upon words, for him to respond to every writer who might disagree with the views he wanted to assert. Third, it was needless, since a positive declaration of the truth should be enough to guard against error.[18] 'But at your request I will briefly consider them particularly.'[19]

And it was particular. At this point the scope of Baxter's disagreement with Owen was narrow indeed, based on only a very few pages of just one book and extending only to two main issues. The first: 'Christ payed not the *Idem*, but the *Tantundum*; not the very same debt mentioned in the threatening, but the value.'[20] Baxter claimed he could not 'well understand Mr. *Owen's* minde' when he defined the *Tantendum* as 'that which is not the same, nor equivalent to it, but onely in the gracious acceptation of the Creditour'.[21] The words 'not equivalent' were at issue and, for Baxter, ambiguous. If Owen meant 'not of equal value' then he had misrepresented Grotius and set up a straw man. 'But if he mean that it is not equivalent in procuring its end, *ipso facto*, delivering the debtor, without the intervention of a new concession or contract of the creditour, (as *solutio ejusdem* doth,) then I confesse Grotius is against him; and so am I.'[22] Either God accepted payment that was less than what was due (and remits the remainder) or he accepted a payment of equal value, but one which he might have chosen to refuse. Grotius argued the latter; Baxter, introducing his own ambiguity, accepted both alternatives and defended Grotius against Owen's attack. Putting it crisply,

> 1. [Owen] overlooketh [Grotius'] greatest Arguments.
> 2. He slightly answereth onely two.
> And 3. when he hath done, he saith as Grotius doth, and yeeldeth the whole cause.[23]

On the first point Baxter outlined Grotius's main argument. The law threatened only the sinner, not Christ, and the punishment was death and eternal torment, something Christ did not deliver in exact kind. 'What saith Mr. *Owen* to any of this?'[24] On the second point, Baxter put off the first argument until later in the discussion 'whereto it belongeth', and rebutted Owen on the second argument. Essentially, Owen opened up the scope of God's pardon too wide by

---

18   Ibid., 123–4.
19   Ibid., 125.
20   Ibid., 133.
21   Ibid., 137, 138. The quote is in Baxter's words. For the original see Owen, *Death of Death in the Death of Christ* (1648): *Works*, x.267.
22   Baxter, *Aphorismes*, Appendix, 138.
23   Ibid., 139.
24   Ibid., 140.

including the whole dispensation of grace, the imputation of sin to Christ and his righteousness to the believer.[25] And on the third point, Baxter assumed that Owen had misunderstood Grotius, thereby losing the whole debate. In several ways Owen's words showed that God had not, in fact, accepted that which was exactly the same,

> but the same in weight and pressure, (therefore not the same in the Obligation, because not fully the same: Not the same numerically; nor perhaps specifically in all respects, if the losse of God's Love and Image, and incurring his hatred, the corruption of the body, the losse of the right to, and use of all the creatures, and the losse of all comforts corporall or spirituall, &c. were any part of the curse.) yet that it was in the greatest respects of the same kinde, I doubt not.[26]

Baxter (and Grotius) believed that the law had been graciously relaxed, not fully executed, in the punishment of Christ and the accepting of his death as satisfaction for sin. Owen did not, but 'I judge that Mr. *Owen* hath no better success in his next assault of *Grotius* on that question ... He that readeth *Grotius* and *Vossius* own words, doth need no further defensative against the force of Mr. *Owens* answers. But this is nothing to me'.[27]

Baxter's response to the first issue was clear enough: Owen had not expressed himself clearly, he had misunderstood Grotius, and he had ended up giving away his own cause. The second issue concerned the timing of the believer's justification: was the believer justified at the Cross, or when they began to believe and fulfilled the conditions? Baxter affirmed the latter and saw in Owen the former. Again, Owen had not made himself clear. He had employed the metaphor of a hostage who is freed from bondage the moment his ransom is paid even though the news of its payment and his actual release may be a long time in coming. Baxter found this absurd. It was God, not the prisoner, who needed the knowledge of ransom paid, and since it was taken to have been paid in Christ's death there was nothing to stop God from bringing about the immediate release of the hostage.[28] Such a belief, of course, would have suited the Antinomians who argued that justification was but the opening of one's eyes to a previous act already complete, even from eternity. 'Whatever this Writer thinketh in this, is nothing to us.'[29]

---

25   Ibid., 140–143.
26   Ibid., 144.
27   Ibid., 145.
28   Ibid., 156–7.
29   Ibid., 159.

Baxter had made no bones about his disagreement with Owen, but it has to be said his tone was relatively measured. He dealt with Maccovius rather more harshly, calling his doctrine 'strange and abhorred', his arguments 'weak', and his beliefs 'erroneous'.[30] On the first point at issue Baxter himself could see that the matter was unclear, though on the second he held no doubts.[31] It is true he was dismissive of Owen's arguments, but he did not go out of his way to insult the man himself. He could even be generous. He did not know Owen's thinking on one point, and 'I will not censure so hardly till I know it'.[32]

I suggest that Baxter did not quite know whom he had taken on, nor quite discerned the dangerous territory into which he had strayed. He had simply been asked by a friend to read a certain portion in a certain book, and he had done as much without going any further than absolutely necessary. His ultimate concern was briefly and clearly stated: 'it grieveth mee to see many of our Divines to fight against Jesuites and Arminians with the Antinomians weapons, as if our cause afforded no better; and so they run into the farre worse extreame.'[33] That was about the extent of his complaint against Owen. The insulting tone that surfaced in other points in the *Aphorismes* was not so much in evidence here.

Yet it is reasonable to assume that Baxter's evident rudeness and lack of tact elsewhere in the book might have coloured the way in which his critique of Owen was read, by Owen and others. It is, at the very least, unfortunate that in the Epistle to the Reader, Baxter criticized those who

> are like superficiall Schollars, who when they have spent many yeares in the Universities, have no way to prove themselves proficients, but to extoll Learning, and cry down the unlearned, that so far they may cast the suspicion from themselves upon others. Even so doe those in crying down errors. I know this small Tract will not relish well with these mens palats; neither is it ambitious of their favour, or yet so quarrelsome as purposely to provoke them; though some words may not be cut meet to their conceits.[34]

Baxter might not have had Owen in mind at all, but Owen could have seen himself intended in Baxter's reflections. Whatever the intent, the effect of the book was regrettable. As F.J. Powicke has discerned, in 1649 Owen was a prominent figure, Baxter merely an upstart interloper. 'For Baxter, then, to criticize the great man – in a first publication – without a hint of self-distrust,

---

[30] Ibid., 146, 147.

[31] Baxter, *Aphorismes*, 31, 35.

[32] Baxter, *Aphorismes*, Appendix, 158.

[33] Ibid., 164.

[34] Baxter, *Aphorismes*, Epistle to the Reader, sig. a3r–v.

did not commend his modesty to strangers; and did actually, to some of those as well as to Owen himself, convey an unfavourable impression of him which they never lost.'[35]

The Death of Christ: A Controversy Sustained

It is a significant fact in itself that Owen chose to respond to Baxter. He did not, for instance, choose to reply to John Horne. He might have penned a response to Horne, had he 'met with any one uninterested person that would have said it deserved a reply'.[36] It would seem that Baxter's book had created a far greater stir than Horne's, with more people pressing Owen for a rejoinder. Yet Horne had launched a sustained attack on Owen in a whole book, while Baxter's comments were more in the nature of an afterthought. Not only that, at the time of writing Owen was in Ireland at the request of Oliver Cromwell, setting Trinity College, Dublin, on a better footing.[37] We know little about the exact nature of Owen's duties in Ireland, but it must have come at some cost to sacrifice time and energy to reply to Baxter. He had been 'attended with more than ordinary weaknesses and infirmities, separated from my library, burdened with manifold employments, and constant preaching to a numerous multitude of as thirsting a people after the gospel as ever yet I conversed withal'.[38] Yet for all those impediments he had gone out of his way to engage with Baxter.

Thus *Death of Christ* – Owen's reply to Baxter's *Aphorismes* – was finished in December 1649 and published in the following year. 'It was in our hopes and expectations, not many years ago', Owen began, 'that the Lord would graciously have turned back all those bitter streams' that through ungrateful pride and carnal wisdom sought to 'overflow the doctrine of the grace of God'. Instead, in these days of freedom for the Church, 'not a few are attempting once more to renew the contest of sinful, guilty, defiled nature, against the sovereign distinguishing love and effectual grace of God'.[39] Owen's initial agenda was invoked once more: preserving God's sovereignty against the attempted usurpation of human free will. The Arminians lay just a breath away from Owen's opening lines. They had been beaten back once; now a revival of similar aims threatened the gospel

---

[35] Frederick J. Powicke, *A Life of the Reverend Richard Baxter 1615–1691* (London: Jonathan Cape Ltd., 1924), 239.

[36] Owen, *Vindiciae Evangelicae* (1655): *Works*, xii.10.

[37] Toon, *God's Statesman*, 36, 39–40.

[38] Owen, *Death of Christ* (1650): *Works*, x.479.

[39] Ibid., x.431.

again. And there could be no doubt that Baxter was among those who were, to Owen's mind, promoting that revival.

That said, though, two further observations might be made. First, Owen also recognized the common ground between him and Baxter in that 'most of [Baxter's] exceptions do lie rather against words than things, expressions than opinions, ways of delivering things than the doctrines themselves'.[40] Here Owen offered his contradictory defence, that in *Death of Death* he was writing in 'the most popular way' and not with 'scholastical' precision.[41] 'Notwithstanding, because I am not as yet convinced, by any thing in Mr Baxter's censure and opposition, that there was any such blameable deviation as pretended.'[42] In this way, *Death of Christ* was Owen's effort to express himself more precisely and clearly. Owen's implication was that, once this was done, the two would be seen to be in substantial agreement (on the two specific issues under discussion, if not on the substance of the *Aphorismes*). Owen echoed Baxter when he explained that the questions under consideration were 'wrapped up in no small darkness, there being in them some things difficult and hard to be understood'.[43] There are grounds, then, for saying *Death of Christ* perpetuated a controversy over extremely uncertain matters and about which the combatants were in substantial agreement, though that would miss the importance of where these arguments led in the way that they were expressed. For Baxter, Owen's language encouraged the Antinomians. For Owen, Baxter's borrowing from Grotius encouraged the Socinians.

The second observation is that Owen chose not to respond to the whole book – he did not have the time – though he wished that others would.[44] In doing so he demonstrated a capacity that Baxter so rarely showed: the ability not to say something that might have been said. As a result, Owen's relatively brief response was very tightly focused on Baxter's two specific criticisms: Owen's position on the satisfaction of Christ in regard to the nature of the payment made; and on the timing of the justification of the believer.

Owen's handling of the first issue was among the most arcane and intricate of all of his writings.[45] If he felt any embarrassment at a lack of scholastical

---

[40] Ibid., x.435. See also, p. 436.

[41] For the contradiction, see above, pp. 73–4.

[42] Owen, *Death of Christ* (1650): *Works*, x.435.

[43] Ibid., 436.

[44] Ibid.

[45] For helpful, detailed discussion on both of these issues under debate, see Trueman, *Claims of Truth*, 206–26; and Matthew W. Mason, 'John Owen's Doctrine of Union with Christ in Relation to His Contributions to Seventeenth Century Debates Concerning Eternal Justification', *Ecclesia Reformanda* 1 (2009): 46–69.

precision in *Death of Death* he more than made up for it here in *Death of Christ*. It is as if he was determined to take up the challenge thrown down by Baxter, even if he lost all but the most dedicated of his readers as a result. To draw out the main features of Owen's response on this first issue, he argued that Baxter had misunderstood and misrepresented his position. Baxter's method was to cast Owen's 'plain, very plain meaning' into distinctions of his own making or terms of his own devising and then demonstrate their falsity.[46] It was the same when it came to Owen's disagreement with Grotius: 'I desire the reader to view the controversy agitated between Grotius and myself, not as here represented by Mr Baxter, so changed by a new dress that I might justly refuse to take any acquaintance with it, but as by myself laid down.'[47] Owen showed how the terms *Idem* and *Tantundum* were inadequate, since even the 'everlasting destruction' of the sinner decreed by the law – the *Idem* – was not an exact payment for sins committed. It was simply appointed to that end. And *Tantundum* did not, in fact, mean of equivalent value, since it was clearly not. Instead, it conveyed that God graciously chose to accept a lesser payment as of equivalent value.[48] In each case, God made up the difference between the price paid, in these two different ways, and the debt that was actually owed. The correct question to ask was whether the punishment Christ underwent was 'the same that was threatened to the transgressors themselves, or whether something else which God accepted in lieu thereof'.[49] Owen affirmed the first. 'The law was executed as to its penalty, relaxed as to the person suffering.'[50] All of this served to reveal the complexity of the issues, much the same point that Baxter had made in the first place. And Owen was also able to show that Baxter had contradicted himself and, as a result, could be shown to agree with Owen.[51] 'Doth not Mr B. labour to prove the same? Where, then, is the difference?'[52] That 'Mr B. affirms the same with me, I can prove by twenty instances'.[53] Once again, Baxter had made the same sort of claim of Owen. The inevitable conclusion is that beneath all the nice language and intricate distinctions, the Latin and the Greek, both men believed the same thing, which raised the question of why the controversy was even necessary in the first place.

---

[46]   Owen, *Death of Christ* (1650): *Works*, x.437, 439.

[47]   Ibid., 442.

[48]   Ibid., 441.

[49]   Ibid., 438.

[50]   Ibid., 447.

[51]   Ibid., 439.

[52]   Ibid.

[53]   Ibid., 448.

The same was true of the second point at issue. Owen vehemently and impatiently denied that he had ever affirmed justification from eternity or from the Cross. 'To have an opinion fastened on me which I never once received nor intimated the least thought of in that whole treatise, or any other of mine, and then my arguments answered as to such an end and purpose as I not once intended to promote by them, is a little too harsh dealing.'[54] 'Do I labour to prove that which I never affirmed, never thought, never believed?'[55] It was an easy thing to make a person's arguments appear 'exceedingly weak and ridiculous' by imputing to them a sense that was never intended. 'I have not only not asserted but positively denied, and disproved by many arguments' that the believer is completely justified before believing. 'To now be traduced as a patron of that opinion, and my reasons for it publicly answered, seems to me something uncouth.'[56]

It was true that Owen denied any change in God towards the believer before and after the Cross, as Grotius had argued, because it was merely human folly to 'measure the Almighty by the standard of a man, and to frame in the mind of a mutable idol, instead of the eternal, unchangeable God'.[57] God did not change his eternal purposes,[58] then, but the accomplishment of those purposes took place in time.[59] At the Cross those good things God purposed for the elect were 'purchased and procured, and all hindrances of bestowing them [were] removed', but they were applied to the individual sinner later, at the moment of belief. 'Hence it is that the discharge of the debtor doth not immediately follow the payment of the debt by Christ ... God reserveth to himself this right and liberty to discharge the debtor when and how he pleases, – I mean as to times and seasons.'[60] The death of Christ was not a real cause that produces its fruit immediately, but a moral cause that does not. The future enjoyment of the benefits of Christ's death was immediately secured for the elect at the Cross along with their actual right to those benefits, but they are not applied until the moment of belief.[61] 'Faith gives us actual possession...'[62]

Two points of dispute, then. On the first, we can discern through the haze essential agreement between Baxter and Owen, despite differences of language.

---

[54]   Ibid., 449.
[55]   Ibid., 472.
[56]   Ibid., 449.
[57]   Ibid., 451. See also, p. 454.
[58]   Ibid., 452.
[59]   Ibid., 457.
[60]   Ibid., 458. See also, p. 459.
[61]   Ibid., 462.
[62]   Ibid., 467.

On the second, Owen simply did not hold the position that Baxter claimed he did. If this is the case, the two men are left in close proximity. Yet it had become a heated exchange. There are scattered throughout Owen's response an increasing number of acerbic comments lobbed in Baxter's direction. In order to convey the tone it is worth repeating a few of them. The *Aphorismes* was 'a large field, and easy to be walked in, [which] lies open on every hand for the scattering of many magisterial dictates, which, with confidence enough, are crudely asserted'.[63] It was a 'most unhappy issue as can possibly be imagined, made up of deceit, weakness, and self-contradiction'.[64] 'There are scarce more lines than mistakes' in one part of it.[65] Owen would like to see Baxter's arguments for a particular assertion, 'but those, as in most other controverted things in this book, he is pleased to conceal'.[66] It was wrong 'that so learned a man should not understand my meaning, unless from his own prejudice'.[67] 'It is far more facile to give the hardest censures than to answer the easiest arguments.'[68] On the immediate effects of the death of Christ, Baxter 'pretends to great accurateness, censuring others for not being able to distinguish aright of them'.[69] The array of words is revealing: harsh dealing, traduced, uncouth, magisterial, prejudice, deceit, weakness, censures. Baxter had 'endeavoured to cast some part of the doctrine of satisfaction and redemption of Christ, as by me delivered, into a crooked frame, and that with some passages of censure as might have been omitted without losing the least grace of his book or style'.[70] It was the tone of the *Aphorismes* as much as the content that had grated on Owen. He took it personally, badly, and his reply was coloured by his impatience with Baxter's seeming arrogance and disdain. The debate had taken a very personal turn, which further evidences the way in which the *Aphorismes* was more generally received. Owen's objection to Baxter's haughty tone was not unique, and Baxter would wear the criticism – with no little justification – for the rest of his days. And while there was space for agreement on these two issues, there was much else in the rest of the *Aphorismes* to which Owen, and others, strenuously objected.[71] Baxter had got off on the wrong foot, to say the least.

---

[63]   Ibid., 445.
[64]   Ibid., 443.
[65]   Ibid., 459.
[66]   Ibid., 460.
[67]   Ibid., 474.
[68]   Ibid., 476.
[69]   Ibid.
[70]   Ibid., 436.
[71]   See, for instance, ibid., 455–6, 461–2.

Bearing Blame

Is this enough, though, to condemn Baxter alone? It is true that he willingly acknowledged his part in starting the debate with Owen in the Appendix to the *Aphorismes*. As a result he resolved not to reply to Owen's *Death of Christ*, allowing him the last word. That implies more credit than he has been given. It seems a rare instance of graciousness and restraint on his part; it conveys a genuine repentance or at least regret; and it reinforces the perception that he never set out to aggravate Owen in the first place, where his language was, for all Owen's indignation, restrained. Baxter broke his self-imposed silence in 1655 and again in 1657. We will come to those responses in Chapter 7; here we can make a brief borrowing to assess his defence against Owen.

Baxter invited Owen's 'tenderest friends' to peruse that part of his book again and to see 'if they can finde a word that is uncivil or abusive'.[72] He had good grounds to do so. Baxter had confined himself to assessing Owen's doctrine; he had not attacked Owen personally. Yet, as he mulled over Owen's reply he observed 'the great pains [Owen] hath taken about my Person (for the caus found him not work enough)'.[73] Baxter had been stung by Owen's personal attack, which he viewed as an over-reaction. Owen had come across as so calm in *Death of Death*, yet so intemperate in *Death of Christ*.[74] Generally Baxter kept to a careful, respectful tone when he dealt with Owen, and he did so in relatively small portions buried in much bigger books. Owen replied in particular titles dedicated specifically to attacking Baxter. At last, Baxter had resolved on silence, 'least I should exasperate'.[75] Baxter's most characteristic presentation of Owen was that of a man much too easily exasperated.

Labelling Baxter as the aggressor, then, sidesteps the issue of Owen's responsibility in choosing to reply. If it was not necessary for him to respond to John Horne, who had written at greater length attacking Owen directly, repeatedly and far more vociferously, why was it necessary to attack Baxter who had in relative terms brought in Owen only as an aside? It is possible that Baxter was on the face of things an ally in the Calvinist cause, while Horne was an Arminian at a time when the Arminians were far from power. Baxter was

---

[72]   Richard Baxter, *Certain Disputations of Right to the Sacraments and the True Nature of Visible Christianity* (1657), 483. A little earlier, in 1654, Baxter had conceded his 'fault in one or two unmannerly words' against Owen. Richard Baxter, *Rich. Baxters Account Given to his Reverend Brother Mr T. Blake of the Reasons of his Dissent from the Doctrine of his Exceptions in his Late Treatise of the Covenants* (1654), Preface, sig. A4r. In *Rich. Baxters Apology*.

[73]   Baxter, *Certain Disputations*, 484.

[74]   Ibid., 483.

[75]   Baxter, *Admonition to Mr. William Eyre*, 36. In *Rich. Baxters Apology*.

showing signs of being a dangerous, unstable and unreliable ally and this, too, may have prompted Owen's response. But if this is a part of the answer, it is not the whole of it. Owen had chosen to read the genuinely haughty tone of the rest of the *Aphorismes* into that section in which Baxter responded specifically to *Death of Death*. He had chosen to take offence when none was intended and, for Baxter, very little was conveyed. Baxter's engagement was reluctant; Owen's was deliberate. Baxter's magisterial tone was not greatly in evidence in his dealing with Owen, but Owen was scathing in reply. Right at the start of the book he questioned why Baxter had brought him into a separate controversy.[76] We might well ask Owen why he chose to prolong it, especially when he appeared to be arguing that the two men essentially agreed on the specific points at issue. Several years after the exchange Owen spoke up in his own defence. Looking back on this first outbreak of controversy between the two men he claimed that 'I gave not the occasion of it; [and] as to the manner of its handling, I carried not on the provocation'. The first assertion is true, the second is not. Nor is it the case that the 'same person [Baxter] both made the beginning and abandoned all moderation'.[77]

Orme's judgement is, therefore, misplaced. Baxter was clearly the beginner of the controversy, something he readily acknowledged. But if anyone was the aggressor, it was Owen. This is not to argue that Baxter was without blame in the matter. He certainly adopted an insulting tone in enough places throughout the *Aphorismes*, and he was naive and careless in so blithely handling Owen's mistakes as he saw them. Owen's response was just one more turn of the whirlwind Baxter's first book had created. But both men must share the blame. It was somewhat to Baxter's misfortune that his anonymous correspondent had drawn him to Owen at the very last moment. That query precipitated a great deal of trouble. Owen's response, which was not strictly necessary and personal in nature, revealed an angry pride all of his own. Indeed, one of the most significant questions is why Owen chose to reply to Baxter. That, as we are about to see, was closely bound up in issues of personality.

---

[76]   Owen, *Death of Christ* (1650): *Works*, x.437.
[77]   Owen, *Of the Death of Christ and of Justification* (1655): *Works*, xii.591. The last few words are in Latin: 'et initium dedit et modum abstulit'.

Chapter 4

Personality

[Owen] was indeed sometimes a little *Impatient* of Contradiction.

[Anon.] *A Vindication of Owen* (1684)[1]

I confess ... I am strongly provoked to blab out any thinge, that I do confidently thinke to be true and weighty.

Richard Baxter (1658)[2]

The strain between John Owen and Richard Baxter was, as much as anything else, a personality clash. So far I have argued that difficulties between them were inevitable given the realities in place before they even met: their contrasting experiences of the first civil war and their competing soteriological agendas. In the same sort of way, their differing personalities also set them on a course of mutual misunderstanding and irritation.

Once again, though, we face the mismatch not just in their capacities and temperaments, but also in the evidence they left behind for us to draw them out. The problem with describing the personality of Owen is that it is so very hard to find. As we saw in the Introduction, it is difficult to imagine anyone as visible as Owen doing such a thorough job of keeping himself hidden. Speaking generally, all we have are his books. In this sense they *are* his personality. And they are not much help, except as evidence of Owen's own self-containment. Coming to an adequate assessment of Owen's personality will, therefore, take quite some digging. But there is some likely terrain in which we might begin a profitable excavation. For the most part, I wish to direct this exercise around a partial description of the development of Owen's career, particularly during the 1650s. This will provide a sufficiently broad basis of activity on which to interpret Owen's actions, and thereby come to a clearer appreciation of his personality and how it was likely to interact with that of Baxter. I have already written elsewhere on Baxter's personality,[3] and here I would like to build upon it rather than repeat it, by considering the main elements of his early life and

---

[1]   [Anon.], *Vindication of Owen*, 38.

[2]   Baxter to Abraham Pinchbecke, 12 October 16[5]8: DWL MS *BC* iv.56r (*CCRB* #508).

[3]   Cooper, *Fear and Polemic*, chapter 2.

career. The danger of this chapter is that focusing so closely on these two men will imply that they acted essentially alone, two fighters in the arena with others serving only as spectators. This impression would be quite wrong. But at the risk of conveying that impression, I do have a very precise task in mind. My intention is to distil the specific aspects of each personality that led to a clash between them – without ignoring others around them nor the similarities between them – in a mix that was never going to blend easily. In fact, we might well conclude that this particular combination of temperaments and talents was a disaster waiting to happen.

John Owen's Career

Owen's story has a consistent strand of patronage running through it from the very beginning. We have already seen that he had a rich uncle to thank for his considerable university education. According to his earliest, anonymous biographer, Owen energetically pursued an *'Ambition* to make himself considerable either in *Church* or *State'.*[4] It was the *'chief motive'* behind his rigorous study habits and his regimen of sleeping less than four hours a night.[5] During those years 'the *honouring of God*, or *serving his Country*, otherwise than to make him capable of *serving himself*, had little room in his Thoughts'.[6] But somewhere in the midst of this endeavour Owen began to feel the stirrings of God's grace, which were sufficiently strong by 1637 to prompt him to leave Queen's College in accord with what would seem to be strong religious scruples against Laudian innovations.[7] John Asty, the second of Owen's two earliest biographers, suggests the abrupt end to Owen's studies and earthly ambitions 'threw him into a deep melancholy, that continued in its extremity for a quarter of a year, during which time he avoided almost all manner of converse, and very hardly could be induced to speak a word, and when he did speak, it was with such disorder as rendered him *a wonder to many'.*[8] This seems a particularly severe form of depression, if

---

[4]   [Anon.], 'Life of Owen', viii.

[5]   Ibid., viii, vi.

[6]   Ibid., viii.

[7]   Ibid., vi . For a description of the Laudian reforms at Oxford University during the 1630s, see Kenneth Fincham, 'Oxford and the Early Stuart Polity', in *The History of the University of Oxford*, vol. 4, ed. Nicholas Tyacke (Oxford: Clarendon Press, 1997), 198–210; and Nicholas Tyacke, 'Religious Controversy' in the same volume, 581–90.

[8]   Asty, 'Memoirs', 4. See also, [Anon.], 'Life of Owen', viii.

that is what it was. Though its early 'violence' lasted only a few months it would be five years before Owen regained a settled footing.[9]

His condition had still not evaporated by the time the first civil war broke out. At that point Owen sided with Parliament, to the annoyance of his uncle who now cut him off. Owen's stand was a brave one, then, but he was separated from his income – 'a great mortification'.[10] More than that, 'all his aspiring Thoughts to be considerable in Church or State, as they then stood, were dash'd at once: But he has often own'd ... that he saw God had made use of his Ambition to qualify him for future service in another manner than what his own Natural Inclinations had propos'd'.[11] The quality of aspiration itself remained undiminished, but those capacities and skills he had already developed were now put to a better use. Shortly afterwards Owen's melancholy finally lifted when he lingered in a London church to hear a sermon from an anonymous preacher. The man 'Answer'd those very Objections which Mr. Owen had commonly form'd against himself' in exactly the method Owen would have used.[12] This happy conjunction resolved all his doubts and established him in a composed assurance of genuine faith. Within a year he had published his first work, *A Display of Arminianism*.

It would seem that Owen had learned from an early age that his advancement depended on patronage. Now, left without that support of his uncle, Owen shrewdly dedicated his *Display* to the Committee on Religion in the House of Lords.[13] He was rewarded with the sequestrated rectory of Fordham, Essex, in July 1643. He was married in the same year, to a Mary Rooke, possibly the daughter of a Coggeshall clothier. Their first child, John, was born in December 1644.[14] All this time Owen had maintained a friendship with a fellow student from Queen's College, Thomas Westrow, who by the mid-1640s had become the MP for Hythe. Westrow (and another MP, Sir Peter Wentworth) nominated Owen to preach to Parliament in April 1646.[15] The connection served to thrust Owen further into national prominence, and it showed once more the merit of having well-placed supporters. About that time Owen was promoted to the

[9] Asty, 'Memoirs', 4.
[10] [Anon.], 'Life of Owen', ix.
[11] Ibid., ix.
[12] Ibid., x. For a full account of the story, see Toon, *God's Statesman*, 12–13.
[13] Carl Trueman calls this an 'astute attempt at flattery and ingratiation', in *John Owen*, 86.
[14] Toon, *God's Statesman*, 17.
[15] Ibid., 16, 19.

vicarage of Coggeshall, 'a much larger and more rewarding assignment than that of Fordham'.[16]

Peter Toon sees that 1646 sermon as a moment of national recognition after which 'his fame and influence steadily grew'.[17] Sarah Gibbard Cook takes a more constrained view. She posits a brief plateau in Owen's career after 1646,[18] before it took off again in 1648: 'In the three short years from 1648 to 1651, Owen was transformed from a locally known parish minister into the dean of Christ Church College, Oxford, and a figure of national prominence.'[19] Cook attributes Owen's success to two related factors. First, and most importantly, the 'catalyst in the transformation was the personal patronage of a succession of leaders in the New Model Army, the Rump Parliament, and the Council of State'.[20] The siege of Colchester in 1648, just a matter of miles from Coggeshall, brought Owen into contact with several influential figures in the parliamentary cause including General Thomas Fairfax,[21] and at least four influential figures in local and national politics: Sir William Masham, Sir William Rowe, Sir Henry Mildmay and Colonel Sir Thomas Honeywood.[22] From there, his range of contacts extended considerably. Second, Owen timed his run perfectly. 'Significantly younger and newer on the national scene than such familiar Independents as [Thomas] Goodwin and [Philip] Nye, he emerged at the very moment when the Independents (by means of their army) achieved supreme power in the English government.'[23] Owen's elevated status was obvious. 'He immediately became one of the Rump's favourite ministers, preaching at least eight times at its invitation and receiving two or three more invitations which he was obliged to decline.'[24] Christopher Hill calls Owen the 'unofficial preacher-in-chief' of the new regime.[25]

---

[16]   Cook, 'Political Biography', 62. Ralph Josselin's diary entry of 31 March 1646 noted that 'Mr Owen removes to Coggeshall'. Alan MacFarlane, ed., *The Diary of Ralph Josselin 1616–1683* (London: Oxford University Press, 1976), 57.

[17]   Toon, *God's Statesman*, 1.

[18]   Cook, 'Political Biography', 418.

[19]   Ibid., 70.

[20]   Ibid.

[21]   Ibid., 79.

[22]   When Owen published his two sermons celebrating the parliamentary victory at Colchester he attached two dedicatory epistles, one to Fairfax and the other to these four men. Owen, *Ebenezer: A Memorial of the Deliverance of Essex County* (1648): *Works*, viii.73–6. See also, Cook, 'Political Biography', 79; Leggett, 'John Owen as Religious Adviser', 14–15.

[23]   Cook, 'Political Biography', 70.

[24]   Ibid., 70.

[25]   Christopher Hill, *The Experience of Defeat: Milton and Some Contemporaries* (London: Bookmarks, 1984), 165.

Owen preached the most significant of those sermons on 31 January 1649, just one day after the execution of King Charles I. It is a remarkable sermon in the circumstances, since it makes no overt reference at all to the events of the day before. It plays on much the same themes as his 1646 sermon, though grounded in a different text.[26] Some of Owen's earlier biographers argued that he was acting only under command and that his sermon should not be read as approving the regicide.[27] That view has been rightly discredited.[28] While he made no overt reference to the regicide, Owen did state that when 'kings command unrighteous things, and people suit them with willing compliance, none doubts but the destruction of them both is just and virtuous'.[29] In the epistle dedicatory, he explained his silence on the regicide in terms that are clearly affirming:

> The foundation of that whole transaction of things which is therein held out, in reference to the present dispensations of Providence, – being nothing but an entrance into the unravelling of the whole web of iniquity, interwoven of civil and ecclesiastical tyranny, in opposition to the Kingdom of the Lord Jesus, – I chose not to mention. Neither shall I at present add any thing thereabout, but only my desire that it be eyed as the granted basis of the following discourse.[30]

In this epistle Owen became almost carried away in a rare display of near-millenarian excitement. He saw 'the days approach for the delivery of the decree, to the shaking of heaven and earth, and all the powers of the world, to make way for the establishment of that kingdom which shall not be given to another people (the great expectation of the saints of the Most High before the consummation of all)'. God had 'called you forth, right honourable, at his entrance to the rolling up of the nation's heavens like a scroll, to serve him in your generation in the high places of Armageddon'.[31] Given this tone, there can be no doubt that Owen supported the decision to execute Charles. There is no evidence to show any

---

[26] 'Let them return unto thee; but return not thou unto them. And I will make thee unto this people a fenced brazen wall; and they shall fight against thee, but they shall not prevail against thee; for I am with thee to save thee, and to deliver thee, says the Lord' (Jeremiah 15:19–20). Owen, *Righteous Zeal Encouraged by Divine Protection* (1649): *Works*, viii.133.

[27] For example, see Orme, 'Memoirs', 67ff.

[28] See Toon, *God's Statesman*, 34; Cook, 'Political Biography', 83–5; and Vose, 'Profile of a Puritan', 54–5.

[29] Owen, *Righteous Zeal Encouraged by Divine Protection* (1649): *Works*, viii.136.

[30] Ibid., 130.

[31] Ibid., 129. Owen was alluding to Hebrews 12:26–7, Daniel 7:26–7, Isaiah 34:4–5 and Revelation 16:16.

reservation, nor, in light of the trajectory of Owen's career, is there any reason to expect it.[32]

On 19 April 1649 Owen preached to Parliament again, welcoming 'these latter days' in which God was setting about to 'so far shake and translate the political heights, governments and strength of the nations, as shall serve for the full bringing in of his own peaceable kingdom'.[33] Owen's audience that day included Oliver Cromwell, the man who would quickly become 'the most influential patron of his life'.[34] A few days after the sermon Owen called on Fairfax to pay his respects. While waiting to see him, Cromwell also arrived and, seeing Owen, crossed the room to lay a hand on his shoulder: 'Sir, you are the person I must be acquainted with.' Owen's reply was suitably demurring: 'That will be much more to my advantage than yours.' Cromwell's response: 'We shall soon see that.'[35] There is no way of assessing the accuracy of this account, but the story is revealing. The awareness of patronage, the mutual balancing of favour, advantage and service, and Owen's perfectly weighted reply, all speak of his ease within the political rhythms of the day and further demonstrate, in the words of Donald Leggett, his 'pursuit for influence'.[36]

Leggett has written a valuable thesis that tracks the development of Owen's relationship with Cromwell. Once again, there is a startling absence of evidence to go on, for both men.[37] There are very few pieces of correspondence between them and what remains is essentially impersonal in nature.[38] Even so, Leggett is able to show that during the 1650s their relationship shifted from an early phase of relative proximity and initial warmth to one of greater distance and eventual strain. Though reluctant to leave his pastoral ministry in Coggeshall, Owen agreed to serve as one of Cromwell's chaplains in the Irish campaign.[39] His work kept him in Dublin – principally surveying the dilapidated state of Trinity

---

[32]   Noel Henning Mayfield claims that Owen offered '[p]erhaps one of the most significant and spirited (if virtually unnoticed by historians) defences of the Regicide' in his sermons from 1649 to 1656. But I am cautious about his argument that Owen and other relevant Independent figures cannot 'be meaningfully regarded as "moderates"' and that Owen's thought contained 'quite radical anti-monarchical tendencies'. His stark distinction between Owen and the Presbyterians seems overdrawn. See Mayfield, *Puritans and Regicide*, 99, 189–98, 242.

[33]   Owen, *The Shaking and Translating of Heaven and Earth* (1649): *Works*, viii.260.

[34]   Cook, 'Political Biography', 70–71. Leggett makes the same point, 'John Owen as Religious Adviser', 78.

[35]   Asty, 'Memoirs', 9.

[36]   Leggett, 'John Owen as Religious Adviser', 22.

[37]   For Cromwell, see Davis, 'Cromwell's Religion', 182–3.

[38]   Leggett, 'John Owen as Religious Adviser', 8.

[39]   Ralph Josselin's diary entry for 16 September 1649 records that 'Mr Owen is going for Ireland'. MacFarlane, *Diary of Ralph Josselin*, 179.

College – so we do not know how much time, if any, he spent with Cromwell.[40] But Cromwell must have been impressed, for he ordered Owen to go with him to Scotland where he 'served to provide and articulate the religious message of the army'; he 'offered an exegesis in defence of pulling down the House of Stuart'; and he provided personal spiritual support to Cromwell.[41] While it is tempting to magnify Owen's relationship with Cromwell, given the latter's increasing importance in England's affairs, it is important to recognize Owen's role in shaping 'the politico-religious identity of the army' and, behind that, his connections with a number of leading Independent Members of Parliament.[42] For several years now Owen had shown himself to be a reliable conveyor of the Congregationalist perspective on England's affairs. And the network of patronage he had built for himself was much broader than just Cromwell, however important he may have been. We must also recognize that Owen accrued this patronage for the purpose of pursuing a specific agenda: godly reform in England, and freedom of conscience. That is why he appended brief treatises on the subject of toleration to two of his earlier, published sermons.[43] Owen knew precisely what he wanted to achieve and deliberately set out to influence religious policy in England. That was most important and, as we shall see, he would place even his relationship with Cromwell at risk for the sake of it.

Owen's service as a chaplain to Cromwell ended on 23 July 1651,[44] but he continued to serve as a chaplain to the Council of State through regular preaching.[45] These efforts only 'furthered his reputation'.[46] He had become 'a valuable state servant'; he was a man 'of genuine importance to his patrons amongst the political Independents'; he had come 'to represent Independent religious credibility'.[47] 'By 1651', says Cook, 'Owen enjoyed the respect and friendship of many of the most politically important Independents in the nation ... [and] he remained an effective and influential member of the party which ruled England'.[48]

---

[40]   Leggett, 'John Owen as Religious Adviser', 27; Toon, *God's Statesman*, 39–40.

[41]   Leggett, 'John Owen as Religious Adviser', 27, 28, 29.

[42]   Ibid., 38, 24.

[43]   See Owen, *Vision of Free Mercy* (1646): *Works*, viii.44–69; and *Righteous Zeal Encouraged* (1649): *Works*, viii.163–206.

[44]   Leggett, 'John Owen as Religious Adviser', 24.

[45]   Again, we do not have much evidence for Owen's work with the Council, apart from his regular preaching each Sunday afternoon. Ibid., 50; Cook, 'Political Biography', 106.

[46]   Leggett, 'John Owen as Religious Adviser', 24.

[47]   Ibid., 31, 34, 38.

[48]   Cook, 'Political Biography', 71. See also, de Sola Pinto, *Peter Sterry*, 19–20.

The rewards accumulated. Parliament conferred £100 per annum for life and appointed him Dean of Christ Church at his former university.[49] Being both a Cathedral and a College, it held a special place.[50] In 1653 Cromwell nominated Owen as his Vice-Chancellor of Oxford University, just at 'the high point of the Independents' power in Oxford';[51] Owen would serve in that role until 1657, by which time their power, and his, had visibly declined. Oxford, of course, was an indispensable element in the project of national reformation, since it produced so many of England's ministers and preachers.[52] By 1650 it 'had become the fiercest ideological battleground in Interregnum England'. Owen 'effectively governed Oxford on behalf of the University',[53] allied with another leading Congregationalist figure, Thomas Goodwin. He was 16 years older than Owen, one of the Dissenting Brethren, a leading Congregationalist figure, and President of Magdalen College. 'Through their closeness to Cromwell the two men gave Oxford an influence on the Cromwellian church at least as great as that which it had exerted on the Laudian church before it.'[54]

But they did not have a free hand. To introduce one important example, John Wilkins was the Warden of Wadham College. While he resists easy classification, Wilkins might be taken to represent Presbyterian interests.[55] Early on, Cromwell included him (along with Owen) on a Council to execute the office of Chancellor.[56] So there was plenty of room for ideological gamesmanship. It is unwise to overstate the differences that existed within the University, but there were clearly competing sympathies that might be too-simply labelled as Congregationalist, Presbyterian and Royalist, not to mention outside pressure from clamorous voices to free the English ministry from both tithes and university training.[57] Such was the arrangement of enemies that the Congregationalists and Presbyterians found cause to co-operate more often than not, the universities ultimately withstood the battering from their

---

[49]   Owen's appointment revived a history of strong Calvinist Deans at Christ Church. See Tyacke, 'Religious Controversy', 569–70.

[50]   Toon, *God's Statesman*, 53.

[51]   Blair Worden, 'Cromwellian Oxford', in *The History of the University of Oxford*, vol. 4, ed. Nicholas Tyacke (Oxford: Clarendon Press, 1997), 741.

[52]   Worden, 'Cromwellian Oxford', 740.

[53]   Collins, *Allegiance of Thomas Hobbes*, 207, 208.

[54]   Worden, 'Cromwellian Oxford', 737.

[55]   See Barbara Shapiro, *John Wilkins 1614–1672* (Berkeley, CA: University of California Press, 1969), 91. Shapiro is cautious about characterizing Wilkins (and indeed other figures) as Presbyterian.

[56]   Shapiro, *John Wilkins*, 88; Collins, *Allegiance of Thomas Hobbes*, 208.

[57]   Worden, 'Cromwellian Oxford', 750–751; Cook, 'Political Biography', 153.

detractors, and there was much that might please the reformers. There were failures and defeats, as we shall soon see, but Owen's general success should not be forgotten.[58] Charles Mallet, who contributed to an early-twentieth-century history of Oxford University, had little sympathy for the godly cause in the 'dark days' of the Interregnum, yet he called Owen 'a remarkable man' and 'a strong and active Vice-Chancellor'.[59] Under his leadership 'the discipline and organisation of the University improved'.[60] He 'left the University stronger than before'.[61] He was 'a strong administrator' who 'pressed his reforms keenly'.[62]

It is the manner in which Owen pursued those reforms, and his reactions to resistance and failure, that are revealing. We can begin with Owen's fundamental posture towards the visitors. This body was one of the principal instruments by which Parliament attempted to reform the universities, especially Oxford, which had of course been the Royalist headquarters during the war.[63] The first visitation had been appointed by Parliament on 1 May 1647. Owen himself had been one of the petitioners requesting a new board of visitors on 8 June 1652,[64] and he was made one of them. A third board was appointed in September 1654 by means of an ordinance – possibly drafted by either Owen or Goodwin, or both – that was ambiguous and badly worded.[65] Owen and Goodwin happily interpreted it as granting power to the visitors to alter the statutes of the University without the approval of Parliament – a handy tool in the service of godly reformation. But the University was horrified. Wilkins carefully laid out the objections: the 'arbitrary' powers of the visitors threatened the ancient liberties of the University; such powers may have been necessary when Royalist Oxford was purged after the first civil war, but not now 'in these more settled times'; even then, the first visitors never presumed to alter the statutes of the University unilaterally; and the effect of these new powers was to subject the University as a whole to 'the will & pleasure of some few of its owne members'.[66]

---

[58]   Worden, 'Cromwellian Oxford', 757.

[59]   Charles Edward Mallet, *A History of the University of Oxford. Volume II. The Sixteenth and Seventeenth Centuries* (New York: Barnes and Noble, 1924), 390, 47.

[60]   Ibid., 391.

[61]   Ibid., 396. See also, Lloyd Gwynn Williams, '*Digitus Dei*: God and Nation in the Thought of John Owen: A Study in English Puritanism and Nonconformity, 1653–1683', PhD Thesis, Drew University, NJ, 1981, 128–32.

[62]   Mallet, *History of the University of Oxford*, 395.

[63]   See Collins, *Allegiance of Thomas Hobbes*, 207–9.

[64]   Bodleian Library: OUA SP/E/4, f.53r.

[65]   See Worden, 'Cromwellian Oxford', 742–4.

[66]   Bodleian Library: OUA SP/E/4, ff.70r–71v. For other petitions in opposition, see ff.62r–v and 68r.

This was a recurrent issue that divided even the visitors themselves: just how much power did they have? Were they empowered to alter even the statutes of the University? Owen consistently argued and acted as if they did. He and Goodwin 'grasped' at these new powers.[67]

One illustration of Owen's tactical style is his long campaign to abolish the wearing of academic habits. He apparently viewed them as 'totally superstitious'[68] and his fixation to see them removed may be part of a consistent anti-formalism. Anthony Wood was there to witness Owen's endeavour 'to put down Habits, Formalities and all Ceremony'. As Vice-Chancellor,

> he, instead of being a grave example to the University, scorned all formality, undervalued his Office by going in *quirpo* like a young Scholar, with powdered hair, snakebone bandstrings (or bandstrings with very large tassels) lawn band, a large set of ribbonds pointed, at his knees, and Spanish Leather Boots, with large lawn Tops, and his Hat mostly cock'd.[69]

This is, it must be said, an unexpected anecdote and it is difficult to know quite what to make of it. There are several potential explanations. In a very hostile critique of the Congregationalists, John Bastwick noted their tendency to dress elaborately: 'you shall find them with cuffs ... and with more silver and gold upon their clothes ... then many great and honourable personages have in their purses'.[70] However overblown this is, perhaps they had a distinctive dress sense that Owen shared. Also, Wood marked Owen for 'a vaine person' who dressed 'as the fashion then was for young men'. It was said in jest that he 'had as much powder in his hair that would discharge eight cannons'.[71] Perhaps vanity plays a part. But the main point that Wood seems to convey is that Owen did not dress in the usual, formal way. He 'scorned all formality'; he deliberately dressed 'in opposition to the prelaticall cut'; he wore his hat – not the customary

---

[67]   Worden, 'Cromwellian Oxford', 742.

[68]   John Gutch, ed., *The History and Antiquities of the University of Oxford in Two Books: By Anthony á Wood, M.A. of Merton College: Now First Published in English from the Original Manuscript in the Bodleian Library* (Oxford: John Gutch, 1796), ii.668. These are Wood's words.

[69]   Wood, *Athenae Oxonienses*, ii.738. To dress 'in quirpo' was to discard the cloak or outer garment, which had the effect of revealing the shape of the body. Source: Oxford English Dictionary online [www.oed.com].

[70]   John Bastwick, *The Utter Routing of the Whole Army of all the Independents and Sectaries... Or, Independency not God's Ordinance* (1646), Epistle to the Reader, sig. D4r. I am grateful to John Coffey for directing me to this reference.

[71]   Andrew Clark, ed., *The Life and Times of Anthony Wood, Antiquary, Of Oxford, 1632–1695, Described by Himself*, vol. 1, *1632–1663* (Oxford: Clarendon Press, 1891), 221.

trencher – to Congregation and Convocation and always kept it 'mostly cocked', a calculated snub towards traditional order.[72] All this indicates the depths of his dislike for traditional academic garb. He certainly went to great lengths to banish it from the University.

The best source for this story is a letter written by a worried John Wilkins.[73] In 1656 he wrote to Jonathan Goddard and Cromwell's brother-in-law Peter French, both well placed men in London with Oxford connections,[74] updating them on Owen's recent manoeuvres and enlisting their aid to obstruct his ambitions. It is true that Wilkins was no ally of Owen's in this context. It is also true that he heard some of the details of his account from others rather than witnessing them for himself. But he may have felt himself to be doing Owen a favour by seeking to rein in what he saw as his determined recklessness; and his account is reinforced by Seth Ward, one of the Proctors at Oxford and another obstacle in Owen's way.

Owen had unexpectedly summoned the members of Convocation to a meeting on the afternoon of Christmas Day 1655, when few members could be present and he was much more likely to get his way. Indeed, the 'very thin delegacy' voted to remove all statutes requiring the use of habits, though it was a short-lived success: Convocation overturned the decision at its next meeting.[75] Owen declared, both in public and in private, that he would give up his attempts to remove habits, but that was hardly true. At a subsequent meeting of Convocation he played a similar stunt. Having declared that he had no more business to propose that day, and once a significant number of the members had departed, he allowed another vote to permit those who wished to, to refrain from wearing habits. This vote also passed, though Wilkins felt it was redundant since that was the practice in any case. Even then, Owen had not finished. At a further meeting of Convocation he bundled several reforms, including the abolition of habits, into one vote. The members were allowed no debate; they had only just seen the wording on which they were to vote; and they were required to vote on the whole package – it was all or nothing. Furthermore, Owen wanted the members physically to divide into groups – a move that was highly unusual – presumably to put more pressure on those who were inclined to vote against

---

[72] Ibid., 300, 359.

[73] The letter is found in the Bodleian Library: OUA SP/E/4, f.91r–93v.

[74] Worden, 'Cromwellian Oxford', 737–8. Late in 1652 they, along with Wilkins and Owen, were appointed members of the commission that effected the work of Chancellor.

[75] The Christmas Day meeting did seem to be highly unusual. The votes were not recorded in the Register of Convocation (Bodleian Library; volume T), though an additional sheet of manuscript was inserted between pages 282 and 283 recording the decisions that were taken, all to do with degree regulations and with no mention of habits. It is as if that vote never took place.

the measures. But they refused to obey Owen's instruction. According to Ward, Owen then declared that the vote had passed without even seeing the results. As Ward delighted to point out, only the Proctors were empowered to declare the results, 'to which he reply'd, *Egregie Procurator tace, Good Mr. Proctor hold your tongue*. Upon this, the Masters, in a tumultory manner rose from their seats, and began to Mutiny, which caus'd the Vice-Chancellor to Dissolve the Convocation'.[76] Wilkins tells us that the members had in fact voted against the package by a majority of some 40 votes, but, according to Ward, Owen called Ward back the next day to attest that the vote had passed; of course, he refused.[77] If Wilkins is correct, Convocation was more than willing to accede to the great majority of the reforms under consideration, but resented the inclusion of the abolition of habits. If Owen had only given way on that point considerable reforms would have been put in place. Instead he held his ground and, faced with defeat, retreated to Coventry with Thankful Owen (a Fellow of Lincoln College and no relation of John Owen) to consider his next move.

His new strategy was to work through the visitors to 'new model' Convocation on the grounds that it had proved itself to be incapable of reforming itself. This was not just an issue of habits. It was claimed that Convocation would have the power to elect a new Chancellor, should the current Chancellor, Oliver Cromwell, choose to resign. Wilkins was unsure that Convocation did have that power, but, in the event, when Cromwell resigned in the following year, he indeed instructed Convocation to elect a new Chancellor.[78] So Owen may have been planning ahead for that moment. Given the fact that his tenure as Vice-Chancellor also came to an end soon after the appointment of the new Chancellor, he may well have had his own security in mind as much as anything else. 'And therefore the whole present frame [was] to bee taken away, and instead some of the power of Convocation to be now put in the hands [of] godly and prudent men.'[79] Not only was this to be done, it was to be done in haste – before Owen had to leave for London – and apparently with the threat of force, if needed.[80] But there was doubt about whether the visitors had any sort of power to remodel Convocation, not just in Wilkins' mind but among the visitors themselves. Apart from Owen they were evenly divided. '[T]he four senior and more sober men (I hear) are against these high acts; and will by no meanes be

---

[76]   Walter Pope, *The Life of the Right Reverend Father in God, Seth, Lord Bishop of Salisbury* (1697), 41–2. I am grateful to Blair Worden for making this account known to me.

[77]   Ibid., 42.

[78]   Bodleian Library: Register of Convocation, T, p. 305.

[79]   Bodleian Library: OUA SP/E/4, f.92v.

[80]   This comment was crossed out in Wilkins' letter: 'and in case the Convocation will not submit to it, they talk of making use of the Major Generall.' Ibid., 92v.

perswaded to consent therein.'[81] They asked that those members of the visitation who were of the gentry and nobility, and who had never been invited to meet with their fellow visitors, be invited to join the discussion. Owen and the other four visitors refused. The reluctant four also asked to wait until they had at least seen their commission in order to ascertain their powers. It seems they had been acting all this time without even that. Again, they were denied. When it became clear that these four were adamant in their resistance Owen scooped up all the papers, still unsigned, leaving no copies with the Registrar, '[i]ntending, as is supposed, to get them confirmed above. And declaring himself resolved to alter the present constitution of Convocation'.[82] He was determined, in the face of even his friends' advice, to fight this battle in London. If Convocation impeded his agenda, he would turn to the visitors; and if they also frustrated his efforts, he would go higher still. So off he went to London, with Wilkins' anxious missive not far behind. 'I need not tell you', he concluded,

> of what huge concernment these actings are. They seem to some of us, to strike at the subversion of all our charters confirmed by so many Acts of Parliament from time to time. And I think wee are the first Corporation in England upon whom any such attempt hath been made.[83]

He asked Goddard and French to do what they could to see common sense prevail and it would seem that they were successful. Owen found a deaf ear in the Lord Protector, and his efforts failed. All he had succeeded in doing was to bring the wearing of habits back into fashion.[84] In July 1658 his old ministerial neighbour from Essex, Ralph Josselin, noted

> how Dr Owen endeavoured to lay down all the badges of schollers distinction in the universities: Hoods, caps, gowns, degrees, lay by all studdie of philosophy; he is become a great scorne, the Lord keep him from all Temptacons, least his great heart turne up into the wind of error, and endeavour some great matter against the truth, I feare about him.[85]

Even Owen's sympathizers, it seems, felt that he had gone too far.

---

[81] Ibid., 92v.
[82] Ibid., 93r.
[83] Ibid., 93r.
[84] Worden, 'Cromwellian Oxford', 745.
[85] MacFarlane, *Diary of Ralph Josselin*, 374.

By then, Owen's days as Vice-Chancellor were effectively numbered[86] and his relationship with Cromwell was in decline. Historians and biographers have assumed that the relationship between the two was very close until cracks appeared in the mid-1650s. There is no evidence to challenge the initial warmth and even admiration but, as Leggett shows, there is also little evidence to prove it. Owen was uncharacteristically effusive in his dedication to Cromwell, attached to two published sermons preached in Scotland. 'I have received from you, in the weaknesses and temptations wherewith I am encompassed, that daily spiritual refreshment and support – by inquiry into, and discovery of, the deep and hidden dispensations of God towards his secret ones – which my spirit is taught to value.'[87] Such scraps as this are suggestive, but inconclusive. And as we have already seen, the patronage of a number of Independent political figures may be more important than that of Cromwell on his own. Even so, the assumption of a positive early relationship between the two can stand in the absence of any evidence to the contrary. This means that the trajectory of their relationship was one of eventual decay and decline.

Cromwell would have agreed with many of Owen's assumptions, not least his tendency to read the hand of Providence in daily affairs and in his attachment to liberty of conscience. But Cromwell did not share Owen's enthusiasm for crafting definite creeds by which to measure doctrinal orthodoxy. I do not wish to offer here the kind of detail and background I will present in the next chapter. It is sufficient only to observe that Owen chose to ignore Cromwell's wishes on that point. In 1654 Owen was a leading figure in an assembly of ministers called by Parliament to identify the fundamentals of religion, a project that did not have Cromwell's full support.[88]

In 1657 Owen became involved in mediation efforts on behalf of the Council of State in a dispute within the Church of Scotland. Here again, Owen pursued his own ends rather than Cromwell's, and his methods were revealing. The division existed between the Protesters – who wanted to reduce the power of synods in a more Congregationalist direction – and the Resolutioners – who preferred the traditional structure and who had supported Charles II. Owen chaired the committee set up to consider the issue and he was clearly partial,

---

86   Worden, 'Cromwellian Oxford', 746; Mallet, *History of the University of Oxford*, 395–6.

87   Owen, *Branch of the Lord the Beauty of Zion* (1650): *Works*, viii.283.

88   Blair Worden notes that while Owen would not have devised a list of the fundamentals without Cromwell's approval, Cromwell 'seems to have distanced himself from them'. Blair Worden, 'John Milton and Oliver Cromwell', in *Soldiers, Writers and Statesmen of the English Revolution*, ed. Ian Gentles, John Morrill and Blair Worden (Cambridge: Cambridge University Press, 1998), 248.

favouring the Protesters.[89] James Sharp, who represented the Resolutioners before the committee, complained that Owen had 'dealt deceitfully with me in the business'.[90] Sharp is not necessarily a source to be trusted, but the kind of manoeuvres he describes are consonant with Owen's behaviour in other settings. In this case he apparently exploited the few days before the committee met to 'prejudice our cause' among its members.[91] He allowed the committee to bully and intimidate Sharp.[92] He took a vote on the final report without the required quorum.[93] And he may have switched reports after the committee had voted so as to reflect his own views before the Council of State.[94] 'Owen had blatantly disregarded procedural niceties in order to accomplish a godly objective.'[95] He had taken 'a heavy-handed approach to securing what he saw as the best way forward for the godly [that] had the potential to damage Cromwell's relationship with the moderate civilians he was trying to court'.[96] In the end Owen did not achieve his aims. Instead, he was 'falling from favour at Whitehall' and, according to Sharp, 'under a cloud at Court'.[97]

That cloud only got darker, and two final episodes touch on Owen's relationship with Cromwell. In May 1657 Cromwell was offered the Crown. Leading army officers were appalled at the prospect. On hearing that Cromwell was planning to accept, his brother-in-law Colonel John Desborough and Colonel Pride instructed Owen to draw up a petition in the name of the army. It was enough to deter Cromwell from proceeding, and Owen's involvement as a 'ghost writer' was sufficient to estrange him from Cromwell who 'made little use of Owen's services in the remaining sixteen months of his life'.[98] Despite later

---

[89]   See James Sharp to Robert Douglas, 6 August 1657: William Stephen, ed., *Register of the Consultations of the Ministers of Edinburgh and Some Other Brethren of the Ministry* (Edinburgh: Scottish History Society, 1921), ii.66–7.

[90]   James Sharp to Robert Douglas, August 1657: Stephen, ed., *Register of the Consultations*, ii.88.

[91]   James Sharp to Robert Douglas, 6 August 1657: Stephen, ed., *Register of the Consultations*, ii.66.

[92]   In particular, see ibid., 68, 86.

[93]   Ibid., 74.

[94]   James Sharp to Robert Douglas, August 1657: Stephen, ed., *Register of the Consultations*, ii.88–9. This accusation seems doubtful. If Owen had such control of the committee, why would he need to switch its reports? Leggett, 'John Owen as Religious Adviser', 53–4. Sharp said 'I know not what or whom to beleeve'.

[95]   Cook, 'Political Biography', 247.

[96]   Leggett, 'John Owen as Religious Adviser', 52.

[97]   James Sharp to Robert Douglas, August 1657: Stephen, ed., *Register of the Consultations*, ii.88.

[98]   Cook, 'Political Biography', 233, 236.

rumours to the contrary, Owen was not among those present with the Protector in his final days.[99]

By the close of 1657 Owen's stock had declined rather badly. A year earlier Wilkins had married Cromwell's sister, Robina. The implication was clear, according to one observer, Thomas Smith: 'From Oxford I am informed, that Dr Wilkins of Wadham is like to prove the man of men there, having very lately married the Protectors sister, Dr Frenches widow, which troubles Dr Owen and others of the Grandees there, who foresee that hee will overtop them all.'[100] They were not far wrong. Bishop Gilbert Burnet later looked back on Wilkins's career at Oxford: 'he married *Cromwell's* sister; but made no other use of that alliance, but to do good offices, and to cover the University from the sourness of *Owen* and *Goodwin*.'[101] And in July 1657 convocation elected Richard Cromwell as the new Chancellor of the University. He had Presbyterian interests at heart. 'Relations between the old vice-chancellor and the new chancellor were destined to be courteous, but far from warm.'[102] And they did not last for long. 'Owen, ill and exhausted, at odds with the protector, gave up the vice-chancellorship in October 1657.'[103] There is a scattering of evidence to suggest that he was pushed out.[104] Whatever the case, his efforts to reform Oxford University were over.

Assessing Owen's Character

This description of Owen's political career during his period of greatest national influence yields numerous insights into his character, temperament and

---

[99]   Owen, *Reflections on a Slanderous Libel* (1670): *Works*, xvi.273–4.

[100]   Thomas Smith to Daniel Fleming, 2 May 1656: *The Flemings in Oxford Being Documents Selected from the Rydal Papers in Illustration of the Lives and Ways of Oxford Men 1650–1700*, ed. John Richard Magrath (Oxford: Clarendon Press, 1904), i.101.

[101]   Gilbert Burnet, ed., *Bishop Burnet's History of His Own Time* (London: Thomas Ward, 1724), i.215.

[102]   Cook, 'Political Biography', 243.

[103]   Worden, 'Cromwellian Oxford', 746.

[104]   James Sharp said that 'Owen is outed of his vicechancellerie of Oxford', in a letter to John Smith, 13 October 1657: Stephen, ed., *Register of the Consultations*, ii.127. Owen's anonymous biographer wrote that 'the notes I have concerning him, say, that he was remov'd from being Vice-Chancellor of the University of Oxford in 1657, which I take to be Proof that he did not thoroughly approve of *Oliver's* Measures. And in 1659 he was remov'd from being Dean of *Christ-Church*. The Authors who mention these things tell us nothing of the Reasons, but there's grounds to believe that both proceeded from some Change in the Times, for we are told he was remov'd from the Deanery soon after *Richard Cromwell* was made Protector'. [Anon.], 'Life of Owen', xxiii. In fact, Owen ceased being Dean in 1660. See Worden, 'Cromwellian Oxford', 770.

personality. But before we begin that assessment, we need to acknowledge that the basis for this perspective is both partial and slanted, in three ways. First, approaching Owen through the prism of his theological writings or (as far as we could recover them) his preaching or pastoral ministry, might offer an impression of the man that is accurate, but quite different from the one presented here – one less calculating and more open. This is perhaps the kind of impression formed on John Asty:

> As to [Owen's] person his stature was tall, his visage grave and majestic, and withal comely; he had the aspect of a Gentleman, suitable to his birth ... As to his temper he was very affable and courteous, familiar and sociable; the meanest person found an easy access to his converse and friendship. He was facetious and pleasant in his common discourse, jesting with his acquaintance, but with sobriety and measure; a great master of his passions especially that of anger: he was of a serene and even temper, neither elated with honour, credit, friends or estate, nor deprest with troubles and difficulties. His carriage was genteel, in nothing mean: He was generous in his favours.[105]

Such a description will have its measure of truth and it provides important ballast to the impression formed by his 1650s political activity. That said, there are grounds to challenge some of Asty's observations. If they were accurate, they must have reflected a later, older, more mature, settled Owen (for what it is worth, Baxter claimed that he improved with age).[106] The 1650s supply ample evidence of quite the opposite tendencies in the man.

The second way in which this is a partial picture of Owen is that it is reliant at key points on the perspective of his detractors, particularly men like John Wilkins, Seth Ward, Anthony Wood and James Sharp, who had an especially personal reason for disliking Owen's style and methods. But if we are forced to rely on such accounts then Owen must bear some of the blame, since he did so little to reveal his own perspective or to shape the way in which he wanted his actions to be interpreted. Also, we can begin to bring in other sources to confirm the views of these men, ones at a greater distance from Owen and much less likely to skew their impressions for personal reasons. And above all it is the patterns that are crucial. Even if there is reason to doubt isolated anecdotes, the recurring dynamics in Owen's behaviour are clear enough.

The picture we are forming is partial also in a third and final way: it is not my intention to offer here a fully rounded appreciation of Owen's personality.

---

[105] Asty, 'Memoirs', 33–4.

[106] Baxter, *Account of the Reasons*, Postscript, sig. M4r.

If it was, this focus on Owen's political activities in the 1650s would be an essential but insufficient basis on which to do so. Instead I have a much more specific purpose in mind: to explain Owen's particular clash with Baxter. Their relationship formed in exactly this period and its difficulties showed up in precisely the field of activity we have been describing. On that basis, therefore, I wish to offer six closely linked observations on Owen's personality as it is reflected in his actions during the late 1640s and 1650s.

The first, the fullest and the most obvious observation is that Owen was a political player, if not always a very successful one. According to one contemporary, he was 'politiquely addicted'.[107] William Guthrie, writing in the eighteenth century, summed him up as 'in all respects a compleat gentleman and a consummate politician'.[108] Today we would call him a 'political animal'. He was a born natural, possessed of the passion, insight and skill necessary for political effectiveness. He was, said Asty, 'well acquainted with men and things, and would give a shrewd guess at a man's temper and designs upon his first acquaintance'.[109] If his preaching is anything to go by, he was eloquent and persuasive. According to Wood, who may well have heard him preach, 'he had a very graceful behaviour in the pulpit, an eloquent elocution, a winning and insinuating deportment and could, by the persuasion of his oratory ... move and win the affections of his admiring auditory almost as he pleased'.[110] He seemed instinctively to understand the system of patronage, making his way up through local politics in Essex with ease and quickly breaking into national prominence, forming a bond with the man who was then the most powerful individual patron of all. His interaction with Cromwell in their first meeting presents a deft performance in the rhythms of deference and power. Later evidence at Oxford shows how Owen could trade on his close proximity to Cromwell to advance his programme of reform.[111] More broadly, the Dissenting Brethren must have recognized the worth of his abilities: despite his youth and inexperience he was quickly absorbed into their group. Owen was obviously a man to watch. As James Sharp put it, 'Dr Owen is no small person here as to courtship'.[112]

---

[107]   John Goodwin to Sarah Goodwin, 24 October 1663: National Archives, London: SP 29/82/39.

[108]   William Guthrie, *A General History of England from Edward the Sixth to the Restoration of King Charles the Second* (London: T. Waller, 1751), iv.1248.

[109]   Asty, 'Memoirs', 34.

[110]   Wood, *Athenae Oxonienses*, ii.741.

[111]   Leggett, 'John Owen as Religious Adviser', 22.

[112]   James Sharp to Robert Douglas, 14 February 1657: Stephen, ed., *Register of the Consultations*, i.368.

There is much we do not know about Owen's post-regicide sermon to Parliament, but it suggests a wide strategic perspective. It is almost as if he had one eye on the Restoration well before it ever came into view. He may have realized how exposed he was simply by the act of preaching so close to the event, and he may have considered how his words would sound in the context of political reversal. What we can say is that, to the amazement of many, he escaped repercussion for his Interregnum activities at the Restoration of Charles II – further testament to his political skill and his ability to foster powerful patrons – a fact that might have been much less likely had he shown himself in 1649 to be a vociferous cheerleader for the bloody demise of the new King's father. As Asty observed, Owen preached at 'a critical juncture, and he was not ignorant of the tempers of his principal hearers; he was then a rising man, and to justify the late action was the infallible road to preferment. But his discourse was so modest and inoffensive, that his friends could make no just exception, nor his enemies take an advantage of his words another day'.[113] His sermon was calculated, restrained and measured. It is another instance of Owen beautifully tailoring himself to the moment in order to win the most advantage, while also standing in continuity with previously declared convictions, arguments and expectations. Indeed, I am not wanting to cast Owen's political activities in a pejorative light, nor do I want to suggest that he changed his convictions according to the need of the moment. The truth is quite the opposite. Owen had a clear sense of what he wanted to achieve and he set out to obtain the power required to achieve it. In this sense he demonstrated a finely tuned 'sense of opportunism',[114] and well-developed political capacities. This does not mean that he was always successful in achieving his ends, of course. His links of political patronage were too closely connected to a particular faction within English politics, and when their astonishing and disproportionate power began to recede, so too did his. Even so, Owen was, among other things, a very astute and capable political operator.

The second observation I wish to make is that there was within Owen a pronounced streak of personal ambition. This is closely tied to the first point: it involved the deployment of much the same set of skills but the goal was not the achievement of an agenda external to himself, it was his own reputation and prestige. Asty said that Owen was 'naturally of an aspiring mind, affecting popular applause, and very desirous of honour and preferment'.[115] At University 'the *honouring of God*, or *serving his Country*, otherwise than to make him capable of *serving himself*, had little room in his Thoughts'.[116] His experience

---

[113]   Asty, 'Memoirs', 8.
[114]   Leggett, 'John Owen as Religious Adviser', 24.
[115]   Asty, 'Memoirs', 3.
[116]   [Anon.], 'Life of Owen', viii.

of religious conversion may have redirected his ambition towards other more noble ends, but it did not entirely eradicate his concern for his own prestige. He could be touchy when it came to slights on his authority.

This is illustrated by the third point: Owen was not a man to be contradicted. In the year after Owen's death, an anonymous admirer vindicated him from the aspersions of, as it happens, Richard Baxter. Near the end of the work, the author was prepared to offer a candid assessment:

> He was indeed sometimes a little *Impatient* of Contradiction (the common Companion of high Esteem) yet on *Cool* Thoughts, or the conviction of *Experience*, he would pay the greater Respects to those, who freely, and faithfully expressed themselves; he was not Nice [shy, reluctant] of receiving Honour, and Respects from others; yet as free to return them, where they were deserved. He had indeed an *humble* Loftiness, and a *lofty* Humility.[117]

Owen did not take kindly to having his will thwarted or to being treated with less respect than he felt he deserved. Two occasions from the Interregnum period illustrate the pattern. In 1654 Owen committed two Quakers to the county jail for 'speaking to the vice-chancellor in the street', probably in an insubordinate manner.[118] A few years later, the *terrae-filius* – the elected jester of the students who routinely mocked the godly – persistently ignored the Vice-Chancellor's warnings 'to avoid profaneness and obscenity, and not go into any personal reflections'. The young man ignored him, and 'several times' Owen ordered him to stop. Next he sent in the beadles to remove the impertinent scholar by force, but the student body pushed them off. Finally, and against the advice of his colleagues, Owen himself grabbed the offender, removed him, and sent him to the Oxford prison. 'I will not see Authority thus trampled on', he said.[119] He later regretted his failure to stop those celebrations 'without having to impose silence on someone among the speakers or, *what is more distressing*, to suffer insults'.[120] Owen could not bear insult from those beneath him. 'The Vice-Chancellor', observed Charles Mallet, 'may or may not have approved of opposition to authority in the case of his colleagues. He was clearly no lover of opposition to his own, and he never faltered in the expression of his views'.[121]

---

[117]   [Anon.], *Vindication of Owen*, 38.

[118]   Mabel Richmond Brailsford, *The Making of William Penn* (London: Longmans, Green and Co., 1933), 97. See also, Cook, 'Political Biography', 179.

[119]   Asty, 'Memoirs', xi–xii. See also Mallet, *History of the University of Oxford*, 395.

[120]   Peter Toon, ed., *The Oxford Orations of Dr John Owen* (Linkinhorne: Gospel Communication, 1971), 31. Emphasis added.

[121]   Mallet, *History of the University of Oxford*, 394.

When his reforms were voted down by convocation 'he took it in bad part' and 'determined, it seems, to break the power of his opponents'.[122]

What this also conveys is, fourth, a ruthless determination in Owen to achieve his desired ends, even if that meant overlooking proper procedure. He resisted efforts to overturn his election to the burgess seat of Oxford even though he should never have been elected in the first place.[123] He was happy to exploit the powers of the visitors even if that subverted the ancient constitution of the university. He engineered votes in convocation in order to ensure the 'correct' outcome; he put pressure on the members to vote in the way he wanted; he declared the result without seeing the final tally; he told the proctor to take his seat and shut up; he tried to bully him into agreeing that the result was the opposite of what everyone knew that it was. And then, when all of that failed, he threatened to use force. It never came to that, of course, but he certainly tried to bend the visitors to his will before going over their heads in London. In the Scottish consultations he made sure his committee made the decision he wanted, allowing various procedural improprieties. In general, he showed 'a willingness to rewrite the rules in order to assure the outcome', and he had no compunction against 'trampling on time-honoured legislative procedures'.[124] His 'pursuit of policy occasionally meant questionable tactics which ignored institutional process'.[125] Owen, armed with a committee, was a formidable opponent. And he was tenacious. He used every last possible means over extended months to banish academic dress: several sessions of convocation; the board of visitors; and, shrugging off good advice, a personal appeal to Cromwell. He was not a man to back down quickly and graciously or accept defeat at its first appearance.

Fifth, Owen reacted angrily when he did not get his way. This is where Asty's observations were the least accurate. Owen was not, in the 1650s at least, 'a great master of his passions especially that of anger'.[126] Once again, there are enough examples to suggest a pattern of behaviour. Owen was 'highly incensed' when Convocation refused to accept the full package of reforms, 'taking all occasions to blow the coale, aggravate it as an unsufferable affront as is not to bee indured'.[127] That Owen 'was extremely incensed', explained Wilkins, 'was evident, both by such expressions as hee let fall in Convocation, and by the like

---

122   Ibid., 395.

123   Cook, 'Political Biography', 185–6.

124   Ibid., 172, 208.

125   Leggett, 'John Owen as Religious Adviser', 49.

126   Asty, 'Memoirs', 34.

127   Bodleian Library: OUA SP/E/4, f.92r. See also, Gutch, *History and Antiquities*, ii.672.

afterwards'.[128] James Sharp endured 'some sharp encounters from D. Owen'.[129] In March 1657 Richard Cromwell noted that 'Dr Owen hath been very angry, and went in great haste oute of London'.[130] Owen himself acknowledged the 'stern' tone of his fourth Oxford oration, delivered in July 1657: 'I beg of you, gentlemen of the University, that you should concede as much to my oration as you believe should be granted to righteous indignation, if it is indignation only that insults and abuses beget.'[131] And in December 1657, Thomas Lamplugh observed that 'Dr. Owen is at last no Vice-Chancellor ... he cannot well digest a private life; but seemes to be angry, at I know not what'.[132] In Cook's view, Owen had become by then 'an angry loser'. 'The adjective most used to describe Owen in 1657 was "angry."'[133]

Sixth, we can see in Owen's behaviour not just a thread of anger, but also a pattern of threats and withdrawal when he did not get his way. When convocation rejected his reforms in April 1656 he 'met his defeat first by withdrawing from Oxford with Thankful Owen and then, fortified by the reflections of that retreat, by threatening on his return to appeal to Cromwell and even to "make use of the major generall"' (either Charles Fleetwood or William Packer).[134] The same kind of pattern is reflected in Richard Cromwell's comment that Owen had been very angry 'and went in great haste oute of London'.[135] When Owen (and Goodwin) were removed from their shared pulpit at St Mary's in 1657, Owen responded by establishing a competing lecture in a different church at the same time. 'I have built the Seats at *Maries*', he is reported to have said, 'but let the Doctors find Auditors, for I will Preach at *Peters* in the East'.[136] That was a later, hostile source, but Thomas Lamplugh confirmed the impression at the time. Owen 'has given over preaching at S Marys upon Sunday afternoons and at the same University hour hath set up a lecture in the Parish Church, it is conceived in opposition,

---

[128]   Bodleian Library: OUA SP/E/4, f.92v.

[129]   James Sharp to Robert Douglas, 6 August 1657: Stephen, ed., *Register of the Consultations*, ii.69.

[130]   Richard Cromwell to Henry Cromwell, 7 March 1657: British Library: Lansdowne MSS 821, fol.324r.

[131]   Toon, *Oxford Orations*, 33.

[132]   Thomas Lamplugh to ??, December 1657: National Archives, London: SP.18.158.58.

[133]   Cook, 'Political Biography', 203.

[134]   Worden, 'Cromwellian Oxford', 745. See also Cook, 'Political Biography', 203–4; and Gutch, *History and Antiquities*, ii.672.

[135]   Richard Cromwell to Henry Cromwell, 7 March 1657: British Library, Lansdowne MSS 821, fol.324r.

[136]   Vernon, *Letter to a Friend*, 28. Anthony Wood was probably repeating Vernon when he said that 'in great scorn, he, out of spite, set up a Lecture at another Church', in *Athenae Oxonienses*, ii.739. (In the next column Wood has a direct quote from Vernon.)

and to drain St. Marye's'.[137] It is possible that these are isolated instances, each with its own explanation, but it is difficult to avoid the impression that when Owen failed to get his way he responded with anger, withdrawal, threats and petulance. Anthony Wood repeats an intriguing piece of gossip: he says that Goodwin dictated the membership of the third board of visitors, weighting it with his own supporters; and that Owen, 'perceiving himself fool'd in this matter ... would not at all act among them, but by way of revenge sides with the University, either to have some alterations made in the said Ordinance or else annulled'.[138] Blair Worden is right – this is highly improbable.[139] And yet it fits the pattern. Perhaps there is a germ of truth that is unrecognizable in the way that Wood has distorted the story.[140]

Finally, and unsurprisingly in light of all these observations, Owen tended to prioritize political ends over personal relationships.[141] The clearest instance of this is Oliver Cromwell. Owen steadfastly followed his own agenda 'even if it meant pursuing a policy against Cromwell's hopes'.[142] He 'was not afraid to jeopardise Cromwell's political stability, or his relationship with him, to secure his aims'.[143] On the other hand, the Congregationalists were such a relatively small faction that they were constantly forced to forge alliances,[144] and Owen proved adept at that, forming alliances across denominational boundaries.[145] The clearest example of that is John Wilkins, something of a Presbyterian and a monarchist.[146] Owen could work closely with him, though only so long as they shared much the same set of goals.[147] To illustrate, in 1654 Henry Bartlett wrote to Richard Baxter seeking assistance in his efforts to reverse Wilkins's decision, made without consultation, to replace two fellows with 'profane drunkards, scoffers at holiness[s]'. The move had 'so far discouraged all the godly, that they are all upon removing'. Bartlett wanted the fellows reinstated,

---

[137] Thomas Lamplugh to ??, December 1657: National Archives, London: SP.18.158.58.

[138] Gutch, *History and Antiquities*, ii.661, 662–3.

[139] Worden, 'Cromwellian Oxford', 746, n. 62. As we have seen, Owen tried to use this board of visitors to remodel convocation.

[140] Toon may be closer to the truth when he speculates that Owen merely disliked the shift in the balance of the membership of the new board and perhaps he blamed Goodwin for that.

[141] Leggett, 'John Owen as Religious Adviser', 49.

[142] Ibid.

[143] Ibid., 54.

[144] Cook, 'Congregational Independents', 347, 355.

[145] Leggett, 'John Owen as Religious Adviser', 77.

[146] See Worden, 'Cromwellian Oxford', 738.

[147] For examples, see Worden, 'Cromwellian Oxford', 748, 751–2, 761; and Leggett, 'John Owen as Religious Adviser', 60.

but 'Dr. Owen is so intimate with the Warden' that there was no way through. Owen himself had apparently put the objectors in their place. So the two men could work easily together, though it was Wilkins who led the resistance to Owen's campaign against habits. 'For the sake of an immediate, specific goal', observes Cook, 'Owen allied himself with the party who shared that goal regardless of long-range affinities and differences'.[148] It seems as if Owen viewed relationships in terms of their potential to advance his own political aims; they were instrumental and dispensable. James Moffatt shrewdly remarks that Owen 'was intensely self-reliant. He learned from few living men, and leaned on none. He had no close friend'.[149] His comment reinforces the impression that Owen was extremely proficient at political networking, but not nearly so capable of, or interested in, deep, lasting, intimate personal friendships. The self-containment of his writings is, in this sense, also evident in his career. In each setting there was a clear purpose immediately to hand and Owen did not give away any more of himself than was strictly necessary.

I need to repeat my earlier point that this is an extremely selective and slanted view of Owen. It is not the whole of the man, and a fuller and more balanced assessment would be rather more flattering.[150] But it is a part of him, and it is particularly apparent in those settings in which he collided with Baxter. Indeed, if Owen's pattern of behaviour in the mid-1650s was new to some, it would have been no surprise to Baxter. He had learned all this the hard way. Even now, it should be clear why Owen's personal style and temperament was not going to mesh easily with Baxter's. Owen bristled at any slight to his authority; he responded with anger and pique; he could demonstrate 'signs of jealousy'; he 'brow-beat every one who had so much manly courage as to appear' against him; he was 'a difficult man to beat'.[151] And this is the man whom Baxter had so visibly slighted in the appendix to his *Aphorismes of Justification*. The result was never going to be pretty.

Richard Baxter in Isolation

In my earlier book I presented Baxter as a man torn between competing tendencies: the one to pursue peace and end controversy; the other to denounce

---

[148]   Cook, 'Political Biography', 192.

[149]   Moffatt, *Golden Book of John Owen*, 20.

[150]   For a more positive assessment, see Orme, 'Memoirs', 347ff.

[151]   Cook, 'Political Biography', 177; Gutch, *History and Antiquities*, ii.668; Mallet, *History of the University of Oxford*, 395.

error and, in effect, to create or sustain controversy.[152] He lacked 'the practical wisdom which adapts means to ends', says George Fisher. 'In this attempt to secure a peace, he excited more contention than he quelled, and a great part of his life was spent in controversies of which he himself was the author.'[153] William Lamont puts it nicely: the 'pathos in his career is the gap between magnanimous aim and divisive means'.[154] The result was, even for a setting as contentious as seventeenth-century England,[155] a very long list of people whom Baxter offended in the course of his life. Both friend and foe alike observed his tendency to come across as magisterial, haughty, arrogant, impervious to correction, blind to his own weakness, incapable of self-doubt and personally disdainful of others. The example of John Humfrey will illustrate this sufficiently. He was the Vicar of Frome, in Somerset, who admired Baxter and joined him in working towards comprehension after their ejection. In 1654 he wrote to commend Baxter's *Aphorismes of Justification*, although 'the thing in your writings which seems most grating is that you seeme to bee sometimes too dogmaticall and confident' where 'a few mollifying words and submission will take better'.[156] This advice was entirely wasted on Baxter and three years later Humfrey had to repeat it. Others were now observing what he had already pointed out, and Baxter was doing himself no favours by persisting in a style 'so violent, eager, sowre, from the very first'.[157]

Baxter was not unaware of the problem. In reply to Humfrey he explained that 'I do not feele any passion or distast against my Brethren any more when I speak so keenly than at other times; but it is my naturall temper to be earnest in speech, and when I write against an error, I am ready to thinke I should lay open the worst of it'. His words may have seemed overly sharp at times but his heart was not heated, nor did he intend to offend. However, 'when I dispute against a sin or errour. I should call it by its owne name, and tell men truly what it is'. The result was that 'I oft goe further than I should, not well consideringe how gratinge and provokinge some truths are to those that are dishonoured by them'.[158] A year later he explained things more simply to Abraham Pinchbeck. 'I confess by the power of truth (if I mistake not) and an estimation of its

---

[152]   See Cooper, *Fear and Polemic*, chapter 2.

[153]   George P. Fisher, 'The Theology of Richard Baxter', *Bibliotheca Sacra and American Biblical Repository* 9 (1852): 136.

[154]   Lamont, *Millennium*, 275.

[155]   N.H. Keeble, '*Loving & Free Converse': Richard Baxter in his Letters* (London: Dr Williams' Trust, 1991), 10.

[156]   John Humfrey to Baxter, 11 May 1654: DWL MS *BC* i.193v (*CCRB* #179).

[157]   John Humfrey to Baxter [c.autumn 1657]: DWL MS *BC* i.197r (*CCRB* #397).

[158]   Baxter to John Humfrey, 13 March 1657/8: DWL MS *BC* i.203r (*CCRB* #437).

interest above any other, I am strongly provoked to blab out any thinge, that I do confidently thinke to be true and weighty.'[159] These words suggested some kind of self-understanding in Baxter but in general he was much more likely to lay the blame elsewhere, on those who could not bear any reproach with humility and graciousness. He continued to write as if he were in sole possession of the truth, without any hint of self-doubt. The tone set in the preface to his *Aphorismes* continued. He regularly offered commentary on others that could just as easily have been applied to himself. In berating those who were over-confident of their opinions and overly ready to share them, he never seemed to discern that others might have resented the same in him. In his 1664 self-review (part of his eventual autobiography) he went so far as to claim that he had all but given up on telling men the error of their ways.[160] If they had been able to read it at the time, his many critics would have found that laughable.

But this tendency was a matter of nurture as well as nature. Here I would like to go beyond my earlier work to identify several shaping forces in Baxter's external environment that combined to cultivate a certain isolation from others, that did nothing to help his lack of tact, that undermined his capacity for compromise, and that circumvented those means by which he might have been shaped in a more tractable fashion.

If we go back to the beginning, Baxter was an only child.[161] Thus he was never engaged in the kind of compromise and rough trading that must go on among siblings. He lacked the opportunity this presented to develop skills in negotiation, or empathy. He had his own way, with no near rival to contradict. (We might bear in mind that Owen, in contrast, was the second of at least five children. This aspect of his upbringing conceivably contributed to his later skills in negotiating and networking.) As we saw earlier, Baxter's family life demonstrated a singularity within the community. His father occasionally reproved 'Drunkards and Swearers' and was roundly abused. Baxter and his parents could hardly hear their Psalms and Scriptures as they read the Bible on the Sabbath, due to 'the great disturbance of the Taber and Pipe and Noise in the Street!'[162] As Anthony Fletcher discerns, this formative experience accentuated in young Richard the 'sense of social isolation' held in common by all Puritans.[163] Baxter was also unmarried, at least until his late forties, and he never had

---

[159]   Baxter to Abraham Pinchbecke, 12 October 16[5]8: DWL MS *BC* iv.56r (*CCRB* #508).

[160]   *Rel. Bax.*, i.126.

[161]   Ibid., 4.

[162]   Ibid., 2–3.

[163]   Anthony Fletcher, 'Oliver Cromwell and the Godly Nation', in *Oliver Cromwell and the English Revolution*, ed. John Morrill (London: Longman, 1990), 215.

children. He saw this as an advantage in his Kidderminster ministry,[164] but he missed once more the opportunity for family life to rub the rough edges off his character.

Not only that, Baxter never went to university. Francis J. Bremer and John Coffey have both shown how attendance at university could establish friendships, networks and alliances that served to bring a young man into community with others.[165] The intellectual exercises of a university education had the potential to moderate existing views under the challenges of disputation and defence. Influential teachers (such as Thomas Barlow, Owen's tutor at Oxford) might mould a student within an existing tradition.[166] This is not to suggest that mavericks were always brought into line during their years at university, but the potential of that community life was never put to the test in Baxter's case. Instead, he was persuaded to live near his family and study under the private tutelage of an ineffectual scholar.[167] After a year and a half he served as a local schoolmaster, eventually turning to pastoral ministry first at Bridgnorth and then at Kidderminster. This was a highly unusual track into ministry, avoiding as it did the traditional path through university. The point is that Baxter was self-taught. He came to his views, in the main, by reading books. But books do not argue back.

In this light, Baxter was an accomplished autodidact. But he was also self-conscious about his lack of formal learning. Early in his pastoral career he was 'conscious of my personal insufficiency, for want of the measure of Learning and Experience which so great and high a Work required. I knew that the want of Academical Honours and Degrees was like to make me Contemptible with the Most, and consequently hinder the Success of my Endeavours.'[168] After the Restoration he was reported to have on one occasion scorned academic trappings. In defending himself, he revealed that he had been ashamed to admit that he had no degrees, so he had declined to wear the proffered tippet.[169] It is just possible, then, that he felt intimidated by Owen's training, which vastly overmatched his. In 1654 Baxter conceded that if he and Owen were 'to joyn

---

[164]   *Rel. Bax.*, i.89.

[165]   See Bremer, *Congregational Communion*, chapter 1; and Coffey, *John Goodwin and the Puritan Revolution*, chapter 1.

[166]   For Barlow, see Trueman, *John Owen*, 2–3, 9–10, 58–9; Sebastian Rehnman, 'John Owen: A Reformed Scholar at Oxford', in *Reformation and Scholasticism: An Ecumenical Enterprise*, ed. Willem J. van Asselt and Eef Dekker (Grand Rapids, MI: Baker Academic, 2001), 185, 191.

[167]   *Rel. Bax.*, i.4.

[168]   Ibid., 12.

[169]   Baxter to John Earle, 12 June 1662: DWL MS *BC* i.98r (*CCRB* #702).

Wit to Wit, and Learning to Learning, and the contest depended on the strength of the Contesters, I should easily yield that he were invincible by such a one as I'.[170] Certainly, their respective academic qualifications were extremely uneven. When Baxter attempted his single work in Latin, in 1681, his writing style was, even in the view of a sympathetic biographer, 'a barbarous imitation of the barbarism of the schoolmen'.[171] There would be no escaping, even then, the effects of that initial gap in his formation.

Geographical isolation was a third shaping factor in Baxter's early development. In 1655 he offered his explanation for the controversy he had provoked over the previous six years. Among other reasons, '[l]ocal distance doth much disadvantage me: it being only those that know me not, or live not within the reach of my converse, that seem offended: and so I have not opportunity to give them that satisfaction, and mollifie their minds, as I doubt not I should do, if I lived among them'.[172] This is another way of saying that no one in Baxter's immediate vicinity objected to his doctrines, which is no great vindication. And yet this was an important factor in Baxter's setting. In 1652 he expressed grave doubts that any efforts of his towards national reconciliation among the godly would bear fruit, 'chiefly for being here confined at such a distance'. For that reason 'I have kept my endeavours in my sphere here in the Country'. John Dury, the devoted unifier to whom he wrote, was 'nearer (in place and Interest) to [that] Power, from which we expect much of what we desire'.[173] Not long after he regretted his inability to keep pace with all the books that were coming into print, the effect of 'living so obscurely and remote from that chief garden where such flowers grow'.[174] Even in 1657, when his influence and reputation might have facilitated a wider circulation, Baxter complained that his 'obscure abode' prevented him from knowing in person so many worthy figures.[175] With due respect to the inhabitants of Kidderminster, Baxter lived a long way from anywhere very useful for his broader purposes. As we have seen, he resided in what had been Royalist territory during the war years with little in the way of promising Puritan ministry: 'We lived in a Country [county] that had but little preaching at all.'[176] He lacked, in other words, the kind of godly

---

[170]   Baxter, *Admonition to Mr. William Eyre*, 36. In *Rich. Baxters Apology*.

[171]   Bates, 'Baxter and Owen', 109. The work was *Methodus Theologiae Christianae* (1681).

[172]   Baxter, *Confession of his Faith*, Preface, sig. d4v.

[173]   Baxter to John Dury, 7 May 1652: DWL MS *BC* vi.90r (*CCRB* #83).

[174]   Baxter to Thomas Bedford, 28 June 1652: Richard Baxter, *Plain Scripture Proof of Infants Church-membership and Baptism Being the Arguments Prepared for (and Partly Managed in) the Publike Dispute with Mr. Tombes*, 3rd edn (1653), 355–6 (*CCRB* #88).

[175]   Baxter to George Ashwell, 30 November 1657: DWL MS *BC* iii.70r (*CCRB* #407).

[176]   *Rel. Bax.*, i.1.

networks open to Owen living in Essex, ones that might have tempered his own views and expression through face-to-face dialogue, though the Worcestershire Association would have helped in part to fill that gap. We might also ponder what Baxter thought of Owen's powdered hair, velvet coat and Spanish leather boots. Coming from the depths of the provinces Baxter was hardly likely to dress, as Owen did, in what 'the fashion then was for young men'.[177] Though he was careful not to be proudly critical of those who followed the fashions, he advised that 'your apparel should express your humiliation; and show that you take more care for the soul'.[178]

Baxter's constant ill health was a further isolating factor in his life. The claims of recurrent sickness from one who lived so long and did so much are difficult to credit, but they should not be wholly dismissed, either.[179] The effects were real enough to him. He regretted how ill health stole away his time and company. 'If I have any ease one day I am sicke another', he explained to John Warren in 1649; 'nay I scarce remember that 2 hours together for this 2 yeares I have bin free from paine in one part or other, except sleeping. My body is able to study but 2 or 3 houres in a day when I am at best'.[180] Baxter's determination to use every moment well meant that he was not one to languish in his sick bed, but recurrent ill health and the internal monitoring attendant on it would have reinforced Baxter's tendency to live in a self-focused state. Owen, on the other hand, enjoyed a strong physical constitution, at least in the first decades of his life.[181] Apart from his earlier encounter with depression, his first mention of any significant 'infirmities' came in 1650.[182]

On more than one occasion Baxter explained how his sickness prevented him from undertaking any considerable travel. For example, in February 1650 Anthony Burgess requested a private conference with Baxter at Birmingham,[183] less than 20 miles from Kidderminster. 'I told you of my weakness', Baxter replied in April, 'which is so great that I am not able to travel, nor to discourse

[177] Clark, *Life and Times of Anthony Wood*, i.221, 300.

[178] Richard Baxter, *A Christian Directory* (1673): *Practical Works*, iv.393.

[179] For analysis of Baxter's ill health see Tim Cooper, 'Richard Baxter and his Physicians', *Social History of Medicine* 20 (2007): 1–19.

[180] Baxter to John Warren, 11 September 1649: DWL MS *BC* vi.96r (*CCRB* #22).

[181] Asty, 'Memoirs', iii. Ralph Josselin's diary entry for 24 October 1647 notes 'Mr Owen very ill of the stone', so his health was not perfect. On 28 May he was 'very ill with a fever'. MacFarlane, *Diary of Ralph Josselin*, 107, 126.

[182] Owen, *Death of Christ* (1650): *Works*, x.479. Of course, he was not one to advertise his bodily condition even if he was sick. See Owen, *Death of Christ and of Justification* (1655): *Works*, xii.594.

[183] Anthony Burgess to Baxter, 13 February [1650]: in Baxter, *Of Justification*, 163 (*CCRB* #38).

to any purpose if I were with you: a few words do so spend me (except when I have a little ease, which falls out perhaps once in a moneth for a few hours unexpected)'.[184] This particular claim certainly stretches credibility. Burgess struggled to believe it;[185] Baxter had sought out a conference with a much nearer disputant, John Tombes, just eight months earlier;[186] and he was able to travel to the eventual conference with Burgess at Birmingham some five months later.[187] Even so, we can believe that Baxter's many ailments at the very least hindered his ability to travel. Thus one means of overcoming the limitations of his geographical location was closed down, and the several dimensions of his isolation were reinforced.

All this is aptly illustrated in the moment of Baxter's soteriological realignment in 1647. In recalling that day, Baxter explicitly played up his isolation.

> I fetched not this doctrine from man ... I did not to my utmost remembrance, receive
> from any Book or Person in the world; but only upon former study of the Scriptures,
> some undigested conceptions stuck in my minde, and at the time of my conceiving
> and entertaining those Notions (about the Nature and Necessity of a twofold
> Righteousnesse, and many the like) I was in a strange place, where I had no book but
> my Bible.[188]

True, the previous few years of daily disputing in the army provided opportunity enough for Baxter's views to be tested and challenged – with little effect, in his case – and these new notions sprouted from the fertile soil of those daily debates. But when the most significant theological alteration in his life came upon him he was far from home, removed from his books and entirely alone. And even later, when reading was possible, his fresh thoughts 'all came in by the way of my own Study of the naked matter, and not from Books'.[189] No wonder Owen would criticize Baxter's views, condemning 'the unscriptural method of these

---

[184]   Baxter to Anthony Burgess, 5 April 1650: in Baxter, *Of Justification*, 165 (*CCRB* #39).

[185]   Anthony Burgess to Baxter, [c. May 1650]: in Baxter, *Of Justification*, 176 (*CCRB* #40).

[186]   Baxter to John Tombes, 11 September [1649]: DWL MS *BC* iii.253r (*CCRB* #21).

[187]   Baxter to My Much Honoured and Highly Esteemed Friend Mr , 12/13 September 1650: DWL MS *BC* i.263r (*CCRB* #48).

[188]   Richard Baxter, *An Unsavoury Volume of Mr Jo. Crandon's Anatomized: Or a Nosegay of the Choicest Flowers in that Garden, Presented to Joseph Caryl by Rich. Baxter* (1654), 5. In *Rich. Baxters Apology*. See also Baxter, *Aphorismes*, Appendix, 110; Baxter to John Warren, 7 November 1649: DWL MS *BT* xiv.88r, item #324 (*CCRB* #25).

[189]   *Rel. Bax.*, i.125.

mysteries which he hath framed in his mind'.[190] Owen would never have offered up anything so idiosyncratic as the *Aphorismes of Justification*.

To identify these factors is not to suggest they were the totality of forces acting on Baxter's natural temperament. There were contexts in which he forged important connections with other people. He had a point when he said that those who were aggrieved all lived at a distance from him, and the bare words on the page were much more likely to cause offence when he was not present to voice them and to invest them with intonation. The building of a new gallery of seating in his church at Kidderminster and the apparent success of his programme of family visitation suggest a considerable capacity to move and impress other people. He must have been a warm and effective pastor. It is unlikely he could have stayed in one place of pastoral ministry for a combined total of 14 years if he had carried himself in the same haughty manner in which he sometimes came across in his published works. By way of illustration, in 1651 the rector of Medbourne, Thomas Doughty, visited his aunt in Kidderminster. Shortly afterwards, he wrote to Baxter to thank him for his 'private converse', recalling Baxter's 'civilitie, mansuetude and indulgence'.[191] That middle archaism speaks of gentleness, meekness or docility.[192] These are not words that have been typically ascribed to Baxter yet, notwithstanding Doughty's flattering posture, they are plausible in the private Baxter, if not always in the printed version. And, in a broader compass, when Bartlett wrote to complain about Wilkins, he urged Baxter to work through his 'friends who are Parliament men', so Baxter was not bereft of political connections.[193] What I am attempting to describe, therefore, is again not the whole of Baxter's personality. But it is an essential dimension of his makeup, it had a particular impact on his relationship with Owen, and it stayed with him. To offer a final example, when Baxter applied for a licence to preach under the 1672 Declaration of Indulgence he was determined to be recorded as a 'Meer Nonconformist'. This fitted in with his middle-way ideology, his concern for Christian unity, and his aversion to religious factionalism, but it also confirms the tendency, identified by Geoffrey Nuttall, 'to see him as an individual figure: as one who agreed with most men about some things but could never agree with any of them about everything; whose determination to

---

[190] Owen, *Death of Christ* (1650): *Works*, x.474.

[191] Tho[mas] Doughty to Baxter, 15 December 1651: DWL MS *BC* iv.182r (*CCRB* #76).

[192] *The New Shorter Oxford English Dictionary*, ed. Lester Brown, 4th edn (Oxford: Clarendon Press, 1993), i.1689.

[193] Henry Bartlett to Baxter, 17 August 1654: DWL MS *BC* vi.144r (*CCRB* #197). Thomas Manton also spoke of Baxter's friends in Parliament in a way that suggested there was a considerable number of them. Manton to Baxter, 27 January 1658/9: DWL MS *BC* ii.320r (*CCRB* #546).

avoid extremes and to take a central position made him, in practice, no founder of a "school" or tradition'. 'In this', he says, 'we are not altogether right'; but this is true only in the sense of a posthumous tradition.[194] While he was alive, Baxter was only ever comfortable when he stood in a party of one.

This quality might charitably be described as a lack of empathy. Too self-absorbed, he did not perceive the effect his words or actions might have on others. This goes a long way to explaining the distinct trail of wreckage among his relationships and the fact that he possessed a small number of staunch admirers who would do anything for him, while a far greater number of others failed to see the attraction. It makes some sense of the stubborn determination with which he held his own opinions. As Baxter explained to a shrewd, supportive correspondent, Peter Ince, 'I am as unapt to yield up my understanding to any mans and goe uppon trust, as most men that ever yet I was acquainted with'. More to the point, 'I am more faulty in being too tenacious of my opinions (I thinke) than in being too mutable'.[195] Indeed. It also helps to account for his tendency to be too severe in his writing style and to cause offence where he never discerned that any was intended or possible. And one of the most significant effects of that was to make him entirely unsuited to the practice of politics. 'Though I offend, I must say that which cannot be hid.'[196] He complained here that his critics had shown themselves to be too prickly, too easily offended. That perspective conveys his blinkered vision of the world, his unshakeable belief that others should conform their beliefs to his, and his failure to see just how individualistic and idiosyncratic those beliefs of his could be.

This is aptly captured in Baxter's relationship with Oliver Cromwell.[197] Remarkably, in the early stages of the first civil war Cromwell and his men had invited Baxter to become their chaplain. His response was typically tactless. 'I sent them a Denial, reproving their Attempt, and told them wherein my Judgment was against the Lawfulness and Convenience of their way, and so I heard no more from them.'[198] One can easily imagine just how condescending Baxter's rebuff would have been. It stands in stark contrast to Owen's beautifully weighted reply to the same man several years later. And it is no surprise that Cromwell and his men chose to say no more. When Baxter met Cromwell a

---

[194]   Geoffrey F. Nuttall, *Richard Baxter and Philip Doddridge: A Study in a Tradition* (London: Oxford University Press, 1951), 1–2.

[195]   Baxter to Peter Ince, 21 November 1653: DWL MS *BC* i.11r,v (*CCRB* #148).

[196]   Baxter, *Confession of his Faith*, Preface, sig. d4v.

[197]   For general description of Baxter's view of Cromwell, see Royce MacGillivray, *Restoration Historians and the English Civil War* (The Hague: Martinus Nijhoff, 1974), 161–3.

[198]   *Rel. Bax.*, i.51.

while later 'he expostulated me for denying them'.[199] Again, the conversation did not go well, for the next time the two men encountered each other, when Baxter finally signed up as army chaplain, Cromwell 'coldly bid me welcome, and never spake one word to me while I was there'.[200] Several years later Baxter was invited to preach before Cromwell. Once again Baxter adopted an abrasive, tone: 'the plainness and nearness I heard was displeasing to him'.[201] We cannot say if the frost ever thawed in their personal interactions, but it is clear that Baxter's estimation of Cromwell steadily rose during the 1650s as he witnessed increasing potential for godly reformation in England under Cromwell's rule. Even so, Baxter bitterly regretted his earlier misjudgement. He might, he thought, have stopped the perversion of the good old cause and prevented the regicide from ever occurring if he had accepted that first invitation and stamped out the flame when 'all the Fire was in one Spark'.[202] The whole, unfortunate episode stands in eloquent testimony to Baxter's striking inability to play the political game, to keep options open, to work with opponents, and to make good any practical, political agenda. Put more positively, the evident ambition in Owen was mirrored in the lack of it in Baxter. He was not without an interest in his reputation, of course, but if he really was a man to pursue ambition he made all the wrong choices. His resolve to remain in Kidderminster shows a commendable lack of concern to make his way up the ladder of preferment. In Baxter, for all these reasons, we see quite a different kind of political creature from Owen.

Putting Owen and Baxter Together

All of this provides a lengthy basis on which to offer a brief conclusion. Owen was 'impatient of contradiction'.[203] Baxter was inclined to 'blab out' the truth as he saw it.[204] Putting the two together was never going to go well. That fact goes a long way towards explaining the strain between them.

This point is a simple one, but it can be fleshed out in several further comments. The first thing to observe is the basic symmetry of their careers in this period. During the 1640s Owen enjoyed a phase of stable pastoral ministry, while Baxter was thrust by events into itinerancy and army chaplaincy. At the end of that season it was Baxter's turn at settled pastoral ministry, while Owen

---

[199]   Ibid.

[200]   Ibid., 52.

[201]   Ibid., 205.

[202]   Ibid., 51.

[203]   [Anon.], *Vindication of Owen*, 38.

[204]   Baxter to Abraham Pinchbecke, 12 October 16[5]8: DWL MS *BC* iv.56r (*CCRB* #508).

moved into itinerancy and army chaplaincy. Owen's experience as Dean and Vice-Chancellor, of course, bears no parallel in Baxter's life, but we can contrast Owen's regular shuttling back and forth between Oxford and London, and the networking and politicking that conveys, with the generally fixed and sustained nature of Baxter's parish ministry. In the background of things lay their relationship with Cromwell. Baxter moved from hostility and dislike to a limited form of appreciation,[205] while Owen travelled in the opposite direction, estranged from Cromwell at his death. And, as we shall see, just as Baxter lauded the regime of Cromwell's son, Richard, Owen was associated in Baxter's mind with bringing it down. The parallels were hardly deliberate and yet it seems somehow apt that when one of these men moved in a particular direction, the other went the opposite way. They were like the twin strands of a double helix, which are always a certain distance apart from each other and in which the chemical sequences progress in opposite directions. Seen in this way, the paucity of Owen's correspondence and the abundance of Baxter's makes a certain sense. Owen had no need to prove his capacity for forging connections and many of his letters might conceivably have been sensitive in the harsh light of later political developments. Conversely, Baxter had to show how he could reach out beyond the confines of his own singular limitations and to demonstrate how he, too, belonged to a widespread and significant community. His correspondence bears witness to his efforts to overcome those pressures within his context and career that tended to isolate him from others.

Second, this assessment helps to make sense of Owen's choice to respond to Baxter's *Aphorismes*. At the heart of things, Owen was a man who expected deference from those around him, who did not tolerate contradiction, and who could become angry when his way was thwarted. Meanwhile, Baxter appeared certain of his own rectitude and blind to his own fallibility, blithely informing the world that Owen had not communicated his thoughts clearly enough. Owen would quite conceivably have been affronted at the over-confidence and haughtiness of one so new to soteriological debate; he would have bristled at the contradiction and misrepresentation of his own views; and he would have been jealous of his reputation at a time when he was coming into a period of influence and ascendency. In his funeral sermon for Owen, David Clarkson declared that, 'as I have observed, he did not affect to be an aggressor, but still was on the defensive, and proceeded with such temper, that he would rather oblige his adversary (if a lover of truth) than exasperate him'.[206] This comment is

---

[205] William Lamont, 'Authority and Liberty: Hobbes and the Sects', in *Liberty, Authority, Formality: Political Ideas and Culture 1600–1900*, ed. John Morrow and Jonathan Scott (Charlottesville, VA: Imprint Academic, 2008), 36, 37.

[206] Asty, 'Memoirs', n.p., sheet h, verso.

important in two ways. Owen was indeed a remarkably fair-minded opponent in the context of seventeenth-century English polemic. He was acutely aware of all the rhetorical tricks at his disposal yet he tended in the main not to deploy them. Even his critics could acknowledge his restraint.[207] For that reason, the lack of restraint he discerned in the *Aphorismes* would have grated on Owen, and that explains why he objected to all those magisterial phrases that were so unnecessary. But the bracketed qualification in Clarkson's comment is also important: if the disputant did not seem a lover of truth, Owen could quickly become aggressive. Baxter carried himself as a lover of his own opinions rather than as one who might perhaps have qualified in Owen's mind as a lover of truth. Bear in mind the 1684 defence of Owen: 'he would pay the greater Respects to those, who freely, and faithfully expressed themselves'.[208] Or as Cook says, it was only towards those 'whom he respected for character and scholarship, and who responded to him with similar respect' that Owen 'exhibited the conciliatory attitude he always advocated among Christians of different denominations'.[209] Baxter's own overbearing, haughty tone rubbed Owen up the wrong way and provoked him to respond. He did not take kindly to contradiction, and most certainly not from one as arrogant as Baxter sometimes seemed to be in his first published work.

The third comment I wish to offer is more speculative: it is easy to imagine that Owen would have struggled to respect Baxter. Certainly the initial impressions formed by the *Aphorismes* were going to make that difficult. Baxter seemed to choose a writing style that Owen found inappropriate. And in person Baxter would have demonstrated his lack of those political capacities that Owen possessed in abundance. Where Owen was generally smooth and adept, Baxter was clumsy and tactless. What this means is that Owen brought to their relationship the skills that might have made their relationship work if he had wanted it to, but Baxter did not. Thus Owen was always going to be more of an influential figure within the Congregationalist stream than Baxter was within the Presbyterian, given the obvious limits of his political skill. Owen tended to weigh relationships for their political potential, which made him less likely to choose to invest in his relationship with Baxter, especially when Baxter may have been seen to work actively against Owen's goals. We have already seen this play out in the area of soteriology and we will soon see the same dynamics in the cause of Church unity.

---

[207] For example, see Anthony Wood's repetition of the sentiments of Edward Stillingfleet and Henry Dodwell, in *Athenae Oxonienses*, ii.740–741.
[208] [Anon.], *Vindication of Owen*, 38.
[209] Cook, 'Political Biography', 189.

Finally, this emphasis on the differences between the two men should not distract us from what they held in common. Once again, it is the similarities that make the differences so important and potentially explosive. To offer up a crude generalization, Owen was self-contained, while Baxter was self-absorbed. These are different qualities with different results – Owen so miserly in his self-revelation, Baxter so profligate – but they are not unrelated. And both men were stubborn and determined. Both could seem like a dog with a bone. There are instances of each man tenaciously and fruitlessly gnawing over the same point, to the exasperation of their opponents.[210] Their competing theological agendas were enough to bring them into extended conflict; but Baxter's tendency to blab out the truth as he saw it, and Owen's bristling at any slight, served only to heighten the tension between them. No wonder their soteriological differences and rejoinders, for example, bounced back and forth in print over a number of years. Neither one was likely to back down first, nor give any genuine ground with ease. The tendencies they shared were as much a problem as those that set them apart.

I am conscious of the danger of taking this analysis too far, of reading too much into the differing temperaments of Owen and Baxter. This chapter has captured each man acting in a particular role. Owen was Vice-Chancellor of a university – exploiting procedure potentially made him a very effective one. Baxter was a polemicist – presenting black-and-white views was what effective polemic required. Both were more rounded than these roles suggest. Yet we cannot ignore personality as a critical factor – among others – that helps to account for the strain between them. Even if they were to an extent acting in role there are aspects of their performance that seemed extreme even to their fellow actors. If Owen and Baxter were to cultivate any sort of warmth in their relationship, they had to overcome far more than just competing agendas and differing soteriological stances. They had their own personalities to confront. And that was always going to be difficult, if not impossible. That is why the next three chapters will show only strain, misunderstanding and mutual frustration.

---

[210]   For Baxter, see Cooper, *Fear and Polemic*, 47–8.

Chapter 5
Unity, Or Not

I confess I would rather, much rather, spend all my time in making up and healing the breaches and schisms that are amongst Christians than one hour in justifying our divisions.

John Owen (1657)[1]

I am resolved ... to speak for Peace, while I have a tongue to speak, and to write for Peace, while I have a hand to write, and to live to the Churches peace, while I have an hour to live, and am able to do anything that may promote it.

Richard Baxter (1658)[2]

The first civil war exposed England's religious divisions. The target of Laudian impositions was obvious enough, but once that was removed the search began for a religious settlement on which all could agree. It never came. The Presbyterian system that emerged from Westminster was partial and abortive. That gave way to several sets of attempts and negotiations as the political landscape shifted, and while there were some successes – the triers and ejectors come to mind as largely effective mechanisms for raising the quality of local ministry – the divisions over even small matters simply proved intractable.

Those divisions were evident from the beginning, in 1643, when the Westminster Assembly first set its face towards the task of 'the settling of the Government and Lyturgy of the Church of England' in order to obtain 'a further and more perfect Reformation'.[3] The most obvious divisions in the historiography have been those between the Presbyterians and the Congregationalists, but there were other, earlier, more surprising divisions that crossed these party lines. Chad van Dixhoorn provides an intriguing account of the Assembly's extensive debates over the place of the early creeds – the Athanasian Creed, the Apostles' Creed and the Niceno-Constantinopolitan Creed – in the worship and doctrinal standards of the Church. This, the longest of all the Assembly's

---

[1]   Owen, *Of Schism: The True Nature of it Discovered and Considered* (1657): *Works*, xiii.95.

[2]   Richard Baxter, *The Grotian Religion Discovered, At the Invitation of Mr. Thomas Pierce in his Vindication, With a Preface Vindicating the Synod of Dort* (1658), 6.

[3]   *An Ordinance of the Lords and Commons Assembled in Parliament for the Calling of an Assembly of Learned, and Godly Divines* (1643), title page and [page 1].

debates, revealed a 'tension between creed and Scripture'.[4] Some wanted to retain the creeds, others of a more Biblicist persuasion wished to omit them.[5] In the end they were omitted, even though they had been deployed pervasively in the Book of Common Prayer.[6] When the Assembly voted on whether to append the Apostles' Creed to its Shorter Catechism, two Congregationalists and three Presbyterians went so far as 'to file a record of their Dissent'.[7] In general, 'although Independents took exception to the creeds, not all who took exception to the creeds were Independents'.[8] What this serves to show is that the most contentious issues in the Assembly's debates were not necessarily the ones most apparent to historians. The place of the creeds in what was, in some ways, a creed-making exercise (in that the Assembly worked to create a doctrinal standard) reveals contemporary tensions in all their fascinating complexity. And if the Assembly was supposed to be a pointer towards English unity on religious issues, it did not bode well.

Indeed, as the Independents came to political power, closely tied to the fortunes of Oliver Cromwell, the search for a permanent settlement continued throughout the Interregnum. As we shall see, progress on these negotiations was hampered by the Erastian aspect of the English Church even after it was disestablished. The Independents were noted for their willingness to give the magistrate a role in protecting and promoting true religion. This raised some very practical questions, such as what 'true religion' actually comprised; the practical freedom allowed to those who held to the agreed fundamentals of the faith while dissenting in some indifferent matters; and how far the magistrate might or might not go in constraining those who publicly preached a variation from agreed orthodoxy. The limits of toleration continued to be very much a divisive issue, especially when the horror of England's various sects and errors was hardly seen to abate with the conclusion of the fighting. And, as before, any agreement that might have been reached among divines on these questions then had to obtain the approval of Parliament (or its subsequent manifestations). This complicated matters considerably and at crucial points purely constitutional and political events derailed progress towards agreement and unity.

The situation was fluid, vexed and fraught, and not just for these reasons: broad agreement on even the most central doctrines of the historical faith was seeming to unravel. Sarah Mortimer measures the escalation of concern in regard to the Socinians in England during the 1650s (or, at least, those who drew on

---

4   van Dixhoorn, 'New Taxonomies', 91, 102.

5   Ibid., 93, 98, 103.

6   Ibid., 100, 102, 105.

7   Ibid., 102.

8   Ibid., 104.

Socinian lines of argument to make their case on particular issues). Even though he had been imprisoned since 1646, the former schoolmaster John Biddle had been able to publish several alarming works in which he relied strictly on reason and a literal reading of Scripture to dismantle the doctrine of the Trinity.[9] He translated into English a version of the Socinians' *Rachovian Catechism* that was published in 1652.[10] He was joined in notoriety by Paul Best – an English soldier who had encountered Socinian ideas while serving on the Continent during the Thirty Years War – and by the MP John Fry.[11] What was so worrying to their orthodox opponents was that they 'received a good deal of sympathy within and without Parliament. They impressed MPs with their evident piety, and above all else, with their reasonableness'.[12] There were other less visible but more commanding scholars and authors who were in their own way casting doubt on the doctrine of the Trinity. And far beyond them, the Quakers also undermined it. By mid-decade these related concerns reached something of a peak. England was witnessing what Philip Dixon calls 'the disintegration' and even 'evisceration' of Trinitarian consensus, a relentless process that would only continue.[13] It demonstrates just how hard it would be to reach a religious settlement if even the most basic Christian doctrines were in doubt.

This is the broad context in which Owen and Baxter both worked towards unity among the orthodox godly. Even this background is sufficient to indicate the kinds of barriers they would have to overcome in order to meet with success. What hardly helped are those pre-existing conditions of personality and experience that served to set them apart; the awareness in each man of how the other had demeaned him in print; and the fact that their preferred methods for achieving unity stood in contrast to each other on a specific set of issues. This chapter and the next one examine their progress, or lack of it, throughout much of the Interregnum. In some ways they supply the very heart of the book, since they help to answer in microcosm the broader and more pressing question: given the extensive common ground between the Presbyterians and the Congregationalists, why could they not come to agreement? The case of Owen and Baxter will serve to illustrate that much wider problem. What it shows is that, indeed, there was an encouraging amount of shared assumptions, convictions and aims. But there were also narrow differences that, while they

---

[9]   See Mortimer, *Reason and Religion*, 160–162.

[10]   Mortimer, *Reason and Religion*, 165. The Catechism had been published the year before in Latin.

[11]   Ibid., 158–60, 164–5; Smith, 'Best, Biddle and Anti-Trinitarian Heresy', 164–5.

[12]   Smith, 'Best, Biddle and Anti-Trinitarian Heresy', 164.

[13]   Dixon, *Nice and Hot Disputes*, 208, 209. On p. 215 he notes that the doctrine of the Trinity survived, even if it was displaced.

may seem small in the scheme of things, were only exacerbated under the force of historical events. Those particular differences generated tremendous amounts of heat, friction and frustration, precisely because the two parties, or the two men, held so much in common.

This chapter, then, lays out the respective agendas of Baxter, first, and then Owen. The next chapter brings them together; it attempts to survey the common ground between them before examining how their narrow tracts of disagreement played a part in, and were widened by, the events of 1654. That is when the two men came together, literally, for the first time in the same room. So it will be necessary once more to allow for personality differences to play their part. But underneath that clash of temperaments lay a more fundamental clash of vision and agenda. While both men pursued unity in the church, the differences in their approach got in the way and hindered the very union they both claimed to seek.

Richard Baxter: Designs and Disappointments

The story of Baxter's schemes for national church unity during the 1650s is one of growing confidence, increasing national prominence, regular disappointment and ultimate failure. In the beginning he was just one more of England's ministers serving in the backblocks of obscurity. He had no university education and few connections.[14] Working in his favour, the *Aphorismes of Justification* had given him notoriety, while the *Saints' Everlasting Rest*, which would run into eight editions before the decade was out, had earned widespread appreciation and acclaim.[15] Other publications followed, along specifically ecclesiological lines. In particular, *Christian Concord* (1653) set out the agreement of the associated ministers of Worcestershire, one that others might also adapt and adopt, with a very long explication written personally by Baxter. Behind the scenes, he wrote letters seeking to enlist others in his project for national church unity. Meanwhile, on the ground in Kidderminster, he worked out his pastoral convictions in practice. In March 1653 he declared himself to be 'in the very beginning of a reformation'.[16] The Worcestershire Association of local ministers was gaining momentum and keenly observed from afar. Such was his reputation that in late 1654 he was invited to join a small group of ministers convened to advise Parliament's sub-committee on the fundamentals of religion. He was,

---

[14]   See *Rel. Bax.*, i.85.

[15]   See Condie, 'The Theory, Practice, and Reception of Meditation in the Thought of Richard Baxter', PhD Thesis, University of Sydney, 2010, 257–82.

[16]   Baxter to [Richard Foley, jun.?], 19 March [1653]: DWL MS *BC* iv.141r (*CCRB* #112).

clearly, well on the way to becoming a figure of national note, if not always influence.

It is a commonplace that Baxter pursued church unity and resisted any tendency towards division and separation.[17] In his 1655 *Confession* he recalled a time 'when I had too Narrow thoughts of the Church of Christ, and little minded the Peace of any in it which I most honoured; and thus was involved in the guilt of Faction'.[18] Whenever that was,[19] and to whatever extent it was true, it quickly gave way to a settled and urgent desire for unity.[20] As he looked about, of course, there was precious little of that to be found. Divisions within the English Church seemed to be calcifying. He also discerned a plot, publicly spearheaded by Hugo Grotius and covertly backed by the Jesuits, to reunite the English Church with the Roman Catholic Church on the basis of the more moderate French Catholicism. Part of the plan, he warned, was 'to hinder all Union of the Learned Godly Ministers, and all exercise of any Discipline, or maintaining of Church Order, that so they may tell the World, we have no Church'.[21] We would do well to bear in mind that for Baxter the stakes were perilously high. Continued disunity was an open invitation to the Jesuits and Papists.

Baxter's plan to correct that problem was simple, but impossible. The earliest evidence we have for his scheme is the second edition (not the first) of the *Saints' Everlasting Rest*, published in 1651. In the dedicatory epistle he disclosed three aspects of his thinking that remained consistent features in all his efforts for

---

[17]   See, for instance, Nuttall, *Richard Baxter and Philip Doddridge*, 5–6, 13.

[18]   Baxter, *Confession*, Preface to the Reader, sig. d3v.

[19]   Geoffrey Nuttall seems to locate this phase when Baxter was 21–23 years old, when he was part of a loose grouping of nonconformists (see *Richard Baxter*, 11); but he also observes that the 'gathering of a separatist congregation was not Baxter's conception of the setting up of the Kingdom of Christ, now or at any time in his life' (p. 13). Baxter himself gave his age as 'eighteen or nineteen', if indeed he was referring to the same episode. See Baxter, *Catholick Theologie*, Preface, sig.a1v.

[20]   William Black (*Reformation Pastors*, pp. 155–6) questions whether Baxter always held his concern for unity in consistently the same fashion. He is suspicious that Baxter's crushed hopes at the Restoration may have distorted his recollections, thus we should not take his recollections in the *Reliquiae* at face value. But I have been struck by the consistency with which Baxter maintained his ecclesiological convictions. All of the main lines of argument he made in his autobiography can be found within his writings in the early 1650s. (I am thinking in particular of *Rel. Bax.*, ii.139–44, where Baxter discusses the four main parties.)

[21]   Richard Baxter, *Christian Concord: Or the Agreement of the Associated Pastors and Churches of Worcestershire. With Richard Baxter's Explication and Defence of it, and his Exhortation to Unity* (1653), Explication, 47. Baxter defended his warning in *The Grotian Religion Discovered* (1658). See also Geoffrey F. Nuttall, 'Richard Baxter and the Grotian Religion', in *Reform and Reformation: England and the Continent c1500–c1750*, ed. Derek Baker (Oxford: Ecclesiastical History Society, 1979), 245–50.

achieving unity during the 1650s. First, he identified the four main parties that might come to a practical union: 'the Moderate Presbyterians, Independents, Episcopal and Erastian'.[22] In *Christian Concord* he clarified this further. The factor all four held in common, he explained, was some degree of attachment to church discipline, without which there was no hope of agreement. This excluded Seekers, Papists and 'Popish Episcopal Divines, who will have all the world come to the Romish Polity'.[23]

Baxter's second observation identified the real obstacle to his scheme: the sinful human heart. 'I make no doubt', he declared, 'but if mens Spirits stood not at a greater distance than their Principles, they would quickly be united'.[24] Baxter's diagnosis identified two related problems: power and party. First, those who happened to be in power used it to impose their way on others. Writing to John Dury in 1652, Baxter explained how each of the parties used 'carnall weapons and advantages' whenever they happened to be in power. First the Episcopal party, then the Presbyterians, and 'now the Independents have power, its like they may thinke it's a losing of the Advantage that God hath given them to sett all right (that is in their way) if they should take themselves as on equall termes' with the other parties.[25] Baxter said much the same thing in *Christian Concord*, though he wisely stopped short of accusing the Congregationalists explicitly.[26] 'Mans proud corrupt heart, will hardly be taken off from the using of his carnal weapons and advantages; but will think that God puts such power and opportunities into his hand, for the promoting of his particular opinions and waies, by force, and not by satisfying the unsatisfied.'[27] A misunderstanding of providence led to an abuse of power, not a display of humility and condescension. 'When you had the advantage of superior and secular Power, your ears were stopt, your hearts were hardened, you thought you had a speedier way to settlement, then by satisfying Dissenters, and condescending to those Brethren, whom you were readier to contemn.'[28]

---

[22]   Richard Baxter, *The Saints' Everlasting Rest: Or, a Treatise of the Blessed State of the Saints in their Enjoyment of God in Glory...The Second Edition Corrected and Enlarged* (1651), Dedication of the Whole, sig. a1v.

[23]   Baxter, *Christian Concord*, Explication, 2v. Baxter thought that reconciliation with Rome 'on just and honest terms' was 'one of the happiest works in the world, could it be accomplished' (p. 96). But he also advertised the 'Grotian design' towards the introduction of popery, which began by dividing the Protestant church in England (p. 46).

[24]   Baxter, *Saints' Everlasting Rest*, 2nd edn, Dedication of the Whole, sig. a1v.

[25]   Baxter to John Dury, 7 May 1652: DWL MS BC vi.90r (*CCRB* #83).

[26]   Baxter, *Christian Concord*, Explication, 96.

[27]   Ibid., 105.

[28]   Ibid., 105–6.

The second, related problem was that men were too much concerned with party. In a 1653 letter to his fellow minister Thomas Gataker, Baxter lamented those who 'are soe passionately adicted to their parties and particular opinions that their zeale for those ... consumeth all notions and inclinations to reconciliation'.[29] For this reason, the very first agreement of the associated ministers of Worcester was 'not to addict ourselves to any Party, nor to set up the Dictates of any as such'.[30] And the *Worcester Petition* (1652) called together those 'least addicted to parties'.[31] All three statements used a variant of 'addicted' in relation to parties – Baxter's characteristic language. On the other hand, there were too few who were 'addicted to promote ... peace and unity'.[32] In 1655 Baxter bitterly attacked 'those men that under pretence of being Orthodoxe, and enemies to errour, are carried so violently in the stream of their party'. They mistook the interests of the whole church for the interests of their own little group, as if they were the church and their interests those of the whole church.[33] This blinkered, partisan perspective kept open the wounds of the church by strictly pursuing the interests of a particular group within it. And it only encouraged 'the common ignorant people' who 'see so many parties, that they know not which one to join with, and think that it is as good [to] be of none at all as of any'.[34] Thus power and party together presented a formidable obstacle not just to Baxter's scheme for unity, which relied on moderation, humility and a willingness to agree to disagree, but also to his related evangelistic concern.

Finally, returning to the *Saints' Everlasting Rest*, Baxter laid out the basic nature of his plan. 'Will God never put it into the hearts of Rulers to call together some of the most Godly, Learned, Moderate and Peaceable of all four opinions (*not too many*) to agree upon a way of union and accommodation!' It is not that Baxter naively expected a happy agreement on every point of principle. The most he hoped for was that these parties might agree on principles as far as they could; where necessary 'unite as far as may be in their Practice, though on different Principles'; and where that was impossible, 'to agree on the most loving, peaceable course in the way of carrying on our different Practices'.[35] The

---

29   Baxter to [Thomas Gataker], 17 October 1653: DWL MS *BC* iii.143r (*CCRB* #137).

30   Baxter, *Christian Concord*, Propositions, sig. A3r.

31   [Richard Baxter], *The Humble Petition of Many Thousands, Gentlemen, Free-holders, and Others, of the County of Worcester to the Parliament of the Commonwealth of England* (1652), 7.

32   Baxter, *Reformed Pastor* (1656): *Practical Works*, iv.406.

33   Thomas Hotchkis, *An Exercitation Concerning the Nature of Forgivenesse of Sin* (1654), Preface [by Baxter], n.p. [p. 8]; Baxter, *Reformed Pastor* (1656): *Practical Works*, Preface, iv.406.

34   Baxter, *Reformed Pastor* (1656): *Practical Works*, Preface, iv.407; see also, p. 408.

35   Baxter, *Saints' Everlasting Rest*, 2nd edn, Dedication of the Whole, sig. B1v. Baxter proposed this plan in other contexts. For instance, see Baxter to Thomas Hill, 8 March [1652]:

same sentiment was more fully fleshed out in *Christian Concord*. There, Baxter explicitly avoided pursuing a 'middle way' on which all parties could agree.[36] 'We are not such strangers to ourselves and mankinde, as not to know, that we must unavoidably be of various Opinions, while we live here in imperfection.'[37] Indeed, each party was allowed its distinctive positions, and each party had some part of the whole truth about it.[38] *Christian Concord* tried only to identify the points of common agreement so the parties could practise them 'unanimously'.[39] Clearly Baxter hoped that such a positive approach, with humility on all sides, might produce a workable harmony – if only the leading figures of the main parties could be shut in the same room and not allowed to leave until agreement was reached. 'The Lord perswade those who have power, to this Pacificatory enterprise without Delay.'[40]

Given his diagnosis, those in power were going to take quite some persuading and Baxter was not in any position to provide it. So in 1652 he reached out to John Dury, 'the apostle of Protestant unity'.[41] Then resident in London, Dury was involved in plans to bring together not just England's contending parties but all European Protestants.[42] The trigger for Baxter's approach was the formation by Parliament of a special Committee for the Propagation of the Gospel,[43] in which Baxter saw an opening through which his plan might be pushed. 'The thing that I propound to you is only that which I have already propounded in the Epis. before the 2[d] edit. of my Treat of Rest.' He proposed that moderate, leading men[44] among each of the parties come together to narrow down their differences to a bare minimum and proceed on the basis of their broad agreement. He also

---

DWL MS *BC* iii.272v–273r (*CCRB* #81).

[36]   Baxter, *Christian Concord*, Explication, 1v.

[37]   Ibid., 2r.

[38]   Ibid., 95.

[39]   Ibid., 9. See also p. 95. Baxter repeated the point more generally in *Reformed Pastor* (1656): *Practical Works*, Preface, iv.407.

[40]   Baxter, *Saints' Everlasting Rest*, 2nd edn, Dedication of the Whole, sig. a1v.

[41]   Trevor-Roper, 'Fast Sermons', 300. For a brief description of Dury's work, see Hugh Trevor-Roper, 'Three Foreigners: The Philosophers of the Puritan Revolution', in *Religion, the Reformation and Social Change and Other Essays*, ed. H.R. Trevor-Roper (London: Macmillan, 1967), 251–2.

[42]   Geoffrey Nuttall surveyed the extended correspondence between Baxter and Dury in 'Presbyterians and Independents: Some Movements for Unity 300 Years Ago', *Journal of the Presbyterian Historical Society* 10 (1952): 4–15. See also, Nuttall, *Richard Baxter*, 75–6.

[43]   See *CJ*, 10 February 1651[/52], vii.86; William A. Shaw, *A History of the English Church During the Civil Wars and Under the Commonwealth 1640–1660* (London: Longmans, Green and Co., 1900), ii.80–82.

[44]   Baxter did not include Owen's name in his thin list of suggestions.

expanded on the main issue. Differences over discipline had 'caused and kept open our wounds: All the rest spring out of that. Here ergo must the Cure begin'. If issues of discipline could be resolved, then differences 'about Doctrinalls would be easily so composed in, or after this, that the Church might yet have peace'. A fine thought, but first 'men must heare each other speake'.[45] So he broached his scheme with Dury.

And Dury liked it.[46] He had, he said in reply, always intended to confer with Baxter on the subject. He had already observed how engagement to party had been caught up in interests of power. He readily agreed that divergence over discipline was the root cause of the church's woes and the only prospect of its cure. And he approved Baxter's idea, though for it to work a lot of other factors would have to come into alignment. Dury was heartened that Oliver Cromwell had a similar thing in mind that would be open to more than just the four main parties, but could not see how such a wide invitation would work.[47] Thus Dury provided important encouragement and essential intelligence on developments in London. There were occasional misunderstandings between the two men,[48] and the Committee for Propagation of the Gospel would prove to be the wrong vehicle for Baxter's idea.[49] Even so, Dury provided a welcome ally as the two men pursued what Dury called at one point 'our designe'.[50]

Dury at last made tangible progress, though it was fleeting. He had tried independently to bring the leading figures of the main parties together, which for a long time proved nearly impossible.[51] He finally achieved his goal early in 1654 when meetings began to take place between the Presbyterians and Congregationalists, and even Cromwell was working in support.[52] By April there had been 'severall considerable meetings' of the 'Chiefe leading men'.[53] They deputized five from each side to make progress towards a full agreement.

---

[45]   Baxter to John Dury, 7 May 1652: DWL MS *BC* vi.90r (*CCRB* #83).

[46]   On the similarity and co-operation between Baxter and Dury, see George R. Abernathy, *The English Presbyterians and the Stuart Restoration, 1648–1663*, Transactions of the American Philosophical Society, New Series vol. 55, part 2 (Philadelphia, PA: The American Philosophical Society, 1965), 8–11.

[47]   John Dury to Baxter, 20 October 1652: DWL MS *BC* vi.83r–v (*CCRB* #99).

[48]   See John Dury to Baxter, 6 January 1652/3: DWL MS *BC* vi.77r–78v (*CCRB* #106).

[49]   John Dury to Baxter, 6 January 1652/3: DWL MS *BC* vi.78v (*CCRB* #106).

[50]   John Dury to Baxter, 9 April 1653: DWL MS *BC* vi.80r (*CCRB* #114).

[51]   John Dury to Baxter, 27 October 1653: DWL MS *BC* vi.81r (*CCRB* #141).

[52]   John Dury to Baxter, 22 February 1653[/4]: DWL MS *BC* v.199r–v (*CCRB* #164). Cromwell was 'continually involved at critical junctures' in the search for a settlement; 'his personal authority proved decisive'. Collins, 'Church Settlement of Oliver Cromwell', 26.

[53]   John Dury to Baxter, 2 April 1654: DWL MS *BC* vi.82r (*CCRB* #173). See also, John Dury, *A Declaration of John Durie, a Minister of Jesus Christ to Witness the Gospell of Peace* (1660),

The Presbyterian nominees were Stephen Marshall, Edmund Calamy, Simeon Ashe, Thomas Manton and Richard Vines. The Congregationalists were Joseph Carryl, Philip Nye, Sidrach Simpson, Samuel Slater and William Carter.[54] Dury was so encouraged that felt he could freely leave for the Continent, but as far as we know all of these efforts came to nothing.

If Baxter's scheme were to succeed it required a deft political hand and an easy manner of speaking. Dury offered those qualities, but not Baxter. He could still seem touchy in places, especially in his very earliest writing. In the first edition of the *Saints' Everlasting Rest* (1650), for instance, he collapsed Congregationalism into outright separation, condemning them indiscriminately as one (he deleted that language from the second edition).[55] And in *Christian Concord* he responded to the objections of the Congregationalists with quite some heat: 'Brethren! Would you have Unity and Peace or no?'[56] In 1655 he had to face apparently widespread accusations that he was proud and too inclined to contradict too many people.[57] As late as 1657 John Humfrey had to remind Baxter, again, that he was still too 'sowre' and 'violent' in his expressions, and 'too engaged in the opinions and matters you take up'. That 'hinders a man from opening his minde freely to you, and receiving the good hee should ... And this temper you shew methinks too much in your business of Association.'[58] In reply, Baxter agreed that his expression could too often convey a personal dislike he did not feel and sometimes he went too far, but 'I rather feare I am too cold than too hott about our Associations'.[59] Baxter's personal style impeded his efforts in this work as well.

And yet, for all that, he demonstrated an unexpected, if limited, capacity for compromise. One of the reasons for this is that many matters of church practice were left unspecified in Scripture so there was much more scope to allow differing opinions and practices. And the stakes were not as high in the issue of ecclesiology as they were in, say, soteriology. By way of comparison, in 1657 Baxter corresponded with Matthew Poole over the question of whether God's predetermination extended towards sinful acts and whether God predestined some to damnation. Baxter denied it, since it would make God the author of

---

23–4. Hunter Powell discerns 'at least four attempts to unite the Godly in early 1654'. See Hunter Powell, 'The Savoy Declaration', MPhil Thesis, Cambridge University, 2008, 57ff.

[54]   John Dury to Baxter, 2 April 1654: DWL MS *BC* vi.82r (*CCRB* #173).

[55]   Richard Baxter, *The Saints' Everlasting Rest: Or, a Treatise of the Blessed State of the Saints in their Enjoyment of God in Glory* (1650), Dedication of the Whole, sig. A4v.

[56]   Baxter, *Christian Concord*, Explication, 34.

[57]   Baxter, *Confession*, Preface to the Reader, sig. b4v.

[58]   John Humfrey to Baxter [c.autumn 1657]: DWL MS *BC* i.197r (*CCRB* #397).

[59]   Baxter to John Humfrey, 13 March 1657/8: DWL MS *BC* i.203r (*CCRB* #437).

sin. 'If you thinke I speake too eagerly about these matters, I pray know ... that to me it is the greatest matter in the world. All my Christianity, belief in God and hopes of salvation lye upon it.'[60] There could be no compromise here, but church practice was a different matter. As he had said to John Lewis a year earlier, 'Scripture commandes us many circumstantialls only *in genere*, leaving it to Church Guides to determine them *in specie*, in which case humane prudence must be judge'.[61] Indeed, Baxter's plan relied on all parties making concessions to the others in the matter of circumstantials, and he set an example. *Christian Concord*, for instance, allowed for people to join congregations in other parishes, if in very strictly defined circumstance, a concession to the Congregationalists.[62] It stipulated that the people had to give their consent to being subject to parish discipline,[63] because the 'want of express Consent is an offense to our Brethren of the Congregationall way'.[64] In a setting where Baxter critiqued the unfortunate abuse of power by those who happened to possess it – where he must have had the Congregationalists in mind, even if he did not name them – he criticized those who engaged in 'secret or open vilifying, deriding, contemning and aspersing your brethren' by wielding the slur of 'Independent'. Now the profane were empowered to use it against 'the most Reverend, and Learned, and godly of that way', thereby weakening the effectiveness of their ministry.[65] His defence of the Congregationalists was a clear statement of collegiality with a differing party.

In the *Reliquiae Baxterianae* there are several documents from the 1650s that provide evidence of Baxter's overtures to others and this reasonably conciliatory stance: a 1655 approach to Sir Ralph Brownrigg, Bishop of Exeter, and 'the finest man to treat with for Concord with the Diocesan Party';[66] an engagement with some unnamed Congregationalists;[67] and an undated communication with Philip Nye. None of these efforts produced any fruit but the papers are revealing. To take Nye as an example, Baxter knew that he had 'very great power' with the Congregationalists 'and he being in the Country [county], I desired him to give me in Writing all those things which of necessity must be granted them by the Presbyterians, in order to Concord and Conjunction in the same Associations

---

[60]   Baxter to M[atthew] Poole, 27 August 1657: DWL MS *BC* iv.256v (*CCRB* #390).

[61]   Baxter to John Lewis, 25 June 1656: DWL MS *BC* ii.126v (*CCRB* #315).

[62]   Baxter, *Christian Concord*, Propositions, sig. B4r.

[63]   Ibid., sig. B2r.

[64]   Baxter, *Christian Concord*, Explication, 13.

[65]   Ibid., 96. Baxter made the same general point in *Reformed Pastor* (1656): *Practical Works*, Preface, iv.407, 408, 409.

[66]   *Rel. Bax.*, ii.172–9.

[67]   Ibid., 193–7.

and Communion'. After a year's delay, Nye identified two issues. 'The first was, that they might have Liberty to take Church-Members out of other Parishes. And the second, that they might have all Church Power to themselves, in their several Congregations.'[68] Heartened, and with Nye's blessing, Baxter offered to blend these into a written basis for agreement. On the first issue, Baxter allowed for inter-parish transfer, even if again on very limited grounds.[69] He also allowed the independence of each congregation as long as they took part in consultative assemblies.[70] 'And thus', Baxter concluded his paper, 'the Presbyterian and Congregational Men are agreed, if they are willing'.[71] But the attempt then foundered on the question of ordination. Baxter could not recognize a pastor who had not been ordained by another pastor, as Nye requested. So 'he receded, and came no nearer to any Agreement with us'.[72]

The engagement shows that the list of sticking points was very small, and that demonstrates just how close – at least in technical terms – the Congregationalists and the Presbyterians really were. Indeed, in 1655 Baxter wrote the first part of *Church Concord* (eventually published in 1691), which demonstrated at length just how close the two parties were on the issues that supposedly kept them apart.[73] And a number of Baxter's pronouncements in other places reveal his proximity to Congregationalist convictions. 'Every Church *Primae magnitudinis* and *speciei*', he said, 'should be as great and no greater, than is capable of PERSONAL Communion'.[74] In effect, church government rested at the local level, with regular synods or associations, such as that developed at Worcester. The local congregation was independent, but not isolated or entirely autonomous. Similarly, Baxter did not allow government by majority vote, but he provided for 'twenty of the ancient and godly Men of the Congregation' to attend monthly meetings with Baxter, his assistants and the deacons, as 'the Trustees of the whole Church, to be present and secure their Liberties ... because all the People could not have leisure to meet so oft, to debate things which required their Consent'.[75] Baxter was regularly asked by correspondents whether

---

68   Ibid., 188.

69   Ibid., 188, 189.

70   Ibid., 188, 189–92.

71   Ibid., 192.

72   Ibid., 188. See also Thomas, 'Rise of the Reconcilers', 56.

73   See Richard Baxter, *Church Concord: Containing, I. A Disswasive from Unnecessary Division and ... II. The Terms Necessary for Concord Among All True Churches and Christians* (1691), 15–59.

74   *Rel. Bax.*, ii.178.

75   Ibid., 150.

Christians within a parish could meet privately, even to take communion.[76] He said yes, though they were not to do so in any way or at any time that suggested they were their own church or congregation, and only as 'a company more sensible of spirituall necessitie, and advantage, and more glad to redeeme time and give diligence for their salvation then the more careless part of the church'.[77] He had no desire 'to coope [Christ] up to the congregations of those few that say to all of the rest of the Church, Stand by, we are more holy than you',[78] but his practice across all his years at Kidderminster of meeting twice a week (on Thursday and Saturday evenings) with the 'more sensible' company in his own parish might have been seen to carry a similar implication. 'I take not a Private Meeting, or a Tolerated Private Church for so odious a thing in it self considered as some do.'[79] Taken together, all this suggests considerable common ground between Baxter and the Congregationalists. No wonder some thought his *Five Disputations* (1659) 'cometh too near the Independents'.[80] And no wonder the list of contentious issues in Baxter's correspondence with Nye was so small.

We can also see that if there was a chance to pursue unity, Baxter took it; if he could overcome the constraints of his geography (through a visit in person, if possible) he did so. Thus a nearby Nye was too big an opportunity to pass up. His paper demonstrates that his scheme was at last potentially workable; it presented a plausible plan. The differing parties could forge agreement 'if they are willing'. There, of course, lay the problem. Finally, it shows a spirit of compromise. Baxter readily made concessions on the issues in dispute, though he could not agree with Nye to recognize pastors that had not been ordained. It is impossible to gauge whether Nye had any genuine interest in reaching agreement or whether Baxter's personal style served to put him off. That it apparently took him a year to respond suggests a lack of enthusiasm, to say the least. In May 1658 he did initiate some sort of discussion with Baxter through the mediation of John Howe, but Howe suspected that Nye was interested in pushing the agenda only of his own party.[81]

---

[76]   For an example of his permission to take communion privately, see Baxter to Michael Edge, 14 February 1655[/6]: DWL MS *BC* iii.102r (*CCRB* #294).

[77]   Baxter to [Thomas Good], [February–March 1655]: DWL MS *BC* ii.232r–v (*CCRB* #219).

[78]   Hotchkis, *Exercitation Concerning the Nature of Forgivenesse of Sin*, Preface [by Baxter], n.p. [p. 18].

[79]   Baxter, *Church Concord*, 1. This portion of the book was written in 1655 (see title page).

[80]   *Rel. Bax.*, i.113.

[81]   John Howe to Baxter, 8 May 1658: DWL MS *BC* iii.196r (*CCRB* #450); and 25 May [1658]: DWL MS *BC* vi.232r (*CCRB* #453).

Baxter was forced to find some sort of compromise much closer to home, within the Worcestershire Association itself, over the issue of Scripture sufficiency in the business of making creeds and constructing doctrinal tests. His position here was adamant, simple, and crystal clear: he refused to go beyond the exact words of Scripture in formulating a common creed. Several other historians have explored his convictions on this point.[82] My interest is specifically in the reasons for Baxter's stance and how he worked through the issue with his colleagues. By late 1652 they were very close to agreement on the doctrinal standard that would be published in the following year in *Church Concord*. Only one obstacle remained: finding an adequate expression for the deity of the Holy Ghost. Here, Baxter faced three related problems. First, the deity of the Holy Spirit could be inferred from the Scriptures but at no point did those same Scriptures make it explicit (nor did the Apostles' Creed, which baldly declared 'I believe in the Holy Ghost'). So if Baxter was to keep to Scriptural language he had to confine himself to wording that was less than perfectly clear on the question. The second problem was the perceived prevalence of the Socinians. Anything less than an explicit statement of the deity of the Holy Spirit would potentially serve their anti-Trinitarian agenda.[83] Therefore, Baxter faced acute pressure to abandon his convictions and, in this one instance, to use a form of wording that while consonant with Scripture and in keeping with his own theology went beyond the exact language of the Bible. The third problem was that the Socinians employed precisely the same lines of argument as Baxter.[84] They too pressed for Scripture sufficiency, believing that taking the Bible in its own terms would serve to bolster their case. So, not only was Baxter's purist stance in danger of giving ground to the Socinians at a time of pervasive concern, it also sounded suspiciously Socinian all on its own.[85] It is not surprising, then, that Baxter's ministerial colleagues balked at his proposed wording on the Holy Spirit: 'we all agreed in each particular word except only about the expressions of the Godhead of the Holy Ghost, and now we are utterly at a losse, though no one among us differ in the thing.'[86]

---

[82]   In particular, see Keeble, *Richard Baxter*, 20–36; Lim, *Pursuit of Purity*, chapter 6; John Coffey, 'A Ticklish Business', 108–36; N.H. Keeble, '"Take Heed of Being too Forward in Imposinge on Others": Orthodoxy and Heresy in the Baxterian Tradition', in *Heresy, Literature and Politics in Early Modern English Culture*, ed. David Loewenstein and John Marshall (Cambridge: Cambridge University Press, 2006), 282–305.

[83]   Lim, *Pursuit of Purity*, 169.

[84]   Ibid., 165–6.

[85]   See Smith, 'Best, Biddle and Anti-Trinitarian Heresy', 172.

[86]   Baxter to [John Dury], 5 February 1652[/3]: DWL MS *BC* vi.94v (*CCRB* #109).

It is important to realize, and easy to miss, that Baxter was not against tests of orthodox belief as such, nor an enumeration of the fundamentals of the faith. After all, *Christian Concord* contained just such a profession of faith.[87] It served as a test for admission to the sacraments and as an instrument whereby churches might come into concord.[88] Clearly Baxter accepted these as legitimate functions of a doctrinal standard. 'We judge it fit withal to require an understanding profession of Assent and Consent to such fundamentals.'[89] Nor was he against doctrinal formulae that went beyond the mere words of Scripture. The essential thing here was the intended audience. 'I dare not express the Godhead of the Holy Ghost (in this Creed which every silly woman must professe, and which must be the test for admitting or not admitting for Communion) in any words but the very words of Scripture.'[90] The point was that Baxter would not use non-Scriptural language 'in this Creed', one to which the most ignorant of the parish would be required to submit. He accepted that a doctrinal test for ministers would yield a place for doctrinal formulations and language more technical than that offered by Scripture, though it should be written '(if possible) in Scripture phrase'.[91] And he accepted a place for historic creeds as a test of orthodoxy, but only the earliest creeds could serve the purpose – the Apostles' Creed and the Niceno-Constantinopolitan Creed. 'Take these two conjunctively for a Test.'[92] If they were a sufficient statement of the unchanging faith then, they must be so now; and there was no need to construct new and more elaborate creeds in the face of every new heresy.[93] There had been a rush of such confessions over the last century.[94] Even in his Epistle to the Reader of his *Aphorismes of Justification* Baxter lamented the 'mischief' of 'Creed makers ... who have a quicke and easy

---

[87]   Baxter, *Christian Concord*, Profession, sig. C2r–C4v.

[88]   Richard Baxter, *Universal Concord...Containing the Particular Terms of Reconciling the Severall Differing Parties that are Reconcileable* (1660), To the Reader, sig. A3r, A3v.

[89]   Baxter, *Christian Concord*, Propositions, sig. B2r.

[90]   Baxter to [John Dury], 5 February 1652[/3]: DWL MS *BC* vi.94v (*CCRB* #109). He made the same point to Thomas Wadsworth, 20 April 1655: DWL MS *BC* ii.252r (*CCRB* #238).

[91]   See Baxter to [John Dury], 5 February 1652[/3]: DWL MS *BC* vi.94v (*CCRB* #109); and Baxter, *Christian Concord*, 13. He was not alone in recognizing this distinction. See Coffey, 'A Ticklish Business', 114.

[92]   Richard Baxter, *Humble Advice: Or the Heads of Those Things Which Were Offered to Many Honourable Members of Parliament* (1655), 3. Technically, the version of the Nicene Creed Baxter referred to was the formula endorsed at the Council of Constantinople in AD381. See Ivor Davidson, *A Public Faith: From Constantine to the Medieval World AD312–600* (Grand Rapids, MI: Baker Books, 2005), 34.

[93]   Baxter, *Universal Concord*, Epistle to the Reader, sig. A3r. See also Baxter, *Reformed Pastor* (1656): *Practical Works*, Preface, iv.410.

[94]   See Coffey, 'A Ticklish Business', 113.

faith as swelled as big almost as *Aquinas* Summes. If one of the Primitive Martyrs were alive among us, and professed but what was in his ancient Creed, hee would scarce be taken by many for a Christian'.[95]

The reason why Baxter held to his stance with such fervency is that Scripture was the only thing on which all Christians could agree.[96] 'We may talk of peace as long as we live', he declared, 'but we shall never obtain it but by returning to the apostolical simplicity'. 'When we once return to the ancient simplicity of faith, then, and not till then, we shall return to the ancient love and peace.'[97] As he asked rhetorically in *Christian Concord*, 'What hope of Union when there is no Uniting Rule or Center agreed on?'[98] New formulations that go beyond Scripture 'are written according to the occasion of their writing'. These new creeds were too much a product of their times. Mounted one on top of the other they became divergent and disordered. And that served only to advance

> the running designe of the Papists ... to draw us to own some other Test of our Religion: and then they think they may freely dispute against it, and charge it with falsity, novelty, etc. which they dare not charge of the Word of God: And they think by this to set us altogether by the Ears, while one is for one Confession and others for another; Whereas in the Scripture we are united.[99]

The only hope for unity lay in a return to Scripture sufficiency and simplicity.[100] Too much was at stake for Baxter to give way. 'There is no hope of Uniting the Churches on any terms but what are Necessary and Divine [and] a new way of union is not to be expected, or attempted.'[101]

But his Worcestershire colleagues pressed for compromise. They proposed the words 'I believe that the Holy Ghost is God one with and proceeding from the Father and the Son'. But he could not bring himself to do it: 'only myself (who as little doubt of the truth of it as they) dare not consent' to that wording. Faced with an impasse, Baxter himself offered up several potential compromises. First, he suggested alternative scriptural wording: 'I believe that the Holy Ghost, the Spirit of the Father and the Son was sent from the Father by the Son to

---

95   Baxter, *Aphorismes of Justification*, Epistle to the Reader, sig. a2v.

96   Baxter to John Lewis, 25 June 1656: DWL MS *BC* ii.126v (*CCRB* #315).

97   Baxter, *Reformed Pastor* (1656): *Practical Works*, Preface, iv.410, 411.

98   Baxter, *Christian Concord*, Explication, 104.

99   Richard Baxter, *The Judgment and Advice of the Assembly of the Associated Ministers of Worcester-shire Concerning the Endeavours of Ecclesiasticall Peace, and the Waies and Meanes of Christian Unity, which Mr John Durey doth Present* (1658), 4.

100   See Nuttall, *Richard Baxter and Philip Doddridge*, 6–9.

101   Baxter, *Grotian Religion Discovered*, 27.

inspire and guide the prophets and Apostles and to be great witness of Christ, and of the truth of his Doctrine, being one with the Father and the word.'[102] His colleagues would not accept it. Then he suggested attaching to the doctrinal test a separate confession that declared 'the Holy Ghost is God', and to which ministers would have to give assent, 'it being fit they should know more than the meere fundamentalls'.[103] Again, the ministers would not budge. Baxter then invited them to search Scripture for better wording. He suggested that the people assent to the Apostles' Creed, and the ministers to the Constantinople-Nicene Creed. He proposed that each minister might have freedom to use a different form of profession in this one section. But his colleagues rejected all of these compromises.[104]

Just at that moment George Hopkins, Vicar of All Saints, Evesham, and a friend of Baxter's, wrote to explain how the ministers in that part of Worcestershire could not agree to the wording in Baxter's draft profession. As well as asking Baxter to reconsider his position, Hopkins suggested that Baxter write to 'two or three of the ablest divines ... desiring their advice'.[105] That constructive and timely suggestion was just the nudge Baxter needed to resolve the dilemma. He immediately wrote to John Dury and Archbishop James Ussher to ask for their opinion. In that letter, he explained with urgent passion his deep sense of conviction:

> God hath possessed my heart with such a burning desire after the peace and unity of the Churches that I cannot forget it, or lay it by. I feele a supernaturall power forcing my strongest zeale, and thoughts that way: and I am afraide under pretence of reconciling to frame an Engine for perpetuall divisions, by giving away the only rule and Centre of reconcilement and unity and so leaving it impossible for I know the Devills last way of undoing is by overdoing, and when it fits his turne, he will seeme more othodoxe and zealous against error than Christ himself.[106]

These were strong and longstanding convictions.[107] They explain why Baxter risked being seen as intractable even with his closest ministerial colleagues.

---

[102]   Baxter to [John Dury], 5 February 1652[/3]: DWL MS *BC* vi.94v (*CCRB* #109).
[103]   Ibid.
[104]   Ibid., 95r.
[105]   Geo[rge] Hopkins, 3 February 1652[/3]: DWL MS *BC* v.236r (*CCRB* #108).
[106]   Baxter to [John Dury], 5 February 1652[/3]: DWL MS *BC* vi.95r (*CCRB* #109).
[107]   In a letter to John Lewis, dated 25 June 1656, Baxter explained that twelve years earlier he had begun to write a book on the subject of Scripture sufficiency; if finished, his first published work might have been on that topic. DWL MS *BC* ii.126v (*CCRB* #315).

As it happens, Dury and Ussher supplied a form of words that satisfied all the parties: 'I believe that God the Holy Ghost the spirit of the Father and Son was sent from the Father by the Son, to Inspire and Guide, etc.'[108] And that, with several clauses tacked on the end, was precisely the wording that appeared in the profession in *Christian Concord*.[109] It was not so different from what Baxter had proposed, if less clumsy. It is possible that the ministers agreed to it more for the authority of Ussher and Dury standing behind it than the particular frame of words. Regardless, the problem had been solved, but only at the local level among ministers who knew Baxter reasonably well. In other places the language on the Holy Spirit was seen as inadequate and there was little hope that, in that form, it would serve as any kind of national profession.

Indeed, there was little hope of church unity at all, something Baxter inevitably learned early on. In 1653 he wrote to the elderly and sympathetic Thomas Gataker in 'a kind of disburdeninge'.

> As for the labour (tending to Concord) ... the face of the Divided Church is so dolefull to me and the Implacablenes[s] and the generall aversnes[s] from reconcilliation is soe great even among the ministry yea the learned and the Godly that it almost overwhelms me with sorrow to thinke of it, when we have done all that we can we cannot get men so much as to set themselves resolvedly, dilligently and with unwearied patience to consult among themselves, to finde out termes of Accommodation.[110]

The problems of party and passion were so great and the number of peacemakers so small that 'I can hardly forbeare of despairinge of our recovery and lookinge on our wounds as incurable in this life, and sayinge I shall never see Unity until I come to heaven'.[111] Gataker could only agree with this bleak assessment.[112]

But Baxter did not stop trying. Writing to Edward Harley in September 1656 (just as Harley took up his seat in the Second Protectorate Parliament as the MP for Herefordshire) he suggested once more that the Committee for Religion might mediate between a few chosen leaders of each party to bring about reconciliation – another version of the idea that seems to have gone nowhere.[113] In 1657 he wrote to John Eliot, missionary to the North American

---

[108] John Dury to Baxter, 22 February 1653/2 [*sic*]: DWL MS *BC* vi.79r (*CCRB* #111).

[109] Baxter, *Christian Concord*, Profession, sig. C3r.

[110] Baxter to [Thomas Gataker], 17 October 1653: DWL MS *BC* iii.143r (*CCRB* #137).

[111] Ibid. Baxter said much the same thing to John Lewis, 25 June 1656: DWL MS *BC* ii.126r (*CCRB* #315).

[112] Tho[mas] Gataker to Baxter, 1 November 1653: DWL MS *BC* iii.145r (*CCRB* #144).

[113] Baxter to Edward Harley, 15 September 1656: DWL MS *BC* i.226r (*CCRB* #324).

Indians, seeking to co-opt his help in his project for unity.[114] As Eliot pointed out in reply, his geographical isolation was more severe than Baxter's.[115] In April 1658 Baxter wrote to John Howe, then a chaplain in Cromwell's household, noting Cromwell's desire for peace and putting forward exactly the same scheme he had promoted for years (with the notable addition of the Anabaptists to his list of the main parties).[116] But there was little to show for his efforts. As he complained in 1658, everyone *said* they were for peace, but no one did anything to bring it about.[117] George Griffith immediately bore that out. He was the man John Dury had left behind to carry on what he had started in 1654, putting the London parties in the same room. Though he was an important leader within Congregationalism, and linked regularly with Owen,[118] Dury said he was 'zealous for the aime of Peace; no wayes engaged in any Party'.[119] So in 1658 Baxter placed his papers in the hands of this man 'who speaketh much for Reconciliation'. But 'when I called for them about a year after, he had shewed them to none, nor made any use of them, which might tend to the desired Concord; and so I took them away as expecting no more success'.[120]

Just how much Baxter's own personality contributed to the failure of all his efforts at national church unity is a question to which I will return. But what of those whose agendas or indifference seemed to impede his plans? During the 1650s Baxter did not name names, yet from all of this it is easy to imagine the kind of person he would view as a rival or opponent: a man who was adept at the deployment of political power: a man closely aligned to the interests of a particular party: a man who pursued sophisticated doctrinal statements as a means of stopping Socinianism in its tracks and of attaining unity in the church – a man, in fact, not unlike John Owen.

---

114   Baxter to John Eliot, 20 January 1656/7: DWL MS *BC* iii.9r (*CCRB* #351).

115   John Eliot to Baxter: 7.8 [October] 1657: DWL MS *BC* ii.274r (*CCRB* #398).

116   Baxter to John Howe, 3 April 1658: DWL MS *BC* iii.200r (*CCRB* #443).

117   Baxter, *Reformed Pastor* (1656): *Practical Works*, iv.406, 407; and *Judgment and Advice*, 2–3.

118   See Richard L. Greaves, 'Griffith, George (1618?–1699x1702)', *Oxford Dictionary of National Biography*, Oxford University Press, September 2004; online edn, January 2008 [www.oxforddnb.com/view/article/39673, accessed 22 May 2009]; and Richard L. Greaves, *Saints and Rebels: Seven Nonconformists in Stuart England* (Macon, GA: Mercer University Press, 1985), chapter 3.

119   John Dury to Baxter, 9 April 1653: DWL MS *BC* vi.80r (*CCRB* #114).

120   *Rel. Bax.*, ii.193, iii.61.

John Owen: Fundamentals and Toleration

If Baxter had any early sympathy for the separatists, it quickly dissipated. If he made any moves in his ecclesiology, he shifted further away from Congregationalism. And if this is true, he might well have met Owen (speaking metaphorically) coming the other way. During the mid-1640s Owen made a pronounced move from Presbyterianism to Congregationalism. It is one more instance of the way in which the career of the one man neatly mirrored that of the other.

Owen offered the fullest account of this early transition in 1657, in a reply to the Presbyterian Daniel Cawdrey. Cawdrey had made a name for himself attacking Congregationalism – and John Cotton in particular – in 1645, with a further expansion in 1651.[121] In 1657 he responded to Owen's defence of Congregationalism in *Of Schism*. Just as Cawdrey finished his book, a copy of Owen's *Duty of Pastors and People Distinguished*, published in 1643,[122] came into Cawdrey's hands. Owen had written that short work of ecclesiology as a Presbyterian. In an appendix, Cawdrey gleefully exposed all the contradictions he thought he saw between Owen's thinking in 1643 and his position in 1657. The effect was to force Owen to clarify the nature of his earlier move. Cawdrey's assault must have struck a nerve: even though it was an appendix in Cawdrey's book, Owen positioned his defence at the beginning of his reply; and, for once, he ventured into autobiography.

In 1643, Owen explained, the conflict between the Presbyterians and the Congregationalists was still young. At the time he had no clear understanding of the issues under dispute, nor had he encountered any actual Congregationalists. So, 'being unacquainted with the congregational way, I professed myself to own the other party, not knowing but that my principles were suited to their judgment and profession'. Having reviewed the matter, and having carefully examined John Cotton's *Keyes of the Kingdom of Heaven*,[123] Owen came to the realization that his principles were, in fact, 'far more suited to what is the judgment and practice of the congregational men than those of the presbyterian'. He was thus prompted to own the Congregationalist position. But this was merely a change

---

[121]   Daniel Cawdrey, *Independencie a Great Schism Proved Against Dr. Owen his Apology in his Tract of Schism* (1657); *Independency Further Proved to be a Schism: Or, A Survey of Dr Owen's Review of his Tract of Schism* (1658).

[122]   The date of publication on the title page was 1644 but this was a publisher's trick to increase the currency of the book. It was actually published in 1643. Owen, *Review of the True Nature of Schism* (1657): *Works*, xiii.222.

[123]   Peter Toon claims (*God's Statesman*, 18–19) that Owen was also swayed by the *Apologeticall Narration*, also published in 1643, but it is not clear what on what evidence he based this assertion.

of label, not principle. 'So that when I compare what then I wrote with my present judgment, I am scarce able to find the least difference between the one and the other.'[124] He repeatedly claimed that he stood by everything he wrote in 1643,[125] with one exception:

> Only, as to the liberty to be allowed unto them which meet in private, who cannot in conscience join the celebration of public ordinances as they are performed amongst us, I confess myself to be otherwise minded at present than the words there quoted by this author do express. But this is nothing to the difference between Presbytery and Congregationalism.[126]

Apart from this, he claimed, his principles had not changed.[127]

Owen's interpretation has never been tested or challenged by historians,[128] and it deserves much greater scrutiny. On the one hand, *Duty of Pastors and People Distinguished* certainly reads like a document that could lend itself to the purposes of the Congregationalists. For example, it made no provision for any higher authority at the level of, say, the synod; it dealt with the authority structure of each congregation in its own terms. It claimed that a pastor was one who was called by God, divinely gifted, and whose authority was recognized by the congregation.[129] There was no discussion of ordination. While Owen allowed no middle ground between the meetings of the whole church body and the gathering together of believers in twos and threes or in families,[130] there was an implicit freedom for believers to encourage each other in the faith.[131] 'In sum ... the people of God are allowed all quiet and peaceable means, whereby they may help each other forward in the knowledge of godliness and the way towards heaven.'[132] Moreover, Owen's explicit context was a church purely reformed, not one in a state of disrepair, which seemed to leave options open in the latter

---

[124]   Owen, *Review of the True Nature of Schism* (1657): *Works*, xiii.223.

[125]   Ibid., 225–7.

[126]   Ibid., 227.

[127]   In a later reply to Cawdrey, Owen stated this categorically: 'Is there any word or tittle in the whole discourse deviating from these principles?' Owen, *Answer to a Late Treatise of Mr Cawdrey about the Nature of Schism* (1657): *Works*, xiii.294.

[128]   See, for instance, Orme, 'Memoirs', 29–30; Cook, 'Political Biography', 53–6. Peter Toon repeats Owen's claim verbatim, with no comment at all (see *God's Statesman*, 27).

[129]   Owen, *Duty of Pastors* (1643): *Works*, xiii.43.

[130]   Ibid., 45–6.

[131]   See, for instance, Owen, *Duty of Pastors* (1643): *Works*, xiii.42.

[132]   Ibid., 47.

case.[133] And there was no contradiction between what Owen wrote in *Duty of Pastors and People* and what John Cotton had set out in *Doctrine of the Church*, even if Cotton went further than Owen. So there was, indeed, much that lay in sympathy with Congregationalist thinking. The shift, when it came, would have been simple enough.

On the other hand, Owen's interpretation obscures one very important change that does go to the heart of the differences between Congregationalists and Presbyterians. The question here is what Owen meant by the liberty of believers to meet in private. Did he intend the right of Christians to form new congregations independent of the local parish church? If so, he was wrong to say that this had nothing to do with the difference between Presbyterians and Congregationalists. It seems more likely that he had in mind merely the right of Christians within a congregation to meet together as a group for private edification. This indeed had nothing to do with ecclesiological differences, since Baxter (not to mention any number of others) also cultivated this practice of private meetings. But if this is true, then Owen glossed over a much more significant shift. Before, he disavowed competing congregations; now, he defended them.

Duty of Pastors and People reveals the extent of that change. As the book reached its conclusion, Owen responded to three objections. The first was that his thinking would foster 'licentious *conventicles* ... as the seminaries of faction and schism in the church of God'. He strongly denied that his thinking would support those

> who have pre-declared themselves to be opposers of the worship of God in the public assemblies of that church wherein they live. Now, the patronage of any such I before rejected. Neither do I conceive that they ought at all to be allowed the benefit of private meetings who wilfully abstain from the public congregations, so long as the true worship of God is held forth in them. Yea, how averse I have been from that kind of confused licentiousness in any church, I have some while since declared in an [unpublished treatise].[134]

The significance lies in a mere three words: that church 'wherein they live'. In 1643 Owen was still working within the traditional parish model in which there was only one church in any given location – a substantial difference from his later thinking. In responding to the second objection Owen criticized those who 'create themselves pastors in separate congregations'. He must have intended

---

133   Ibid., 39.
134   Ibid., 47.

the regular gathering together of believers in distinct congregations formed in competition with the local parish church.[135] Owen's final summation of his book carried the same implication: 'To conclude, then, for what I have delivered in this particular, I conceive that I have the judgment and practice of the whole church of Scotland, agreeable to the word of God, for my warrant.'[136] This could be the case only if he was denying any place for competing congregations within the same parish, and not just the liberty of Christians within a congregation to meet privately.

The magnitude of Owen's shift, then, lies in his abandonment of the national church structure formed around geographical units. In 1643 he naturally assumed that structure; in 1657 he dismissed it. Christ had instituted no 'parochial, diocesan, metropolitical, patriarchal' church structure.[137] Owen now believed 'this constitution is human ... and arbitrary'.[138] He refused to accept that the Bishop of Oxford, where he lived in 1657, had any sort of Christ-instituted jurisdiction over Owen himself or that Owen was obliged to meet with a congregation over which the Bishop ultimately presided.[139] In fact, he went much further than that, defending the right and even the necessity of godly Christians to separate from an unreformed parish church.

> Is this yoke laid upon me by Christ, that, to go along with the multitude where I live, that hate to be reformed, I must forsake my duty and despise the privileges that he hath purchased for me with his own precious blood? Is this a unity of Christ's institution, that I must forever associate myself with wicked and profane men in the worship of God, to the unspeakable detriment and disadvantage of my own soul? I suppose nothing can be more *unreasonable* than once to imagine any such thing.[140]

He refused to accept a believer was obliged to meet with the one parish church, no matter how dead or ungodly it might have been.

> I ask whether it be schism or no for any number of men to reform themselves, by reducing the practice of worship to its original institution, though they may be the minor part lying within the parochial precincts, or for any of them to join themselves

---

135   Ibid., 49.
136   Ibid.
137   Owen, *Of Schism* (1657): *Works*, xiii.141.
138   Ibid.
139   Ibid., 187.
140   Ibid., 200.

> with others for that end and purpose not living within those precincts? I shall boldly say this schism is commanded by the Holy Ghost.[141]

Separation from the parish church structure could be not just a right but a duty. And that is not what Owen had said in 1643, when the national church structure stood firm in his mind and he would brook no separation.

Owen's extended thinking here raises two important questions: what did 'a unity of Christ's institution' look like, and how would it be achieved? *Of Schism* supplied an answer, if only implicitly. The book itself appeared like Melchizedek, without genealogy, without mother or father, in that it carried with it no preface, no introduction, and no specific context. William Orme thought Owen was prompted to write the book by the Congregationalist minister, Thomas Beverley.[142] In February 1657 Beverley had written an impassioned letter suggesting that the well-placed Owen might do more to defend the Congregationalist cause. He expected more than silence from 'you, who see more, and have more Advantages every way, than any before you, for whom even to appear in the Cause, is in effect to gain the Victory'.[143] However, in the epistle to the reader of Owen's follow-up book, dated 9 July 1657, Owen stated that *Of Schism* was 'published about a year ago'.[144] Either Owen's recollection was mistaken or the book was written at least eight months earlier than Beverley's letter.[145]

The precise trigger for the book remains something of a mystery, then, but the cause is clear: Owen defended the Congregationalists from the accusation of schism.[146] Using Paul's first letter to the Corinthians as a basis he audaciously defined schism not as separation from a church (its customary meaning) but as division within it. This nicely negated any criticism of the Congregationalists because a Presbyterian congregation could be marked by schism (internal division) just as easily as a Congregationalist one. Owen also distinguished three senses of the word, 'church'. First, there was the church militant, or the catholic church, the '*church of the elect*, redeemed, justified, sanctified ones, that are so built on Christ, and these only'.[147] Schism from the church in this sense

---

[141]   Ibid., 199–200.

[142]   Orme, 'Memoirs', 196–7.

[143]   *CJO*, 97.

[144]   Owen, *Review of the True Nature of Schism* (1657): *Works*, xiii.209

[145]   George Thomason put the date of 17 June on his copy of the book, presumably accepting the year date of 1657.

[146]   For general background on the dispute with Cawdrey, and Owen's view of the Church, see Nuttall, *Visible Saints*, 64–9; and Collins, *Allegiance of Thomas Hobbes*, 231–6.

[147]   Owen, *Of Schism* (1657): *Works*, xiii.126,

was impossible, since the elect could never fall away. Second, the 'church visible' was marked out not by any particular structure, but by shared doctrine. Thus to break from the visible church was not a sin of schism, but a sin of apostasy, or heresy.[148] Finally, there was the particular church, the local congregation, which was detached from any superimposed national structure. As long as each congregation was rightly ordered there could be no schism as Owen defined it.

Unity, therefore, was not structural or organizational, but invisible (by virtue of being members of the body of Christ) and doctrinal.

> Now, that this union be preserved, it is required that all those *grand and necessary truths of the gospel*, without the knowledge of which no man can be saved by Jesus Christ, be so far believed as to be outwardly and visibly professed, in that variety of ways wherein they are or may be called out thereunto.[149]

So there was 'a variety of ways' of organizing church congregations but they all would share in the same doctrine.

Two things were required for this kind of unity to be attained. First, believers had to agree on what those essential, saving truths would be. 'These are commonly called fundamentals, or first principles; which are justly argued by many to be clear, perspicuous, few, lying in an evident tendency to obedience.' If they were 'savingly believed', a person was made 'a member of the church catholic invisible'. And 'the profession of those truths' instated a person 'in the unity of the church visible'.[150] This was the impetus behind Owen's campaign to identify the fundamentals of religion. An approved, agreed list was a necessary, practical precursor to unity of the visible church. 'The belief and profession of all the necessary saving truths of the gospel ... is the bond of the unity of the visible professing church of Christ.'[151]

The second requirement for unity was toleration.[152] *Of Schism* contrasted 'two general ways fixed on respectively by sundry persons for the compassing

---

[148]   Ibid., 170.

[149]   Ibid., 146.

[150]   Ibid.

[151]   Ibid., 147.

[152]   See Paul Lim, 'The Trinity, *Adiaphora*, Ecclesiology, and Reformation: John Owen's Theory of Religious Toleration in Context', *Westminster Theological Journal* 67 (2005): 281–300; and a variant on that article, '*Adiaphora*, Ecclesiology, and Reformation: John Owen's Theory of Religious Toleration in Context', in *The Development of Pluralism in Modern Britain and France*, ed. Richard Bonney and D.J.B. Trim, vol. 2 (Oxford: Peter Lang, 2007), 243–71. See also Gary S. De Krey, *London and the Restoration, 1659–1683* (Cambridge: Cambridge University Press, 2005), 100–105.

of peace and union among Christians': uniformity enforced by a secular power; and toleration. Owen drily noted that a uniformity imposed by force had lost its reputation of late. The previous hundred years or so had proved just how ineffectual and counterproductive the policy was: it had brought continual violence and disruption rather than tranquillity; it had deadened people's affection and respect for religion; and it better served dissemblers than conscientious professors.[153] Instead, Owen promoted a policy of toleration. This was not a limitless toleration of all beliefs, nor did it leave no place for the civil magistrate, but it was 'our present condition' and the best means of attaining 'peace and union among Christians'.[154] These two requirements complemented each other: defining the fundamentals also served the purpose of shielding those secondary questions on which there would be toleration of belief and practice.[155]

A year earlier, in 1656, Owen had set forth his vision for England in a sermon to Parliament:

> That the *people* of God be delivered from the hands of their cruel enemies, that
> they may serve the Lord without fear all the days of their lives, in righteousness and
> holiness; – that, notwithstanding their present differences, they may live peaceably
> one with, or, at least, one by another, enjoying rule and promotion as they are fitted
> for employments, and as he gives promotion in whose hand it is; – that godliness and
> the love of the Lord Jesus Christ be preserved, protected, and secured, from a return
> of the hand of violence upon it.[156]

This aim was 'no other than my heart hath been fixed upon for many years, and which I have several times, on one account or other, intimated or pressed unto the parliament'.[157] This, then, is the end Owen had in mind: godly unity predicated on agreement with prescribed fundamentals and toleration. We can now go back to the beginning in order to show how he developed that vision across those 'many years', how he adapted his stance as he moved from Presbyterianism to Congregationalism, and how all of this brought him into competition with Baxter.

When Owen published his first sermon to Parliament in 1646 he attached 'A Short Defensative About Church Government, Toleration, and Petitions about

---

[153]   Owen, *Of Schism* (1657): *Works*, xiii.95–6.

[154]   Ibid., 96.

[155]   John Coffey, 'The Toleration Controversy During the English Revolution', in *Religion in Revolutionary England*, ed. Christopher Durston and Judith Maltby (Manchester: Manchester University Press, 2006), 49.

[156]   Owen, *God's Work in Founding Zion* (1656): *Works*, viii.419.

[157]   Ibid.

these Things'. It was his first obvious attempt to shape national religious policy, it supplies a fascinating glimpse into his transition out of one ecclesiological camp into another, and it reveals a further inconsistency in Owen's later recollections. Daniel Cawdrey had charged Owen at numerous points with abandoning the Presbyterians.[158] Owen denied the accusation. But, while it was technically true that he had never been a member of a strictly Presbyterian system,[159] it was misleading to say that he did not 'plead for their Presbyterian way in the year [16]46'.[160] Even in the preface to his essay on church government he continued to 'plead for presbyterial government in churches'.[161] And the essay itself, which he had 'long since' written,[162] promoted a generally Presbyterian frame. Far from having abandoned the parish system Owen merely wanted to revise the existing boundaries. He proposed new ones no greater than eight or 10 miles in diameter, containing a population base of between 100 and 500 souls.[163] These new parish churches would comprise 'visible saints, men and women of good knowledge and upright conversation' who had joined 'by their own desire and voluntary consent'.[164] Thus the scheme blended the concerns of the Presbyterians (one church in one parish) with those of the Congregationalists (membership of the consenting godly). It was not designed to 'erect churches amongst churches and against churches', since it was 'a mere forming of one church with one presbytery'.[165] Owen argued that his proposal would satisfy both groups. We can see, then, how his later claim that his principles were consonant with Congregationalist belief and practice made some sense. But we can also see that his abandonment of the parish structure, of which he was later so dismissive, remained a major change still to come even by mid-1646.

Having dealt with church government Owen then moved on to make his first published case for toleration. Here again there is a fascinating glimpse into the process of transition. In the sermon itself Owen had dismissed those who

---

[158]   Cawdrey, *Independencie a Great Schism*, 8, 60–61, 181

[159]   Owen, *Of Schism* (1657): *Works*, xiii.195; *An Answer to a Late Treatise of Mr Cawdrey about the Nature of Schism* (1658): *Works*, xiii.297. See also Orme, 'Memoirs', 29.

[160]   Owen, *An Answer to a Late Treatise of Mr Cawdrey about the Nature of Schism* (1658): *Works*, xiii.301.

[161]   Owen, *Of Schism* (1657): *Works*, viii.47. The context of this quote is that Owen had been criticized in the past for doing this. But there is no hint that he was doing so no longer and the essay he was publishing proposed a generally Presbyterian model.

[162]   Owen, *Of Schism* (1657): *Works*, viii.47.

[163]   John Owen, 'A Short Defensative about Church Government, Toleration, and Petitions about these Things', appended to *Vision of Free Mercy* (1646): *Works*, xiii.50–51.

[164]   Ibid., 51.

[165]   Ibid., 52.

were so concerned about the weeds among the corn.[166] But in the essay he used the same image to different effect. Here he agreed with 'every just call, to oppose, suppress, and overthrow' those heresies that challenged the fundamentals of the faith, 'to root them up and cast them out, that they may not, as noxious weeds and tares, overgrow and choke the good corn, amongst which they are covertly scattered'.[167] Thus Owen seems to have written the essay as a Presbyterian and preached his sermon as a Congregationalist. But the fact that he published his essay as a Congregationalist shows that he was still, even then, content to work within parish boundaries. So we can say that in April 1646 his views had still not fully matured.[168] This suggests that the difference between Presbyterianism and Congregationalism lay not just in matters of ecclesiological principle, it was also a way of seeing the world, one that was less concerned by the apparent existence of heresy and error.

Owen again advanced his plan by attaching an essay on toleration and the role of the civil magistrate to his published post-regicide sermon to Parliament. On 16 January 1649, just a few weeks earlier, the Commissioners of the General Assembly of the Church of Scotland had publicly rebuked some of their brethren in England. They denounced the push for 'a Toleration unto all Errours ... but expresse Popery and compulsion'.[169] 'We know that such a way is looked upon by some as the best foundation of safety, but we know nothing more like to bring ruine and destruction.'[170] Owen strongly disagreed, though there is ambiguity and subtlety in his reply. The magistrate, he said, had a positive role to support by material means the places and preachers of the nation's declared religion.[171] The magistrate was also empowered to dismantle 'any public places for (in his judgment) false and abominable worship'.[172] But he was not to involve himself in 'minute differences' such as those between the Presbyterians and the Congregationalists.[173] And he was not to act with force against heretics for

---

[166]   Owen, *Vision of Free Mercy* (1646): *Works*, viii.28.

[167]   Owen, 'Short Defensative about Church Government': *Works*, xiii.58. He obliquely referred to the parable of the wheat and the tares again on p. 66, where he seems to allow that both truth and error 'should grow together until harvest'.

[168]   See also Lim, 'Trinity, *Adiaphora*, Ecclesiology, and Reformation', 285; and '*Adiaphora*, Ecclesiology, and Reformation', 247–50.

[169]   Commissioners of the General Assembly of the Church of Scotland, *A Solemn Testimony Against Toleration and the Present Proceedings of Sectaries and their Abettors in England in Reference to Religion and Government* (Edinburgh, 1649), 2.

[170]   Commissioners, *Solemn Testimony Against Toleration*, 10.

[171]   John Owen, 'Of Toleration: And the Duty of the Magistrate about Religion', appended to *Righteous Zeal Encouraged* (1649): *Works*, viii.192.

[172]   Owen, 'Of Toleration': *Works*, viii.194.

[173]   Ibid., 193.

their heresy, only for their public disturbance: 'actual disturbances, indeed, must have actual restraint'.[174] Owen argued that the same crime could be judged by two authorities but distinct aspects of the crime were being judged in each case. In the crime of heresy that led to public disturbance the two aspects were heresy and disturbance: the church judged the heresy; the magistrate judged the disturbance. On the latter, 'none denies it to be the magistrate's duty to interpose with his power'.[175] But the former was to be constrained not by physical punishment but by spiritual means: the admonition of believers, 'gospel conviction'; and 'the sword of discipline'.[176] In the first 300 years of the church such means had effectively prevented heresy.[177] But as the civil magistrate took up an active role in punishing error by physical means, heresies such as Arianism (the ancient ancestor of Socinianism) gained ground,[178] and 'the man of sin walked to his throne'.[179] Non-toleration was simply 'the old Roman way'.[180] Instead, spiritual officers should use spiritual means: 'admonition, avoiding, rejection, excommunication, will be the utmost that can be inflicted on them; which, for my part, I desire may be exercised to the utmost extent of the rule.'[181] 'Spiritual ways of healing are known to all – let them be used.'[182]

One of the problems Owen identified in his essay was the absence of an agreed list of 'publicly owned and declared truths'.[183] It was not 'known and confessed what articles in religion are fundamental'.[184] Such statements of doctrine were the 'constant practice of the churches in former ages'; they served as 'a discriminating [symbol] of their communion in doctrine'. But they were lacking now, and that absence exacerbated the confused state of English churches and prevented a right ordering. England urgently needed its own list of fundamentals.

> If this be done by the authority of the magistrate, – I mean, if such a declaration of
> the truth wherein the churches by him owned and protected do consent be held out
> as the confession of that truth which he embraceth, – it will be of singular use unto,

---

[174] Ibid., 195.
[175] Ibid., 201.
[176] Ibid., 170–171.
[177] Ibid., 183, 184.
[178] Ibid., 184.
[179] Ibid., 184–5.
[180] Ibid., 178.
[181] Ibid., 200.
[182] Ibid., 205.
[183] Ibid.
[184] Ibid., 198.

yea, indeed, most necessarily precede, any determination of the former question [of church order].[185]

Agreed doctrine preceded church order, though both were pressing, and the magistrate carried the responsibility of authorizing that agreement.

By 1649 Owen was on the verge of becoming 'the architect of the Cromwellian Church',[186] and increasingly well placed to help remedy the problem. Recent scholarship provides impressive scrutiny and re-evaluation of Owen's attempts to engineer a list of fundamentals. One of the shifts underway is to be less accepting of Baxter's perspective, within which Owen and his fellow Congregationalists pursued a narrowly partisan agenda to secure their own interests. Most notably, Michael Lawrence argues that those efforts were

> far removed from Baxter's characterization. Rather than being narrowly doctrinaire and stubbornly factious, Goodwin and his colleagues occupied an unexpectedly moderate position, both on the structure of the church and its doctrine. Moreover, the various attempts at confessional settlement were anything but polarizing. Instead they were at the centre of a concerted effort to reunify the English church around a doctrinal platform that was broadly protestant and truly 'catholic'.[187]

This is an important recognition, though it ignores the tightening of the doctrinal limitations that he discerns in each iteration of the fundamentals. They had the effect, by 1654, of ruling out Arminians.[188] More recently, Sarah Mortimer has seen the importance of this. As the 1650s progressed Owen became increasingly concerned by the influence of Socinianism in England, embodied in influential authors (such as Grotius, Henry Hammond, and, as we shall see, even Baxter) and presented in variants that could almost pass for orthodox Protestantism. In response, Owen helped to craft a doctrinal formulation much more tightly aligned with Reformed Calvinism.[189]

On 10 February 1652, Owen, Thomas Goodwin, Philip Nye and Sidrach Simpson presented a petition to Parliament.[190] Regrettably, its content is not extant. In response, the Commons established two sub-committees to consider the petition, 'to confer with these ministers' and to consider 'such Proposals as

---

[185]   Ibid., 203.

[186]   Worden, 'Toleration and the Cromwellian Protectorate', 204.

[187]   Thomas Michael Lawrence, 'Transmission and Transformation: Thomas Goodwin and the Puritan Project 1600–1704', PhD Thesis, Cambridge University, 2002, 143–4.

[188]   Lawrence, 'Transmission and Transformation', 174–5.

[189]   See Mortimer, *Reason and Religion*, chapter 8.

[190]   *CJ*, 10 February 1651[/52], vii.86.

shall be offered for the better Propagation of the Gospel'.[191] Those proposals were published later that year as the *Humble Proposals*. This brief tract put forward a series of ideas that would be regularly floated and sometimes implemented as the nation searched for a permanent settlement in religion during the following decade. Lawrence sees it as 'a compromise document' that was 'almost presbyterian': 'there was something in the *Proposals* for both sides to cheer'.[192] It provided for the official recognition of authorized pastors in each congregation and proposed what would become in time the system of triers and ejectors. In line with Owen's views on toleration it allowed for 'persons dissenting from the Doctrine and Way of Worship owned by the State' to meet together in venues notified to the magistrate without the right to propound any views deviating from 'those Principles of the Christian Religion'.[193] Parliament asked the authors to specify what those principles were, and their answer was published in December that year as the *Proposals for the Furtherance and Propagation of the Gospell in this Nation*.[194]

They make for interesting reading. Mortimer is right to say that the Socinians had been only a smokescreen for a different agenda.[195] Apart from affirming that 'God is one in three persons, or substances' the proposals said nothing about the deity of the Holy Spirit.[196] Instead, the real target was the sects who were rightly alarmed by the seeming betrayal of their former allies, the Congregationalists.[197] Lawrence also explains that 'the authors were essentially expounding the Apostles' Creed'.[198] And they did so in language that was resolutely (if not pristinely) biblical. Each section began with a brief summary statement that was then backed up by a considerable number of biblical proof texts printed in full. Baxter, of course, wanted nothing less than exclusively scriptural language, but we should recognize that this set of proposals came close to that ideal.

As for Baxter's impressions of the document, we do not know. Certainly they did not match his general prescription published some six years later: 'the terms

---

[191] Ibid.

[192] Lawrence, 'Transmission and Transformation', 150, 149, 151.

[193] Owen et al., *Proposals for the Furtherance and Propagation of the Gospell in this Nation: As...Also, Some Principles of Christian Religion, without the Beliefe of which, the Scriptures doe Plainly and Clearly Affirme, Salvation is not to be Obtained* (1652), 5–6. Hereinafter, *The Humble Proposals*.

[194] Lawrence, 'Transmission and Transformation', 151.

[195] Mortimer, *Reason and Religion*, 196–200, 205.

[196] Owen et al., *Proposals for the Furtherance...of the Gospell*, 9.

[197] See Carolyn Polizzotto, 'The Campaign against *The Humble Proposals* of 1652', *Journal of Ecclesiastical History* 38 (1987): 569–81; Coffey, 'A Ticklish Business', 120.

[198] Lawrence, 'Transmission and Transformation', 152.

of an Universal Concord or Peace, must be purely Divine, and not Humane; Necessary, and not things unnecessary; Antient, according to the Primitive simplicity, and neither New, nor yet too Numerous, Curious or abstruce.'[199] Closer to the time, on 8 March 1652, he wrote to Thomas Hill, Master of Trinity College, Cambridge. Baxter wanted Hill to petition Parliament to adopt his plan of a meeting between the leading figures of the four main parties. Baxter fretted that 'the Rulers do nothing for setling the church, nor the Ministers for Accommodation'.[200] In fact, that was not quite true. The *Humble Proposals* represented an effort to settle the church and to reach accommodation. But Baxter chose not to interpret developments in that way: 'I heare the Independents are now about cutting out all themselves.'[201] Though important, this statement has been made to carry more weight than it can bear.[202] All it reveals is what Baxter had heard – he merely passed on the opinion of others. He had not seen the *Humble Proposals* for himself, which had not yet been published, and we can only surmise that they triggered his comment. But it does suggest Baxter's inclination to believe what he had heard, to interpret the actions of Owen and his fellow authors as part of a narrowly partisan agenda, and to urge another course of action in competition, or at least in precedence. 'It will be sad to the church, if such an Accommodation [as Baxter suggested] precede not their Settlement. I pray you ... set a foote such a petition presently.'[203] As it happens, the proposals were never authorized,[204] but what this shows is that, even then, it seems, Owen and Baxter were on course for a collision. The clash finally came in 1654.

---

[199]   Baxter, *Grotian Religion Discovered*, 29.

[200]   Baxter to Thomas Hill, 8 March [1652]: DWL MS *BC* iii.272v (*CCRB* #81).

[201]   Ibid., 273r.

[202]   See Nuttall, *Richard Baxter*, 79; Polizzotto, 'Campaign', 575; and Lawrence, 'Transmission and Transformation', 147.

[203]   Baxter to Thomas Hill, 8 March [1652]: DWL MS *BC* iii.273r (*CCRB* #81).

[204]   The sub-committee for the propagation of the gospel reported back the proposals a year later with telling amendments that were overruled by Parliament (see *CJ*, 11 February 1652[/53], vii.258–9, and 25 February 1652[/53], vii.262). Progress stopped when Cromwell dissolved Parliament in April 1653. See Lawrence, 'Transmission and Transformation', 164–5; Shaw, *History of the English Church*, 80–84.

Chapter 6

1654

I had rather suffer any thing in the World, than be guilty of putting among our Fundamentals one word that is not true.

Richard Baxter[1]

The previous chapter laid out the ecclesiology and schemes for unity of John Owen and Richard Baxter. We are now in a place to evaluate them together and to see how they played out in practice. The specific focus is 1654, when Parliament summoned a number of ministers to advise on the creation of an authorized list of fundamentals. The particular context of the ministers' work cast into relief the differences between Owen and Baxter, and cast into shadow the much more extensive range of agreement. It is necessary, then, first to assess what those points of agreement were before examining in detail how factors of disagreement and personality conspired to make the meetings of 1654 an exercise in frustration.[2] In doing so, we should recall the discussion of personality in Chapter 4. Owen seems to have been in charge of the ministers' proceedings and we have already observed his managerial style at work in a committee setting. It is easy to believe that he manipulated affairs to the fullest possible extent to achieve his ends. But Baxter was no easy opponent. We have seen his belligerence, his inability to keep his mouth tactfully shut, and his willingness to contradict others in service to the truth as he saw it. The events of late 1654 were, therefore, both a personality clash and a meeting head-on of two fixed and contrasting agendas in church unity. It is unfortunate that the common ground was overlooked, and the narrow factors of divergence so painfully accentuated.

---

[1]   *Rel. Bax.*, ii.204.

[2]   Neil Keeble also sees that behind the obvious points of difference 'lay incompatibilities of temperament and doctrinal emphasis', in 'Orthodoxy and Heresy in the Baxterian Tradition', 285; while John Coffey also sees areas of agreement and disagreement between Owen and Baxter, in Coffey, 'A Ticklish Business', 109, 129.

Common Ground – And Its Limits

There was much that Owen and Baxter held in common. To begin with the broadest and most obvious factor, both wanted the same thing – church unity. Said Owen, 'I would rather, much rather, spend all my time in making up and healing the breaches and schisms that are amongst Christians than one hour in justifying our divisions, even therein, wherein, on the one side, they are capable of a fair defence'.[3] And one could point to any number of places in which Baxter, sometimes with great eloquence and passion, declared his 'burning desire after the peace and unity of the Churches'.[4] Of course, this is not saying all that much. No one within the mainstream of English Christianity applauded the fractious state of the church and advocated its continued disunity.[5] 'Religious division is the great anxiety of early modern Europe', especially for those who lived through the Thirty Years War or experienced firsthand the English Civil War.[6] It is also true that Owen employed overt language of unity only rarely. He was much more likely to speak the language of toleration (though toleration was ultimately in the service of unity).[7] The contrast with Baxter is substantial: unity was, for him, a recurrent rhetorical motif. It is easier to see his repeated affirmations as expressing genuine sentiment than it is for Owen's more occasional pronouncements.

And, a final qualification, both men could be accused of professing a desire for peace, yet employing methods and postures that would serve only to hinder its fulfilment. Owen was seen as too much of a party player and sometimes carried himself as such. As Carl Trueman concludes, Owen's 'theology was self-consciously developed in part in sharp opposition to Arminianism', which 'scarcely provided the opportunity for building a broad Protestant consensus'.[8] Owen had the kind of access to power needed to bring about unity, but not a sufficiently broad theological inclusiveness. Baxter was more inclusive, but lacked the access to power and influence. This was not just another trick of geography;

---

³   Owen, *Of Schism* (1657): *Works*, xiii.95.

⁴   Baxter to [John Dury], 5 February 1652[/3]: DWL MS *BC* vi.95r (*CCRB* #109).

⁵   Owen made this point in his essay on church government: *Works*, viii.53–4. See also, Davis, 'Religion and the Struggle for Freedom', 529: 'the consensus emerging amongst historians in recent years has been that religious unity remained a virtually universal priority among the godly in the 1640s and 1650s'.

⁶   Worden, 'Toleration and the Cromwellian Protectorate', 210.

⁷   For an example of the link between toleration and unity, see Owen, *God's Work in Founding Zion* (1656): *Works*, viii.422, 424. See also Worden, 'Toleration and the Cromwellian Protectorate', 210.

⁸   Carl Trueman, 'Richard Baxter on Christian Unity: A Chapter in the Enlightening of English Reformed Orthodoxy', *Westminster Theological Journal* 61 (1999): 61.

his personality and peremptory style too often got in the way. It is significant that Baxter's schemes came closest to fruition when others, such as John Dury, acted as his agents. In all Baxter's approaches to various Congregationalists there was a common pattern: they essentially ignored him, doing nothing with his papers for months on end, then handing them back. This might have reflected their own unwillingness to compromise or it might have been that while the proposals had merit in themselves, Baxter was simply not the man to promote them. Even George Griffith, admittedly a Congregationalist figure but selected by John Dury and with an evident desire for unity, seems to have demonstrated a distinct lack of interest in Baxter's proposals. And why is it that the Worcestershire ministers readily accepted the proposed wording of Dury and Ussher on the deity of the Holy Spirit when it was not all that different from what Baxter had offered up in the first place? Perhaps it was their stamp of authority that made the difference; on his own, Baxter could not get his colleagues to budge. Maybe that was why George Hopkins suggested that Baxter approach other respected divines for their suggestions. After all, Baxter was still at that point only in the early stages of his career and influence. Therefore, in these different ways, Owen and Baxter each lacked what was necessary to achieve the unity they professed to desire. Even so, both men would, with justification, have felt themselves to be working towards a common goal. In early 1654 while Baxter was encouraging Dury from Kidderminster, Owen was also backing him from Oxford.[9] The two were closer than they realized.

They were also close on two central planks in their plans for unity: toleration and the importance of church discipline. The first is not as surprising as it may appear. 'It may seem perverse', writes Blair Worden, 'to present Owen ... as an opponent of toleration', but that is what he does (using the term in its modern sense).[10] That conceivably places Owen closer to Baxter, who has more obviously been seen as an opponent of toleration, and not without reason.[11] At times he sounded distinctly cold on the idea, especially when he had in mind his experience of civil war soldiers – their many aberrant ideas, coupled with a

---

[9] Owen et al. to the Evangelical Churches of Europe [March 1654?]: *CJO*, 68–70; Dury, *Declaration of John Durie*, 24.

[10] Worden, 'Toleration and the Cromwellian Protectorate', 207. Worden distinguishes Victorian 'toleration' from early modern 'liberty of conscience', p. 209. See also, p. 214. John Coffey accepts Worden's presentation of Owen (if not of the sectarian tolerationists), in 'Puritanism and Liberty Revisited: The Case for Toleration in the English Revolution', *Historical Journal* 41 (1998): 961, 963–4.

[11] For instance, see Thomas, 'Rise of the Reconcilers', 57–60; Worden, 'Toleration and the Cromwellian Protectorate', 201; Trueman, 'Richard Baxter on Christian Unity', 57.

tendency to talk up toleration.[12] He always feared that a 'universal toleration' would bring in the Papists.[13] But this was not Baxter's only voice on toleration. He never published a work specifically on that subject (though in 1659 he intended to write one)[14] but we can discern this more positive line of thinking in several sources. In a very early letter of 1646 he ventured (rather tentatively) that 'it seemes to pervert the order of God in Nature, in making one mans judgment the guide of another mans judgment or actions [that] the Magistrate must chase out, and the people depart from ... whom others judge a hereticke'. It was wrong to force another person to go against their own judgement. And it encroached on Christ's prerogative to say 'wee must believe this, and submit to that, upon there [*sic*] bare word'.[15] In *Christian Concord* he prayed that 'our Rulers may avoid these two destroying extreams, of giving *too much* Liberty, or *too little*'.[16] He repeated the point in a letter of 1656, in which he put forward the outlines of a church settlement to Edward Harley, but in a way that showed where his preference lay. 'In a doubtfull case, I had rather erre in granting too much liberty, then too little.' In a similar way to Owen, Baxter contended that physical punishment should not be brought to bear on the heretic – that was like 'Popery [that] resteth so much on humane strength and violence' – but church discipline administered by orthodox ministers. It was better to support the orthodox in parish discipline than make martyrs out of heretics by putting them in jail. He also argued that no one should be prosecuted merely for holding an errant belief; 'it is the seducing of others by the teaching of those untruths' that should be constrained.[17] 'And this may be restrayned in consistency with Liberty that is granted in the Instrument of Government.'[18] Later, in the *Reliquiae Baxterianae*,

---

[12]   Richard Baxter, *A Holy Commonwealth, Or, Political Aphorisms, Opening the True Principles of Government: For the Healing of the Mistakes, and Resolving the Doubts, that Most Endanger England at this Time* (1659), Addition to the Preface, n.p. [see his discussion on Proposition 6].

[13]   See, for instance, *Rel. Bax.*, ii.203.

[14]   Baxter, *Holy Commonwealth*, Addition to the Preface, n.p. [in his discussion on Proposition 6].

[15]   Baxter to ??, March [1646]: DWL MS *BC* i.39v (*CCRB* #7).

[16]   Baxter, *Christian Concord*, Explication, 105.

[17]   This sentiment was not unusual. 'Even the stoutest champions of orthodoxy conceded that conscience could not be forced.' Worden, 'Toleration and the Cromwellian Protectorate', 208.

[18]   Baxter to Edward Harley, 15 September 1656: DWL MS *BC* i.226v (*CCRB* #324). For similar thoughts on toleration, see Richard Baxter, 'An Answer to the Overturners and New Modelers of the Government About a Senate, Toleration and Tithes', dated 30 November 1659 and reproduced in Richard Schlatter, ed., *Richard Baxter and Puritan Politics* (New Brunswick, NJ: Rutgers University Press, 1957), 130.

Baxter repeated his endorsement of Cromwellian toleration. That policy had been good for godliness:

> I shall think that Land happy that hath but bare Liberty to be as good as they are willing
> to be; and if *Countenance* and *Maintenance* be but added to *Liberty*, and tolerated
> Errors and Sects be but forced to *keep the Peace*, and not to oppose the Substantials of
> Christianity, I shall not hereafter much fear such Toleration, nor despair the Truth will
> bear down Adversaries.[19]

Owen would have said no less. 'I speak not against a toleration of godly, tolerable men', said Baxter in 1659, 'episcopal, Presbyterian, independent, Anabaptist, &c. that will walk in charity, peace and concord'.[20] Again, this is all Owen ever asked for.

The two men also shared many of the same convictions when it came to church ministry and discipline. By the mid-1650s Baxter's model of pastoral visitation was beginning to generate impressive momentum and success. He arranged for every willing family in his parish to visit him once a year for a spiritual health check, testing their knowledge of Scripture and the early creeds and employing catechisms.[21] That practice lay at the heart of the pastoral plan with which he challenged all of England's ministers in the *Reformed Pastor*, published in 1656. Baxter saw his responsibility as extending well beyond his Sunday duties. He was not alone in that sort of sentiment, of course, but Owen, at least during his own years of parish ministry, may not have been much different. He published two catechisms for use among his congregation,[22] and he explained how he had taught them both 'publicly and from house to house'.[23] That was a straight borrowing from Acts 20:20 and the example of the Apostle Paul, so we should perhaps not take it too seriously.[24] He was also at that point still a Presbyterian: in his country essay on church government he again urged ministers to visit their parishioners in their own houses.[25] But the language persisted. In the *Humble Proposals* ministers were to visit their flock, 'instructing [them] from house to house'.[26] And in his 1649 essay on toleration Owen grieved for 'the great disorder of the

---

[19] *Rel. Bax.*, i.87. See also, p. 86.

[20] Baxter, *A Treatise of Self Denial* (1659), Epistle Monitory: *Practical Works*, iii.357.

[21] Baxter, *Reformed Pastor* (1656): *Practical Works*, Preface, iv.359, and 454–69. See also, Black, *Reformation Pastors*, esp. pp. 93–5.

[22] Owen, *Two Short Catechisms* (1645): *Works*, i.463–94.

[23] Ibid., 465.

[24] Peter Toon is prepared to take it at face value. See *God's Statesman*, 17–18.

[25] John Owen, 'Short Defensative about Church Government' (1646): *Works*, viii.50.

[26] Owen et al., *Humble Proposals*, 5.

churches of God amongst us'. Right discipline was the cure. 'Were the precious distinguished from the vile, churches rightly established, and church discipline [so] exercised that Christians were under some orderly view' the problem would be easily solved.[27] True, those phrases disguise differences with Baxter, but their vision of what the conscientious minister should do among his congregation and the effect that could have on godly unity was broadly similar.

It might be said that both Owen and Baxter were merely drawing on the same pool of commonplaces, but that is the point. They drew from the same well. And the similarities extend to more specific comparisons. Like Baxter, Owen was realistic about the potential extent of doctrinal and practical agreement. In 1646 he hoped for agreement as far as possible, and then 'a peaceable dissent in some smaller things, disputable questions, not absolutely necessary assertions'.[28] Ten years later he ventured that Christians might at least 'live peaceably with or, at least, one by another'.[29] So both men recognized these practical limits to church unity. Baxter could say of the triers and ejectors, an important component of Owen's scheme, that 'they have done much good'.[30] Notably, Baxter averred that 'I question not the Magistrate's coercive power'.[31] And both men lamented the pernicious effect of power and party, though Owen did so with rather less credibility. 'Every one', he complained in 1657, 'if not personally, yet in association with them of some peculiar persuasion with himself, would be the head; and because they are not, they conclude they are not of the body, nor will care for the body, but rather endeavour its ruin'.[32] Those words could have been Baxter's. A year later he complained that any party's idea of reconciliation was keeping all the others in subjection and in their place.[33] Toleration, then, was Owen's solution to the twin problem of power and party, since it involved freedom, not coercion. For this reason he could claim that 'I acknowledge myself to no party'.[34] Once again, we should not necessarily take these assertions at face value. They are stylized and polemical, and hardly unique. But this does not deny that there were vast swathes of common ground and common assumptions between them. Both sat comfortably within the puritan tradition with its pressing desire

27   Owen, 'Of Toleration' (1649): *Works*, viii.203.
28   Owen, 'Short Defensative about Church Government' (1646): *Works*, viii.47.
29   Owen, *God's Work in Founding Zion* (1656): *Works*, viii.419.
30   Baxter to Edward Harley, 15 September 1656: DWL MS *BC* i.226v (*CCRB* #324).
31   Baxter to ?, March [1646]: DWL MS *BC* i.39r (*CCRB* #7). See also DWL MS *BT* i.294r–297v, item #15; and Baxter, 'Answer to the Overturners', reproduced in Schlatter, *Richard Baxter and Puritan Politics*, 128ff. Lamont, *Millennium*, 63–5.
32   Owen, *God's Work in Founding Zion* (1656): *Works*, viii.415.
33   Owen, *Of Schism* (1657): *Works*, xiii.97.
34   Owen, *Review of the True Nature of Schism* (1657): *Works*, xiii.220.

for church and social reformation. There was so much on which both could nod their heads in agreement.

But that common ground had its limits and there were two issues in particular on which they could not see eye to eye. The first has to do with parish boundaries. Owen blithely dismissed them as a human invention. He disdained the idea that he would be forced to attend the one church along with the most ungodly and dissolute of his neighbours. 'I grant no such thing as a national church.'[35] In contrast, Baxter firmly held to a parish-based national church. While he could make some concessions to inter-parish transfer in very limited circumstances,[36] the idea of two competing congregations within the same location went against every grain. In a very early letter to a group of friends being tempted into Congregationalism, he passionately rebuked the 'evill of separation'.[37] By distilling the best and removing them from the local church, the Congregationalists fatally weakened the church they left behind. In an unwitting echo of Owen's 1646 speech to Parliament, Baxter declared that the church was 'a Corne Field, where Corne and Thistles grow together: But if instead of weeding out the Thistles, any will weed out and remove the Corne, and leave the soil to the Thistles, then it is no Corne field'.[38] The first part of Baxter's *Church Concord*, written in 1655 and published in 1691, also bears this out. It is an impressive document written with the aim of showing that all the main points of division between the Presbyterians and the Congregationalists were not genuine reasons for division at all. But it also reveals how the integrity of parish boundaries was a line beyond which Baxter could not be pushed. He began by demonstrating the disaster that was 'Divided and Private Congregations' when 'in one and the same Parishes ... there shall be divers Churches, one Publick, and one Private'.[39] And at the end, having explained why the differences between the two parties were not real obstacles, he still asked that for 'order sake, let Parishes be the ordinary bounds of Churches'.[40] Having made his own concessions, this was the point on which he expected the Congregationalists to move. But there was no hope of that, and even in Baxter's post-Restoration approach to Owen this would remain the greatest outstanding point of difference.[41] The issue reflected a broad ecclesiological divergence. For the Congregationalists especially, 'truth lay in the

---

[35] Ibid., 272.

[36] See Baxter, *Christian Concord*, 34–7; *Rel. Bax.*, ii.191, 195.

[37] Baxter to [A Person at] Shrewsbury [c. 1649]: DWL MS *BC* v.51r (*CCRB* #13).

[38] Ibid., 51v.

[39] Baxter, *Church Concord*, 1. See also, pp. 4, 10–11.

[40] Ibid., 48.

[41] 'I knew scarce any of you that did not by an *unjust espousing of your few*, do the People a double Injury, one by denying them their Church-Rights, without any regular Church Justice, and

spirit rather than the institution, in the power rather than the form'.[42] So for Owen the very nature of church unity and belonging was invisible, intangible, doctrinal and spiritual. For Baxter, the church was much more institutional, organizational, tangible and physical. His ministry and model were nothing if not parish-based.

The second insurmountable difference lay in the formulation of a list of fundamentals, but it is essential to recall the narrow scope of the disagreement. To repeat an earlier point, Baxter was not against the idea of the fundamentals as such. He had little problem with the method Owen proposed. But he denied that an additional, personal profession of faith and a specific 'account of the manner of their conversion' was necessary for people to be received into fellowship,[43] and he was adamant that the fundamentals should be expressed only and exclusively in language drawn from Scripture itself. Owen's *Proposals for the Furtherance and Propogation of the Gospell* came impressively close to Baxter's ideal, but not close enough; he would not give an inch. Once again, the issues that divided Owen and Baxter were narrow and insurmountable at the same time. To illustrate this further, in that first part of *Church Concord* Baxter made the case that the right response to heresy was church discipline; as long as heresy was not actively promoted, coercion had no place. As we have seen, that was Owen's line as well. But Baxter offered that line in the context of a discussion of Scripture sufficiency. In this light, the imposition of new, man-made creeds was an act of coercion just as misguided as physical coercion. 'We must not make new Laws, every time the old ones are misinterpreted or broken.'[44] Baxter had an aversion to imposed non-scriptural fundamentals in the same way that Owen had an aversion to coercion over indifferent matters of faith and practice. Because of a broadly shared commitment to toleration, the differences over Scripture sufficiency were crucial. In a related way, Sarah Mortimer is not wrong to say that there were 'in effect, two rival plans for Church settlement in these years – underpinned by two very different conceptions of Christian unity. One was associated with Owen, Thomas Goodwin and other Independent ministers ... The second plan can be traced to Richard Baxter'. The first centred around the magistrate, toleration and the fundamentals; it emphasized purity of doctrine. The second worked through the vehicle of the associations to produce unity on

the other by lazily omitting most that should have been done for their Salvation.' Baxter to John Owen, 16 February 1668[/9]: *Rel. Bax.*, iii.67 (*CCRB* #771; and *CJO* #73).

[42]   Worden, 'Toleration and the Cromwellian Protectorate', 207. See also, Bremer, *Congregational Communion*, 132.

[43]   Baxter, *Christian Concord*, 38.

[44]   Baxter, *Church Concord*, 14.

the ground; it emphasized an ethical and moral concern.[45] This distinction, at once narrow and broad, explains so much of the clash of 1654. It is regrettable that when the two men finally met in person for the very first time they were forced to do so in circumstances that did nothing to accentuate the vast common ground between them. Instead, the conditions did everything to confront them with this one narrow, but ultimately irresolvable, issue of disagreement. Their relationship, such as it was, already fraught, could only get worse.

Forging the Fundamentals

England gained a written constitution on 3 December 1653: the Instrument of Government.[46] One of the effects of that was to give new energy to the ongoing search for a religious settlement. Article 35 asserted that 'the Christian Religion, as contained in the Scriptures, be held forth and recommended', with a publicly funded ministry. Articles 36 and 37 offered protection and freedom from coercion and restraint to those who differed from 'the Doctrine, Worship or Discipline publickly held forth'.[47] On 11 September 1654 the first Protectorate Parliament, barely a week into its existence, came to debate those articles. Seeing the need for a clear expression of what that public profession of religion would be, it resolved that each Member should nominate one godly minister from within his county who would meet with eight representatives from Ireland and eight from Scotland, as well as one from each of the universities, 'to offer their Advice concerning such Matters of Religion as shall be proposed to them by the Parliament'.[48] By 5 October that plan had been replaced by a more manageable scheme of summoning 'twelve or twenty' ministers to offer their advice to a small sub-committee of MPs who would, in turn, advise the Lord Protector.[49] The ministers met in the Jerusalem Chamber of Westminster Abbey, where the

---

[45]   Mortimer, *Reason and Religion*, 221. Paul Lim makes a similar point, in *Pursuit of Purity*, 181. Baxter certainly disliked an environment that rewarded people for professing all the right beliefs while ignoring love and practice. See DWL MS *BT* ii.168r–v, item #38(2).

[46]   Technically, though, the document was never ratified by Parliament. Worden, 'Toleration and the Cromwellian Protectorate', 219.

[47]   C.H. Firth and R.S. Rait, eds, *Acts and Ordinances of the Interregnum 1642–1660*. Vol. II, *Acts and Ordinances from 9th February, 1649, to 16th March, 1660* (London: His Majesty's Stationery Office, 1911), ii.821–2.

[48]   *CJ*, 11 September 1654, vii.367.

[49]   John Towill Rutt, ed., *Diary of Thomas Burton esq. Member in the Parliaments of Oliver and Richard Cromwell from 1656 to 1659...with an Introduction Containing an Account of the Parliament of 1654 from the Journal of Guibon Goddard, Esq. M.P.* (1828), vol. ii, p.xlvi; Thomas Grove to Baxter, 4 November [1654]: DWL MS *BC* iii.169r (*CCRB* #204).

Westminster Assembly had conducted its own discussions.[50] They began to meet on 4 November and carried their deliberations on into December,[51] working towards an authorized 'confession of faith'.[52]

A surprising coalition of voices had been calling for exactly that. For example, when Marchamont Nedham, editor of the parliamentarian newsbook *Mercurius Britanicus*, defended the Instrument of Government in 1654 he saw within Articles 36 and 37 the hint of 'a Publick profession intended to be held forth by the Magistrate'. Regretting the 'innumerable parties and Factions [parading] under the banner of Religion', he declared it 'high time for our Governours to lay a healing hand to these mortall wounds and breaches, by holding forth the Truths of Christ to the Nation in some solid Establishment, and not quite to lay aside or let loose the Golden reins of Discipline and Government, in the Church'.[53] On 5 August 1654, in the dedication to *True Christianity*, Baxter asked for just the same thing. He urged that the 'right means' be used for healing England's divisions. Those means were the liberty for local or national church assemblies and the formulation of 'one Scripture creed, or confession of faith, agreed on by a general assembly of able ministers, duly and freely chosen hereunto, which shall contain nothing but matter of evident necessity and verity' and which would serve as a test of the orthodox. Such a confession, he noted, like Nedham, was that 'which it seems is intended in the 37th article of the late formed government'.[54] Geoffrey Nuttall is right to doubt that Baxter's proposal prompted the actions of the new Parliament in the following month (though the similarity with its first plan is tantalizing) since the book was unlikely to have been available in time.[55] More than that, as Nedham's comments reveal, there was a number of voices clamouring for such a confession, including, no doubt, Owen's. And the final result differed from Baxter's suggestion in two important ways. It was not 'a general assembly of able ministers' but something much more confined; and it did not intend a 'Scripture creed' in quite the way that Baxter had in mind. Even so, he approached the project with considerable sympathy for its general aims.

---

[50]   Keeble, 'Orthodoxy and Heresy in the Baxterian Tradition', 285.

[51]   For a fuller account of developments in the weeks preceding the first meeting, see Lawrence, 'Transmission and Transformation', 168–9.

[52]   *CJ*, 16 November 1654, vii.385.

[53]   Marchamont Nedham, *A True State of the Case of the Common-Wealth of England, Scotland and Ireland* (1654), 42, 43–4. Cromwell later endorsed Nedham's conclusion. Worden, 'Toleration and the Cromwellian Protectorate', 216, 218.

[54]   Baxter, *True Christianity*, Dedicatory Epistle (1654): *Practical Works*, iv.783.

[55]   Nuttall, *Richard Baxter*, 77.

It goes almost without saying that Owen also supported the work of this small assembly of divines. To the extent that he was the architect of the Cromwellian Church he engineered the development. By 1654 England urgently needed to settle the fundamentals and reach agreement if only because the Socinian threat was looming ever larger. In that year the Council of State commissioned Owen to write a reply to John Biddle. He was an easy target compared to other better-placed scholars who were also borrowing from Socinianism. This worrying development threatened to derail any attempts at unity by casting doubt on even the most central of Christian doctrines. The Socinian separation of Christianity and natural law 'was potentially the most damaging of all to [Owen's] own plans for the English Church. It implied that religion was an individual and voluntary matter which need not concern the magistrate and it suggested that humans could live quite independently of God or religion'.[56] Owen needed to secure the fundamentals before the rising tide of Socinianism swept away any possibility of general agreement.

It was Baxter's misfortune to arrive late, after the ministers had begun their work. And it was typical of Owen's management that he did not wait for a voice that would not quite speak his language. We do not know the precise makeup of the group but Owen was certainly one, and he seems to have led proceedings. Other names were, among the Congregationalists, Thomas Goodwin, Philip Nye and Sidrach Simpson; and among the Presbyterians, Stephen Marshall, Francis Cheynell, William Reynor, Richard Vines, Thomas Manton and Thomas Jacomb.[57] Lord Broghill, a member of the sub-committee of MPs, also nominated Archbishop Ussher; he declined, but suggested Baxter in his place.[58] Broghill evidently agreed.[59] On the very day the ministers began to meet, Thomas Grove (another member of the sub-committee) wrote to Baxter inviting him to travel to London to join them.[60] Grove was one of a trio of figures, all known to each other, who had in private correspondence applauded Baxter's plans for church

---

[56]   Mortimer, *Reason and Religion*, 207.

[57]   See Lawrence, 'Transmission and Transformation', 169; and *Rel. Bax.*, ii.197. Thomas Grove's list was slightly different. He included Henry Jessey and Daniel Dyke, both Baptists. See Thomas Grove to Baxter, 4 November [1654]: DWL MS *BC* iii.169r (*CCRB* #204) and its footnotes in *CCRB*.

[58]   *Rel. Bax.*, ii.197.

[59]   For the similarity of Broghill's views with Baxter, see Mortimer, *Reason and Religion*, 223; David L. Smith, 'Oliver Cromwell, the First Protectorate Parliament and Religious Reform', *Parliamentary History* 19 (2000): 45–6; and Patrick Little and David L. Smith, *Parliaments and Politics* (Cambridge: Cambridge University Press, 2007), 204. Baxter stayed with Broghill while in London (*Rel. Bax.*, ii.205).

[60]   Thomas Grove to Baxter, 4 November [1654]: DWL MS *BC* iii.169r (*CCRB* #204).

unity.[61] While Grove noted and appreciated the 'miscelany' of men among the ministers with their 'severall interests and judgements',[62] he was clearly aware of Baxter's agenda and supported it. We should not ignore the fact that the balance lay in favour of the Presbyterians, which may reflect a defensive shift in the face of sectarian and Socinian threat.[63]

The fullest account we have of the work of the ministers is Baxter's autobiography, written around 10 years after the event.[64] There is no avoiding his account, but it must be used carefully as it reflects that later time. For instance, the way in which Baxter couched his objections to the ministers' way of contriving the fundamentals (even proposing the word 'essentials' as a preferred alternative)[65] was quite different from the way in which he approached the subject in the mid-1650s (when he himself used the word 'fundamentals' without reservation).[66] Therefore, I intend to employ his account principally for several important facts it relays and the impression it gives of Baxter's own carriage among the ministers – he comes across as supremely unconstructive even in his own recollections.[67] But I will not use it to assess Owen's role in the committee. It is not that Baxter's impressions are without truth – in fact, given

---

[61]   The other two were Peter Ince and Henry Bartlett. For approving comments, see Thomas Grove to Baxter, 13 November [1652]: DWL MS *BC* iii.170r (*CCRB* #102); Peter Ince to Baxter, 16 November [1652]: DWL MS *BC* iv.181v (*CCRB* #103); and Henry Bartlett to Baxter, 30 December 1652: DWL MS *BC* iv.178r (*CCRB* #105). As for connections between the three, both Grove and Ince referred to Bartlett in postscripts to their letters; Bartlett mentioned talking to Grove and Ince in his letter; in 1647 Grove had nominated Ince to the rectory at Donhead St Mary, Wiltshire (see the headnote to *CCRB* #102); and Bartlett was a neighbour of Ince, who was a 'close friend' of Grove (see the headnote to *CCRB* #94).

[62]   Thomas Grove to Baxter, 4 November [1654]: DWL MS *BC* iii.169r (*CCRB* #204).

[63]   Lim, *Pursuit of Purity*, 161.

[64]   *Rel. Bax.*, ii.197–205. There is also a second, later account among Baxter's papers, but it is very brief and offers no additional significant information. It was published as 'Original Letters and Papers from Richard Baxter's MSS', *Monthly Repository* 20 (1825): 287–9.

[65]   I have in mind here the top half of *Rel. Bax.*, ii.198.

[66]   For instance, in a letter to Peter Ince of 21 November 1653, Baxter urged Ince to 'bottom uppon Christ and the great fundamentalls', DWL MS *BC* i.12r (*CCRB* #148). In a letter dated 5 July 1654, Baxter urged Abraham Pinchbecke in his preaching to 'dwell much on the fundamentall truthes', and to join with ministers who 'live in unity holding the fundamentalls of Christian faith and practice', DWL MS *BC* iv.168r, v (*CCRB* #190). In a paper he presented to the ministers of the 1654 assembly Baxter used the word 'essentials' only once, and not in any way that suggested a preference for it; otherwise, he continued to speak of the fundamentals. *Rel. Bax.*, ii.200. Even in 1658 he continued to speak of 'fundamental verities', in *Confirmation and Restauration* (1658): *Practical Works*, iv.340.

[67]   William Orme also came to this view. See 'Memoirs', 114.

what we know of Owen's manipulation of other committees and procedures,[68] they are all too plausible – but because there is too great a risk that Baxter's memory when he wrote this part of the *Reliquiae Baxterianae* in 1664 had been coloured by the events of 1659. Later in this book, I will suggest that Owen's alleged part in the downfall of Richard Cromwell transformed him in Baxter's mind into the 'great doer',[69] not to mention the 'great ... breaker'.[70] I am, therefore, too distrustful of Baxter's post-1659 perceptions of Owen. It is far safer, and indeed more than sufficient, to exploit Baxter's pre-1659 observations on Owen's behaviour. They are hidden, but not beyond reach.

Baxter was clearly a square peg in a round hole. In the marvellously apt words of Paul Lim, 'Baxter's main role during the assembly became that of a dissenting maverick'.[71] It would have taken only a very short time for everyone to work that out, because Baxter's position was simple and pure, he could not accept any formulation of authorized doctrine that went even one syllable beyond the words of Scripture. It was an absolute position on which he could not compromise. As soon as that fact was made plain there was nothing the ministers could do except to adopt Baxter's stance – that they could not do – or to reject it. It would have had almost the same effect on the outcome, and it would have made more friends, if Baxter had simply taken the next coach home. As it was, he stayed for the several weeks' duration of the deliberations, acting as little more than a thorn in the side of most, if not all, of his fellow ministers, and of Owen in particular.

Those ministers felt they had a good reason for rejecting Baxter's purist policy: Socinianism. In Baxter's account, he suggested 'the *Creed*, the *Lord's Prayer*, and *Decalogue* alone as our Essentials or Fundamentals; which at least *contain all* that is necessary to Salvation'. They refused to accept it: '*A Socinian or a Papist will Subscribe all this*.' 'I answered them, So much the better, and so much the fitter it is to be the Matter of our Concord', because the answer to a new heresy (or even an old one) was not a new formulation of faith. If God had not crafted a statement that no one could misinterpret or give their own sense to, why try to create one? Such a move would only forestall unity, not advance it. 'These Presumptions and Errours have divided and distracted the Christian Churches, and one would think Experience should save us from them.'[72] As Lim discerns, the conflict lay in the distinction between Baxter's 'essentialist' position of Scripture sufficiency and the more 'context-specific' awareness of

[68]   See above, pp. 114–15, 121
[69]   *Rel. Bax.*, ii.198.
[70]   Ibid., 61.
[71]   Lim, *Pursuit of Purity*, 161.
[72]   *Rel. Bax.*, ii.198.

Owen and others among the ministers.[73] The most pressing problem in that particular context was Socinianism.

It is surprising that Baxter did not simply offer up the 'Profession of the Associated Churches in Worcestershire', which served the purpose of the ministers in terms that Baxter could live with.[74] In fact, he may well have made that suggestion (if so, it is another way in which his later account is insufficient) though the result was the same. Owen and Baxter later quibbled with each other over how much time they had spent in each other's company while working together in London. Owen played it up, in order to complain that in all their conversations Baxter never mentioned his *Confession of Faith*, which was about to be published and in which he criticized Owen.[75] In his turn, Baxter played it down.[76] Whatever the amount of their conversation together, the context gives a sense of their discussions. Clearly, one subject was the Worcestershire Profession. Owen believed it was an open door for Socinians to walk through. It 'differs from the known confession of the Socinians' only 'in one expression at most' and 'in sundry particulars gives so great a countenance to their abominations'.[77] Most importantly, it seemed to differentiate 'the only God' from 'the Lord Jesus Christ our Redeemer'.[78] Baxter was outraged to hear it. Owen had wilfully misread the document and completely ignored 'the sense I had told him in my explication' of the Profession.[79] So the two men had talked about the Profession during the course of the assembly, which in turn suggests that Baxter had proposed it but they had simply talked past each other. Owen could never accept the Profession as a solution because it let in the Socinians as easily as did the early creeds. Baxter did not deny it, but for him that was a virtue. His fellow ministers could not see it that way.

Of all the ministers in England with whom Baxter might have clashed, Owen was the most obviously concerned with Socinianism. A year earlier he had published *A Dissertation on Divine Justice*, which argued that God was bound by his justice to punish sin. The book specifically attacked the Socinians, who 'place all their hopes of overturning the doctrine of the satisfaction of Christ in opposing this justice', as well as other mistaken (but well-meaning) divines such as Samuel Rutherford and William Twisse who inadvertently played into their

---

73   Lim, *Pursuit of Purity*, 162.

74   Baxter, *Christian Concord*, Profession.

75   Owen claimed he had 'much conference with him at London'. *Death of Christ and of Justification* (1655): *Works*, xii.592.

76   Baxter, *Certain Disputations*, 486.

77   Owen, *Death of Christ and of Justification* (1655): *Works*, xii.594.

78   Ibid., 595.

79   Baxter, *Certain Disputations*, 487.

hands.[80] Then on 2 March 1654 the Council of State asked Owen to respond to John Biddle.[81] This exercise would have made him excruciatingly aware of just how Socinian Baxter could sound. In the Preface to his *Brief Scripture Catechism*, published earlier that year, Biddle encouraged his readers to be

> addicted to none of those many factions in Religion, whereinto the Christian world
> hath to its infinite hurt been divided; but rejoice to be *a meer Christian*, admitting (as
> I have elsewhere declared) no other Rule of Faith, then the Holy Scripture, (which all
> Christians, though otherwise at infinite variance amongst themselves in their opinions
> about Religion, unanimously acknowledge to be the Word of God).[82]

This sounded uncannily like Baxter, and Owen's reply, finished by April 1655, canvassed exactly this comment.[83] The assembly of late 1654, then, most likely interrupted him in the process of writing that book. His mind was, if nothing else, focused on the issue. And his reputation was coming to rest in large part on his role as England's public defender against Socinianism in all its forms.

Baxter was no Socinian. He had made that clear as early as the *Aphorismes of Justification*. 'I have read little of their writings; but that little gave me enough, and made me cast them away with abhorrence ... Most accursed Doctrine!'[84] But that did not forestall the accusation. Baxter was seen by many 'to draw too near Socinianisme'.[85] William Robertson, for example, accused him of defending 'Jesuitical, Arminian, and Socinian principles'.[86] And Owen was, in effect, also about to level the accusation.[87] All of this frustrated Baxter. 'When men plead reason for Christianity and Scripture authority, [others] say, It is Socinianism: when we plead for the sufficiency of Scripture alone, and appeal to it; they say, This is Socinianism too.'[88] This overlooks other grounds on which he might have been charged with Socinianism, but that was Baxter's experience among the

---

[80]   Owen, *Dissertation on Divine Justice* (1653): *Works*, x.506, 507–8, 551–4.

[81]   Smith, 'Best, Biddle and Anti-Trinitarian Heresy', 175.

[82]   John Biddle, *A Brief Scripture Catechism for Children: Wherein, Notwithstanding the Brevity Thereof, All Things Necessary unto Life and Godliness are Contained* (1654), Preface, sig. L3r–v.

[83]   Owen, *Vindiciae Evangelicae* (1655): *Works*, xii.70.

[84]   Baxter, *Aphorisms of Justification*, 306–7.

[85]   Richard Vines passed on the comments in a letter to Baxter, 1 July 1650: DWL MS *BC* ii.15r (*CCRB* #44).

[86]   William Robertson, *An Admonitory Epistle unto Mr Rich. Baxter, and Mr Tho. Hotchkis* (1655), 2.

[87]   See Owen, *Death of Christ and of Justification* (1655): *Works*, xii.591–616.

[88]   Baxter, *Confession*, 16.

ministers. This was why they could not accept his purist position. They wanted to lock the door against Socinianism; Baxter's way seemed to let the Socinians walk right in.

With the substantive issue raised by Baxter's arrival now recognized and dealt with, the ministers then continued to thrash out the exact details of their formulation. It is easy to imagine Baxter sitting by himself in the back row lobbing objections. It was Philip Nye's view at the time that Baxter 'puzzles the framers of the ... Confession of Faith'.[89] The dynamic would have shifted. It became the clash of personalities that had long been waiting to happen. It seems from Baxter's account that most of the group sat in silence while Baxter battled single-handedly with Owen and 'his Assistants'.[90] Owen, as we have seen, was not one to be contradicted; all Baxter offered in these meetings was contradiction. He later recalled that 'those that managed the Business, did want the Judgment and Accurateness which such Work required, (though they would think any Man supercilious that should tell them so)'.[91] No doubt Baxter did tell them so. It is even now astonishing that Baxter could say to Owen's face – the Vice-Chancellor of Oxford University, the regime's first-choice defender of Christian orthodoxy, 'the pre-eminent Puritan and ecclesiastical authority of the Interregnum'[92] – that he lacked judgement and accuracy. Baxter, still the new boy on the block, would have seemed patronizing and insulting. No wonder they accused him of being supercilious: 'haughtily contemptuous in character or demeanour; having or expressing an air of contemptuous indifference or superiority'.[93] All that Owen might have suspected from Baxter's written style was confirmed by his personal presence as he set about to make himself an irritant. 'When I saw they would not change their Method, I saw also that there was nothing for me and others of my Mind to do, but only to hinder them from doing harm, and trusting in their own Opinions or crude Conceits, among our fundamentals.'[94]

Baxter's account is mostly taken up with one issue that can serve as an example of the extensive discussion around '[m]any other such crude and unsound passages'.[95] Owen wanted to begin with the conviction that 'no man could know God to Salvation by any other means' than Scripture.[96] This reflected the first

---

[89]   Quoted in Lim, *Purity and Unity*, 162.
[90]   *Rel. Bax.*, ii.199.
[91]   Ibid., 198.
[92]   Keeble, 'Orthodoxy and Heresy in the Baxterian Tradition', 284.
[93]   Leslie Brown, ed., *The New Shorter Oxford English Dictionary on Historical Principles* (Oxford: Clarendon Press, 1993), ii.3146.
[94]   *Rel. Bax.*, ii.199.
[95]   Ibid.
[96]   Ibid.

of the 1652 proposals: 'That the holy Scripture is that rule of knowing God, and living unto him, which who so doth not believe, but betakes himself to any other way of discovering truth, and the minde of God instead thereof, cannot be saved.'[97] Baxter was horrified. What about those who believed before the Scriptures were written? What about those in remote places who relied on oral tradition? 'After a deal of wrangling about these things' Baxter, apparently feeling both ill and outnumbered, asked if he might put his objections in writing. He did. And they apparently ignored it. This was a typical pattern: Baxter claiming ill health or perhaps retreating behind the excuse of it;[98] and writing a paper of which no one took any notice.[99]

In fact, Baxter's piece was not entirely disregarded: 'After this Paper they new worded the Article.'[100] It now read, 'All the means of Revealing Jesus Christ are subordinate and subservient to the Holy Scriptures; and none of them co-ordinate.' On the one hand that choice of language was a world away from the scriptural sufficiency Baxter held to. But on the other, it seems to indicate at least some concession to his perspective on the principle it conveyed, since it allowed for other means of salvation apart from Scripture. And the two sides might have come closer to agreement than Baxter allowed in 1664. He claimed in a second paper written at the time of the assembly for the purposes of critiquing the new wording that 'we thought that all had been brought to Agreement'.[101] It may have been that Owen had manipulated the discussion back into a shape with which he was more comfortable. Or it may be that Baxter failed to see the way in which his fellow ministers were trying to give some concession to what he was saying. Whatever the case, Baxter again retreated from open discussion to written words in that second paper.[102] He regretted that he again had cause to delay proceedings; he exposed the absurdity of the new wording, as he saw it; and he offered a heartfelt description of his motives:

> I earnestly crave that the offering of these Reasons, as my Dissent, may not be offensive
> to you; seeing I apprehend the Case to impose on me a Necessity; there being no
> Means in the world (that I remember) more like to be an Engine to tear in pieces
> the Church, than an unsound composure of Fundamentals; I mean, as Imposing of
> those things as Fundamental which are not sound; whereby the most deserving may
> be ejected from the Ministry, and censured to Damnation. We are framing a means

---

[97]   Owen et al., *Humble Proposals*, 5.

[98]   See Cooper, 'Richard Baxter and his Physicians', 3.

[99]   Baxter included the paper in his autobiography. See *Rel. Bax.*, ii.200–203.

[100]   *Rel. Bax.*, ii.203.

[101]   Ibid.

[102]   Ibid., 203–5.

of Union, not of Division. And though it grieves me to be offensive to my Brethren, yet I had rather suffer any thing in the World, than be guilty of putting among our Fundamentals one word that is not true.[103]

That is a very important quote. It clearly distils how the 1654 assembly exquisitely exposed the differences in the agendas between Baxter and Owen. The issue of the fundamentals of religion so narrowed, focused and concentrated their disagreement on this one issue – like sunlight through a lens – as to cause a searing heat, if not outright conflagration. Both men were seeking unity, but their preferred means were opposed. Baxter could never allow one word beyond that of Scripture, the only basis for agreed truth. For that reason he saw the entire project as a means of division, not the work towards unity it was meant to be. It is a strange irony that Baxter's passionate concern for unity forced him into a singular disunity with his fellow divines.

In the end he was overruled. The Scriptures were, in the final wording of the assembly, 'the Word of God, and the only Rule of knowing him savingly, and living unto him in all holiness and righteousness, in which we must rest; which Scriptures, who so doth not believe but rejecting them, doth instead thereof betake himself to any other way of discovering the mind of God, cannot be saved'.[104] And Baxter fared little better on all the other issues he fought on. He managed to prevent Sidrach Simpson's notion ('He that alloweth himself or others in any known sin, cannot be saved') from being included in the fundamentals, but that was about his only victory. 'Other Exceptions there were: but they would have their way, and my opposition to any thing did but heighten their Resolution.'[105] That was about the sum of it. By the end of the proceedings Baxter had lost influence and credibility with his endless quibbles. At one stage he even attempted some sort of joke that fell badly flat, since it vaguely insulted the Congregationalists. They 'marvelled what I meant'.[106] So the proposals submitted by the ministers would have pleased Owen, but not Baxter, who would have been quietly relieved when 'the Parliament was dissolved' in January 1655 'and all came to nothing'.[107]

---

[103]   Ibid., 204.

[104]   The principles were never published as such, but 300 copies were made for MPs. Parliament strictly ordered that only the Members should see it (*CJ*, 12 December 1654, vii.399). Fortunately, George Thomason laid his hands on one. It is informally titled 'A New Confession of Faith', Thomason Tracts E 826(3).

[105]   *Rel. Bax.*, ii.199.

[106]   Ibid.

[107]   Ibid., 205. For a summary of the progress of the proposals up until the point of dissolution, see Worden, 'Toleration and the Cromwellian Protectorate', 219; and Shaw, *History of*

The assembly of the ministers was just one more missed opportunity at producing anything like a settlement of religion, but it did a great deal of damage to the already fragile relationship between Owen and Baxter, and we will see in the next chapter how their public writings took on a new aura of contempt after 1654. There is no specific evidence of what Owen thought of Baxter's behaviour in the committee though his constant contradictions would indubitably have grated on Owen, a man not inclined to receive contradiction graciously. But there is evidence of what Baxter thought of Owen, even if he did not mention him by name. In the preface of his *Confession* of 1655 he claimed the 'most destructive engine ... that ever was used to divide that Church, were Humane, superfluous, and questionable Rules, in imposed Confessions, intended by proud and ignorant men, for the Unity of that Church, and the security of the Truth'.[108] When Baxter wrote in 1656 to the MP Edward Harley with his ideas for church settlement, he included 'a covert reference' to 1654 that exposed what he saw as a hidden agenda.[109] 'I have observed some leading men that are for Toleration' to depart from Scripture sufficiency and devise 'many nicetyes and controverted points ... and at last I suspected, it was to undoe all by overdoing; and to force able sober men to seeke for Toleration'.[110] In the *Reformed Pastor* of 1656 he criticized those who followed the dictates of party; who copied the Papists' example of establishing 'new fundamentals'; who 'look not only after new discoveries in lesser things, but they are making us new articles of faith, and framing out new ways tó heaven'; and who question the orthodoxy of those who differ from them by wielding unthinking, unworthy labels.[111] He also cloaked his disgust in a Latin quote from the fifth-century work of Vincent of Lérins, the *Commonitory for the Antiquity and Universality of the Catholic Faith Against the Profane Novelties of All Heresies*:

> I cannot sufficiently wonder at the madness of certain men, at the impiety of their blinded understanding, at their lust of error, such that, not content with the rule of faith delivered once for all, and received from the times of old, they are everyday seeking one novelty after another, and are constantly longing to add, change, take away, in religion, as though the doctrine 'Let what has once for all been revealed suffice' were

---

the *English Church*, ii.86–92.

[108] Baxter, *Confession*, Preface, sig. b3v.

[109] *CCRB*, p. 223.

[110] Baxter to Edward Harley, 15 September 1656: DWL MS *BC* i.226v (*CCRB* #324).

[111] Baxter, *Reformed Pastor* (1656): *Practical Works*, Preface, iv.410, 411.

not a heavenly but an earthly rule – a rule which could not be complied with except by continual emendation, nay, rather by continual fault-finding [or, correction].[112]

It is another irony that at least some among Vincent's intended targets were semi-Pelagians and Nestorians, and quite the opposite in their views from Owen. He would have been appalled by the allusion. Yet even that was not the end of it. In 1658 Baxter again publicly criticized those 'proud men' who 'thrust their own Opinions into the Churches Creed, and un-Church all that hold not such Opinion', thereby 'lacerating the Churches'.[113] But the strongest words were those of 1655. With the 1654 committee still fresh in his mind, and in the context of those 'proud and ignorant men' with their 'questionable Rules', Baxter claimed 'I have judged it my duty to promote as much as I could, Christs means for our recovery, and to oppose as much as I could the Enemies designs and endeavours for our ruine'.[114] That is exactly what Baxter had come to believe. Yes, England needed a new confession of faith. But in his 'blinde zeal',[115] in his departure from Scripture sufficiency, and by insisting on his own dubious ideas, Owen was simply doing the devil's work.

Assessing Their Actions

Neither the plans of Owen nor the plans of Baxter came to fruition during the 1650s. England never did find that long-sought-for permanent settlement in religion. The church remained a divided thing. In June 1656 Baxter despaired at any prospect of unity: 'I have looked every way for a remedy and can find none.' He had given up any hope of anything beyond a 'smal imperfect closure', and

---

[112]   Ibid., 410–411. The translation is taken from Vincent of Lérins, *A Commonitory for the Antiquity and Universality of the Catholic Faith Against the Profane Novelties of All Heresies*, trans. C.A. Heurtley, in *A Select Library of Nicene and Post-Nicene Fathers of the Christian Church*, 2nd ser., ed. Philip Schaff and Henry Wace, vol. xi (Edinburgh: T&T Clark, reprint 1991), 146. The original Latin is 'Mirarisatisnequeotantumquorundumhominumvaesanium, tantamexcoecatae mentis impietatem; tantampostremo errand libidinem, utcontenti non sinttraditasemel et acceptaantiquitus credenda regula; sed nova ac nova in diem querunt, semperquealiquidgestantreligioniaddere, mutare, detrahere: quasi non coeleste dogma sit quod semelrevelatumessesufficiat, sedterrenaintitutio, quae aliterperfici nisi assiduaemendationae, immorpotiusreprehensione non posit'. I am grateful to my former colleague, Professor Ivor Davidson, for his help in tracking down the original source.

[113]   Baxter, *Judgment and Advice*, 4.

[114]   Baxter, *Confession*, Preface, sig. b3v.

[115]   Ibid.

even that seemed impossibly distant.[116] Writing to Edward Harley in September 1656 he explained how his experience of the Worcester Association proved it was 'no impossible worke' to bring the parties together in unity, but there was no immediate prospect of a national assembly resolving matters: 'at present I feare they would be so divided amonge themselves' that a convocation 'would rather widen than close the wound'.[117] Things looked bleak, then. The Humble Petition and Advice of 1657 promised a confession of faith, but it never came.[118] A year later Baxter was still calling for 'a Profession of the Christian Faith; That which we require to prove a single person fit to be a member of the Church'.[119] No doubt Owen would have desired the same thing, if in different terms, but by 1658 his influence and his hopes were receding. In a sermon to the second Protectorate Parliament in 1656 he discerned England to be still in the wilderness, still on its way to the Promised Land. 'In the last assembly of Parliament' the cloud rested over the tabernacle rather than guiding the people on, so 'that they could not see how to take one step forward'.[120] Even that second assembly would disappoint him. Yet he claimed to have hope. In 1657 he had his plans for unity between the Presbyterians and the Congregationalists that 'I may offer, ere long'.[121] And in the following year: 'I am not yet without hopes of seeing a fair coalescency in love and church-communion between the reforming Presbyterians and Independents.'[122] It was not to be.

The 1654 assembly itself was not a failure. It was merely – in the scheme of things and in terms of tangible progress – irrelevant. The ministers succeeded in drafting a new confession of faith, and who can say how it might have fared if not for the dissolution of Parliament. Yet it was one more step in the greater failure to reach a religious settlement during the 1650s and in itself it did little to foster mutual understanding and amity among the differing parties. How, then, should we evaluate the contribution of Owen and Baxter to the outcome?

Perhaps surprisingly, given that most of what we have was supplied to us by Baxter, there is little evidence of Owen's manipulation of the assembly. But we should not be so naive as to think that it did not go on. Owen was 'politically

---

[116]   Baxter to John Lewis, 25 June 1656: DWL MS *BC* ii.126r (*CCRB* #315).

[117]   Baxter to Edward Harley, 15 September 1656: DWL MS *BC* i.226r (*CCRB* #324).

[118]   Gardiner, ed., *Constitutional Documents of the Puritan Revolution*, 454; Worden, 'Toleration and the Cromwellian Protectorate', 227; Shaw, *History of the English Church*, i.366, ii.94ff.

[119]   Baxter, *Judgment and Advice*, 4.

[120]   Owen, *God's Presence with a People the Spring of their Prosperity* (1656): *Works*, viii.441–2.

[121]   Owen, *Review of the True Nature of Schism* (1657): *Works*, xiii.258.

[122]   Owen, *Answer to a Late Treatise of Mr Cawdrey about the Nature of Schism* (1657): *Works*, xiii.296.

the most influential clergyman of the 1650s'.[123] The draft confession was exactly what he wanted. There are much clearer examples of Owen employing questionable tactics to achieve his ends and we might assume he orchestrated similar machinations here as the need arose. Perhaps he was responsible for the re-worded first proposal just as Baxter felt they had all reached an agreement, one that Baxter was bound to dislike. We have also seen Owen make some claims about his previous positions that are dubious at best.[124] While he could no doubt rationalize such claims, it was not always possible to trust what he said. For what it is worth, Baxter did present Owen as the 'great doer of all that worded the Articles', and 'the hotter, and better befriended in that Assembly'.[125] In his account of the proceedings Baxter made a comment in the manuscript that he later crossed out. Having called Owen the 'great doer', he said in brackets that Owen was 'a man whom I will give no character of, because he hath written so much against me, that I take myself to be unmeet for that action'.[126] This restraint may have prevented Baxter from offering more specific evidence of Owen's handling of the assembly. What evidence we have may be tainted, partial or circumstantial, then, but we can assume that Owen engineered events to his own ends as far as possible.

Even so, it is Baxter who comes off so badly in 1654 and it is easy to see why he would have proved such an irritation to Owen. Two other anecdotes will help to illustrate this. First, a short time after the assembly, Cromwell invited Baxter to speak with him on two occasions about liberty of conscience. Baxter felt that both meetings were a tedious waste of his precious time and he proposed that 'two sheets' would do the work of 'many days' spent in such pointless discourse. Cromwell 'received the paper after, but I scarce believe that he ever saw it'.[127] If we are keeping count, this is the fifth time during the 1650s that Baxter fell back on written proposals – he placed them in the hands of George Griffith;[128] Philip Nye;[129] some unnamed Congregationalists;[130] the assembly of ministers; and now Cromwell – and it presents a curious, even slightly dysfunctional pattern. Perhaps a retreat to the written word was a necessary way for Baxter to

---

123   Worden, 'Toleration and the Cromwellian Protectorate', 207.

124   I have in mind the claim that he did not change his principles in his move to Congregationalism, and that he did not plead for the Presbyterians in 1646. See above, pp. 157–60, 163.

125   *Rel. Bax.*, ii.198, 199.

126   DWL MS *BT* iii.114r, item #62(2).

127   *Rel. Bax.*, ii.205.

128   Ibid., ii.193, iii.61.

129   Ibid., ii.188.

130   Ibid., ii. 193.

overcome those isolating factors in his life, and it played to his strengths. Or, to put that another way, maybe it reflects his inadequacy in person. He simply was not equipped to bring people to his point of view because it was so entrenched, because he lacked an easy political facility, because he could not help but convey a scornful arrogance. What he never recognized, it seems, is how utterly unsuccessful this strategy was. Putting his thoughts on paper gave people the time and space to ignore them. In none of these instances did he get the result that he wanted. In 1668 he would employ exactly the same tactic with Owen, with exactly the same outcome.[131] Baxter's abilities were ill-suited to politics and not well matched to the art of the possible, and to that extent he was not a very helpful or constructive player in negotiations of a political nature.

That is borne out in a second anecdote some six years later. In the wake of the Restoration the Presbyterians debated among themselves what sort of settlement they hoped to obtain from the new King. In his later work of history,[132] Gilbert Burnet regretted that they gave so much credence to Baxter: he pursued the ideal settlement 'without considering what was like to be obtained, or what effect their demanding so much might have in irritating the minds of those [the Anglicans] who were then the superior body in strength and number'. At the Savoy Conference that quickly followed, the Presbyterians then debated with the Anglicans on the issue of whether to exclude from communion those who did not kneel at the sacrament. Here, Baxter represented the Presbyterians; Peter Gunning (then Master of St John's College, Cambridge) the Anglicans. Burnet could hardly think of a worse choice. They 'were the most unfit to heal matters, and the fittest to widen them, that could have been found out'. '*Baxter* and he spent some days in much logical arguing, to the derision of the town, who thought they were a couple of fencers engaged in disputes, that could never be brought to an end, nor have any good effect.' Nothing was achieved before the time was up.[133]

Historians have generally agreed with Burnet's dismal appraisal of Baxter's performance. Robert Bosher concludes that his 'combativeness and voluble self-

---

[131]   Ibid., iii.62.

[132]   He wrote the *History* over three decades, beginning in 1683, and with a substantial rewriting in 1704. See Martin Greig, 'Burnet, Gilbert (1643–1715)', *Oxford Dictionary of National Biography*, Oxford University Press, September 2004; online edn, January 2008 [www.oxforddnb.com/view/article/4061, accessed 15 May 2009].

[133]   Gilbert Burnet, ed., *Bishop Burnet's History of His Own Time*, vol. 1 (London: Thomas Ward, 1724), 207–8. Baxter himself respected Gunning's ability and demeanour. *Rel. Bax.*, ii.364. For a very hostile description of Baxter's 'clownish' actions, see [Samuel Young], *Vindiciae Anti-Baxterianae: Or, Some Animadversions on a Book, Intituled, Reliquiae Baxterianae; Or, the Life of Mr. Richard Baxter* (1696), 126–7.

assertion was [*sic*] highly exasperating to the Anglicans, and militated against any friendly rapprochement between the two parties'.[134] For all his evident sympathy for Baxter, A. Harold Wood agrees.[135] So, too, does E.C. Ratcliff. 'Baxter suffered from defects which made him as awkward an ally as he was a difficult opponent.' Because he had never been to university, he had not been trained in the art of disputation. This, combined with his zeal for the truth as he conceived it, made him too aggressive in debate. 'While, therefore, he sincerely desired accommodation with the bishops, he was not the most likely figure to bring it about, or promote it.'[136] To identify a particular example, the new liturgy offered up by the Presbyterians – crafted by Baxter single-handedly in the space of two weeks – 'offered the bishops nothing which they were able to use', forcing them to promote 'a conservative revision of the Prayer Book'.[137] This example illustrates that Baxter's political missteps were shared and enabled (or at least not resisted) by his colleagues. But there is no mistaking the significance of his own interventions. 'Ecclesiastical politics, like secular, is the art of the possible. Baxter, a visionary, had little conception of the art.'[138] Ratcliff goes so far as to suggest that the two parties just might have reached a compromise (though it would have been stillborn) had Baxter not been a member of the delegates.[139] Anne Whiteman aptly identifies the problem of Baxter's political incapacities:

> It would be difficult to find a sadder example of misapplied zeal than Baxter's determination to strive with the Anglicans almost single-handed in these discussions … A man with a more flexible political sense must have grasped that whatever wider concessions might have been hoped for at an earlier stage in the negotiations, Anglican fortunes had now risen so decisively that there was no longer any question of attaining the Puritan ideal; it was merely a matter of what could be salvaged from the wreck of their hopes … Baxter's burning sincerity and indefatigable spirit, merits though they were, were less useful to the Puritans at this juncture than political suavity and *finesse* could have been.[140]

---

[134]   Robert S. Bosher, *The Making of the Restoration Settlement: The Influence of the Laudians 1649–1662* (London: Dacre Press, 1951), 229–30.

[135]   Wood, *Church Unity Without Uniformity*, 173–4, 212.

[136]   E.C. Ratcliff, 'The Savoy Conference and the Revision of the Book of Common Prayer', in *From Uniformity to Unity 1662–1962*, ed. Geoffrey F. Nuttall and Owen Chadwick (London: SPCK, 1962), 108–9.

[137]   Ibid., 125.

[138]   Ibid., 127.

[139]   Ibid.

[140]   Whiteman, 'Restoration of the Church of England', 77–8. See also, p. 84: the Presbyterians 'were certainly unfortunate in that no clerical leader with first-rate political capacity

It is not as though Baxter was alone in this. For example, A.H. Drysdale made the point that the leaders of the Westminster Assembly had earlier pressed for too much in the circumstances: they 'were better divines than tacticians'.[141] But Baxter offers a distinctive and notable example of this tendency. He held out for the ideal even when it was impossible, and because he refused to abandon a point of principle he was incapable of delivering anything substantial in practice.

The same was true in 1654. Baxter may have shown an ability to compromise in places, but some things he would not see in any other way than his own. 'It is easy to see', says John Coffey, 'why Owen and his colleagues found [Baxter] frustrating in 1654 – they were not, after all, drafting a basis of faith for the World Council of Churches, but for the Reformed Church of England, an evangelical Protestant institution'.[142] Would it really, in practice, have been that harmful to church unity to draft a confession in language that went beyond Scripture? Could that credibly be called the devil's work? Was it not preferable to have that confession in place, though hardly ideal, than to have none at all? Baxter never seems to have allowed these kinds of questions. For someone who claimed to accept that peace was impossible in this world he was not prepared to accept something less than perfect while he remained within it. Thus he was working to his own agenda just as much as Owen was. It is just that Owen was better at it.

Another example of Baxter's fixed perspective in all this was his diagnosis of England's ills and the twin problem of party and perspective. It is not that his diagnosis was gravely mistaken – others came to the same conclusion and there is still much to commend it. The problem was that Baxter struggled to see beyond it. If he observed something he disagreed with, it was all too easy to ascribe that to party interest. So as he looked back on the events of 1654 he thought he saw 'the tincture of Faction' that 'hindered their Judgment'.[143] No doubt Owen was acting with any eye to the interests and concerns of the Congregationalists, but we should also bear in mind Michael Lawrence's welcome correction: Owen was

---

emerged from their ranks'.

[141] Drysdale, *History of the Presbyterians in England*, 347. Drysdale sees Baxter as a figure of compromise in 1660, joining other Presbyterians in seeing that a place for episcopacy was necessary (p. 374); but Baxter was always comfortable with a reduced episcopacy and would demonstrate no compromise on the narrower issues that he considered essential. Geoffrey Nuttall accepts this negative picture of Baxter but points out the difficulty of the context and the inevitability of the outcome, in *Richard Baxter*, 89–90. Likewise, Walter Douglas is sympathetic to Baxter, but also concedes that he could be an 'embarrassment' even to his colleagues at the Savoy. Walter B.T. Douglas, 'Richard Baxter and the Savoy Conference of 1661', PhD Thesis, Manchester University, 1972, 134, 185.

[142] Coffey, 'A Ticklish Business', 128.

[143] *Rel. Bax.*, ii.198.

also pursuing what he felt to be the good of the godly as a whole.[144] And he did not have a majority among the members of the assembly. There were, as far as we can make out, at least as many Presbyterians as Congregationalists, if not more, so the outcome of the deliberations cannot be judged solely as a work in party politics. But Baxter failed to see that and he seemed to disregard the other, more senior Presbyterian figures. Stephen Marshall, for example, was entering the last year of his life, one marked by considerable political acumen, moderate leadership, judicious pragmatism and service to the cause of unity going back 20 years and more.[145] And Thomas Manton, by then 'the principal Presbyterian voice on protectorate committees',[146] was well on his way to becoming 'one of the greatest divines among the Presbyterians. His industry and learning, his talent as a preacher, his moderation, his activity and learning and address in the management of their public affairs, in all which he was a leading man, are mentioned with respect, by several writers'.[147] These were not men to be easily walked on. In dismissing them, Baxter failed to register just how much on a limb he was. No doubt Owen's actions gave him every encouragement to read the management of the assembly as an exercise in power, but his conclusion reveals more about Baxter's own preconceptions and blinkered perspective than it does about any manipulation by Owen. Historians have routinely relied on Baxter's interpretation of 1654, in which Owen played the part of the villain. The truth is not nearly so clearly cut, and it is time that Baxter himself is seen to be also at fault in these proceedings. Neither one made things easy for the other.

What we see in 1654, then, is an unfortunate combination of factors. First, there was the force of historical events. Owen and Baxter met for the first time in the most unhelpful of circumstances. Rather than meeting in conditions conducive to highlighting the many ways in which they shared the same assumptions and priorities, they were confronted with one of the few points of intense and principled disagreement between them. The similarities brought them together, since they both wanted an authorized confession of faith, but the points of difference drove them apart. It was the similarities that made the

---

[144]   Lawrence, 'Transmission and Transformation', 150, 149, 151.

[145]   See Tom Webster, 'Marshall, Stephen (1594/5?–1655)', *Oxford Dictionary of National Biography*, Oxford University Press, September 2004; online edn, October 2007 [www.oxforddnb.com/view/article/18148, accessed 15 May 2009].

[146]   E.C. Vernon, 'Manton, Thomas (*bap.* 1620, *d.* 1677)', *Oxford Dictionary of National Biography*, Oxford University Press, September 2004; online edn, May 2008 [www.oxforddnb.com/view/article/18009, accessed 15 May 2009].

[147]   James Grainger, *A Biographical History of England* (London: T. Davies, 1769), ii., part 1, p. 210. Manton was five years younger than Baxter but more prominent, especially within London Presbyterian circles.

differences so important, heated and divisive. But that is in part the product of historical circumstances. The precise way in which events played out hindered any mutual understanding and served only to exacerbate conflict. But that, too, might have been ameliorated if different personalities had been involved. Meeting together in the same physical space inevitably brought out the personality clash. It was there in the writings, to be sure, but so much more potent in person. In fact, meeting each other (in these circumstances) quickly confirmed the worst of their prior suspicions and perceptions. But there also were, finally, genuine theological differences. They may have been relatively narrow in scope, at least compared to the broad areas of overlap and commonality, but they proved insurmountable. While the assembly managed to agree, at least by majority, on a new confession, Owen and Baxter did not come to any sort of agreement. The pressure cooker environment further soured their relationship. And that new tone of hostility was evident when further conflict broke out between them just a few months later. We turn to that next.

Chapter 7

Silence and Speech

I purposed to have said nothing to this Reverend Brother Doctor *Owen*; but ...

Richard Baxter (1655)[1]

I was in some hope to have escaped this trouble ... I must profess my thoughts arose only from his long silence.

John Owen (1655)[2]

In April 1655 Francis Tallents ventured his opinion on the gulf between Owen and Baxter: 'I conceive it not so wide as it appears in your dispute but that in the Maine you in effect agree.'[3] Tallents was not far wrong. As we have seen, for all the controversy between the two men there was a lot of common ground. It is an important point to which, in this chapter, we will return. Baxter's reply, coming some months later in January 1656, was brief, measured and faintly defensive:

> So much the better as to the thing: And if you had instanced in any words of mine where I wrong him, I should have reviewed them, that I might have reversed them: If you refer mee to his owne discourses, I say, I shall make as good use of them as I can, but I have not the felicity or facility of believing all that good and learned men expect I should believe.[4]

This is not the issue that Tallents had broached, but what Baxter knew in April 1655 – and Tallents probably did not – is that he had recently added to the number of those 'words of mine'. And by the time he replied, Owen had issued his response. No wonder Baxter sounded so sullen. Here we will consider this new round of public sparring.

Stung by Owen's *Death of Christ* in 1650 Baxter had lapsed into significant silence, but the argument between them was merely suspended. He broke his silence, such as it was, with the publication of his *Confession of his Faith* in 1655. In the meantime, of course, just a few months earlier, the two men had met

---

[1]   Baxter, *Confession*, Preface, sig. e1.

[2]   Owen, *Death of Christ and of Justification* (1655): *Works*, xii.591, 592.

[3]   Fra[ncis] Tallents to Richard Baxter, 24 April 1655: DWL MS *BC* ii.161r (*CCRB* #243).

[4]   Baxter to Francis Tallents, 7 January 1655[/6]: DWL MS *BC* ii.169v (*CCRB* #286).

for the first time in a context that had served to worsen their already fragile relationship. Those events lent a new tone of hostility in this second round of soteriological dispute. The added contempt stemmed as much from Owen's unfortunate firsthand experience of Baxter's temperament as from this fresh frustration at having to answer questions he felt he had fully answered some years ago. And Baxter, who lacked the capacity to let sleeping dogs lie, felt the backlash of one who was in his view far too easily exasperated. The exchange was edifying for neither party.

Once again this chapter risks presenting the two men as if they existed in a world of their own. They certainly did not. Inasmuch as there is no avoiding a close examination of their printed exchange in the years from 1655 to 1657, there is also no ignoring the wider world in which they each believed the stakes of their argument were very high indeed. The essential differences between them had not changed and those issues tied into much broader debates and concerns. For a start, the question of exactly when the believer became justified in the sight of God – from all eternity or at the point of conversion – was a source of tension even among the Westminster divines. Justification from eternity was an Antinomian position, but that did not prevent some of the divines from arguing for it against the majority. Chad van Dixhoorn suggests that Antinomianism was a much greater and more immediate fear in the Assembly even than Catholicism, thus 'Baxter-like theological concerns, taken broadly, [were] uppermost'.[5] Indeed, the Assembly concluded that believers 'are not justified, untill the holy Spirit doth in due time, actually apply Christ unto them'.[6] But this hardly stopped Antinomianism in its tracks, nor did it prevent Baxter from fretting about it. Even if his anti-Antinomian concern was at last beginning to subside by 1655 there was no conceivable prospect of his giving ground to any author who seemed to argue for justification from eternity.[7] So as he came around publicly to clarify his soteriological convictions in the turbulent wake of the *Aphorismes* he was confronted by a still-pressing need to address this question in strong terms.

At the same time, Owen and his allies had become 'genuinely anxious about the spread of Socinian ideas – and there was some truth in their fears'.[8] Socinianism had been rearticulated in order to enhance its appeal for orthodox

---

[5]   Chad van Dixhoorn, 'The Strange Silence of Prolocutor Twisse: Predestination and Politics in the Westminster Assembly's Debate over Justification', *Sixteenth Century Journal* 40 (2009): 405–6.

[6]   *The Confession of Faith and Catechisms, Agreed upon by the Assembly of Divines at Westminster* (1649), xi.4 [pp. 26–7].

[7]   For the subsidence of Baxter's concern around 1655, see Cooper, *Fear and Polemic*, 135–6.

[8]   Mortimer, *Reason and Religion*, 205.

Protestants, which only amplified the threat.[9] Owen was worried about 'the new vogue' for historicizing theology represented especially by Hugo Grotius's *Annotationes*, essentially a compilation of commentaries on all the books of the Bible that served to show that God's revelation was changeable across time.[10] They were published in England during the 1640s and they enjoyed significant success and influence within the intellectual climate of the 1650s.[11] Henry Hammond, to offer the most relevant example for this chapter, had been part of the Great Tew Circle in the 1630s. He still held to the doctrine of the Trinity, but he also worked along the same lines as Grotius and Socinus in seeing the teaching of Christ as a new revelation.[12] Preferring to push human responsibility and godly living, Hammond also denied that faith was a free gift of God. 'By the 1650s, that model was losing its grip both in England and on the continent, and Hammond's writing was helping to ensure that it would be replaced by one in which the agency of humans played a much greater part.'[13] So we should not be at all surprised to see Owen lining up Grotius, Hammond and Baxter for attack.[14] They were in his mind part of the same broad trend. His renewed attack on Baxter was not just the personal pique that it might seem – much more hung in the balance.

And Owen was far from alone in his concern. The Scottish Presbyterian, Robert Baillie, for instance, held grave fears about Baxter's orthodoxy and influence. In 1655 he worried that Baxter's *Confession* 'seems to be stuffed with grosse Arminianisme'. He urged that something be done to bring him to heel.[15] Baillie's correspondent, the Presbyterian minister Simeon Ashe, replied with the news that despite the attempts of Anthony Burgess and Richard Vines, Baxter remained 'tenacious in his mistakes'.[16] Three years later nothing had changed. Baillie urged that someone, anyone, would take Baxter 'to task in all his errors, which truely he has a way to insinuate more than any heterodox I know in this side of the sea. I entreat that some of yow would advise how to get this dangerous

---

[9]   Ibid., 206.

[10]   Ibid., 209, 122–3.

[11]   Ibid., 228.

[12]   Ibid., 125–6.

[13]   Ibid., 127.

[14]   Smith, 'Best, Biddle and Anti-Trinitarian Heresy', 172.

[15]   Robert Baillie to Simeon Ashe, 31 December 1655: David Laing, ed. *The Letters and Journals of Robert Baillie, A.M. Principal of the University of Glasgow* (Edinburgh: Robert Ogle, 1842), iii.304.

[16]   Simeon Ashe to Robert Baillie [January 1656]: Laing, ed., *Letters and Journals of Robert Baillie*, iii.307.

evill remeded [*sic*], at leist stopped'.[17] It was not just Congregationalists like Owen who fretted over Baxter's influence.

This renewed controversy, then, serves several purposes. First, it illuminates this wider context. Second, assessing their respective arguments allows us more fully to understand the theological differences between them and the driving forces that propelled them in opposite directions. Third, the way in which Owen and Baxter conducted themselves in the debate indicates the condition of their relationship by the mid-1650s. Finally, tracking the argument will further enable us to attribute responsibility for the poor repair of that relationship. Even if Owen responded too sharply, it is Baxter who must take the lion's share of the blame for the revival of their controversy. All the least appealing aspects of his dogmatic style showed themselves once again. And, for the second time, it was he who began it, when he chose to break his long singular silence.

Baxter's Cautious Silence: 1650–5

Owen had replied to Baxter in *Death of Christ*, published in 1650. Baxter made no response, at least not until 1655: five years of silence. This is significant, since he was rarely silent on anything, let alone on a topic of such personal urgency as suspected Antinomianism and in the presence of such specific and personal provocation. In his autobiography Baxter categorized those works written against him – at that stage he could count 'about Fifty Books'.[18] 'To many of these I have returned Answers', he explained, 'and that some others remain unanswered, is through the restraint of the press'.[19] It seems Baxter's intention was to reply to every opponent if he possibly could. Yet he chose not to respond to Owen. Baxter's deliberate restraint suggests that he had learned the hard way how dangerous it was to provoke him. Indeed, what little mention he made of Owen in these years was striking in its reserve and respect.

Baxter was willing enough to explain his silence. In the *Reliquiae Baxterianae* he offered another apology for the *Aphorismes of Justification*, in which he saw two main faults. The first involved some infelicitous expression. And the second:

> I medled too forwardly with Dr. *Owen*, and one or two more that had written some passages too near Antinomianism. For I was young, and a stranger to mens tempers, and thought others could have born a Confutation as easily as I could do my self; and

---

17   Robert Baillie to Simeon Ashe, 29 November 1658: Laing, ed., *Letters and Journals of Robert Baillie*, iii.391.

18   *Rel. Bax.*, i.106.

19   Ibid., 107.

I thought that I was bound to do my best publickly, to save the World from the hurt of published Errours; not understanding how it would provoke men more passionately to insist on what they once have said ... But indeed I was then too raw to be a writer.[20]

We might note here Baxter's knack for delivering insults in the guise of a personal confession: the real problem here was Owen's temper and touchiness, not Baxter's demeanour. Even so, he clearly regretted his entanglement with an author seemingly so easily provoked and that regret may be enough in itself to explain Baxter's unwillingness to re-engage. Somewhat burnt by the experience, he decided to leave well enough alone.

This silence was impressive, but not quite total. In 1654 Baxter published his *Account Given to his Reverend Brother Mr T. Blake* (the first part of his *Apology*). In the preface, dated 1 August 1653, Baxter offered three reasons for not replying to Owen. First, he could see that the dispute 'containeth so little matter of reall difference between him and me'. On the first issue of dispute, the *Idem* and *Tantundum*, Owen 'yieldeth as much as I need'. Indeed, Baxter would never again hold that particular issue against Owen. Second, Baxter saw no need to reply. And, third, he was too aware of his 'temerity in being so foolishly drawn to begin with him' and his 'fault in one or two unmannerly words of him'. 'It is not fit', he concluded, 'that I should both begin and end'.[21] Baxter also briefly touched on Owen in his *Admonition to Mr William Eyre* (the fourth part of his *Apology*), but only because Eyre had declared Owen the victor in the dispute between them. Baxter repeated his reluctance to reply; while acknowledging Owen's superior wit and learning, he declared the truth to be on his side; and he regretted that Eyre had forced him to say even 'this much, which else I would not have said, least I should exasperate'.[22] It was another indication that Baxter might have learned his lesson in so confidently entangling himself with Owen. His reticence here is especially impressive, since Eyre's book had come with a preface from Owen in which he lamented 'too great evidence of very welcome entertainment, and acceptance, given by many to an almost pure *Socinian Justification* and *Exposition of the Covenant of Grace*'.[23] Baxter felt that Owen was referring to him, and he probably was.[24] If so, Owen had just accused him of an almost-Socinianism. Yet Baxter chose not to pick up on the slight, at

---

[20]   Ibid.

[21]   Baxter, *Rich. Baxters Account*, Preface, sig. A4r. In *Rich. Baxters Apology*.

[22]   Baxter, *Admonition to Mr. William Eyre*, 36. In *Rich. Baxters Apology*.

[23]   Eyre, *Vindiciae Justificationis Gratutiae*, Owen's Preface.

[24]   Baxter, *Confession*, Preface, sig. e1. Owen would develop the Socinian accusation in *Death of Christ and of Justification* (1655): *Works*, xii.594–5, 597–602.

least here in his reply to Eyre.[25] He was extremely cautious about what he said of Owen. The lengths to which he went to avoid further exasperation are really quite remarkable.

The issue also cropped up in private correspondence where, again, Baxter showed his restraint. In the middle of June 1652 Baxter worked on a reply to John Wallis, Savilian Professor of Geometry at Oxford University and one of those who had sent private and mostly agreeable animadversions on the *Aphorismes*. In the unfinished document Baxter offered the same explanation for his silence: he left Owen's book unanswered 'to avoid any shew of contention', because he 'was foolishly drawne in to be the beginner, and so in Justice I must first desist', and there was no clear call from God or from others to offer up a defence. But the issue – the *Idem* and *Tantundum* – was, *pace* Wallis,[26] and *pace* his later comment to Blake, 'of so exceeding great weight' that he was prepared to justify his disagreement with Owen at length, though he made no further mention of Owen himself.[27] Even in private he could be entirely respectful.

Richard Baxter's *Confession* (1655)

Almost six years on from the *Aphorismes* the debate between Owen and Baxter resurfaced in Baxter's *Confession of his Faith*. The book – nearly 500 pages long – must have appeared either at the very end of December 1654[28] or very early in January 1655,[29] which makes it almost certain that he wrote the book before he met Owen in London.[30] As he explained in his autobiography, Baxter wrote the *Confession* as a substitute for amending his *Aphorismes*. He had intended 'only to correct two or three passages and elucidate the rest', but this new project blossomed into a massive restatement of his doctrinal convictions at the same time as he 'opened the whole Doctrine of Antinomianism'.[31] The two main

---

[25]   Baxter finally responded to Owen's assertion in *Confession*, Preface, sig. e1r–v.

[26]   He said the question was not 'of any great consequence' and unlike Baxter he dealt with it very briefly. DWL MS *BT*, ii.27v, item #21(2). Wallis did not respond to the Appendix so he did not mention Baxter's critique of Owen in particular. See f.42.

[27]   DWL MS *BT*, ii.13r, item #21(2).

[28]   That is, after the assembly of ministers had dispersed, since Owen did not know of it during their sessions. See Owen, *Death of Christ and of Justification* (1655): *Works*, xii.592.

[29]   George Thomason added it to his collection on 8 January and changed the publication date on the title page from 1655 to 1654. See *Thomason Tracts*, ii.98.

[30]   In fact, Baxter claimed to have written his *Confession* before Owen was made a Doctor of Divinity. Baxter, *Certain Disputations*, 485. The title was conferred on 23 December 1653. [Anon.], 'Life of John Owen', xvi.

[31]   *Rel. Bax.*, i.111.

targets in Baxter's view were William Eyre and John Crandon; their paired names were mentioned frequently throughout the text. Yet there were several places where Owen was almost certainly in Baxter's mind even if he was not mentioned by name. Most pertinently, in referring to those critics who had accused Baxter of pride, it 'may be worth their labour to search, how much Pride may lie in their impatiency of contradiction, and making a man an offender for a word, and being such that a man knows not how to speak to them for fear of seeming contumelious, by withdrawing, or not giving them the honour they expect'.[32] Owen surely lay just beneath the surface of a comment like this.

Overt references to Owen were rare and reluctant: Baxter's reserve still held. He dealt with him only because the particular issue at hand gave him no other choice.

> I purposed to have said nothing to this Reverend Brother Doctor *Owen*; but when I came to answer the Arguments for Justification, or Absolution, or Remission before Faith, I found myself engaged to do it, because I knew none that had said so much as he there doth; and because (since the publishing of my Apology) two or three reverend Brethren told me that, as to that part, it was thought necessary.[33]

Even then, Baxter did not refer to Owen at all until page 190, then again on pages 219, 222 and 228.[34] These references were both brief and respectful: Owen was 'the most sober and learned man that I know of, that writes this way'.[35] Clearly Baxter had learned his lesson. And he responded only because a matter of genuine importance was at stake: 'Though I offend, I must say that which cannot be hid.'[36]

The most concentrated engagement with Owen began on page 254, in a section that introduced 20 objections to the doctrine of justification from eternity. 'I shall the rather speak to this Objection, because the late mentioned learned man Mr. *Owen* builds so great a Fabrick on it.'[37] Here Baxter unpicked the second section of *Death of Christ*, in which Owen had denied affirming justification from eternity. Baxter never responded explicitly to Owen's distinction between a real cause (which bore fruit immediately) and a moral cause (which bore fruit at a later time and in a manner of God's choosing), one

---

[32] Baxter, *Confession*, Preface, sig. b4v.

[33] Ibid., sig. e1r–v.

[34] This does not include Baxter's response to Owen's accusation of Socinianism, in the Preface, sig. e1r–v.

[35] Baxter, *Confession*, 219.

[36] Ibid., Preface, sig. d4v.

[37] Baxter, *Confession*, 254. In the original, Owen's name is asterisked in the margin.

of the main planks in his defence, but it is clear that Baxter found it irrelevant. There are two main reasons for this. First, there could be no talk of rights being given to those creatures who were not yet in existence.[38] Second, if any rights were procured, it was Christ's right to dispense pardon, since he was, obviously, in existence at the time.

> If you pay a summe to the Turk for a 1000 slaves, thereby buying them absolution into your own power; I do not believe that they have any more Right to freedom then they had before: though you have [a] Right to free them, if you please. They are now your own; you may do with them as you will. Or if you resolve to free them, that gives them no Right.[39]

More than that, it 'was not that I Merited but Christ, and I am no further under it, then to partake of the Fruits of it, and that is by Degrees, in what time and measure he seeth meet to give them out to me: which is not all at once, nor all perfectly, till another world'.[40] These words drifted close to Owen's discussion of real and moral causes, but Baxter skirted that to return to the progressive justification outlined in the *Aphorismes* and to his fundamental objection to the Antinomians. Here Baxter could quote Owen's own language that Christ 'Merited on their behalf [the elect]: Yea, in their stead, they dying with him'.[41] Such words sent a shudder down Baxter's spine: 'Here is the heart of the whole Controversie, and (if I may have leave to speak as confidently as your self,) the Root of many dangerous errors, I think very plainly subverting the Christian Religion'.[42] The unspoken word, 'Antinomian', can be heard distinctly.

Indeed, that was increasingly the drift of Baxter's argument though he came as close as he possibly could without having to make the accusation explicit. In an adept manoeuvre, Baxter extended Owen's argument for him. He linked the merit earned for the elect by Christ at the Cross to a pardon or absolution similarly earned for them in the eternal decree between the Father and the Son infallibly to save the elect. This move widened the grounds on which Owen might be accused of Antinomianism, since it shifted a justification from the Cross towards a justification from eternity, and immediately Baxter became carried away by extending the logic (absurdly) towards other relations: 'Was *Edward* the 6*th* King of *England*, or *Elizabeth* Queen from the time of Christs death? Or was Mr. *O*. Mr *E*. Mr. *C*. or any now living, a pastor of a Church

---

38   Ibid., 260, 267.
39   Ibid., 262.
40   Ibid., 265.
41   Ibid., 266, quoting Owen, *Death of Christ* (1650): *Works*, x.468.
42   Ibid., 266.

when Christ dyed? I hope none will say that God decreed not these, or that Christ merited them not?'[43] This was the only place in the book when Baxter grouped Eyre, Crandon and Owen together. Perhaps realizing he had gone too far, he took a step back. 'I put both together [that is, both Christ's death and the decree] because I deal with men that somewhat differ. Some [that is, Owen] do not so openly or plainly own the Eternity of Absolution as others do.'[44] Whether Owen did, 'I am uncertain: By some passages I should hope better: but these words' – a further quote – 'make me doubtful'.[45] Yet the effect was the same. In the remainder of the section, Owen was implicitly taken to hold justification from eternity.

That quote was the last time Baxter drew explicitly on *Death of Christ* but it would have been very easy for the reader to miss the change. Initially he continued to speak as if he were addressing Owen,[46] but his discussion steadily aligned itself into a hammering away at the consequences of what he had just taken to be Owen's position. The common formula is this: 'If we are Justified, Absolved, or pardoned, and have right to heaven, from eternity, or from the time of Christs undertaking or suffering, or before our Conversion, then ... But the Consequent is purely Antinomian: therefore so is the Antecedent.'[47] At the very least, it was not clear that Baxter had ceased to include Owen, and the words 'as aforesaid' were often inserted into this formula to encourage the reminder. So the discussion proceeded for some 20 pages as Baxter drew out the implications of justification from eternity as he perceived them. 'And thus', he concluded at the beginning of the next section, 'I have shown you somewhat of the face of these Doctrines of the Antinomians.'[48]

Two final observations on this exchange are pertinent. First, Baxter explicitly disagreed with Owen that the dispute between them was simply a matter of words rather than substance.[49] Something far more important was at stake. Second, Baxter's tone was extremely respectful, though he was not above the odd moment of insult and irony. In a marginal comment he exclaimed, 'If you could make the Lawyers believe this strange Doctrine, you would make a great change in *England*'. He quietly mocked Owen's use of an evasive and open-ended loophole, 'in some sense or other'. And he mimicked one of Owen's own

---

[43] Ibid., 268.
[44] Ibid.
[45] Ibid.
[46] Ibid., 269.
[47] Ibid., 281.
[48] Ibid., 289.
[49] Ibid., 228. 'By this much it may be gathered where our difference lyeth in sense, as well as terms'.

accusations against him: 'It might easily have been foreseen that somebody in the world would require better proof of this then bare affirmation.' This comment revealed that Baxter had taken due note of Owen's insults.[50] But all these instances appeared on a single page.[51] In the main, Owen could have few complaints about the tone of Baxter's response. As far as possible, Baxter tried to dismantle the ideas, not the man.

Had he accused Owen of Antinomianism? No, and yes. Nowhere had he explicitly called Owen an Antinomian. Technically, the most he had done was to say that Owen held to some positions that were used by others who were genuinely Antinomian. He had claimed not to be sure that Owen held to justification from eternity. But this would be a very technical answer to the question. The weight of what Baxter had written was sufficient to force Owen together with the Antinomians. Baxter had explicitly put him in the same company as Eyre and Crandon. He had used Owen's own words to show something like strict imputation, which he had already explained was the very foundation of Antinomianism. It is hard to conceive of a way in which Baxter might have come closer to accusing Owen without making it explicit. And there were certainly grounds for Owen to believe that he had been accused. His defence appeared within months.

John Owen's *Of the Death of Christ and of Justification* (1655)

Owen greeted Baxter's *Confession* with despair: 'must we have no end to this quarrel?'[52] Yet he chose to extend it himself, and he placed his reply in a most uncomfortable setting for Baxter. In 1655 he published *Vindiciae Evangelicae*, his massive critique of John Biddle and the Racovian Catechism. He tacked another much shorter work onto the end, his *Review of the Annotations of Hugo Grotius*, which replied to Henry Hammond's *Second Defence of Hugo Grotius*, also published in 1655. In between he sandwiched his reply to Baxter, in a relatively brief appendix entitled *Of the Death of Christ and of Justification*. Owen's deployment conveyed the point well enough: Baxter was hardly in auspicious company. The very context itself signalled the implication of Socinianism well

---

[50]   Owen had said of Baxter: 'Had he attempted the proof of this assertion, perhaps he would have found it a more difficult undertaking than barely to affirm it.' Owen, *Of the Death of Christ* (1650): *Works*, x.455.

[51]   Baxter, *Confession*, 261.

[52]   Owen, *Death of Christ and of Justification* (1655): *Works*, xii.592.

before Owen raised the subject explicitly, and Baxter was shrewd enough to discern it.[53]

Owen's appendix may be brief, but it was heated and pointed. By now he felt himself to have been grievously insulted. It is easy to read into his words a tone that is by turns offended, bitter, sarcastic and bewildered. He repeated his earlier denials; he criticized Baxter's arrogance and method; he engaged with the latest provocation point by point; he clarified the pertinent aspects of his soteriology; he amplified his previous cutting tone. His reply reveals him at his most devastating, using every means available to demolish Baxter: the placement of the text itself; visibly and uncharacteristically excessive Latin and Greek quotations; deft irony and, in places, sarcasm; and clear, defiant, forceful rejoinders. Owen placed his learning and skill on show. He conveyed in very clear undertones that Baxter's efforts were not to be suffered.

Owen would have preferred to remain silent.[54] That was always his intention, at least following the publication of *Death of Christ* in 1650. Baxter's 'long silence' had given hope that the dispute was at an end.[55] More than that, when Owen met Baxter for the first time in 1654, Baxter had kept quiet about his forthcoming *Confession*. Owen could only assume that the book had been printed by then and Baxter did not want to waste his time and effort, nor the printer his investment, in withdrawing it.[56] It may be that Owen exaggerated his discourse with Baxter, but his silence regarding the impending *Confession* was inexplicable and uncharacteristic and, for that reason, intriguing. It may suggest that Baxter, who was intimidated by so few people and willing to tell anyone the facts as he saw them, was daunted by Owen and reluctant to raise the matter of his *Confession* before it was published. We cannot know. But we can be certain that Owen took this as unfair dealing. He was forced to find out through rumour and print what Baxter might have told him to his face.

Once again, Owen objected to the tone in Baxter's writing: 'nothing but self-fulness, oscitancy, and contempt of others'.[57] First, there was in Baxter's writings this 'self-fulness', a self-obsession that Owen found distasteful:

> I dare not look upon myself of any such consideration to the world, as to write books
> to give them an account of myself (with whom they very little trouble their thoughts);
> to tell them my faith and belief; to acquaint them with when I am well and when I am
> sick; what sin I have mortified most; what books I have read; how I have studied; how

---

53 Owen positioned it here 'to intimate that I belonged to that Party'. *Rel. Bax.*, i.111.
54 Owen, *Death of Christ and of Justification* (1655): *Works*, xii.591.
55 Ibid., 592.
56 Ibid.
57 Ibid., 607.

> I go, and walk, and look; what one of my neighbours says of me, and what another; how I am praised by some and dispraised by others; what I do, and what I would have others do; what diligence, impartiality, uprightness, I use; what I think of other men: so dealing unmercifully with perishing paper.[58]

Owen meant what he said: his own writings show exactly the reverse, a steady determination not to make himself the focus. And his comments show an astute measure of, and a capable familiarity with, Baxter's works (at a relatively early stage, and long before the *Reliquiae Baxterianae*, which would only have confirmed Owen's impressions). The point is, for Owen, that Baxter made himself the measure of all things. In saying this he was beginning to wrestle with the central enigma of his dispute with Baxter. Why did his opponent not accept his outright denial of those positions he was said to have taken? Owen had specifically disavowed justification from eternity, yet Baxter continued to accuse him. Why? One possible reason was that he did not arrive at his conclusions in a manner that pleased Baxter. 'I dispute as well as I can against justification from eternity, and that I cannot do it like Mr B. is my unhappiness, not my crime.'[59] He dismissed Baxter, in Latin – the only place I have found where Owen alluded to Baxter's lack of academic training: 'There was nothing more contrary to what is right than this unlearned fellow who considers nothing correct which he does not himself do.'[60] There was also the hint that Baxter had been swelled with his own increasing status and achievements: 'Real or reputed success gives great thoughts and pretexts for any thing.'[61] His works were exercises in 'polemic, self-promotion and self-justification'.[62]

The second word in Owen's trio, 'oscitancy', refers to indolence, negligence and inattention. Baxter 'ought to have known' one point; there was evidence of 'a failure of Mr B.'s memory' on another.[63] He just did not listen. If Owen had to carry on a debate, he would prefer to do so 'with them that, understanding my meaning, will fairly, closely, and distinctly, debate the thing in difference, and, not insisting on words and expressions to no purpose'.[64] Baxter did not. His method was 'from words of mine, which from several places of my treatise are put together, he makes sundry inferences, and opposes to them all two

---

[58]   Ibid., 594.

[59]   Ibid., 603.

[60]   Ibid., 594. The Latin is 'Homine imperito nunquam quidquam injustius, / Qui, nisi quod ipse facit, nihil rectum putat'.

[61]   Ibid., 603.

[62]   Ibid., 591. This is a translation from the Greek: 'logomachia, periautologia, apologia'.

[63]   Ibid., 602, 603.

[64]   Ibid., 605.

conclusions of his own'.[65] Thus Owen's own words were turned into something else – altered by inferences and conclusions of Baxter's own making – which further helps to explain why Baxter could extend the controversy in the face of Owen's clear denials. Even though Baxter did not want others to read the *Aphorismes* except through the filter of his *Confession*, he was more than willing to take Owen's words in different books and contexts, and stitch them together in a fashion that Owen never intended.[66] This resulted in a strange warping of Owen's position. It was Baxter's logical inferences from and extensions of Owen's disparate words that were ultimately the problem, which led Baxter to claim that Owen had destroyed 'all the merits of Christ' even when Owen's dearest aim was to magnify those merits.[67] Essentially, Owen was saying that Baxter saw too much of what he wanted to see, and too much that reflected Baxter's own suppositions. He did not show the discipline (or the moral rectitude) of dealing with what Owen actually said and intended. That is why Owen was confident enough in places simply to point the reader to his previous works,[68] certain that a fair reader would recognize where Owen ended and Baxter began in the dispute at hand.

The final quality, a 'contempt of others', stemmed from Baxter's own arrogance and was reflected in the way he had handled Owen's earlier denials. In a quote that demonstrates Owen's use of irony, he questioned how this could be in a man who was professedly humble and teachable:

> I verily believe that if a man (who had nothing else to do) should gather into one heap all the expressions which in his late books, confessions, and apologies, had a lovely aspect towards himself, as to ability, diligence, sincerity, on the one hand, with all of those which are full of reproach and contempt toward others, on the other, the view of them could not but a little startle a man of so great modesty and of such eminency in the mortification of pride as Mr B. is.[69]

Owen concluded 'that a humour of disputing and quarrelling was very predominant' in Baxter.[70] He seemed to know Owen's mind better than Owen did himself, or at least he carried himself as if he did, interpreting Owen's sense for all the world in ways that surprised their original author.[71] Baxter's writings,

65 Ibid., 605–6.
66 Ibid., 604.
67 Ibid., 604–5.
68 Ibid., 596, 603.
69 Ibid., 593–4.
70 Ibid., 594.
71 Ibid., 603.

said Owen, were full of 'pride and passion ... magisterial insolence, pharasaical, supercilious self-conceitedness, contempt of others, and every thing that is contrary to the rule whereby I ought to walk'.[72] These were hardly words of mutual admiration.

Owen's response consisted initially in directions to earlier works. 'But what should a man do in this case? I have already published to Mr B. and all the world that I believe neither of these propositions' that Baxter repeatedly accused him of promoting.[73] It was a fair point and if it had been left at that, this would have been a very brief reply indeed. But these gave way to a point-by-point rebuttal of those passages in the *Confession* that specifically mentioned Owen. The debate had extended to include the issue of exactly how justification was terminated in the conscience, but this was mostly a rehearsal of previous positions and there is little need to restate them in any detail here. Owen was at pains, perhaps in the hope this might be enough to close the dispute this time around, to be very clear in what he did and did not affirm. On some points he clarified his thinking and even restructured earlier sentences, suggesting that for reasons of 'great haste' he had not expressed himself as carefully as he should.[74] This gave some encouragement to Baxter, but not much. Owen continued to insist that the elect had a right to the benefits of salvation before they were born, even if it was not actionable until the moment of belief.[75] On several occasions he located his thinking in the covenant of redemption, which meant that while the elect did not have a right to Christ at his death, Christ had a right to the elect.[76]

This last point was similar to what Baxter had claimed, but there was little in the way of common ground here and no hope of mutual understanding. 'I am enrolled into the troop of Antinomians', Owen complained.[77] Baxter had cast 'the aspersion of me for an Antinomian'.[78] Admittedly, Owen recognized the distinction Baxter tried to maintain between 'the ruder sort' and those accused of 'laying the foundation of Antinomianism'.[79] But he still resented the implication of Antinomianism, 'now so strenuously opposed by Mr B.'.[80] Owen replied in kind, virtually accusing Baxter of Socinianism, in three ways. First, there was the placement of his reply between two anti-Socinian

---

[72]   Ibid., 615.

[73]   Ibid., 592.

[74]   Ibid., 602. See also p. 603.

[75]   Ibid., 609.

[76]   See Owen, *Death of Christ and of Justification* (1655): *Works*, xii.607, 608, 611 and 615.

[77]   Owen, *Death of Christ and of Justification* (1655): *Works*, xii.601.

[78]   Ibid., 592.

[79]   Ibid., 602.

[80]   Ibid., 614.

treatises. Second, he showed how the Worcestershire Confession was capable of conveying a Socinian understanding of the Trinity.[81] Third, and most explicitly of all, Owen assembled over 40 substantial Latin quotations from Socinian authors asserting beliefs that were similar to those promoted by Baxter.[82] In essence, both Baxter and the Socinians believed that faith, repentance and obedience were the condition whereby we come to be justified before God, not by the imputation of the obedience and righteousness of Christ. For example, 'God has appointed eternal life only to those who practise faith and virtue to the extent of their ability. That faithfulness is … an essential cause – as they say the necessary antecedent condition – of our justification'.[83] Having accused Baxter again of being an 'almost Socinian',[84] and having laid out those quotes, 'now let the Christian reader judge whether I had any just occasion' to do so.[85]

Thus by 1655 the dispute between Owen and Baxter had degenerated into a sophisticated exercise in name-calling. Owen was a near-Antinomian; Baxter was an almost-Socinian. Owen treated Baxter in the same way that Baxter had treated him. And again we need to consider their respective soteriological agendas and how each one stood in the way of the other, making accusations like these at least possible. It is true that Baxter had given the flame of controversy a fresh burst of oxygen. But we might also observe that Owen had chosen to respond quickly, and in the midst of a great many other very heavy labours.[86] The sharp tone – so severe, so hostile, so dismissive – made his distaste for Baxter perfectly clear. While he protested a desire to keep the peace and the silence he was quick to break them both, if only to end it once and for all. 'This may perhaps be the close of the controversy', he hoped. Even if Baxter did respond, Owen would say no more.[87] And indeed, this extended phase of soteriological controversy between the two men was coming to something of a close, but not before Baxter slipped in a final word.

---

[81]   Ibid., 594–5.

[82]   Ibid., 597–601.

[83]   Ibid., 598. The original Latin is 'Interim tamen sic habendum est, cum Deus non nisi illis, qui fidem virtutemque pro sua virili parte colunt, vitam sempiternam designaverit, fiduciam istam ne quidem causam meritoriam, aut principaliter efficientem, sed causam sine qua non (ut loquuntur) justificationis nostrae esse. — Volkel, de Vera Relig. lib. 4 cap. 3'.

[84]   Owen, *Death of Christ and of Justification* (1655): *Works*, xii.601.

[85]   Ibid.

[86]   Owen, *Vindiciae Evangelicae* (1655): *Works*, xii.9–10.

[87]   Owen, *Death of Christ and of Justification* (1655): *Works*, xii.615.

The 'displeasure of the Reconciled'

Writing in the early 1660s, Baxter looked back and claimed that he had let Owen have 'the last word' in their dispute 'because I had begun with him'.[88] This is not entirely true. Right at the end – page 480 to be precise – of his *Certain Disputations of Right to the Sacraments*, written against Thomas Blake, Baxter summed up the entire affair from his perspective. His account is dated 1 October 1655,[89] a matter of months after Owen's reply was published, though the work itself did not appear until 1657.

The first thing to observe is the sense of woundedness and even dislike. Baxter had been personally attacked, 'voluminously slandered' and loudly 'Caluminated' as 'hypocritically proud'.[90] Owen and 'his Brethren' had ganged up on him to 'publish abundance of Calumnies of mee to the world, telling them not onely that I am a Papist, but what books they were that made mee a Papist, and what emissaries I have in all parts of the Land, with much more of the like'.[91] John Crandon seems the main culprit here, but there is little to link him with Owen and no evidence that Owen ever repeated the claims. Yet, as Baxter saw it, when he tried to defend himself from their accusations Owen came along 'to proov mee proud for contradicting them; forsooth for talking so much of myself'.[92] If Baxter seemed self-absorbed it was only because he had been so personally attacked. Instead of understanding, he found 'ingenius malice'.[93] Owen was the contradictory voice of Shimei, sent by God to do David good; he was 'a messenger of Satan to buffet me' and keep him humble.[94] These are strong sentiments indeed, and overdrawn. But if we take them at face value they suggest that Baxter was incapable of finding that mutual understanding that might lead to genuine goodwill. There is of course a noticeable irony in all of this to which Baxter was characteristically blind. Much of this might have been said against him by Owen and others, with good reason. But if we set the irony aside we can discern the struggle Baxter had in trying to appreciate Owen. There was

---

[88]   *Rel. Bax.*, i.111.

[89]   Richard Baxter, *Certain Disputations of Right to the Sacraments and the True Nature of Visible Christianity* (1657), 523.

[90]   Baxter, *Certain Disputations*, 484.

[91]   Ibid., 486.

[92]   Ibid.

[93]   Ibid., 487.

[94]   Ibid., 486. Shimei pelted King David with stones and curses as he fled Jerusalem during his son Absalom's revolt; David accepted Shimei's curses as from the Lord (2 Samuel 16:5–14). To keep him from becoming proud over his visions and revelations, the Apostle Paul was given 'a thorn in my flesh, a messenger of Satan, to torment me' (2 Corinthians 12:7).

nothing, it seems, to endear him. And even by 1655 their relationship faced little prospect of healing and understanding.

Second, Baxter responded directly to many of Owen's lines of attack in ways we can measure. For instance, Owen's friends accused Baxter of disrespectfully denying him the title of Doctor. Baxter's response was simple: 'when my papers were written hee was not Doctor, though he was when they came out of the press.'[95] This is very likely. The Preface clearly refers to 'this Reverend Brother Doctor *Owen*', so Baxter was not unwilling to use the title.[96] On the other hand, Baxter was much less credible when he claimed that Owen was 'unable to produce a syllable of mine' to show that Baxter had accused him of Antinomianism. 'I think this dealing is not fair.'[97] Baxter was fooling himself here. He had gone just as far towards calling Owen an Antinomian as Owen had gone towards calling him a Socinian. Baxter could hardly take umbrage at Owen's manoeuvre yet deny his own. As we have seen, Owen had good reason to believe he stood accused. Baxter asserted he had brought in Owen only in one particular section; 'will it thence follow that I fasten on him all the errors that I mention in the precedent or subsequent pages?'[98] He claimed to be astonished that 'so learned a man should make such a stir upon the pretence of a charge that was never brought against him, but onely against others, a leafe before the mention of his name'.[99] This is hard to believe. Having linked Owen so closely to the Antinomians it is difficult to accept he was merely saying that Owen gave them encouragement.

Baxter's rebuttal, therefore, was very far from being uniformly credible and convincing. But what would have most infuriated Owen was Baxter's claim that Owen 'seems to disclaim the Absolution of Unbelievers' – justification from eternity. Here Baxter's blinkered vision was most apparent. From beginning to end Owen had denied justification from eternity. He did not deny it in the same way that Baxter did, but he did deny it, clearly and repeatedly. Yet Baxter ignored his protestations and then claimed a victory by reading into Owen's words a concession. 'I must confess I do somewhat the less repent of those disputes that so much offend men, when they have so good an issue for the matter, though som accidental evils are occasioned by them. When a bad caus is disowned, I

---

[95] Baxter, *Certain Disputations*, 485.

[96] Baxter, *Confession*, Preface, sig. e1r. On the other hand, Owen professed his indifference to it, and claimed that it was awarded 'in my absence, and against my consent', in *Answer to a Late Treatise of Mr Cawdrey about the Nature of Schism* (1657): *Works*, xiii.302.

[97] Baxter, *Certain Disputations*, 485.

[98] Ibid.

[99] Ibid.

have the thing that I intended.'[100] If Owen ever read those words, and we can assume he did, he must have ground his teeth in frustration. Baxter had claimed victory for a concession Owen had never given. He did well to hold to his resolve not to enter into the debate again. Perhaps he saw that by then there was nothing to be gained.

And so we come to what Baxter called 'the displeasure of the Reconciled', the state in which he now viewed their relationship. Owen had disavowed his bad cause and the two men were in broad, if heated, agreement. 'And though it bee very angrily that wee agree, and close with somwhat a sharp collision, yet it's well that we agree.'[101] What seemed to surprise Baxter was the tone of Owen's concession. 'I marvailed to finde a man with such high indignation endeavouring to proov himself of his opponents minde; and that we should agree more passionately than wee seemed to differ.' Baxter would not have believed he was of the same view as Owen, 'but hee hath hotly and haughtily proved it; and therein also I rejoice. As long as wee com nearer, and error goeth away with the disgrace, wee may the better bear the displeasure of the Reconciled'.[102] It is difficult to take Baxter's words at face value here. Did he really believe that Owen was using the most scathing language and methods he ever used to make a concession? Was he genuinely surprised at the hostile tone? It would be impossible to prove – and uncharacteristic for Baxter – that he was using irony to twist the knife in Owen, to speak of a change of mind and concession knowing full well that none had been made. But if he meant what he said this is one of the clearest instances of Baxter's stubborn self-absorption, what came across to his critics as haughty presumption. He never allowed for a moment that his interpretation of Owen had been mistaken. Nowhere did he give any indication of entertaining the remotest possibility that he might have been wrong. Instead, he fitted Owen's denials into his own implacable perspective, one in which Owen had somehow become the errant novice, now graciously corrected by the condescending master.

Significant Silences

This was, it has to be said, a very strange debate, and this the most unusual of endings. Two dynamics made it strange, ones of speech and silence. First, when it comes to what Owen and Baxter said to each other the commonalities are

---

[100]   Ibid., 483.
[101]   Ibid.
[102]   Ibid., 484.

impressively extensive. In this sense, Baxter was right. It seems strangely distorted that two men with so much in common should come to such bitter verbal blows, rather like the parent and child who are so similar they clash, criticizing in the other what annoys them about themselves, or overlooking in themselves what irritates in the other. There was a similarity in the fundamental accusation they lobbed at each other: Owen was the near-Antinomian; Baxter the almost-Socinian. That, said Baxter, was 'the hardest measure of all', yet he measured Owen in just the same sort of way. Owen criticized Baxter for taking the opinions of others and rendering them 'so changed by a new dress that I might justly refuse to take any acquaintance with it'.[103] But he was the one who employed his own paraphrase of Baxter's position to highlight the Socinian resonances. Baxter complained that Owen had 'put it into as odious a dress' as he possibly could and he denied the Socinian-sounding paraphrase, saying they 'never fell from any pen' of his, 'nor came into my thoughts with any approbation'.[104] Just as Owen regretted that Baxter had not told him of the *Confession* to his face, so Baxter objected to Owen's interpretation of the Worcestershire Confession, 'contrary to the sense that I had told him in my explications wee took the words in'.[105] Owen claimed he could not win: Baxter refused to believe his outright denials.[106] Likewise, Baxter claimed he could not win: either he denied Owen's accusations of pride, and seemed proud; or he accepted the rebuke, and seemed falsely modest.[107] All the while, each man questioned the professed humility of the other.[108] Owen was amazed that someone who praised him so highly treated him so badly;[109] Baxter was astonished that Owen demonstrated his agreement with such 'high indignation'.[110] I realize that the dynamics of debate in seventeenth-century England would make any two combatants take up arms and methods similar to each other and that in responding specifically to Owen, Baxter was bound to throw back in Owen's face the same sort of accusations that had been aimed at him. But all this bitterness fell out between two men who at different points in the conflict claimed that they agreed with each other, and the similarities are remarkably extensive. The structure of polemic, in which one drove one's opponent to the extremes, thereby masking any common ground, simply reinforced the curious dynamic of the dispute between Owen and Baxter.

---

[103]   Owen, *Death of Christ* (1650): *Works*, x.442.
[104]   Baxter, *Certain Disputations*, 487, 488.
[105]   Ibid., 487.
[106]   Owen, *Death of Christ and of Justification* (1655): *Works*, xii.592.
[107]   Baxter, *Certain Disputations*, 484.
[108]   Ibid., 483.
[109]   Owen, *Death of Christ and of Justification* (1655): *Works*, xii.596.
[110]   Baxter, *Certain Disputations*, 484.

The many commonalities between them amplified their genuine differences. They also reinforce the perception of a clash of personalities.

So the way in which the two men spoke to each other had a bearing on the strange nature of their disagreement. In a similar way, two central silences served to accentuate the oddness. The first silence was Owen's. In *Death of Christ* he had explained that it was 'not at all in my thoughts to engage myself into the chief controversy' of the *Aphorismes*, though he hoped others would.[111] In his 1655 Appendix he said 'I must assure the reader that I have other thoughts of the great transaction of the business of our salvation in the person of our Representative than are consistent with Mr B.'s principles, or than I have yet published'.[112] He consistently kept himself only to the two specific issues under dispute and here he essentially claimed that his position was not so different from Baxter's. This meant that he went into combat over the two areas on which he actually agreed with Baxter and said nothing at all about the many other aspects of the *Aphorismes* with which he would clearly have disagreed. It might have been a more conventional dispute if Owen had published those 'thoughts' he kept to himself and kept to himself those thoughts he actually offered.

There was also a significant silence in Baxter, one that can be traced back to that brief postscript to the main portion of the *Aphorismes*. There he mentioned a 'few pages' on the issue of universal redemption. He never did publish them, though five months before his death in December 1691 he passed on a manuscript to Joseph Read with the intention of seeing them printed. Read had become Baxter's assistant at Kidderminster in 1657. 'Some of the first work he put me upon was to transcribe these papers of [universal] Redemption, which he designed for the Press.' Those papers were the product of a series of Thursday lectures given by Baxter to ministers in the Worcestershire Association. But they were written at a time 'when the opposition of the Learned of differing Opinions had sharpen'd his Pen, and made him critically exact in considering what he intended for the Press'.[113] Or, as Baxter explained it to John Howe in April 1658, 'I suppress them for peace'.[114] The main reason was 'because many narrow minded Brethren would have been offended with it'.[115] Thus the papers had lain beside Baxter unpublished for almost four decades, though their immediate context was the period from 1655–1657.[116] They are worth examining, for two

---

[111]　Owen, *Death of Christ* (1650): *Works*, x.436.

[112]　Owen, *Death of Christ and of Justification* (1655): *Works*, xii.604.

[113]　Joseph Read, 'To the Reader', in Baxter, *Universal Redemption*.

[114]　Baxter to John Howe, 3 April 1658: DWL MS *BC* iii.200r (*CCRB* #443).

[115]　*Rel. Bax.*, i.123.

[116]　Hans Boersma speculates that Baxter wrote what Boersma calls part four of the book between 1647 and 1649, and that these are the 'few pages' that Baxter referred to in the Postscript

reasons. First, they help to clarify an essential aspect of his soteriology that stood in contrast to Owen's. Second, they throw more light on the tone and content of Baxter's disagreement with Owen.

On the first of those aspects, Baxter affirmed that 'Christ Died for All Men, and not only for the Elect'.[117] He laid out his thinking in a way that showed how the fundamental framework of the system he developed in the *Aphorismes* was still very much in operation, especially the central distinction of God as *Dominus* and *Rector*.[118] As *Dominus*, God 'useth such means with all his Elect as shall infallibly succeed, to bring them to Faith and Perseverance'.[119] At the end of the book was a short piece designed to prove that 'Christ Died with a Special Intention of bringing Infallibly, Immutably, and Insuperably certain Chosen Persons to Saving Faith, Justification, and Salvation'. He wrote it against those – the Arminians – who believed God's intention was to save '*only Believers* in *General*, or *All men Conditionally* if they will Believe'.[120] The 'main inequality', then, 'is not in the Mercies which he gives as Legislator [*Rector*], (till their own Faith or Unbelief makes the difference) but in the Mercies which he gives as absolute Lord, which flow from his secret *Decree de rerum Eventu*'.[121] The elect were clearly distinguished in the decree and in its fulfilment.

But this did not mean that Christ died only for the elect. The 'greatest Ambiguity in our Question is the term "For"'.[122] The way in which the Spirit worked 'in such seasons and measure' to arrange the means by which he brought faith to life was never in the same way twice. In this sense Christ died 'for' each man or woman in a unique way, with a different arrangement of 'providential occurrences and removal of temptations and hindrances'. So it was foolish to distinguish between how Christ died 'for' the elect and 'for' the non-elect, since the answer changed even within those groups.[123] Not only that, the gift of

---

to the first portion of his *Aphorismes*. See Boersma, *Hot Pepper Corn*, Appendix A, 333–8. I find this unconvincing for two main reasons. First, that section is 286 pages in length. It is not a 'few pages' in Baxter's words, nor 'a relatively brief treatise' in Boersma's. Second, there are several pages that refer to Owen (139ff.), and I have argued earlier that Baxter was not aware of Owen's *Death of Death* when he wrote the Postscript. It remains possible that *Universal Redemption* was written in installments, as Boersma says. But I suspect the 'few pages' Baxter wrote were never published in that form and are not part of the final work.

[117] Baxter, *Universal Redemption*, 1.
[118] See above, p. 77.
[119] Baxter, *Universal Redemption*, 20.
[120] Ibid., 481, 483.
[121] Ibid., 20.
[122] Ibid., 4.
[123] Ibid., 20.

faith was not tied directly to the death of Christ.[124] Instead, it had its origins in predestination.[125] Thus Baxter distinguished between the redeemed – which is everyone – and the elect.[126] The general sacrifice of Christ for all was common to both groups; what set apart the elect was the conjoined decree of election.[127] He also distinguished again God's role as *Rector* and *Dominus*. As *Rector*, God perfectly extended the terms of the new covenant to everyone equally; as *Dominus* he did not do all that he might have done, since here he acted above and beyond and in distinction to his rectorial government as redeemer.[128] This did not cast any slight on Christ, nor make him out to be an imperfect redeemer.[129] At no point in the Bible was there any promise that Christ would save all those for whom he died and satisfied.[130] Baxter saw no great obstacle in that, nor did he see any inconsistency between the specifically targeted nature of election and the general ransom of all: the distinction simply lay in Christ's differentiated roles as *Rector* and *Dominus*.[131] All of this kept alive God's intention infallibly to save through sovereignly designated means a specific number of individuals known as the elect (something Owen could readily have agreed with) without having to say that Christ died only for the elect.

A second important distinction was that between the old law and the new covenant. 'All Mankind *immediately* upon Christ's Satisfaction, are redeemed and Delivered from that Legal necessity of Perishing which they were under.'[132] While this dealt with the threats of the old law it did not touch on the requirements of the '*New Law*'.[133] There are several points to note here. First, Baxter's language is at least suggestive of a right or status accruing to men and women immediately upon the death of Christ. This is something like what Owen argued for in the first place, and which Baxter denied. But the impression is fleeting: Baxter immediately affirmed that no right was given directly to anyone, except Christ's right of 'the Redeemer as their owner and ruler, to be dealt with upon terms of mercy which have a tendency to their recovery.'[134] Second, the old law was suspended at the death of Christ so that every person

---

[124]   Ibid., 425, 426, 431.
[125]   Ibid., 425.
[126]   Ibid., 432, 434.
[127]   Ibid., 432–3.
[128]   Ibid., 414–15.
[129]   Ibid., 415, 426.
[130]   Ibid., 408.
[131]   Ibid., 279.
[132]   Ibid., 36.
[133]   Ibid., 53.
[134]   Ibid., 36.

was now freed from the punishment of death it demanded. Baxter had moved on from his earlier position that the curse of the law remained even to the elect. Third, this release was entirely temporary and conditional upon the eventual faith of each person. It was not 'Actually done' until belief, 'nor ever shall be to the final Rejectors'.[135] '[W]e are conditionally pardoned whether we believe or not. But we shall not be actually pardoned till we believe [and persevere].'[136] It was 'undeniable' that Christ gave to the non-elect 'some Faith, some Taste of his word and the power of the World to come; [and] sanctifyeth them by the Blood of the Covenant'.[137] This accounted for those who seemed to fall away from the faith in much the same terms that Owen used.[138] But the elect would infallibly come to full salvation. So Baxter's scheme did not make God out to be weak – one of Owen's repeated objections to Arminian doctrine – only generous. It avoided the possibility that no one would be saved by the death of Christ, without abandoning a decisive place for the faith, obedience and perseverance of the believer. Fourth, the distinction answered one of Owen's other main objections to universal redemption. He could not agree that Christ died for the sins of all people, since logically that would include the very sin of unbelief that would finally damn them. Baxter held that the only sins for which Christ satisfied were those defined under the old law; the conditions required under the new law were exempt – and they were not supplied to the elect by Christ acting in their place – and therefore remain outstanding in those who are finally impenitent, even though Christ could rightly be said to have died for their sins.[139] This meant that all those who perish are responsible for their choice to resist that grace that might have brought them closer to God.[140]

It pays to bear in mind that even at 500 pages Baxter's book was a long way from being finished. He stopped it only because other books that argued much the same cause had appeared in the press,[141] and Baxter was not one to waste his time on unnecessary labours. This shows up the contrast with Samuel Hoard, for example, whose much briefer book was capable of only a one-dimensioned assault. Baxter's was much more expansive. Almost effortlessly he assembled 50 propositions here, 60 theses over there, another 30 arguments beyond that. He was capable of endless variation. But, inevitably, the two lines of attack launched against Owen resurfaced. First, Baxter argued that 'all' really did mean 'all' in

---

135   Ibid., 41.
136   Ibid., 40.
137   Ibid., 66.
138   See Owen, *Doctrine of the Saints' Perseverance* (1654): *Works*, xi.90.
139   Baxter, *Universal Redemption*, 383, 385.
140   Ibid., 434.
141   Ibid., 376, 480.

the context of the satisfaction of Christ, and 'world' really did mean 'world', not 'the elect'.[142] When the Scriptures say plainly that Christ died for all we should believe them.[143] 'The Doctrine of Universal Redemption thus delivered, runs with the whole Scope of Scripture, and hath not the least inconvenience; when the denial of it, contradicteth a multitude of express Texts, and bringeth on more desperate consequences than can be easily conceived.'[144] Second, Baxter showed up the inadequacy of limited atonement when it came to grounds for assurance. He included a fictional conversation between a minister who favoured limited atonement and one of his poor parishioners (even if one possessed of an implausible degree of theological acumen).[145] The point was to show that there was no assurance to be gained from limited atonement, since the main message was that Christ did not die for the non-elect – which included the anxious parishioner, for all he knew. In several places, and with examples out of Johannes Maccovious and William Perkins,[146] Baxter showed how those who argued for limited atonement in printed disputations were forced to adopt universal redemption in their preaching. Their 'way of Preaching for the Conversion of Sinner, doth plainly intimate Universal satisfaction; For they use to lay all the blame on the Wills of Sinners (and justly) as that only which can deprive them of the benefits of Christs sufferings'.[147]

All of this brings us to Owen specifically, though he appeared in only a very small dose.[148] On the question of the *Idem* and *Tantundum*, 'Mr. O, (against me) seems stiffly to maintain it to be the *Idem*, but yielding it to be not *per eundem*, and the Law to be relaxed so far, doth yield as much as I need, and gives up the whole cause; and made me think it is useless to reply to him'.[149] At least Baxter acknowledged what Owen had said and was precise in the concession. But he continued to imply he had been vindicated; he treated Owen dismissively in asserting Owen had betrayed his own cause; and there was no mention of his more noble desire to allow the last word. He also took Owen's 'unsound' and 'strange' doctrine to deny the sufficiency of Christ's death for all men and women if they believe.[150] Baxter argued that the point of Christ's death

---

142   Ibid., 293.
143   Ibid., 285–6.
144   Ibid., 64.
145   Ibid., 226–8.
146   Ibid., 169, 176, 184,
147   Ibid., 153.
148   Apart from the instances mentioned here, Owen was referred to only briefly and in passing on pages 70 and 84.
149   Baxter, *Universal Redemption*, 78.
150   Ibid., 139.

was to offer satisfaction for sins, and if he did that only for the elect then there was nothing gained for the non-elect even if they did believe. So after quoting Owen at some length Baxter uncovered what he felt was the 'absurdity' of his position.[151] 'How can he say "there is sufficient merit" where there is no merit at all? The death of Christ hath no merit as to the Pardon of Devils, or any for whom it never suffered.'[152] Owen's only confidence in preaching Christ to all was the conviction that only the elect among them will believe.[153] The sufficiency he saw in Christ's death for all was only the excess funds in the purse of a rich man that have might have been used to purchase the liberty of a few kidnapped souls, but he will expend only what is required to save a select few.[154] Therefore, those of Owen's mind needed to 'new model their Doctrine' or stop saying that Christ's death was sufficient for all if they believe, 'for that is notoriously false (according to them)'.[155]

Baxter was offering an accurate description of Owen's thinking here. 'It was', said Owen, 'the purpose and intention of God that his Son should offer a sacrifice of infinite worth, value, and dignity, sufficient in itself for the redeeming of all and every man, if it had pleased the Lord to employ it to that purpose'.[156] He distinguished between the limitless sufficiency of the death of Christ and its limited efficacy in its application only to the elect in order to resist the conclusion that God 'had failed in his design' by not saving all those for whom he might be said to die for that purpose.[157] And he argued that the proponents of universal redemption themselves undervalued the sufficiency of the death of Christ, because 'its true worth consists in the immediate effects, products, and issues of it' and a general sufficiency did nothing to guarantee any such immediate fruit.[158] So both Owen and Baxter argued that the other's position rendered the satisfaction of Christ, to use Baxter's word, 'useless'.[159]

---

[151] Ibid., 142.
[152] Ibid., 140.
[153] Ibid., 141.
[154] Ibid.
[155] Ibid.
[156] Owen, *Death of Death in the Death of Christ* (1648): *Works*, x.295.
[157] Ibid., 296.
[158] Ibid., 297.
[159] Baxter, *Universal Redemption*, 142.

The Quarantined Cross

It is possible now to stand back and to assess the respective soteriologies of Owen and Baxter. It is not enough simply to consider the shape of their systems; the dynamic is all-important. We must ask not just what and how, but why, since each man's convictions were not developed in isolation from important external forces. For Owen, his nonconformist upbringing combined with his university learning and his experience of encroaching Laudianism at Oxford to forge an understanding of doctrine that precluded anything that might look like human merit in the process of salvation. He did this in a phase of intense political developments, at a time when Laudian influence in England peaked and then receded. In his 1646 sermon to Parliament he specifically identified Arminianism as the threat and one that, even then, might still not be vanquished. More than that, at just that moment the new face of human autonomy – the Socinians – began to emerge as an increasingly significant marker in the mind of Owen and others of a growing independence in human thought and aspiration. They were enough of a threat to convince Owen that his system was ideally robust to repel Socinian soteriology as well as Arminian. Judging by the request of Parliament to reply to John Biddle, significant others were convinced of that as well. Again, this is not to reduce Owen's soteriology to mere pragmatism, only to recognize that he crafted his belief in a particular context under identifiable pressures and with discernable aims. Thus his soteriology did everything to preserve God's sovereign choice, working by his Spirit through voluntary human agency to bring about infallibly the salvation of the elect, all the while falling short of outright determinism.

For Owen, the beginnings were important. The eternal decree of God to save particular individuals was as good as securing their full salvation even though the incidentals of their being brought to belief were located in time and space. The death and resurrection of Christ also effectively secured the salvation of the elect. The Cross gave them a moral right that could never be denied or impeded. Owen's understanding of the covenants led him to link Christ's death and resurrection with his ministry of intercession (a link Baxter largely overlooked in his own writings),[160] both of which were specifically and only for the elect. So there was never any doubt of their eventual, full salvation from the Cross or even from eternity, since the sovereign freedom of God provided the adamant certainty of his decrees and the infallible aims of the death and intercession of Christ. The relative solitude and ease of Essex supplied a conducive environment

---

[160]   There is a 'virtual absence of the threefold office from Baxter's discussion of Christ's work as mediator, as opposed to its centrality to Owen's argument'. Trueman, *Claims of Truth*, 241.

for Owen to contemplate the timeless, eternal decrees of God. I realize this is unfair to Owen. He was far too capable a thinker for this impression of isolated complacency to hold true and the course of the civil war did interrupt his life on occasions in the late 1640s and early 1650s. But he was much freer to focus on the far off and remote – the aims of the war, or the sovereign purposes of God worked out in but unsullied by the vagaries of human circumstance.

Baxter was not. And for him the endings were important. During the war he confronted the overpowering force and sometime-brutality of historical events, driven by all-too-human actions and ideas.[161] Indeed, he discerned what seemed to him a direct link between actions and ideas. Ironically, both Owen and Baxter shared a concern for excessive human freedom. Owen disliked the autonomy the Arminians and Socinians granted to the human will. Baxter condemned the liberty allowed by the Antinomians, which reflected itself in practical rebellion and disobedience. And both could trace each version of excessive human freedom back to a misunderstanding about what had been achieved, and not achieved, at the Cross of Christ. Baxter quarantined the Cross. Each of his many twofold distinctions was a paling in the fence he built with a wide circumference around the Cross but the central distinction, the one that did the most work, was that between God's activity as *Dominus* and *Rector*. It gave Baxter a way of preserving God's infallible election of particular individuals – a conviction he could state just as strongly as Owen – while making certain that no one, not even the elect, was let off the hook of moral responsibility. Baxter distinguished the particular salvation of the elect (which was rooted in the eternal decree of God) from the work of Christ on the Cross (in that all men and women were equally redeemed by his death). He distinguished between what Christ did in terms of the old law from what all men and women, including the elect, were called to do under the terms of the new law. In this fashion he kept open a space for human responsibility. That is why it was so necessary for him to circumscribe what was achieved at the Cross and to shift his attention to what took place in time and season, to what would be complete only on that great day of judgement. This was the end that mattered, and inasmuch as those who were elect and those who repented and perseveringly believed were precisely the same group of individuals, nothing was finally secure until that End. This is why he could claim that 'the main Body of Divinity stands or falls according to the Resolution' of the question of the *Idem* and *Tantundum*.[162] And this, ultimately, is why he could not avoid a confrontation with Owen, who did so much to secure the salvation of the elect at the beginning of things, in the Cross of Christ: 'I found

---

161   Lamont, *Millennium*, 92.
162   Baxter, *Universal Redemption*, 78.

my self engaged to do it, because I knew of none that had said so much as he there doth.'[163]

The result of putting the two men together, therefore, was bound to be a clash. While they had much in common – most notably in the shared Calvinist conviction that God would by his Spirit and through means bring the elect infallibly to full salvation – the governing dynamic of each one's system moved in the opposite direction. So it could look at times like they met head on. Certainly Owen would have found repugnant Baxter's conviction that Christ did not save all those whom he had redeemed. It explains why he found Baxter's criticism that he emptied the Cross of Christ of its merit entirely absurd. He was right to reply that those merits were his dearest treasure – they were. His whole theology was designed to preserve them. And if anyone it was Baxter who diminished those merits by distinguishing redemption from salvation. In his turn, Baxter's twin objections to Owen centred on the Cross of Christ: did he stand in the place of the elect and were any rights attached to the elect at that point? Baxter answered No to both questions; Owen said Yes. But this is the point: Owen shared his answer with the Antinomians who loaded every significance on the Cross of Christ and none at all on their own response and responsibility. Baxter shared his answer with the Socinians who saw in the satisfaction of Christ merely an exemplary model of righteous suffering. In the context of seventeenth-century polemic, the respective accusations were predictable and inevitable. Here, both men took much the same stance. They built up their case by context and circumlocution, coming within a hair's-breadth of accusing the other of Socinianism or Antinomianism. Neither accusation was valid, but each could be seen to be giving encouragement to and sharing some ideas in common with those dreaded groups.

It is also possible now to revisit the question of blame. In Chapter 3 we saw that while Baxter was the beginner of the dispute, Owen – in replying so quickly, specifically and heatedly – can be seen as the aggressor. Having examined the second round of their 1650s soteriological dispute, it is fair to say that Baxter's share of the blame increased substantially. His principal crime lay in ignoring Owen's protestations that he had never asserted justification from eternity and then claiming a retraction where there was none. His behaviour reinforces the accusation of arrogance. Baxter was one who saw what he chose to see. If others claimed not to see it, even those who were said to propose it, then they were wrong and he was right. His implication that most disputants were not as capable as he was in distinguishing and reasoning hardly helped any claims to humility.[164]

---

[163]   Baxter, *Certain Disputations*, Preface, sig. e1v.

[164]   For example, see Baxter, *Universal Redemption*, 1.

Moreover, Baxter's denial that he had ever accused Owen of Antinomianism did him little credit. He may not have used the exact words, but his careful arrangement of context and assimilation carried the message loud and clear. To then accuse Owen of being overly sensitive by making exactly those connections was disingenuous. So too was his claim to have allowed Owen the last word. He did no such thing. Of course, in the same place as he offered his final response to Owen he claimed not to have written a particular response to Thomas Blake – this at the end of a 500-page book against Blake.[165] Baxter, it seems, avoided writing replies by ... writing replies. His final thoughts on Owen, as brief as they were, themselves comprised the 'last' word in their soteriological dispute, at least in public and at least for now. 'I have said as much as I now intend in the conclusion of these Disputations.'[166] At this stage in their disagreement Baxter was showing the same signs that appeared in the many other disputes with other people. He would not let a matter rest, he was determined to believe only his own interpretation and he wore people down with his intransigence, thereby eroding goodwill even in relationships that had been showing promise.[167]

So we can understand Owen's frustration and many of his lines of attack. They were not without validity. Bishop Edward Stillingfleet is reported to have said: 'Dr. *Owen* dealt with [Baxter] like a Gentleman; Mr. *Baxter* like a Thresher. He had no good manners.'[168] 'Certainly', Owen himself claimed, 'never was a man more violently pressed to a warfare than I to this contest'.[169] But the earlier criticisms of Owen can be reasserted here. Baxter only ever critiqued him in briefer passages hidden away in much larger works. Yet Owen chose to reply in specific works targeted at Baxter. While his first reply might have been unnecessary, the second was more genuinely provoked. But Owen could have been content to let the reader judge between him and Baxter by going back to what Owen had said before in his own defence. If the two men agreed, as he claimed, then his main purpose in replying was to protect his reputation by clearing himself from the accusation of Antinomianism. This is an entirely reasonable thing to do, especially in the face of Baxter's belligerence, but Baxter was right to suspect that Owen's own pride played a part in keeping the exchange alive. And it is

---

165   Baxter, *Certain Disputations*, 480, 515.

166   Ibid., Preface, sig. e2.

167   For an example of this, see Cooper, *Fear and Polemic*, 47–8.

168   [Young], *Vindiciae Anti-Baxterianae*, 121. See also, p. 191. A thresher was one who beat the straw to separate the grain. Certainly Stillingfleet had no love for Baxter's angry way of writing. See Edward Stillingfleet, *The Unreasonableness of Separation: Or, an Impartial Account of the History, Nature, and the Pleas, of the Present Separation from the Communion of the Church of England* (1681), Preface, lxix–lxi.

169   Owen, *Death of Christ and of Justification* (1655): *Works*, xii.596.

no surprise that Owen's ironic, biting tone and his own accusations of pride wounded Baxter. We do not know why Owen chose not to take up with Baxter a third time: 'I shall have no itch to be scribbling to no purpose.'[170] It suggests a genuine restraint on his part. But we might still recognize the ways in which he had helped to sustain the controversy between them. Neither man was innocent in their war of words.

Finally, this second round of soteriological debate reveals more of the condition of the relationship between Owen and Baxter by 1657. It was clearly in poor repair. Baxter had done himself no favours by essentially ignoring Owen's earlier protestations of innocence. Yet he showed himself to be careful and generally restrained in his response. He was clearly aware by now that Owen was not a man to provoke. He countered Owen only when the issue at hand demanded it. But we should recognize his own self-blindness and the formidable capacity to believe the best of himself and his own interpretations of doctrine. It made him come across as haughty and self-absorbed. On the other hand, Owen had learned a thing or two as well, and his respect for Baxter was at a very low ebb. Yet he also had shown himself to be prickly and easily provoked. So by 1657 the two men had lapsed back into silence over soteriology: Baxter resolving to say no more; Owen holding – perhaps only by the barest thread – to his earlier resolution to keep the peace. There was, then, a low-level simmering hostility, with no hope at all of mutual understanding any time soon. The best the two could hope for was that the peace would last. As it happens, that was not the way of things at all, and the seeds of mutual dislike sown through the Interregnum were about to bear fruit in a most dramatic and permanently unconstructive way.

---

[170]   Ibid., 609.

Chapter 8

1659

[I] never had a hand in, nor gave consent unto, the raising of any war in these nations, nor unto any political alteration in them, no, not to any one that was amongst us during our revolutions.

John Owen (1664)[1]

Dr. *Owen* and his assistants did the main work.

Richard Baxter (1664)[2]

In 1659 all of the Interregnum experiments came to an end. So did many of the hopes and dreams of John Owen and Richard Baxter. Owen spent the last few years of the decade trying to shore up the visibly sinking fortunes of the Congregationalists in England (in a way that was continuous with his earlier efforts to find unity among the godly) and to preserve England's allegiance (such as it was by the late 1650s) to Reformed orthodoxy. In this light we will consider the *Declaration of Faith* that emerged from the deliberations of the Congregationalists in 1658 as well as Owen's concerted efforts to help find some sort of stability through the increasingly fluid and unsettling political events of 1659. Those events, particularly the downfall of Richard Cromwell, proved to be the dashing of all Baxter's hopes, just as his hopes were at their highest. The last few years of the 1650s were marked by an unusually bright optimism in Baxter about the cause of peace, but the events of 1659 permanently shattered that optimism. Above anyone else, Baxter came around to blame Owen for the fall of Richard Cromwell, a fall from which there would be no salvation. For this reason we will evaluate Baxter's claim that Owen was the unseen hand that engineered Richard Cromwell's demise. It was a claim, as we shall see, that long outlasted the end of the Protectorate and the dark, depressing developments of 1659.

---

[1]   Owen, *A Vindication of the Animadversions on 'Fiat Lux'* (1664): *Works*, xiv.190.

[2]   *Rel. Bax.*, i.101.

The Savoy Declaration

England's Lord Protector died around three o'clock on the afternoon of 3 September 1658; within hours the Council of State informed Richard Cromwell that he had been nominated by his father as the new Lord Protector, a fact proclaimed in London the following day. The country received the news with universal calm and in some measure genuine warmth.[3] 'Indeed', wrote John Thurloe, Richard's Secretary of State, 'there is among us all that can be wished of tranquillity and unanimity, a good reason to hope the same for the future'.[4] In his autobiography Baxter recalled the smooth transition: it seemed to put an end to any hopes the royalists might have held for a restoration of the former monarchy, and even those who were inclined to oppose Oliver felt compelled to support Richard.[5] We know now that the Restoration was merely a matter of months away; at the time, it seemed more distant than ever before.[6] As Ruth Mayers has cautioned, we should be careful not to assume that the Restoration was imminent or even likely in the middle of 1659, let alone near the close of 1658.[7] Richard's seamless and painless ascension seemed to offer the prospect of peace and stability; it appeared as a token of God's continued presence and blessing in England's national affairs. How soon things changed.

As William Lamont has shown, Baxter's attitude towards the Protectorate regime had steadily improved during the 1650s: 'he had moved from his frigid position in 1650 to one where he was seeking active co-operation with the Protectorate in 1659.'[8] That shift had involved a growing appreciation for Oliver Cromwell,[9] but he reserved a far greater esteem for Richard, the one who was more clearly of Presbyterian sympathies and without all the baggage

---

[3]   Woolrych, *Britain in Revolution*, 707, 710; Godfrey Davies, *The Restoration of Charles II 1658–1660* (San Marino, CA: Huntington Library, 1955), 6–8; Peter Gaunt, 'Cromwell, Richard (1626–1712)', *Oxford Dictionary of National Biography*, Oxford University Press, September 2004; online edn, May 2008 [www.oxforddnb.com/view/article/6768, accessed 27 October 2009].

[4]   John Thurloe to ??, 9 September 1658: National Archives, London: SP 78.114.159.

[5]   Baxter, *Rel. Bax.*, i.100.

[6]   Baxter later recalled that the Restoration of the King 'we thought next impossible'. *Rel. Bax.*, i.100.

[7]   Ruth Mayers, *1659: The Crisis of the Commonwealth* (London: Royal Historical Society, 2004), 2–3.

[8]   Lamont, *Millennium*, 104. See also, pp. 178, 197, 203; William Lamont, 'False Witnesses? The English Civil War and English Ecumenism', in *The Development of Pluralism in Modern Britain and France*, ed. Richard Bonney and D.J.B. Trim (Oxford: Peter Lang, 2007), i.105–6; and Goldie, *Entring Book of Roger Morrice*, i.252.

[9]   Lamont, *Millennium*, 169, 182. See also, Coffey, *John Goodwin*, 254.

of the 1640s. Baxter took the opportunity to address the new Lord Protector by dedicating two books to him. Together these works identified Baxter's most urgent concerns of national significance in the late 1650s. In the first, *A Key for Catholicks*, he exposed the continued manipulation of English affairs by the Catholics with the aim of reconciliation with Rome. In the second, *Five Disputations of Church of Church-Government and Worship*, he addressed the main issues that continued to stand in the way of a religious settlement.[10] These dedicatory epistles came in for criticism.[11] In a passage he later deleted from the manuscript of his autobiography, Baxter defended himself from the charge that he had been rather too supportive of Richard Cromwell and claimed that he was simply enlisting him in the cause of the Church's peace.[12] But one dedication would have been sufficient; writing two was excessive. He noted how 'the Nation generally rejoyceth in your peaceable entrance unto the Government' and speculated that Richard might be 'the Healer of our breaches', specially kept from shedding blood – just as King Solomon, not David, was allowed by God to build the temple.[13] And Lamont is right to say that the content of the books, along with *A Holy Commonwealth* published later in 1659, betray his 'enthusiasm for the regime'. In that deleted section Baxter worried that he had inadvertently triggered Richard's eventual fall by sending a copy of *A Key for Catholicks* to 'some of the Major Generalls'.[14] This suggests an intriguing connection between the book and the regime if its publication was enough (at least in his mind) to precipitate such a dramatic response. But the fall of the Protectorate was still some months in the future, and nowhere on Baxter's horizon.

Richard Cromwell's ascent was, therefore, no bad thing for Baxter and by late 1658 he was markedly upbeat about the prospects for Church unity.[15] I suspect the ascension of Richard Cromwell was the principal cause of his new optimism, along with the realignment that succession seemed to promise in the context of broader changes. 'Indeed at the time there was real hope for the Reconcilers that

---

[10]   The book 'was written (hastily and imperfectly) on purpose to carry on the busyness of Reconciliation'. DWL MS *BT* iii.110v, item #62(2). These two issues were, of course, closely connected. The Catholics worked their manipulation by fostering division in the English Church. Baxter alerted the nation to their ploy in *The Grotian Religion Discovered*, also published in 1658.

[11]   *Rel. Bax.*, i.100, marginal note.

[12]   DWL MS *BT* iii.110r, item #62(2).

[13]   Richard Baxter, *Five Disputations of Church of Church-Government and Worship* (1659), Epistle Dedicatory, sig. A1v. For the biblical allusion, see 1 Chronicles 22:6–10. Other biblical allusions were a common ingredient in the many public addresses welcoming Richard; see Davies, *Restoration*, 11.

[14]   DWL MS *BT* iii.110r, item #62(2). See also, Lamont, *Millennium*, 299–300.

[15]   He was in a 'buoyant mood', to quote Lamont, *Millennium*, 57.

their cause was making solid progress.'[16] The Association movement was bearing impressive fruit, and even if he was not the sole inventor there were many who looked to the Worcestershire Association and to Baxter in particular for example and inspiration. His ministry in Kidderminster was a thriving going concern. He was looking every bit a national figure at the height of his publishing powers. He had produced nine books in 1657; eight more followed in 1658, including such devotional classics as *A Call to the Unconverted* and *Directions and Persuasions to a Sound Conversion*; the *Saints' Everlasting Rest* appeared in its seventh edition. Now he contemplated the timely appearance of Richard Cromwell:

> Your Highness hath a fair opportunity for this happy work: You enter in a season when we are tired with contention, and sensible of our loss and danger, and tenderer than formerly of one another, and the most angry parties are much asswaged, and there is not so much reproach and bitterness among the Godly, as lately there hath been. A Spirit of Peace and Healing is lately risen in the hearts of many thousands in the Land, and Ministers that differed, do lovingly associate, and most do feel the smart of our Divisions, and are so prepared for a perfecter closure, that they wait but for some Leading hand.[17]

The Baptists supplied impressive evidence of this fresh mood for agreement – Baxter was then in discussion with key figures about a basis for unity. This said as much about Baxter as it did about the Baptists. In a letter to John Howe, written in April 1658, Baxter made a striking amendment to his otherwise unaltered scheme for unity: he proposed a meeting between representatives of the five main ecclesiological parties, not just four – the Baptists were now included.[18] And in August he hurried off a letter – written on the Sabbath, no less – to Barbara Lambe, in which he strongly asserted his warmth towards the Baptists.[19] That began a series of correspondence with Barbara Lambe and her husband Thomas, and with William Allen, both moderate London Baptists whose congregations would soon rejoin the fold of the orthodox godly. These letters were so important to Baxter that even decades later he instructed his editors to include them in his autobiography.[20] They disclose exactly the same positive

---

16   Thomas, 'Rise of the Reconcilers', 67. See also, Abernathy, *English Presbyterians*, 16–17.

17   Baxter to Richard [Cromwell,] Lord Protector, [c. November 1658]: *Five Disputations*, Epistle Dedicatory, sig. A3r–v (*CCRB* #515).

18   The parties he listed were 'Episcopall, Presbyteriall, Congregationall, Erastian, Anabaptist'. Baxter to John Howe, 3 April 1658: DWL MS *BC* iii.200r (*CCRB* #443).

19   Baxter to Barbara Lambe, 22 August 1658: *Rel. Bax.*, Appendix, 54–8.

20   *Rel. Bax.*, Appendix, 54–107. See also ii.180–181, and the headnote to *CCRB* #473.

sentiment that Baxter offered to William Allen, in a letter probably written about the same time, in November 1658:

> I have felt that in my own Soul, and seen that upon my Brethren for these two or three Years past, which persuadeth me that God is about the healing of our Wounds, having communicated more healing Principles and Affections, and poured out more of the Spirit of Catholic Love and Peace than I have perceived heretofore ... The Prince of Peace erects his Banner, and the Sons of Peace flock in apace.[21]

Agreement with the Baptists, on the basis of Baxter's own generous and minimalist principles,[22] looked increasingly likely through the early months of 1659. John Durie reported positive progress in London,[23] and leading Baptists held meetings there to discuss Baxter's proposals.[24] Fortunately, all this effort was not derailed by his typically tactless assertion that they were responsible for the killing of the King, delivered in *A Key for Catholics*.[25] Though he vehemently protested their innocence,[26] Allen pronounced himself unoffended and not 'set back by a Hair's Breadth in my earnest desire to general Communion'.[27] Baxter had every reason to hope that, at long last, his efforts to foster unity between rival parties might actually bear tangible fruit.

Baxter also seemed generously inclined towards the Congregationalists. At the beginning of 1659 several notable London Presbyterians wrote to ask for his assistance in a new effort to mend the division between Congregationalists and Presbyterians. Both the tone and the content of the letter made it clear that such mending would be made only on Presbyterian terms. They asked Baxter for his opinion of their proposal; for 'strong arguments' supporting the Presbyterian case; for answers to the Congregationalists' 'specious' objections; and reasons against separation.[28] Baxter, of course, was hardly short of such material. Just a

---

[21]   Baxter to William Allen, 6 November 1658: *Rel. Bax.*, Appendix, 81–2 (*CCRB* #519).

[22]   See Baxter to William Allen, 6 November 1658: *Rel. Bax.*, Appendix, 89 (*CCRB* #519).

[23]   John Durie to Baxter, 20 Xbr [December] 1658: DWL MS *BC* i.96v (*CCRB* #531).

[24]   Will[iam] Allen to Baxter, 8 March 1658[/9]: DWL MS *BC* iv.272r (*CCRB* #561); Will[iam] Allen to Baxter, 18 April 1659: DWL MS *BC* iv.270r (*CCRB* #567).

[25]   The regicide 'was the work of Papists, Libertines, Vanists, and Anabaptists'. Richard Baxter, *A Key for Catholicks: To Open the Jugling of the Jesuits, and Satisfie All that are but Truly Willing to Understand, Whether the Cause of the Roman or Reformed Churches be of God* (1659), 323.

[26]   Will[iam] Allen to Baxter, 30 May 1659: DWL MS *BC* iv.187r–v (*CCRB* #576).

[27]   Will[iam] Allen to Baxter, 12 July 1659: *Rel. Bax.*, Appendix, 90 (*CCRB* #584).

[28]   [London Presbyterian Ministers] to Baxter, [late January–early February 1659]: DWL MS *BC* ii.278r (*CCRB* #549). The ministers who signed the letter were Edmund Calamy, Thomas Whitfield, William Jenkyn, Simeon Ashe, William Cooper, William Wickins and Matthew Poole.

few months earlier, in a letter to Thomas Lambe, he had strongly asserted the responsibility to care for the needs of all members of the parish and denounced the sheer laziness of those who would draw away the good and the godly and serve them only. Touchingly, he described how the very poorest of the parish would come to him for instruction, leaving a 'plentifull' supply of lice to inhabit Baxter's chamber 'for a competent space of time'. 'If I durst have gathered a separated Church here, I could have had one large and numerous enough, or such as would allow me ease; but I think Parish Work the best.'[29] So Baxter had no lack of sentiment to draw on, in response to this request of the London Presbyterians, but his response was guarded. He was prepared to help, but only if the

> businesse be principally for healing and concord, rather than defense of the presbyterian cause, and confutation of the Independents and if they meddle no further with disputinge their differences than is necessary for the Church and consistent with that reconciliation which is their end, and that in a manner that shall not obstruct it, drawing as neere and graunting as much as justly and easily we may.[30]

The Presbyterians had asked Baxter to move 'suddenly' and 'with all your speed'.[31] But he offered to send some material only once he had three things: an assurance that these conditions would be met; a better idea of how his thoughts would be deployed; and a guarantee his 'words or name' would not be used in the debates.[32]

What makes his response so interesting is that over the previous year his correspondents, on whom he was so reliant for intelligence, had given him more than enough cause immediately to condemn the Congregationalists if he had chosen to do so. Two examples will suffice. First, John Howe was at that point a struggling young chaplain in the household of Oliver Cromwell. Experiencing a 'near catastrophe' in his fledgling ministerial career he was 'out of his depth,

---

[29]   Baxter to Thomas Lambe, 29 September 1658: *Rel. Bax.*, Appendix, 63 (*CCRB* #503)

[30]   Baxter to Matthew Poole, [February–March 1659]: DWL MS *BC* iii.190r (*CCRB* #558).

[31]   [London Presbyterian Ministers] to Baxter, [late January–early February 1659]: DWL MS *BC* ii.278r (*CCRB* #549).

[32]   Baxter to Matthew Poole, [February–March 1659]: DWL MS *BC* iii.190r–v (*CCRB* #558). Poole provided these assurances in a letter of 23 March 1658[/9]: DWL MS *BC* vi.164 (*CCRB* #565). Baxter's papers were published in [Matthew Newcomen], *Irenicum, Or An Essay Towards a Brotherly Peace and Union Between those of the Congregational and Presbyterian Way* (1659). The Epistle to the Judicious Reader (sig. a1r) rejoiced that 'the God of Peace hath stirred up the heart of a faithful and able Minister of the Gospel (whose name would adde authority to this work, though hee see cause to conceal it) in a new way to attempt a brotherly agreement'.

at times depressed and increasingly desperate to escape a difficult situation'. Thus he turned to Baxter for advice, who took the chance 'effectively to recruit Howe as his agent at Whitehall'.[33] Howe had no axe to grind, which would have made his reflections on Philip Nye all the more persuasive. On 13 April 1658, Howe indentified Nye as a man so close to Cromwell that he would decisively either help or hinder Baxter's schemes, and he seemed unlikely to help.[34] On 7 May, Howe conveyed the specific nature of Nye's disagreements with Baxter's plan.[35] By 25 May Howe had lost any hope of co-operation from Nye. 'I perceive [in him] so steady a resolution to measure all indeavours of this kind by their subserviencie to the advantage of one partie.'[36] This was no more than Baxter had been saying for many years and Howe's assessment should only have confirmed his perspective.

The second example is Matthew Poole, one of those Presbyterian ministers in London who wrote to Baxter asking his aid. Poole had been involved in a scheme to establish godly young men at the universities. In August 1658 he wrote to Baxter in despair:

> the Congregationall men had a meeting at Oxford wherein two or three things were resolved[.] I know one was to set up Associations against Associations[.] But the other was (I am sure) to set up a designe against our university designe to chuse other Trustees and to maintaine lads in their way[.] I am informed from good hands that they intend plainly to carry it on in the way of a party.[37]

Poole was anxious that such a move would not only heighten existing divisions, it would irritate Oliver Cromwell 'who will not suffer the nation to bee a cockpit for two parties'.[38] That would have concerned Baxter as well, and given his high hopes for the Association movement he would have been alarmed to hear about any prospect of rival associations.[39]

Just two days later Poole was able to follow up with assuring news. Moderates among the Congregationalists had scuttled any plans for rival schemes and Nye was proving to be 'more inclinable to Accommodation than formerly', not because he had changed his stripes but because the political winds had shifted: Oliver Cromwell 'is much for agreement and because Associations grow every

---

33   Sutherland, *Peace, Toleration and Decay*, 42, 43.

34   John Howe to Baxter, 13 April 1658: DWL MS *BC* iii.198r (*CCRB* #447).

35   John Howe to Baxter, 8 May 1658: DWL MS *BC* iii.196r (*CCRB* #450).

36   John Howe to Baxter, 13 April 1658: DWL MS *BC* vi.323r (*CCRB* #453).

37   Ma[tthew] Poole to Baxter, 14 August 1658: DWL MS *BC* v.78r (*CCRB* #476).

38   Ibid.

39   His reply to Poole is not extant.

day more considerable, they lesse'.[40] No doubt this was one more ray of light in Baxter's relatively sunny disposition at the end of 1658, but several aspects of the exchange should be noted. First, Nye remained a leading figure, if not *the* leading figure, among the Congregationalists in the late 1650s. Second, he had shown himself once again to be a partisan player of the political game (or, at least, that is what Baxter was told). Third, and most significantly, Poole's letter offers telling evidence of Baxter's relationship with the Congregationalists at the time. Having successfully warded off these rival schemes Poole pleaded with Baxter to say no more. 'I beg of you that you do not upon any termes declare to Mr. N[ye] or any other indifferency as to the carrying of their work on in distinction from us, that will certainly much animate them to carry it on whereas now they are pretty well of[f] it.'[41] All it would take for the Congregationalists to revive their rival schemes was one word from Baxter asking them not to. It is clear that by now he had become a man with whom the Congregationalists simply could not deal. There was nothing positive to be said about their relationship. If Baxter asked for one thing they would do the opposite just to spite him. This evidence, coming from a Presbyterian figure with no motivation to inflate the dysfunction in this particular relationship, says it all. After his behaviour throughout the 1650s, Baxter had no sway with the Congregationalists; none at all.

So there was no love in them for him. And yet he did not quickly rush to hammer them when those Presbyterian ministers asked him to in early 1659. Coming on top of the other indications of Congregational partisanship, Baxter refused to be partisan himself. This seems to be one of those rare occasions when, acceding to Poole's entreaty, Baxter kept his mouth shut. That restraint and his positive mood present Baxter possibly at his most optimistic and conciliatory during the Interregnum (and, indeed, thereafter). But as the year progressed his posture changed. It may have begun to alter when he first saw the *Declaration of Faith and Order* put forward by the Congregationalists after their conference at the Savoy in October 1658.

A leading hand in that project was of course John Owen, whose career and experience once more presents the mirror image of Baxter's. If he was enjoying a rare phase of relative promise and optimism, Owen most certainly was not. Twelve months earlier he had been removed as Vice-Chancellor of Oxford University, one more indication of a deepening estrangement from Oliver Cromwell. We might recall that about that time the adjective most often used to describe Owen was 'angry'. In the season that followed Oliver's death, Owen and his fellow Congregationalists found themselves increasingly on the defensive. In

---

[40]   Mat[thew] Poole to Baxter, 24 August 1658: DWL MS *BC* vi.113r (*CCRB* #485).

[41]   Ibid.

some ways that reactionary stance is reflected in Owen's publications through 1658 and 1659, many of which concerned themselves with buttressing the reliability of Scripture in the face of a rising rationalist tide.[42] This slotted in nicely with Owen's anti-Socinian concern during the previous decade but his defence of Hebrew vowel-pointing, for example, was just another instance of a losing battle.[43] One gets the sense that Baxter would have had far more cause to enjoy his writing than Owen had during these worrying months. And it was not the only context in which Owen felt that hard-fought gains were slowly slipping away. Nowhere is that more apparent than in his final published sermon to Parliament, preached on 4 February 1659.[44] Despite its title, *The Glory and Interest of Nations Professing the Gospel*, there was very little glory about it.

Owen chose for his text Isaiah 4:5, which delivered God's word to the remnant of Israel: 'Upon all [Israel] the glory shall be a defence.' The context itself reveals just how far Owen had come from his first sermon to Parliament, preached so many years earlier, in 1646. Then, he was filled with a bright optimism about the wonders God was working in England. This positive tone continued to colour all his sermons to Parliament, even through the early 1650s. But by the middle of the decade it had become clear just how far away the Promised Land still lay. There is a readily discernible arc in the trajectory of Owen's sermons and by the late 1650s it was drifting inexorably downwards. Here at last, at the very beginning of 1659, Owen advertised 'the *overflowing flood of profaneness*, and opposition to the power of godliness, that is spreading itself over this land'. England 'begins to be overwhelmed by the pouring out of a profane, wicked, carnal spirit, full of rage, and contempt of all the work of reformation that has been attempted among us'. That spirit already had 'a visible prevalency' about it. 'And are not these the sad evidences of the Lord's departing from us?' For that reason, Owen was deeply worried for the future:

> I pray God we lose not our ground faster than we won it. Were our hearts kept up to our good old principles on which we first engaged, it would not be so with us; and the temptations of these days have made us a woful prey. *Gray hairs are here and there*, and it will be no wonder if our ruin should come with more speed than did our deliverance.[45]

---

[42]   See Owen, *Of the Divine Original, Authority, Self-Evidencing Light and Power of the Scriptures* (1659), which also included *A Vindication of the Hebrew and Greek Texts* (1659).

[43]   For brief context to the debate, see Benedict, *Christ's Churches Purely Reformed*, 301.

[44]   He later preached to the Rump Parliament on the day after its return but the sermon was not published. Woolrych, *Britain in Revolution*, 724.

[45]   Owen, *The Glory and Interest of Nations Professing the Gospel* (1659): *Works*, viii.467–8.

Very clearly, times had changed. Once again the contrast with Baxter is stark. In 1646 Baxter despaired while Owen dared to hope. By the opening of 1659 their respective postures had been entirely reversed. Now it was Baxter's turn to be brightly optimistic.

Owen's 1659 sermon, then, presented a frank assessment of England's present condition. He was more blunt and direct than normal. Pointedly, he declared that the world (by which he meant the ungodly, or those who had no true interest in the ways and the people of God) sat under judgement, no matter how powerful and glorious it might appear. 'In all the glittering shows of their wealth and riches, in the state and magnificence of their governments ... they are, in the eye of God, a filthy and abominable thing, – a thing that his soul loatheth.'[46] Such was England's present Parliament if it did nothing to shore up the interests of the godly. In 1646 Owen had preached as an insider; now he appeared as an outsider, one who feared that his audience was drastically out of alignment with his own interests and concerns, and beyond his control. So Owen spoke up, but he did so as a sick man who groans without any real expectation of becoming well.[47] He urged his hearers each to claim Christ for himself, to work to oppose the prevailing spirit of ungodliness and to close with the truly godly.[48] They embodied the remnant, the presence of God in England; and England's fortunes were tied inextricably with their interests. If they were promoted, God's grace would work for the nation's deliverance; 'but where they are diminished, there the glory is eclipsed'.[49] So the country's hope lay not with councils and armies, though God had used them in the past, but only with the preservation of the godly cause.[50] Though Owen claimed to be representing no party,[51] it would not have been difficult to read into his sermon that God was on the side of the Puritans and on that of the Congregationalists in particular. Their political influence was receding; Owen equated that with the Lord departing.

This is the context of declining political fortunes in which the Congregationalists held their meeting at the Savoy, in October 1658.[52] The project began some two months earlier on 12 July when a significant number

---

[46]   Owen, *Glory and Interest* (1659): *Works*, viii.463. 'Sin, with honour, with wealth, with power, with wisdom, is a deformed and contemptible thing' (viii.464).

[47]   Owen, *Glory and Interest* (1659): *Works*, viii.456.

[48]   Ibid., 466–71. He defined the truly godly at the bottom of p. 469.

[49]   Ibid., 462.

[50]   Ibid., 464–5.

[51]   Ibid., 470.

[52]   For description, see A.G. Matthews, ed., *The Savoy Declaration of Faith and Order 1658* (London: Independent Press Ltd, 1959), Introduction; and R. Tudur Jones, *Congregationalism in England 1662–1962* (London: Independent Press Ltd, 1962), 34–8.

of Congregationalist ministers happened to be present in Oxford for the Oxford Act. They agreed that an assembly was necessary.[53] George Griffith – the Congregationalist whose actions on unity proved so disappointing to Baxter – issued the invitations in a series of letters, probably beginning on 20 August. The delegates were to send their replies to Henry Scobell, master of the Savoy Palace and Clerk of the Executive Council.[54] Around 200 congregational elders and messengers were present.[55] They met on 11 days between September 29 and October 12,[56] in two groups. The larger group met together to formulate advice to Congregationalist ministers on matters of discipline and organization, after a period of years when the number of congregations had grown rapidly.[57] The second group consisted only of Thomas Goodwin, Philip Nye, William Greenhill, Joseph Caryll and John Owen. Their task was to devise a confession of faith. Each day the work of this small committee was ratified by the whole body, which resulted in the agreed Confession.[58] And the fruit of that was *A Declaration of the Faith and Order Owned and Practised in the Congregational Churches in England*. It opened with a preface that has long been attributed to Owen.[59] He may have been the guiding figure in its composition but it lacks the sustained sophistication typical of his writing to be just his work alone.[60] The Confession itself was modelled on the Westminster Confession, with 32 chapters. Finally, there was another declaration comprising 30 chapters that concerned specifically Congregational church polity. The whole work was published seemingly some time later. George Thomason entered his copy on 15 February 1659, with the typically caustic comment, 'Philip Nie and his Confederat Crew of Independents'.

---

[53]   *Mercurius Politicus*, Thursday 14 October 1658, no.438.

[54]   Powell, 'Savoy Declaration', 7.

[55]   Matthews, *Savoy Declaration*, 11.

[56]   *A Declaration of the Faith and Order Owned and Practised in the Congregational Churches in England* (1658), Preface, sig. a1r. This does not count two Sabbaths and the first day during which they discussed how to proceed. See *Mercurius Politicus* (Thursday 14 October 1658, no.438) for the start date; and Powell, 'Savoy Declaration', 3.

[57]   Matthews, *Savoy Declaration*, 24.

[58]   See Powell, 'Savoy Declaration', 3.

[59]   For instance, see Matthews, *Savoy Declaration*, 11, 16; Lawrence, 'Transmission and Transformation', 186; Woolrych, *Britain in Revolution*, 717.

[60]   James Sharp believed that 'D. Owen and D. Goodwin are the compilers of that Confession; and though in their preface they speak of 11 or 12 dayes only taken up about it, yet it hath been told some of them here that it is knowen they have been above so many moneths employed in framing it'. James Sharp to Robert Douglas, 8 March 1659: Stephen, ed., *Register of the Consultations*, ii.158.

Thomason's barb illustrates the difficulty of identifying the appropriate contexts for the *Declaration*. In part that reflects the weakness of the Preface. It is reasonably clear what the Preface is saying; it is not clear why it is saying it. Two possible contexts offer themselves. The first is a distinctly Congregational setting in which the *Declaration* was a purely Congregational exercise. In this light, the Confession was merely the authorized benchmark of belief for Congregational churches. 'And such *common Confessions* of the Orthodox Faith, made in simplicity of heart by any such body of Christians, with concord among themselves, ought to be entertained by all others that *love the truth as it is in Jesus*, with an answerable *rejoicing*.'[61] Perhaps this was why the Preface is framed around '*four remarkable Attendants*',[62] including the relative speed with which the delegates came to agreement,[63] to show that this confession of the Congregationalists was as worthy as any other and vouchsafed by the Spirit's working. Moreover, the delegates acknowledged that there had been divisions 'in some of our Churches' but this confession evidenced their present unity.[64] 'And this experimented event from out of such divisions, hath more confirmed us, and is a lowder Apologie for us, then all that our opposites are able from our breaches to alleadge to prejudice us.'[65] In this context, then, the Confession was an apology for Congregationalism. This is how it has largely been understood in the historiography, most notably by A.G. Matthews, the self-identified Congregationalist who edited a publication of the Declaration with his own too-casual introduction in 1959.[66] He closely linked the Savoy exercise with the waning political fortunes of the Congregationalists vis-à-vis the Presbyterians,[67] and he denied that they would have had any interest in union with them.[68] 'We must envisage the Declaration as a relic of the greatest period of Congregational history; a high-tide mark on the sands of time. It stands in isolation.'[69]

But a second, much broader context is also possible if we zoom out, as it were, and see the Savoy as one more instalment in the almost continuous search for settlement that trekked through the *Humble Proposals* of 1652, the

---

[61]   *Declaration*, Preface, sig.A1v.

[62]   Ibid., sig.A2v.

[63]   Ibid., sig.a1r.

[64]   Ibid., sig.a3r.

[65]   Ibid., sig.b1v.

[66]   Matthews, *Savoy Declaration*. He writes of 'our churches', 'our platform' and '[o]ur church system', on pp. 30, 36, 38.

[67]   Ibid., 10–11.

[68]   Ibid., 16.

[69]   Ibid., 39. What he meant by 'isolation' is that the confession had no precursor or successor within the Congregational movement.

meeting of divines in 1654 and the call for a national confession in the *Humble Petition and Advice* of 1657. Hunter Powell, building on the thoughts of Austin Woolrych, Michael Lawrence and Francis Bremer,[70] persuasively locates the Savoy in this wider context. He notes the continuity of personnel: essentially the same names involved in this confession were closely involved in all those earlier efforts.[71] He argues that Scobell was acting in an official capacity as Clerk of the Executive Council, suggesting some degree of state interest and even sponsorship – enough for one of the invitees, Vavasor Powel, to be extremely wary of the political machinery inevitably at work in such close proximity to the Lord Protector.[72] He points out that the role of the Magistrate was included in the Confession, something that would not have been included if this was simply a matter of Congregational belief.[73] And he tracks the continuities and changes in the theology of the various confessions of the 1650s, and in particular with the Westminster Confession. While there were clear developments in the Savoy Confession there was fundamentally no great departure; all these statements of belief were essentially of a piece.[74] This case is compelling and the Preface is able to carry the weight of it. The whole world, it affirmed, 'may now see after the experience of many years ran through (and it is manifest by this Confession) that the great and gracious God that ... kept us in that common unity of the Faith and Knowledge of the Son of God, which the whole Community of Saints ... have arrived unto.'[75]

So we have before us two plausible contexts for the Savoy *Declaration* and we need not choose between them. Both are important. One way of bringing them together is to borrow from the observations of James Sharp. He, of course, was the man who acted as the London agent for the Scottish Resolutioners and who tangled with Owen in doing so. In March 1659 he offered the following report:

> I find that those who pass under the notion of Presbyterians are still in jealousie [of] the Independent party who do stickle[76] more now than ever to strengthen their faction

---

[70]   Bremer, *Communion*, p. 201; Lawrence, 'Transmission and Transformation', 183–7; Austin Woolrych, *Commonwealth to Protectorate* (Oxford: Clarendon Press, 1982), 373; Woolrych, *Britain in Revolution*, 716–17. Peter Toon also sees the possibility, in *God's Statesman*, 101.

[71]   Powell, 'Savoy Declaration', 3.

[72]   Ibid., 7–8. See also, Matthews, *Savoy Declaration*, 16–17.

[73]   Powell, 'Savoy Declaration', 13.

[74]   Ibid., 70.

[75]   *Declaration of Faith and Order*, Preface, sig. A4v.

[76]   To stickle is 'to be busy, stirring or energetic; to strive or contend pertinaciously; to take an active part (in a cause, affair)'. Source: Online *Oxford English Dictionary* [www.oed.com].

and to get into the sadle. They have published a confession ... on designe upon sitting downe of the Parliament to prevent the imposing (as they say) of the Assemblie's Confession, which they feared the Parliament might doe. This Philip Nye told it one who had spoke it to me.[77]

Sharp's interpretation was acutely aware of current political conditions, but it also connected with the ongoing search for a religious settlement. The publication of the Savoy Confession may have been a pre-emptive move on the part of the Congregationalists to prevent the Westminster Confession from being forced upon them, but if so theirs was something of a counter offer in advance, one consciously modelled on Westminster. Indeed, by April 1659 'the Commons were debating in grand committee the adoption of a "public profession" of the nation's faith, and ordered that it should consist of the doctrinal articles of the Westminster Confession'.[78] So this pre-emptive concern makes sense not just of the Preface but also of Thomas Goodwin's assurances to the new Lord Protector when he came to present the Confession. The Savoy delegates had 'unanimously and through the Grace of Christ, without the least Contradiction, assented and agreed' to the Westminster Confession.[79] Therefore, we should locate the Savoy within the long search for settlement, but it came at a time when the high-flying Congregationalists were beginning to sink. Yes, much the same players were involved but it is surely telling that now, for the first time, they met and deliberated on their own. The Savoy was, in Powell's words, the 'final confession of the Puritan era',[80] the last of several; but in the end it belonged only to the Congregationalists and no one else.

John Owen fits nicely into this mix of contexts. To the extent that he was a leading figure within it, the Savoy is further evidence of his agenda for a national religious unity that nurtured the godly while tolerating minor differences among them. It reflected a continuation of his efforts begun so many years before but carried on now in drastically altered political circumstances. So Sharp's view of the Congregationalists continuing to jostle for influence and strategically pre-empting likely political developments is more than plausible. Here we have, once more, Owen the political player in pursuit of godly unity, but only on his own terms or at least only with safeguards for his own central convictions about toleration. And here we have again another failed, truncated effort to

---

[77]   James Sharp to Robert Douglas, 8 March 1659: Stephen, ed., *Register of the Consultations*, ii.157–8.

[78]   Woolrych, *Britain in Revolution*, 717. See also, Little and Smith, *Parliaments and Politics*, 218.

[79]   *Mercurius Politicus*, Thursday 14 October 1658, no.438.

[80]   Powell, 'Savoy Declaration', 1.

achieve a settlement of any sort. The Puritans were, as we now know, to enter the Restoration period still with no agreement and with any hopes of a national settlement on anything like their terms forever dashed. Thus the outcome of the Savoy would have done nothing to lift Owen's mood heading into 1659.

What all this serves to demonstrate is that the Savoy event was capable of multiple understandings and interpretations depending on the relative position of the observer and what the observer chose to see. Even within the Congregationalist movement there may have been differences. Hard-line sectarians may have seen it as a welcome firming of boundaries; the moderates and conciliarists (those who turned up for the assembly) would have viewed it as a viable basis for reconciliation among the godly.[81] Moving outside, those Presbyterian ministers who wrote to Baxter asking for his help late in 1658 consciously and publicly understood their own efforts as advancing 'the good design begun at the *Savoy*'.[82] But Baxter himself was, not surprisingly, only dismayed by the outcome of those deliberations.

Standing alone among his unpublished papers is a three-page, unfinished, undated postscript to another work. Exactly what that work was is unclear,[83] but it must have been along the lines of church unity: his 'despondencie' at the Savoy *Declaration* tempted him 'to cast away these Pages' as the prospect 'of Peace began to seeme so much more hopelesse than it was before'. What grated most on Baxter was that the 'most erroneous and dividing' positions 'published formerly by particular men' seemed to have caused 'the moderate healing concessions of Mr Norton, Mr Cotton, and others of old England yea, of My Nye and Dr Goodwin to be left out'.[84] These words are most remarkable. In particular, note 'the moderate healing concessions ... of Mr Nye'. It is, of course, possible that Baxter had evidence to go on of which we are unaware. Perhaps he had good reason to see Nye as a conciliator. But given what his correspondents had only recently told him, and given Baxter's own disappointing experience with the man, his inclusion of Nye (and Goodwin) as a man of healing, moderate principles is striking. I suggest something else is going on: Baxter was clearly pointing to Owen without going so far as to name him. He skirted around him

---

[81]   I am grateful to Joel Halcombe for this observation. Indeed, I would like to thank both Hunter Powell and Joel for various conversations on the Savoy.

[82]   [Newcomen], *Irenicum*, title page.

[83]   It is possible those pages were the ones written at the request of the London Presbyterians and published anonymously in [Newcomen], *Irenicum*. Thomason's entry for that work is dated 24 April 1658 and the title page referred to the Savoy. Roger Thomas suggests the papers were the first part of what was published as *Church Concord* in 1691 but that was written in 1655, not this late in the decade. See Thomas, 'Rise of the Reconcilers', 68.

[84]   DWL MS *BT* vi.203r, item #201.

in a way that made his absence from the list of names glaringly obvious. It was a way of blaming Owen without having to use the actual words. It is difficult to think of any Congregational figure of comparative significance who is *not* mentioned in Baxter's list; thus Owen is guilty by implication.

Baxter arrived at this judgement on the basis of more than just a bare reading of the text itself. He had himself talked 'with some of that Assemblie' and received 'credible report from others'. This intelligence gave him confidence that 'many good and peaceable men that were there present intended' the Confession not to be read in any 'dividing distant sense'. Indeed, if key words and phrases were understood in their proper sense, the *Declaration* did indeed offer the basis for unity. All of this served to underscore the problem: the undue 'influences of a few that seem resolved against a healing course'. Baxter hoped for 'a Peacemaking Ruler' to arise to put those few in their place.[85] Thus for all Baxter's stated grief his essential optimism and even generosity were not extinguished. On the question of private ministry, for instance, 'we take it gratefully, that they [the Congregationalists] yield so much'.[86] He agreed that the 'Protecting Coercive Power of the Magistrates is some way needfull', and, in a similar way the 'Power of Ordaining Pastors is some way needfull'. That said, he qualified both statements; and if the Congregationalists seriously believed that a congregation without officers simply 'receive all Power from Christ' then that was 'very false' and 'very dangerous'.[87] The manuscript breaks off unfinished, but it is worth noting two things. First, Baxter had discussed only the ecclesiology of the *Declaration*, not its soteriology. And, second, his tone was relatively moderate and conciliatory. Having vented his bitterness towards Owen's destructive engineering (even if he did not name him explicitly) he quickly became more positive and generous. Owen was only one man and only one of very few who, in Baxter's mind, were so resolutely set against unity. The *Declaration* itself (if read correctly) and so many of those present at the Savoy gave some prospect of peace. Baxter's optimism through the winter of 1658/9 had taken a hit, but it was not yet defeated. After all, Richard Cromwell – England's promising Lord Protector and perhaps that hoped-for 'Peacemaking Ruler' – remained in power. But not for long. The Savoy may have been a troubling event all on its own; much worse was still to come.

---

[85]   Ibid.

[86]   Ibid.

[87]   Ibid., 203v.

The Downfall of Richard Cromwell

Richard Cromwell's tenure as Lord Protector may have begun well enough but it ended badly and relatively quickly. In essence the Protectorate regime proved itself too divided to stand for long and Richard himself was incapable of holding the competing interests in check. The problem was exposed most starkly in the Council of State where 'the rift between the civilian and military parties was widening'.[88] The army had been losing ground since 1656 and now feared its ascendency might be displaced. On 21 September 1658 Charles Fleetwood presented Richard with an address of loyalty on the army's behalf but it was 'qualified by a reminder that Oliver had "in his armies ... reckoned the choicest saints his chiefest worthies", and by an exhortation to "carry on that good old cause and interest of God and his people"'. In the following month a petition from the junior officers demanded that Fleetwood be given much greater powers and independence from the head of state.[89] Clearly the army retained its place as political force in London, agitating for payment of arrears and for the cause of freedom and godliness – however that was understood – for which so many of its members had died. But the army itself was fragmented. According to Edmund Ludlow (an army officer, a regicide, and a member of the Council of State in 1659) it was 'divided into three parties, and neither of them much superior to the other in number'. The first group were those attached to the aspirations of the commonwealth, comprising several senior officers 'with divers captains and other inferior officers'.

> The second party was known by the title of Wallingford House, or army-party, who had advanced Mr. Richard Cromwell in expectation of governing as they pleased: of these were Lieutenant-General Fleetwood, Col. [John] Desborough, Col. [William] Sydenham, Col. [John] Clark, Col. [Thomas] Kelsey, Col. James Berry, Major Hainese, treasurer Blackwel, and some others.

Wallingford House was Fleetwood's residence in London where the senior officers routinely gathered. His party attempted to secure its own aims without alienating the support of the junior officers and soldiers.[90] Ludlow's third grouping was loyal to Richard, 'who having cast off those that had taken the pains to advance him, joined himself to [these] men that were more suitable to his inclinations'. They included many English officers 'and more particularly

---

[88]   Woolrych, *Britain in Revolution*, 710.
[89]   Ibid., 708–9.
[90]   Ibid., 713–14.

those that were officers in the Scots and Irish forces'.[91] As we shall see, these internal divisions played a decisive role in bringing down the Protectorate.

The civilian interest was hardly united, either. A republican core sat in the Commons, led by Sir Henry Vane and Sir Arthur Haslerig, too small to shape its deliberations but big enough to be more than troublesome.[92] Opposed to the Protectorate, they shared alliances with the commonwealth faction in the army; with the sects; and with a small number of crypto-Royalists in the Commons who worked to frustrate the efforts of government and who, naturally, rejoiced in its demise.[93] They lay behind a concerted pamphlet campaign in the autumn of 1659 designed to reassert the 'Good Old Cause'.[94] So it was left to Richard's courtiers and loyalists to advance his agenda in the face of mounting debt, unclear policy aims and these many and varied opponents. Perhaps that is enough to explain why the new Parliament called in early 1659 failed to enact a single Bill.[95] In religious terms Richard's ascendency heartened the Presbyterians. This caused no little amount of apprehension among the sectaries,[96] and led to attacks on the Congregationalists.[97] Though there seemed good reason to hope at the beginning of things, all of these pervasive, longstanding and deep-rooted divisions would prove fatal.

On 22 March 1659 John Thurloe wrote to Henry Cromwell: 'It is a miracle of mercy, that wee are yet in peace, consideringe what the debates are, and what underhand workeinge there is to disaffect the officers of the army.'[98] He was right to marvel, but the lull during which he wrote was just about to break. Just days later the Wallingford House party tried without success to seek an *entente* with the parliamentary republicans.[99] According to Ludlow, with whom they met, they were 'finding themselves abandoned by Mr. Richard Cromwell, and being very desirous, if not to get the whole power into their hands, yet at least to preserve what they were already possessed of, and to render themselves

---

[91]   C.H. Firth, ed., *The Memoirs of Edmund Ludlow Lieutenant-General of the Horse in the Army of the Commonwealth of England 1625–1672* (Oxford: Clarendon Press, 1894), ii.61.

[92]   Woolrych, *Britain in Revolution*, 711–12.

[93]   Barry Coward, *The Cromwellian Protectorate* (Manchester: Manchester University Press, 2002), 107–10; Woolrych, *Britain in Revolution*, 712–15.

[94]   Woolrych, *Britain in Revolution*, 715.

[95]   Davies, *Restoration*, 84.

[96]   Woolrych, *Britain in Revolution*, 713.

[97]   See, for instance, Firth, ed., *Memoirs of Edward Ludlow*, ii.61.

[98]   Thomas Birch, ed., *A Collection of the State Papers of John Thurloe, Esq. Secretary, First, to the Council of State, and Afterwards to the Two Protectors, Oliver and Richard Cromwell* (London, 1742), vii.636.

[99]   Woolrych, *Britain in Revolution*, 718; Davies, *Restoration*, 74–5; Firth, ed., *Memoirs of Edmund Ludlow*, ii.63–5.

formidable, desired to renew a correspondence with the Commonswealth men'.[100] Not long after they persuaded a reluctant Richard to summon a General Council of Officers. But 'they grossly overestimated their influence over their unruly juniors. They probably hoped to enlist republican support just far enough to make Richard give up his preferred counsellors and bring the army back to its political eminence of earlier years, but they soon found that they could not ride the tiger'.[101] The resulting petition carried alarming overtones, ominously offering to help 'in plucking the wicked out of their places'.[102] Parliament responded only with further provocation. On 18 April the Commons resolved that the Officers of the Army were forbidden to meet together without the permission of Oliver Cromwell.[103] As one of Henry Cromwell's informants put it, the Commons had 'voted ... the dissolution of the Generall assembly of officers at wallingford house' – a pre-emptive strike against a rival irritant. After the vote 'his highnesse having sent for [the officers] into his presence did declare their assembly dissolved and inhibited them to assemble againe'. The informant felt confident that this move would 'prove a stable foundation of a lasting settlement'.[104] But that confidence was badly misplaced. The manoeuvre met with opposition in the Other House; there was 'no chance' of it being enforced.[105] On 21 April Fleetwood gave orders for a general rendezvous of all the regiments the following day; Richard ordered a counter-rendezvous for the same time at Whitehall. He received only a very small response. That night, Fleetwood and Desborough met with him, pressuring Richard to dissolve Parliament and promising to take care of him – something they did not do.[106]

> It was the second time that the army had broken a parliament without knowing what it was going to put in its place ... The officers at Wallingford House who precipitated it had no desire to bring the Protectorate to an end, but only to manipulate Richard and ensure he exercised his authority through councillors of like mind to themselves. They wanted to consolidate their power over the army, but they found themselves having to share it with the men whom Oliver [Cromwell] had wisely purged, and to bow to the

---

[100]   Firth, ed., *Memoirs of Edmund Ludlow*, ii.63.

[101]   Woolrych, *Britain in Revolution*, 719.

[102]   Ibid.

[103]   *CJ*, 18 April 1659, vii.641.

[104]   D.W. Loftus to Henry Cromwell, 19 April 1659: British Library: Lansdowne MSS 823, f.297r.

[105]   Woolrych, *Britain in Revolution*, 720.

[106]   Ibid., 721.

pressure of subordinates whom they could no longer control ... [The] only group who achieved their aims in the short term were the parliamentary republicans.[107]

The republicans successfully argued for the restoration of the Rump parliament 'as the one way of redeeming the nation's "backsliding"'.[108] The Wallingford House group reluctantly conceded, with conditions. And on 6 May the first of the Rump members took their seats. On 25 May Richard, who had not gone down without a fight, finally 'signed a dignified submission to the restored Rump's authority that came as close as need be to a resignation'.[109] The Protectorate was no more.

Richard Cromwell's demise was a depressing black cloud that quickly and permanently obscured Richard Baxter's relatively sunny optimism. He received the news of Parliament's dissolution on 25 April, just as he neared the end of his manuscript of *A Holy Commonwealth*, which would be published a few months later.

> When I had gone thus far, and was about to proceed a little further, the sudden News of the Armies Representations, and of the dissolving of the Parliament, and of the displeasure against my Book against Popery, called, *A Key for Catholicks*, and some other passages, interrupted me, and cast me upon these MEDITATIONS and LAMENTATIONS following.[110]

Those lamentations reflected on the mysterious ways of God's providence in the world and the seeming senselessness of these latest events. Just when he 'thought that Charity was reviving in the world ... new storms arise; our hopes delude us; we find our selves in the tempestuous Ocean, when even now we thought we had been almost at the shore'.[111] Inexplicably, God's people were once more 'tost up and down in the world, as a Sea-rackt vessel, as the football of contempt'.[112] Baxter's choice of imagery is suggestive. The mournful tone of these meditations returned him to the late 1640s and to the *Saints' Everlasting Rest*, where he compared the wars to a pond unleashed. Now that great body of waters was larger still: this 'Ocean' a frightening, powerful, uncontrollable thing. To make his despondency more acute, God had allowed his people to be cast adrift just as they had almost reached safe harbour. Surely the sovereign God

---

[107]   Ibid., 721–2.
[108]   Ibid., 722–3.
[109]   Ibid., 725.
[110]   Baxter, *Holy Commonwealth*, 491.
[111]   Ibid., 492.
[112]   Ibid., 491.

could have brought them home, had he wished. 'How easily could he dispel our darkness, and reconcile our minds, and heal our breaches, and calm our passions, and subdue corruptions, and bring us into the way of pleasant Peace?'[113] But to wish for such things was to wish for a heaven on earth; to desire comfort over affliction; to expect too much of sinful people; to expect the perfect End before its time.[114] 'And as it is necessary that Heresies arise, that those which are approved may be made manifest; so it is necessary that Warres, confusion, and rebellions arise, that the meek, and peaceable, and obedient may be manifest.'[115]

Baxter knew whom to blame: the army. He knew from his own experience as a chaplain how the corrosive effect of a war environment steadily altered the moral reasoning of the soldiers in such a way as to rationalize any crime or atrocity: 'a slip into excess is excused there as a necessary evil'.[116] When he wrote a preface to the whole work some weeks later,[117] he addressed it to 'all those in the Army or elsewhere, that have caused our many and great eclipses since 1646'.[118] He insisted that 'a *special presence of God was with that Parliament*, which you then pull'd down, or forced out'.[119] He had written the manuscript 'while the Lord Protector (prudently, piously faithfully, to his immortal Honour, how ill soever you have used him) did exercise the Government'.[120] In September 1659 Baxter dedicated *A Treatise of Self Denial* to Colonel James Berry, a key leader in the army and a member of the congregation that met at Wallingford House. He had been a close friend of Baxter's, the one who had 'provoked me to this sweet, though flesh-displeasing life of ministry, in which I have chosen to abide'.[121] So Baxter addressed him with the wounds of a friend, alluding to Berry's sins in 'resisting and pulling down of governments'.[122] Later, when he wrote his autobiography, Baxter would be more explicit about Berry's part in Richard Cromwell's demise, and that of the army as a whole.[123]

---

[113]   Ibid., 492.

[114]   Ibid., 494–500.

[115]   Ibid., 498.

[116]   Ibid., 511.

[117]   He referred to the 'remaining Members' of the long Parliament 'that now sit again'. Baxter, *Holy Commonwealth*, Preface, sig. B1v. The *CCRB* (letter #575) dates it around late May.

[118]   Baxter, *Holy Commonwealth*, Preface, sig. A3r.

[119]   Ibid., sig. A4v.

[120]   Ibid., n.p.

[121]   Baxter, *Treatise of Self Denial* (1659): *Practical Works*, iii.359 (*CCRB* #603). 'You brought me into the ministry', iii.361.

[122]   Ibid., 356.

[123]   *Rel. Bax.*, i.57–8, 101–2.

So the army was clearly the target of Baxter's anger and disappointment at the turn of events but they were not solely to blame. After all, he addressed his preface to those 'in the Army *or elsewhere*'. Others were complicit. If we return to his immediate meditations, there is another sort of figure in view. This was someone who saw himself as a servant of God; who was a familiar friend; who called upon God in the cause for which he was engaged; who was 'too blind, too selfish, sinfull, and infirm to be the Guardian of the Church'; who was 'pulling down the Church, supposing they are building it'; who was full of 'self-conceit, and think none so fit to govern Countries and Nations as they'; who does not suspect his own understanding; who is too inclined towards his own honour; and who has a 'potent carnal Interest'.[124] It is impossible to know who Baxter had in mind when he penned these bitter reflections. James Berry is a possibility, though he could hardly be described as a guardian of the church. We cannot be sure who this represents, though we might note that Baxter's description is not far removed from how he viewed John Owen.

Indeed, at some point – and it may have been this early; we do not know – Baxter came to hold Owen responsible for bringing down Richard Cromwell. Here I would like to assess the plausibility of Baxter's claim. In the following chapter I will argue that Owen's perceived culpability in 1659 permanently vitiated Baxter's view of him and rendered their relationship, such as it was by 1659, beyond repair. In that context Owen's actual guilt or innocence are largely incidental; what matters is what Baxter believed and a passing plausibility was all that was needed. It is important to note that nowhere during 1659 did he explicitly blame Owen for Cromwell's demise, so the evidence for Baxter's understanding of Owen's part in proceedings comes from the Restoration period. I have been careful throughout this book to draw evidence as far as possible only from the period under examination. But it is necessary here to bring in several later pieces of evidence in order to convey the outlines of Baxter's view so that the notion of Owen's culpability can be tested.

In the first part of the *Reliquiae Baxterianae*, written in 1664, Baxter claimed that

> Dr. Owen and his assistants did the maine work: His high spirit now thought the place of Vicechancellor and Deane of Christs Church, to be too low: and if the Protector will not do as he would have him, he shall be no Protector: He gathereth a Church at Lieutenant Generall Fleetwoods quarters, at Wallingford howse, consisting of the active Officers of the Army! ... Here fasting and prayer, with Dr. Owen's magisteriall

---

124   Baxter, *Holy Commonwealth*, 500, 501, 503, 505, 507, 508.

counsel, did soon determine the Case, with the proud and giddy headed Officers, that Richards Parliament must be dissolved, and then he quickly fell himself.[125]

In the third part, written in 1670, Baxter repeated the point: 'Dr. *Owen* was ... the greater persuader of *Fleetwood, Desborough,* and the rest of the Officers of the Army who were his *Gathered Church,* to compel *Rich. Cromwell* to dissolve his Parliament; which being done he fell with it.'[126] In the early 1690s when Edmund Calamy was helping Matthew Sylvester to edit the *Reliquiae,* Baxter's reflections on Owen's actions were a topic of intense discussion between the two men. Sylvester told Calamy that during those crucial days in April 1659 Thomas Manton

> was summoned to the meeting at Wallingford House, and as he was passing into the room in which the company met, heard Dr. Owen give his sense with great warmth, about the matter that was the occasion of the summons given. Of which Mr. Sylvester had a distinct account both from Mr. Richard Stretton, and Mr. Wm. Taylor, (who had it directly from Dr Manton) as well as several others.[127]

Finally, Calamy offered the actual words allegedly uttered by Owen in Manton's hearing – 'He must come down, and he shall come down' – though he confused matters by saying that Manton made the connection between Owen's words and Richard's fall only 'after the event'.[128] If this is the case, why did he feel the need to turn around and go home? Be that as it may, this could well be the basis on which Baxter staked his claim: Manton overheard Owen urging the demise of Richard Cromwell.

That, then, is the shape of Baxter's indictment against Owen, but just how plausible is it? It is certainly true that Owen had gathered a church that included among its members the leading officers of the Wallingford House party and that they met together at Wallingford House. In March 1659 James Sharp informed his Scottish masters that the Congregationalists 'have their party both in the

---

[125] British Library: Egerton MS. 2570, f.26r. This is the manuscript version of Baxter's comments, which is longer, more pointed and more bitter towards Owen. For the abridged edited version, see *Rel. Bax.,* i.101.

[126] *Rel. Bax.,* iii.42.

[127] John Towhill Rutt, ed., *Edmund Calamy: An Historical Account of My Own Life With Some Reflections on the Times I Have Lived In (1671–1731)* (London: Henry Colburn and Richard Bentley, 1829), i.378–9.

[128] Samuel Parker, ed., *Edmund Calamy: The Nonconformist's Memorial: Being an Account of the Ministers Who Were Ejected or Silenced After the Restoration...Now Abridged and Corrected by Samuel Parker* (London: W. Harris, 1775), i.154.

Court and Parliament, which they own and cry up to the disparaging of those who are not for them: Owen hath lately erected a congregation about Whythall, of which Fleetwood, Desburrie [Desborough], Lambert, Berrie, Whaley, are members, upon a state project'.[129] It is also true that Owen had been a key player in the various negotiations that went on. For instance, on 30 April Sir Archibald Johnston of Wariston (the only Scottish member of the Council of State) 'mett with Doctor Owen, Col. Sydenham, Mr King, Griffeth and at last with my Lord Fleetwood' to discuss what should happen next. He

> told them largly my reasons against calling the Long Parliament. I heard they had agreed to byde one be another and manteane civil and spiritual libertyes already obteaned, and submit to what gouverment God shal incline them to. I heard the Protector was not very sensible of his condition tho Doctor Owen spak thryse to him.[130]

While this meeting took place after the dissolution of the former Parliament it does indicate just how enmeshed Owen was in the exchanges between the Wallingford Party and Richard Cromwell. The circumstantial evidence is fairly damning, especially if we link these events with those of 1657 when Owen was instrumental as a 'ghost writer' in the attempts of Fleetwood and Desborough to dissuade Oliver Cromwell from accepting the Crown.[131] There, Owen proved himself to be loyal to the aims of the army officers, even if that meant displeasing the Lord Protector. It requires no great leap of the imagination to see Owen doing much the same thing precisely two years later. Baxter may well have been right.

John Asty, Owen's early biographer, did not think so. He directly challenged the *Reliquiae Baxterianae* and rightly observed that it might have been helpful if Baxter had aired his accusation while Owen was still alive to rebut them.[132] He also offered some intriguing background, quoting from a letter from a Reverend James Forbes of Gloucester:

---

[129]   James Sharp to Robert Douglas, 8 March 1659: Stephen, ed., *Register of the Consultations*, ii.158.

[130]   James D. Ogilvie, ed., *Diary of Sir Archibald Johnston of Wariston: Volume III 1655–1660* (Edinburgh: T and A Constable Limited, 1940), 106.

[131]   Daniel Neal also makes this connection, and concludes it is 'very probable' that Owen was complicit, in *The History of the Puritans, Or, Protestant Non-Conformists from the Death of King Charles I to the Act of Toleration by King William and Queen Mary, in the Year 1689*, 4 vols (Dublin: Brice Edmund, 1755), iv.178. But Neal was not a neutral commentator.

[132]   Asty, 'Memoirs of Owen', xviii.

There is yet a worthy minister alive, who can bear witness that Dr. Owen was against the pulling down of *Richard Cromwell*, for there came a person to him with this request; you must preach for Dr. Owen such a day in the *Chapel* at *Whitehall*, for he is sick, and is not able to preach, and the cause of his present illness is his dissatisfaction at what they are doing at *Wallingford*-House, with respect to the Protector. This minister is my intimate acquaintance; and this he gave me under his hand.[133]

Though we are once more relying on hearsay, this is tantalizing evidence. It suggests that Owen was seeking to defend the interests of Richard Cromwell. At the very least it is possible that he saw himself as a mediator between the two parties and not serving one alone, and that he was 'sick with worry' at the way that matters were falling out.[134]

Even though he did not live to read the *Reliquiae Baxterianae*, Owen's alleged crime was brought to his attention on several occasions. In late 1659 or 1660 Thomas Truthsbye (possibly a pseudonym for Thomas Taylor, but certainly a Quaker) wrote a bitterly hostile letter to Owen 'relating to the intendments of Wallingford-house'. 'Does not the light within thee witness to thy wrinkled face, that thou *John Owen* wast instrumental, and by thy close jugling with a gathered Brood in *Wallingford-house*, didst countenance, promote, vigorously act to the downfall of that timorous *Richard*, and dissolution of that famous Parliament?'[135] If Owen deigned to reply it is not extant. But he did respond to George Vernon, who published *A Letter to a Friend Concerning Some of Dr. Owen's Principles and Practices* in 1670. Among his many criticisms, Vernon asserted that Owen 'became the Instrument of Ruine' to Richard Cromwell.[136] In reply, Owen denied bringing down Richard, 'with whose setting up and pulling down I had no more to do than himself [that is, Vernon]'.[137] Earlier, in 1664, Owen had defended himself against the more general accusations of John Cane. Owen presented himself as 'a person who never had a hand in, nor gave consent unto, the raising of any war in these nations, nor unto any political alteration in them, no, not to any one that was amongst us during our revolutions'. Though he immediately conceded, referring to himself in the third person, that 'he lived and acted under them the things wherein he thought his duty consisted, and challengeth all men to charge him with doing the least personal injury unto any,

---

133   Ibid., xix.

134   Woolrych, *Britain in Revolution*, 724.

135   Thomas Thruthsbye to Owen, [1659/60]: *CJO*, 118.

136   Vernon, *Letter to a Friend*, 28.

137   Owen, *Reflections on a Slanderous Libel* (1670): *Works*, xvi.274. This defence is one of two elements in *An Expostulatory Letter to the Author of the Late Slanderous Libel against Dr. O*, published anonymously by Sir Thomas Overbury in 1671. See Asty, 'Memoirs of Owen', xix.

professing himself ready to give satisfaction to any one that can justly claim it'.[138] Finally, and second-hand, Calamy claimed that when faced with the accusation, 'this [Owen] himself and his friends solemnly denied'.[139] All of this is about as much evidence as we can assemble.

Let us allow ourselves for a moment to believe that Owen is guilty as charged. We might begin with this rebuttal in 1664. It is stretching things well beyond the bounds of plausibility to say, as Owen did, that he 'never ... gave consent unto, the raising of any war in these nations'. Technically he was not a notable voice when the war first began, but he was a consistent supporter of its aims and he became a very visible champion of the cause. His many sermons to Parliament give ample testimony to that. It is also quite untrue that he never gave his consent to any 'political alteration' – he was a key advisor in the search for a frame of politics through which God's providential blessing might be experienced. Likewise, his reply to Vernon claiming he had nothing to do with pulling down Richard Cromwell strains credibility. Peter Toon is right to conclude that in 'saying this, Owen was claiming too much'. The fact that he stayed in London rather than returning to Oxford and the fact that he preached to the newly restored members of the Long Parliament 'do involve him to some degree in culpability for what occurred'. Owen 'certainly had some part, howbeit a small and indirect one, in the fall of Richard'.[140] We have also seen before that Owen's claims in his own defence could be dubious. We might ungenerously see in his 1664 defence the slippery words of a well-practised politician; they were capable of a very wide latitude of interpretation. Furthermore, the notion of Thomas Manton turning back with his hand at the door has a compelling specificity about it, and as a reported comment of Owen's it is not unique. In 1657 James Sharp claimed that Owen 'professeth he will lay out himself to the outmost against Presbyterians'.[141] Once again this seems a strongly asserted sentiment, though one that is also open to doubt. In this light, Owen surprisingly shares Baxter's great weakness in common. For Baxter, his methods always defeated his aims – he sustained division in the pursuit of peace. Likewise, we should not doubt Owen's genuine aspiration to reconcile the godly in England, but his methods – those illustrated most acutely in his exchanges with Sharp – tarnished his credibility. He was genuinely a lover of peace and concord, though his partisan methods and dubious tricks powerfully conveyed otherwise.

---

[138]   Owen, *A Vindication of the Animadversions on 'Fiat Lux'* (1664): *Works*, xiv.190.

[139]   Parker, *Nonconformist's Memorial*, i.154.

[140]   Toon, *God's Statesman*, 114. See also, Dale, *History of English Congregationalism*, 347.

[141]   James Sharp to Robert Douglas, August 1657: Stephen, ed., *Register of the Consultations*, ii.88.

Even so, there is also good cause to doubt the evidence against him. Manton may well have been at the door but he may have mistaken the voice, misheard the words or misunderstood their context. William Orme goes too far in suggesting that Owen's words 'might allude to the Pope, or the Grand Turk, as well as to Richard Cromwell',[142] but the underlying point is valid. The story, as Calamy has it, passed from Manton through Taylor through Sylvester to Calamy. The evidence is not only second-hand but relatively circumstantial and ambiguous. Also, there is the possibility that Owen really was made sick by the developments of April 1659. The letter from which Asty quoted is itself another instance of hearsay long after the fact but we might note that Owen does come across as a mediating figure. He met with the junior officers at St James as well as with the senior officers at Wallingford House.[143] Austin Woolrych is inclined to think that in gathering his congregation, which included more than just the Wallingford House officers, Owen 'had probably intended to try and heal the breach that had opened between Richard's supporters and the Wallingford House faction'. He concludes 'there is no evidence that Owen did or said anything positive to Richard's prejudice, and indeed it is unlikely, but the fact that he preached before the Rump on the day after it returned to power made it appear that he at least condoned the change in government'.[144] Appearances such as these were the biggest problem he faced, especially in choosing to gather a church at Wallingford House. From the beginning his move 'hath divers constructions put upon it', observed Arthur Annesley, 'and is not that I can heare very well liked at Whitehall'.[145] In Toon's view, 'Owen was probably tactless to engage in the role of pastor of such a church since its very existence ... was open to misunderstanding. His aims were honourable'.[146] If this is so, both he and Baxter were heartsick at the turn of affairs. If Baxter had ever chosen to enquire, he might have been surprised by the extent to which Owen shared his disappointment.

---

[142]   Orme, 'Memoirs', i.213. In this sequence of pages Orme surveys the evidence against Owen and concludes that it can have had no basis in fact.

[143]   Richard Baker, *A Chronicle of the Kings of England* (1682), 659; Woolrych, *Britain in Revolution*, 724.

[144]   Woolrych, *Britain in Revolution*, 724. This is a departure from Woolrych's early view that 'Fleetwood in particular ... was much influenced by Dr John Owen'. '[W]hen Owen gathered a church at Wallingford House ... there was good reason for the anxiety felt at Whitehall, for with this leader of the Independents preaching the good old cause its call was no longer merely sectarian.' Woolrych also then accepted Baxter's claim without question. A.H. Woolrych, 'The Good Old Cause and the Fall of the Protectorate', *Cambridge Historical Journal* 13 (1957): 146–7.

[145]   Arthur Annesley to Henry Cromwell, March 15 1658[/9]: British Library: Lansdowne MSS 823, f.272r.

[146]   Toon, *God's Statesman*, 110.

Owen's claim to have had nothing to do with Richard Cromwell's demise was untrue, but so was Baxter's contention that Owen 'did the main work'. Wherever the truth lies, it sits in between those two perspectives. All the evidence we have for Owen's complicity is circumstantial – plenty of smoke, but no actual fire. It certainly makes sense to see him working 'hand in glove' with the army officers to achieve their political ends.[147] That would be entirely consistent with his past behaviour. But it also makes sense that he was trying his best to hold things together in the most difficult of circumstances and deeply troubled by the turn of events. The fact is, there was plenty of blame to go around. The momentum against the Protectorate, regardless of the person who filled the office of Protector, had been building for several years and from different directions.[148] The parliamentary royalists, the republicans and the Commonwealth men worked assiduously to undermine the Protectorate in a way that Owen certainly never did. Fleetwood and Desborough must shoulder responsibility for what Godfrey Davies calls the 'military *coup d'état* which had forced the Protector to dissolve Parliament'.[149] Richard's own supporters at court proved themselves to be inept; they hardly helped his cause.[150] And Richard was no mere victim of events beyond his control. In the summation of Davies, he

> had neither the will nor the wish to prevail when occasions arose that required stern measures. The father [Oliver] often hesitated until his mind was made up, but then he struck like lightning; the son [Richard] continued to drift until upon the rocks. Difficulties similar to those that ruined the son – and more besides – had been overcome by the father. But the religious enthusiasm, fiery energy, and iron determination which had enabled Oliver to overcame every obstacle were all wanting in Richard.[151]

Patrick Little and David Smith are more generous. They think Richard 'displayed considerable skill in handling the difficult and complex circumstances that he inherited from Oliver'. The military coup should be seen as a sign of the army's fear that he was doing rather too well in achieving political stability in a way that diminished its influence.[152] Perhaps Baxter was right to think that Richard had

---

[147]   Matthews, *Savoy Declaration*, 10.

[148]   This comes through most clearly in Austin Woolrych's early article, 'The Good Old Cause and the Fall of the Protectorate'.

[149]   Davies, *Restoration*, 86.

[150]   Woolrych, *Britain in Revolution*, 708, 712.

[151]   Davies, *Restoration*, 17.

[152]   Little and Smith, *Parliaments and Politics*, 169–70.

governed 'prudently, piously, faithfully'.[153] Whatever the case, the point is clear: even with his proximity Owen was hardly in a position to bend such varied forces to his will.[154]

He continued to have a hand in events as they unfolded through the second half of 1659, but those events 'took the control of the future out of the hands of most of those who formed the church in Wallingford House'.[155] By the beginning of May momentum began to turn towards the recalling of the Long Parliament; the only questions were any conditions or limitations that might be placed upon it, the possible creation of a senate to replace the Other House, and the continuing status of the Lord Protector.[156] Owen was privy to those discussions,[157] and we know he preached to the restored members of the Long Parliament the day after they first sat. Regrettably, we do not know what he said. Given a later comment by Thomas Truthsbye – that Owen called them 'dry Bones breathed into' – his text may have been Ezekiel 37, in which God breathed life into dry bones.[158] Whatever the case, the occasion was clearly momentous (in a similar way to his preaching the day after the regicide) which demonstrates just how closely he was involved in these events. In October the army, led by John Lambert, effectively closed down the Parliament for the third time, again not knowing what to put in its place.[159] General George Monck, then stationed in Scotland, began to involve himself in developments. On 19 November Owen wrote to Monck to clarify his role in things – he had been absent from London for five weeks, during which time the latest dissolution occurred – and to plead with Monck to assist in the 'fixing on a free Commonwealth; and in such a way' as to preserve 'the true interest of Christ, and that of men sober and godly'.[160] Monck sent a reassuring reply but made it clear that he would seek 'to see my

---

[153]   Baxter, *Holy Commonwealth*, Preface, n.p.

[154]   Detailed accounts of Richard's demise can offer explanations that are plausible enough without once mentioning Owen's supposed machinations. For example, see Gerald R. Cragg, 'The Collapse of Militant Puritanism', in *Essays in Modern English Church History in Memory of Norman Sykes*, ed. G.V. Bennett and J.D. Walsh (London: Adam and Charles Black, 1966), 76–103; De Krey, *London and the Restoration*, chapter 1; and Little and Smith, *Parliaments and Politics*, chapter 7.

[155]   Toon, *God's Statesman*, 115. See also, Jones, *Congregationalism in England*, 42–6.

[156]   Woolrych, *Britain in Revolution*, 724.

[157]   Ogilvie, *Diary of Sir Archibald Johnston of Wariston*, iii.107–8.

[158]   'As for Parliaments, didst thou not preach up and down the Rump? After its resurrection thou calldst them dry Bones breathed into, and in a short time with Lambert, Desborough, etc. help rebury them, and preach their second Funeral Sermons.' Thomas Truthsbye to Owen, [1659/60]: *CJO*, 118.

[159]   Woolrych, *Britain in Revolution*, 741.

[160]   Owen to George Monck, 19 November 1659: *CJO*, 106–8.

Country freed (as much as in mee lies) from that intolerable slavery of sword Government, and I know England cannot, nay, will not endure it'. Monck called on Owen, 'knowing the interest you have in Lord Fleetwood', to tell him 'that hee should restore the Parliament to sit with safety and freedome'.[161] On 21 December, Owen was present at a meeting at Wallingford House called in response to news of desertions among the army.[162] The Wallingford Party had clearly lost control. The Long Parliament was permitted to reconvene: it sat in its final session from 26 December to 16 March, joined from 21 February by its long-excluded members. Monck arrived in London on 3 February. In a telling sign of the shift in political fortunes, on 13 March 1660 the full Parliament cast out the Dean of Christ Church, Oxford.[163] Owen's proximity to power had very visibly come to an end.

Owen can hardly have enjoyed these winter months; and neither did Baxter. Richard Cromwell's end had stabbed a hole in his earlier optimism. A new tone of bitterness and disappointment took its place. In the dedicatory epistle to his *Treatise of Self Denial*, written in September 1659, Baxter put this rhetorical question to James Berry: 'How long have some been longing, and praying, and moving, and labouring for peace among the professed sons of piety and peace in England; and all (for aught I see) almost in vain; unless to the condemnation of a selfish, unpeaceable generation!' Evidently, not long enough. 'Little would you or I have thought, that after professors of godliness were in power, so many years should have been spent in destroying charity and unity.'[164] In October he marvelled at the utter failure to achieve unity among the godly, when the godly had been in power. He and Archbishop James Ussher had agreed on a form of Church government in the space of half an hour.[165] 'And that it should be harder to agree with the Congregational Brethren, is incredible. Why then is there not long ago a settled concord among all these?' That the work should be resisted and frustrated was shameful and astonishing, 'especially of some that have been the hinderers ... by their self-blinding and Church-troubling pride'.[166] This is,

---

[161]   George Monck to Owen, 29 November 1659: *CJO*, 110–12.

[162]   Ogilvie, *Diary of Sir Archibald Johnston of Wariston*, iii.160.

[163]   For these dates, see Davies, *Restoration of Charles*, 256; and Toon, *God's Statesman*, 115–16. Also see Spalding, *Diary of Bulstrode Whitelocke*, 573, 576.

[164]   Baxter to James Berry, 12 September 1659: *Practical Works*, iii.356, 357 (*CCRB* #603).

[165]   Baxter never tired of pointing this out, but R. Buick Knox suggests that the two men were further apart than Baxter realized and that Ussher's scheme 'never was a promising guide to ecclesiastical comprehensiveness', in 'Archbishop Ussher and Richard Baxter', *Ecumenical Review* 12 (1959): 60 (and p. 59).

[166]   Baxter to the Reader, 17 October [1659]: in John Tombes, *True Old Light Exalted Above Pretended New Light* (1660), To the Reader, sig. B4r–v (*CCRB* #611).

quite possibly, the closest he came to blaming Owen explicitly. But he had also lumped in the Baptists in a letter to William Mewe, dated 6 August, offering the inescapable logic that if unity with the Congregationalists and the Baptists was possible it would have happened by now. 'I had all most accomplish it with many pastours of the Anabaptist Churches in London.' They had been happy to proceed but Richard Cromwell's demise had been seen to be their elevation: 'the turne set them up and then they were to [*sic*] high for accommodation'.[167] This must have rubbed salt in the wound, to come so close and be denied. It gave Baxter one more reason to resent Owen and to see him as the destroyer of all his dreams.

Therefore, as the Interregnum came to an end Owen and Baxter were further apart than ever before, though for all that they still had much in common. Each one had witnessed the failure of cherished dreams and each one would have felt that to some extent the other was to blame. It remains to be seen just how those perceptions continued to shape and limit the relationship between them as it developed throughout the Restoration period.

---

[167]   Baxter to William Mewe, 6 August [*recte* September] 1659: DWL MS *BC* iv.281r (*CCRB* #600).

Chapter 9
Fatal Memory

I thought it my Duty without any thought of former things, to go to [Owen], to be a Seeker of Peace ...

... I told him, that I must deal freely with him, that when I thought of what he had done formerly, I was afraid lest one that had been so great a breaker, would not be made an Instrument in healing.

Richard Baxter (1670)[1]

In 1696 Richard Baxter got in one last, glancing blow at the reputation of John Owen – not a bad effort for a man who had been dead for five years. Despite all his earlier contrition at having been the beginner of the controversy between them, despite his stated intention to allow Owen the final say, Baxter made sure that he had the ultimate Last Word, spoken from the grave and delivered with all the advantages of being dead: unanswerable, and far beyond all rebuke or correction. By then Baxter had been nursing carefully chosen words a very long time. He had begun to write his autobiography in 1664, adding to it in progressively finer instalments as the decades advanced. In that first part Baxter accused Owen of having done 'the main work' in bringing down Richard Cromwell. In 1696 – more than 30 years later – this device that Baxter had laid in the ground finally detonated. The *Reliquiae Baxterianae* exposed Owen's alleged part in Richard's fall for all to see.

It is important to appreciate the sense of wounded indignation felt by those who cherished Owen's memory. This is what William Orme alluded to when he explained that 'Baxter seldom omitted an opportunity of hitting a blot in Owen's conduct and writings; and not content with wrangling during his life, he left a legacy of reproach on the memory of his brother, which continued to operate long after his death'.[2] We see this woundedness most clearly in the commonplace book of John Asty – a document that has only just come to light.[3]

---

[1] *Rel. Bax.*, iii.61.

[2] Orme, 'Memoirs', 89.

[3] I am deeply indebted to Hunter Powell, a PhD candidate at the University of Cambridge, who spotted the significance of this document in the course of his own research and alerted me to its existence. It is 'New College Comm 2', held at the University of Edinburgh Library. There are two main reasons to think it is the work of John Asty. First, and most obviously, he signed his

In this book Asty devoted some 60 pages to defending Owen against Baxter's accusation. Regrettably, Asty was able to offer nothing in the way of specific evidence in his defence. Indeed, that was the genius of Baxter's method, publicly proclaiming Owen's crime 'when all or most that were acquainted with the transactions of those times were dead and gon, it being above 30 yeares from the laying down to the publishing Mr B. Life'.[4] Asty was reduced – plaintively, repetitively and ineffectually – to bemoaning Baxter's own lack of evidence for Owen's guilt. But merely lamenting Baxter's lack of proof was to shut the stable door well after the horse had bolted, enjoyed a long retirement in distant fields, and died. So it is no surprise that Asty never published these pages, and his defence of Owen in the memoirs he did publish was far more effective and concise.[5] But it lacks the sense of mystifying betrayal so touchingly conveyed in the commonplace book. 'For personal Reflections on eminent Persons gon to Rest, especially Those whose Labours have been eminently usefull in the Church of God, and may be so in future ages, can hardly be justified; because it may prepossess Men with Prejudice against their Writings, and so prevent the Advantage that might otherwise be reaped by them.'[6] Baxter had besmirched Owen's reputation entirely without proof.

Of course Baxter's intentions could yet have been thwarted if the editors of his manuscript had judiciously chosen to delete his reflections on Owen. That very nearly happened. When Matthew Sylvester and Edmund Calamy edited the *Reliquiae Baxterianae* they debated what to do with those portions of the manuscript that did not reflect well on certain individuals. Calamy was all for discretion and sought to delete or soften as many as he could; Sylvester could hardly bring himself to tamper with Baxter's creation. As it turned out,

---

name in the last few pages. Second, it contains long passages on the life of Owen that are identical in phrasing to Asty's published 'Memoirs of the Life of Dr. Owen' – we may surmise this is his first draft. Moreover, language used in a later section defending Owen from the accusation of bringing down Richard Cromwell is identical to that used by Asty. I am also grateful to the University of Edinburgh Library for supplying me with a PDF copy of the document. The original has no foliation, and blank pages may have been omitted from the PDF copy, which makes assigning folio numbers difficult. To help the reader, I can say that I have adopted page numbers, one number for each side of the sheet, which is the numbering I use in these notes. Asty's defence of Owen begins on page 113 (beginning 'But having pleased Mr Baxter...') and ends on page 178, with two-thirds of a page of shorthand. Therefore, to consider the similarities between this and Asty's memoirs, compare 'New College Comm 2', 150, 152, with 'Memoirs', xviii.

   [4]   University of Edinburgh Library: 'New College Comm 2', 126. See also pp. 125, 154, 156, where Asty repeats the point.

   [5]   See Asty, 'Memoirs', xvii–xix.

   [6]   University of Edinburgh Library: 'New College Comm 2', 129.

regrettably, Calamy badgered Sylvester into making some modest amendments.[7] 'But our greatest difficulty', Calamy recalled years later, was

> with relation to Dr. Owen, upon whom there were several reflections. Some of these, (after frequent debates) he did allow me to blot out, and I did it, cheerfully, with my own hand. But, as to the main reflection upon him, with regard to the affair of Wallingford House, and his concern in it, on which Mr. Baxter laid a considerable stress, (and which Mr. Sylvester had often heard Mr. Baxter discourse of with great freedom,) he would not by any means give his consent to have that out.[8]

Sylvester rightly felt that to omit the episode entirely was a betrayal of the integrity of the account that Baxter wished to leave the world, but he is due more credit than Calamy gave him. He wrote a Preface to the Reader, dated 13 May 1696, that demonstrates that he was not naive about the likely reception of Baxter's conclusions, nor one-sided. He explained that he had written to Owen's widow (his second wife, Dorothy) to ask for a written defence in reply to Baxter's accusations so that he might put it in the margin. He even offered to 'expunge that passage'. 'But this offer being rejected with more contemptuousness and smartness than my Civility deserved, I had no more to do than to let that pass upon Record.'[9]

These related events are extremely revealing. Clearly Owen's part in the downfall of Richard Cromwell was a central issue for all concerned, not least Baxter himself. He continued to lay 'a considerable stress' on Owen's actions 'often' and 'with great freedom'. He continued to vent his feelings long after the Protectorate had collapsed. As far as he was concerned this was the defining event in his relationship with Owen; he carried it with him to his death. More than that, we see Owen's prominence in the *Reliquiae*, if only because he was the one who came in for most criticism. Sylvester recognized this in his Preface, pairing Owen with Oliver Cromwell as the ones in particular who 'seem to be *sharply* censur'd by him'.[10] Ranking anyone with Cromwell, in late-seventeenth-century England, speaks for itself.

---

[7] Calamy's preferences are abundantly clear in his own reshaping of Baxter's autobiography, where he omitted any mention at all of Owen. 'But the Assembly at *Wallingford-House* did the main Business. It was there determin'd, *That Richard's Parliament must be dissolv'd*; and then he quickly fell himself.' This was decidedly not what Baxter wished to say. Edmund Calamy, *Abridgement of Mr. Baxter's History of His Life and Times* (London: Thomas Parkhurst, 1702), 72.

[8] Rutt, ed., *Edmund Calamy: An Historical Account of My Own Life*, i.377.

[9] *Rel. Bax.*, Preface to the Reader, §vii. Sylvester also broached the subject in §viii.

[10] Ibid., §viii. The italics are in the original.

We have already considered the plausibility of Owen's part in the fall of Richard Cromwell; to Baxter, it was more than plausible. During the 1650s the two men had stored up a treasury of wounds, insults and aggravations. Thus when April 1659 came around Baxter was already predisposed to believe the worst of Owen, not the best. No doubt he felt he had seen and experienced enough of Owen's methods to make his complicity in Richard's demise not merely a possibility, but a certainty. While his account does spread the blame more widely than just Owen, no other figure or party is forced to carry so much culpability. This was Owen's unforgiveable sin. Almost at a stroke, the events of April 1659 had transmogrified Owen into Baxter's caricature of a church wrecker, a destroyer, a scatterer. All of Baxter's Interregnum disappointments came to be personified in and focused on Owen, making it impossible for the two men to come together in any sort of unity or agreement.

Such darkened memories lay not just in Baxter's mind; Owen had no good reason to remember Baxter kindly. We have much less evidence here to go on but we can well imagine that as he tended his own regrets over the failed experiments of the 1650s, when he considered just how close God had brought the English nation towards that glorious reformation, he too would have felt that Baxter had been an obstacle to the cause; a belligerent, haughty, infuriating and stubborn irritation. So when Sylvester made his approach to Dorothy Owen she 'resented the motion', in Calamy's words, 'and was free in her reflections'.[11] It seems reasonable to conclude that her response reflects the bitterness Owen himself felt towards Baxter, expressed to his wife in private, if not to anyone else in print. For her part, Dorothy claimed to have nothing to say: 'I am but of Yesterday, and know Nothing of those Proceedings, but what I had from his own Mouth.'[12] Regrettably, even Asty did not pass on what Owen had said to his wife and he could offer no specific defence. Instead he seems to have been taken by surprise. No one had brought up the matter before, not even in 'common discourse', and now all of Baxter's 'friends' swallowed it whole 'as if it had been infallible'.[13] But Baxter was not infallible, far from it, as this chapter will show.

Even as the seventeenth century drew to a close, then, the hostility between Owen and Baxter continued to vitiate discussions. That is its greatest significance. It is unfortunate enough that the relationship between the two men never healed, but the impact and influence of that strain was felt beyond just these two individuals. Restoration nonconformity itself was tainted to some degree by the stagnant pool of memories from which Owen and Baxter drew in the final

---

[11]   Rutt, ed., *Edmund Calamy: An Historical Account of My Own Life*, i.378.
[12]   University of Edinburgh Library: 'New College Comm 2', 120.
[13]   Ibid., 122.

decades of their lives. In this chapter I wish to evaluate that aspect of memory – fatal memory – by assessing Baxter's construction of Owen's mid-1659 activities and how it continued to colour his perception of the man throughout the Restoration period. I intend to show how Baxter's memory altered and distilled over time, and to evaluate the extent to which the vitiated relationship between Owen and Baxter may have contributed to – or hampered – the development of Restoration nonconformity.

1659: The Construction of a Crime

J.C. Davis argues persuasively that mid-seventeenth-century English autobiographical writing did not signal any marked rise of individualism; instead, the self was essentially broken down in the presence of God's own agency and providence. Using John Bunyan's autobiography, *Grace Abounding*, as an example, Davis claims that '[p]ersonal autonomy, the agency of the self, is indeed hard to find in this classic of spiritual "autobiography". Rather we are presented with a series of divine actings on the blank canvas of Bunyan's personality and experience.' Other examples also illustrate Davis's point: in the relating of one's life, 'memory is a field of divine agency'.[14] But if this is the case Baxter's autobiography (which he began to write two years before Bunyan first published his) is an exception. It is not that Baxter omitted any recognition of providence, but there is throughout an unmistakeable sense of self and a determination where he thought necessary to blame human agency and specific human agents. Agents like John Owen.

Baxter was explicit in his criticisms of Owen only in the *Reliquiae Baxterianae*. The restraint that he showed in other contexts finally gave way in a document that he knew would be published only after his death. He wrote the work to give his interpretation of events in which he had played a part and it was inevitable that he should broach the sad end of Richard Cromwell along with Owen's hand in it. Here Calamy may have failed in omitting the matter completely, but he certainly succeeded in softening the tone. As Geoffrey Nuttall discerned in 1955,[15] there is a stark difference between the manuscript version of Baxter's comments and the published version. This is what Sylvester and Calamy allowed into print:

---

[14] Davis, 'Living with the Living God', 31–5.

[15] Nuttall, 'The MS.of *Reliquiae Baxterianae*', 73–9.

> Dr. *Owen* and his assistants did the main work: He gathereth a Church at Lieutenant General *Fleetwood's* Quarters, at *Wallingford* House, consisting of the active Officers in the Army (this Church-gathering hath been a Church-scattering Project). In this Assembly it was determined that *Richard's* Parliament must be dissolved, and then he quickly fell himself.[16]

But this is the full text of the original manuscript version, written in 1664:

> Dr. Owen and his assistants did the maine work: His high spirit now thought the place of Vicechancellor and Deane of Christs Church, to be too low: and if the Protector will not do as he would have him, he shall be no Protector: He gathereth a Church at Lieutenant Generall Fleetwoods quarters, at Wallingford howse, consisting of the active Officers of the Army! (This Church-gathering hath bin the Church-scattering project.) His parts, and confidence, and busybodiness, and interest in those men did give him the opportunity to do his exploits; and quite put Hugh Peters besides the chaire (who had witt enough to be against the fall of Rich: Cromwell, as seeing how quickly his owne would follow). Here fasting and prayer, with Dr. Owen's magisteriall counsel, did soon determine the Case, with the proud and giddy headed Officers, that Richards Parliament must be dissolved, and then he quickly fell himself.[17]

To add another layer of complication Baxter himself crossed out one line and rewrote it. This is what he deleted: Richard 'must downe, for favouring Parliaments and Presbyterians so much, and he little'. The words 'must downe' are almost certainly a specific allusion to the report of Thomas Manton, the likely basis on which Baxter made this claim.[18]

His original version is much more specific, personal and bitter. Owen was not just one in a number of players, he was the engineer, exploiting his connections with well-placed figures to shape events. This is a very hostile interpretation of Owen – the proud busybody, the magisterial manipulator – that built on Baxter's earlier engagements with him. This one extract presents Baxter's ongoing bitterness in its most distilled essence. It also shows how his memory, even as early as 1664, was unreliable: Owen had ceased being Vice-Chancellor of Oxford University two years before Richard fell.

But this was not the only place where the original manuscript was altered. Two pages later Owen appeared again. Jeremiah Burroughes, a Congregationalist

---

[16]   *Rel. Bax.*, i.101.
[17]   British Library: Egerton MS. 2570, f.26r.
[18]   See above, p. 249.

Minister and one of the Dissenting Brethren at the Westminster Assembly, had died in 1646. It was then that

> Dr. *John Owen* arose, not of the same Spirit, to fill up his place; by whom and Mr. *Phillip Nye*'s Policie the Flames were encreased, our Wounds kept open, and carried on all as if there had been none but they considerable in the World; and having an Army and City Agents fit to second them, effectually hindered all remedy till they were dash'd into all pieces as a broken Glas. O! What may not Pride do? And what Miscarriages will not false Principles and Faction hide?[19]

This was strong enough but the original was more bitter still and more focused on Owen: he 'arose with a contrary spirit to fill up his place: This one mans *Pride*, and Mr. Philip Nye's Policie, increased the flame'.[20] And when, on the next page, Baxter blamed the Congregationalists, he really blamed these two figures. 'So much could two men (Dr Owen and Mr Nye) do',[21] but his editors omitted the names.[22]

Nuttall spotted all these alterations in Part I of the *Reliquiae Baxterianae*, but there were others.[23] First, Baxter regretted how the Savoy Confession contradicted the epistle of James. What is missing from the published version is the reason: 'I suppose to shew the zeale of Dr Owen and some few others against the doctrine of Justification which I had asserted.'[24] The actions of the Congregationalists were being driven, in Baxter's mind, by Owen's grudge against him. Second, Baxter described Owen's reply to his *Confession* in more detail than appears in the published version: he said that Owen's answer was 'full of Pride and Scorne, and painted with Adages and sentences',[25] which it was. Third, and most substantially, several lines were omitted when Baxter explained that the Congregationalists as a whole did not support Richard's downfall. The published version says this: 'Yea, Mr. *Nye*, that was then thought to be engaged in the same Design, doth utterly disclaim it, and profess that his Consent or Hand was never to it: *But Pride usually goeth before Destruction*.'[26] This makes no

---

[19]   *Rel. Bax.*, i.103.

[20]   British Library: Egerton MS. 2570, f.27r.

[21]   Ibid., f.27v.

[22]   *Rel. Bax.*, i.104.

[23]   Nuttall, 'The MS of *Reliquiae Baxterianae*', 78–9. A perusal of the markings in the version of the *Reliquiae* that Nuttall used to make the comparison suggests that he was fully aware of these other omissions but chose not to mention them in his article.

[24]   British Library: Egerton MS. 2570, f.27v.

[25]   Ibid., f.31v.

[26]   *Rel. Bax.*, i.101–2.

sense. If the Congregationalists disapproved and if Philip Nye never agreed then who was to blame? Whose pride was at fault? The original is a great deal clearer:

> Yea Mr Nye that was then thought to be Dr Owens second in it, doth utterly disclaime it, and profess that his consent or hand was never to it. But no wonder if God infatuate those whom he will destroy! That they should be so blind as not to see, the imprisonments and hangings they were preparing for themselves, and their companions. But thus Pride goeth before destruction.[27]

No wonder this, too, was deleted. Baxter seemed to be comparing Owen with Haman, the evil Agagite who sought to engineer the destruction of the Jews only to be hanged on his own gallows.[28] The effect of naming Owen in this section is to focus what is a remarkably bitter paragraph on only him. The effect of leaving him out is to empty the paragraph of its decisive force.

Judicious changes also occurred in the second part of the autobiography. It is not entirely certain but it may have been Baxter himself who made these deletions, perhaps as he reviewed the manuscript at a later date.[29] When Oliver Cromwell died, the 'Military Anabaptists ... set up his Son, and pulled him down again, and set up others, and pull'd down them, and never ceased rebelling and overturning all before them'.[30] But this failed to name the particular villain: they pulled Richard down 'especially at the instigation of Dr. John Owen'.[31] And when Baxter described the 1654 sub-committee on the fundamentals he claimed that the 'great doer of all that worded the Articles was Dr. *Owen*: Mr. *Nye*, and Dr. *Goodwin* and Mr. *Syd. Sympson* were his Assistants; and Dr *Cheynall* his Scribe'.[32] Once again a bracketed comment had been left out of the published version: Owen was 'a man whom I will give no character of because he hath written so much against me, that I take myself to be unmeet for that action'.[33]

There is also at least one place where Owen is not mentioned explicitly, but was surely in view, enough for Samuel Young to spot his presence.[34] In the section that followed Baxter's main accusation against Owen he bitterly targeted 'the *weaker and younger sort of Professors*, [that] have been prone to be puft up with high Thoughts of themselves, and to over-value their little Degrees of Knowledge

---

[27]   British Library: Egerton MS. 2570, f.26v.

[28]   For the biblical reference, see the book of Esther, chapter 7.

[29]   The deletions in Part I were silent; here lines and even whole pages were crossed out.

[30]   *Rel. Bax.*, ii.180.

[31]   DWL MS *BT* iii.109v, item #62(2).

[32]   *Rel. Bax.*, ii.198–9.

[33]   DWL MS *BT* iii.114r, item #62(2).

[34]   [Young], *Vindiciae Anti-Baxterianae*, 42–3.

and Parts ... and all this under the Pretense of the Purity of the Church'. They and the sectaries undermined legitimate authorities, 'at last attempting to pull them all down', all the while claiming to do so in the cause of the gospel.

> Yea, though they thought themselves the most understanding and conscientious People of the Land, yet did the Gang of them seldom stick at any thing which seemed to promote their Cause; but whatever their Faction in the Army did, they pleaded for it and approved it: If they pull'd down the Parliament, imprisoned the godly, faithful Members, killed the King, if they cast out the Rump, if they chose a Little Parliament of their own, if they set up *Cromwell*, if they set up his Son and pull'd him down again, if they sought to obtrude Agreements on the People, if they one Week set up a Council of State, and if another Week the Rump were restored ... in all these the Anabaptists, and many of the Independents in the Three Kingdoms followed them; and even their Pastors were ready to lead them to consent.[35]

It is difficult to think of any other issue on which Baxter was so utterly scathing. All of these events were seamless in that they were part of the same cause and perpetrated by the same 'Gang' who were led, in Baxter's mind, by Owen himself. In making sense of the Interregnum Baxter discerned a clear link between Owen and the 'Sectaries (especially the Anabaptists, the Seekers and the Quakers)'. He would later return to make that connection even more explicit.[36]

Even the published version of the *Reliquiae* supplies sufficient indications of Baxter's ill-feeling towards Owen. Adding in the omissions amplifies that feeling and indicates the extent to which his editors went when they tried to reduce the number of times Owen was mentioned and to soften the impression that Baxter deliberately intended to make. It is possible that there were other deletions in relation to Owen that we know nothing about, as the relevant portions of the original manuscript are no longer extant. Even so, Baxter's vitiated view of Owen, consolidated by 1664, is abundantly clear. It would prove to be very significant.

Comprehension, Toleration and Indulgence

The manuscript of the *Reliquiae Baxterianae* offers us a significant glimpse into Baxter's thoughts towards Owen during the Restoration period, thoughts he kept mostly to himself at the time. It helps us, therefore, to evaluate the effect of that memory and the effect of their broken relationship on the shape

---

[35]   *Rel. Bax.*, i.102.

[36]   See below, pp. 284–5.

of nonconformity. In order to make this assessment I would like to examine a particularly relevant and significant season in the story of nonconformity, one for which we can assemble evidence for this fatal memory at work. The story begins in 1667 and ends in 1673; it entails a series of discussions concerning the twin issues of comprehension and toleration; and it culminates in the issuing and subsequent retraction of Charles II's Declaration of Indulgence.[37]

To relate these events briefly, the Restoration settlement had been a frustrating and bitter outcome for moderate Presbyterians like Richard Baxter: though they fervently believed in a national church, they had been shut out of the restored Church of England. They 'were separatists who did not believe in separation.'[38] Not surprisingly they continued to advocate for comprehension wherever they could, hoping to find their way back into the national church on terms they could accept. In theory this should not have been difficult: the differences between the restored churchmen and moderate Presbyterians in 1662 were 'sometimes scarcely perceptible.'[39] In practice, it proved impossible. The alternative was toleration, either within the national church or without. Clearly this had been the consistent ambition of the Congregationalists, who were far less concerned than the Presbyterians at the prospect of going their own way. Toleration proved intolerable to the Cavalier Parliament, heavily stacked with restored churchmen; all such schemes quickly came to a dead halt. It did not help that these two agendas could be played off against each other, to the detriment of both. A third, close alternative was indulgence. Worryingly, this implied the right of the Crown to override established laws. But the bigger problem here, for Presbyterians at least, was that indulgence seemed to solidify their place outside the national church.[40] Yet this was the only viable scheme on offer in this period, and only for a relatively brief time.

All of this had yet to be proved in 1667, which in many ways seemed to present a propitious context for progress. The nonconformists had gained a new

---

[37] I will borrow the shape of this story from Roger Thomas's older (but still useful) essay, 'Comprehension and Indulgence', in *From Uniformity to Unity 1662–1962*, ed. Geoffrey F. Nuttall and Owen Chadwick (London: SPCK, 1962), 189–253. But see also John Spurr, 'The Church of England, Comprehension and the Toleration Act of 1689', *English Historical Review* 104 (1989): 933–5; Spurr, *Restoration Church of England*, 56–65; Spurr, 'From Puritanism to Dissent', 244–7; and Sutherland, *Peace, Toleration and Decay*, 1–10.

[38] Goldie, *Entring Book of Roger Morrice*, i.276. See also, Drysdale, *History of the English Presbyterians*, 392; and C.G. Bolam and Jeremy Goring, 'Presbyterians in Separation: The Cataclysm', in *The English Presbyterians: From Elizabethan Puritanism to Modern Unitarianism*, ed. C. Gordon Bolam et al. (London: George Allen and Unwin Ltd, 1968), 84–5.

[39] Goldie, *Entring Book of Roger Morrice*, i.227. See also, John Spurr, *England in the 1670s: 'This Masquerading Age'* (Malden, MA: Blackwell, 2000), 227–8.

[40] Goldie, *Entring Book of Roger Morrice*, i.236–7.

public esteem for their ministerial faithfulness in London during the plague and the fire of the previous two years; a depression in trade suggested that that persecution – nonconformists were strong in trading quarters – had been bad for business; and Sir Orlando Bridgeman replaced Edward Hyde, First Earl of Clarendon, as Lord Chancellor.[41] In this favourable context, Sir Robert Atkyns prepared a 'Comprehensive Bill' that would remove the main barriers towards conformity.[42] In the course of those manoeuvres, Atkyns consulted with Thomas Manton, 'accounted the leader of the Presbyterians',[43] who in turn consulted by letter with Baxter. A series of conferences ensued in which Manton, Baxter and William Bates represented the Presbyterians.[44] At about the same time George Villiers, second Duke of Buckingham, worked towards a toleration Bill.[45] So there were two projects moving in parallel: comprehension and toleration. Neither one had enjoyed any kind of success before the parliamentary session ended in May 1668.

Around this time a disturbing division manifested itself within Presbyterianism. Put simply, the older generation of moderate Presbyterian leaders, who earnestly favoured comprehension, found themselves confronted by a younger generation of Presbyterian leaders, led by Samuel Annesley, who were growing increasingly comfortable with the idea of an existence outside the national church. Sir Joseph Williamson (then assistant to the Secretary of State, Lord Arlington) dubbed these two groups the 'Dons and Ducklings'.[46] They had been coalescing since at least the mid-1660s and the division they represented would, in fact, only grow and consolidate. It marked an unmistakeable shift from comprehension to toleration within Presbyterianism, and the significance

---

[41] Thomas, 'Comprehension and Indulgence', 195–6.

[42] For the text of this Bill, see Arthur West Haddon, ed., *The Theological Works of Herbert Thorndike, Sometime Prebendary of the Collegiate Church of St. Peter, Westminster*, vol. 5, *The True Principle of Comprehension* (Oxford: John Henry Parker, 1854), 304–6. For an illuminating regional focus on the effort for comprehension, see Newton E. Key, 'Comprehension and the Breakdown of Consensus in Restoration Herefordshire', in *The Politics of Religion in Restoration England*, ed. Tim Harris, Paul Seaward and Mark Goldie (Oxford: Basil Blackwell, 1990), 191–215.

[43] Thomas, 'Comprehension and Indulgence', 198.

[44] *Rel. Bax.*, iii.24–5; Walter Simon, 'Comprehension in the Age of Charles II', *Church History* 31 (1962): 440–48; Goldie, *Entring Book of Roger Morrice*, i.239, ii.354; Thomas, 'Comprehension and Indulgence', 198–9.

[45] For Buckingham and toleration, in a slightly later context, see Nicholas Tyacke, 'The "Rise of Puritanism" and the Legalising of Dissent', in *From Persecution to Toleration: The Glorious Revolution and Religion in England*, ed. O.P. Grell, J.I. Israel and N. Tyacke (Oxford: Clarendon Press, 1991), 36–7.

[46] *Calendar of State Papers Domestic*, 1671–2 (13 December 1671), 28.

was not lost on Baxter.[47] It represented an alarming drift towards effective Congregationalism from within his own ranks.[48] The London Minister, Vincent Alsop, became a central figure in that development.[49]

In June 1670 Charles II signed the secret Treaty of Dover in which he agreed to support the French in the present war with the Dutch and later to declare himself a Roman Catholic. This drove his interest in indulgence (over against comprehension) since it could be extended also to include the Catholics. Hints of this policy emerged in 1671, then in March 1672 Charles issued his Declaration of Indulgence, one that did indeed include the Catholics.[50] On the morning of 28 March, Owen willingly presented thanks to the King on behalf of the Congregationalists;[51] in the afternoon, less willingly, Manton presented his thanks on behalf of the Presbyterians.[52] Philip Henry, an ejected Presbyterian minister, crisply summarized the varying reactions to the Indulgence: 'the Conformists generally displeas'd at it, the Presb[yterians] glad, the Indep[endents] very glad, the Papists triumph'. He also identified the 'Trilemma' facing moderate Presbyterians: 'either to turn flat Independents, or to strike in with the conformists, or to sit down in former silence and sufferings, till the Lord shall open a more effectual door'.[53] As it happens that door remained open for only a year; in March 1673, under pressure from a hostile Commons, Charles was forced to close it once more.

That was hardly the end of efforts towards comprehension and toleration, but it provides sufficiently wide ground in which to observe the effect of the strained relationship between Owen and Baxter, and of Baxter's poisoned memory of 1659. Indeed, it helps to put the matter in some perspective. On one level, the difficulties between the two men were largely irrelevant. As always, very powerful political forces determined outcomes and there was nothing

---

[47]   *Rel. Bax.*, iii.42–3.

[48]   Thomas, 'Parties in Nonconformity', 95; Keeble, *Literary Culture of Nonconformity*, 58. See also, *Rel. Bax.*, iii.43.

[49]   See R.A. Beddard, 'Vincent Alsop and the Emancipation of Restoration Dissent', *Journal of Ecclesiastical History* 14 (1973): 161–84, esp. pp. 175–7. See also, Goldie, *Entring Book of Roger Morrice*, i.237.

[50]   For the broader background to these years, see Spurr, *England in the 1670s*, chapters 1 and 2, and esp. pp. 35–6.

[51]   The text of Owen's address was first published in *Gentleman's Magazine*, June 1761, 253. It was reprinted in Orme, 'Memoirs', 272–3. See also Thomas, 'Parties in Nonconformity', 98: the Indulgence 'satisfied Owen'.

[52]   Thomas, 'Comprehension and Indulgence', 209; *Rel. Bax.*, iii.99; *Calendar of State Papers Domestic*, 1671–2 (13 December 1671), 609.

[53]   Matthew Henry Lee, ed., *Diaries and Letters of Philip Henry, M.A., Of Broad Oak, Flintshire A.D. 1631–1696* (London: Kegan, Paul, Trench and Co., 1882), 250.

the nonconformists could do to improve their fortunes.[54] They remained at the mercy of the politically dominant restored churchmen and a parliament determined not to give an inch to any policy that might have the potential of recreating all the chaos of the civil war and Interregnum. In this sense, it hardly mattered whether Owen and Baxter were the best of friends or the worst of foes. And yet, if we delve more deeply into the detail of story there were ways in which the strain between the two men came to the surface. While that might have had only a negligible effect in the realm of high politics, it did help the Anglican cause that the differing parties within nonconformity could be played off against each other. Therefore, their evident strain sheds light on the failure of the nonconformists to shift the established order, on the growing fracturing within nonconformity, and on the persistence of old divisions.

Owen and Baxter: Front and Centre

The first point to note is the continuing centrality of Owen and Baxter in these events. To begin with Owen, he was the leading non-parliamentary figure in the push for toleration. In 1667 he published *Indulgence and Toleration Considered: In a Letter unto a Person of Honour*. In it, he promoted toleration indirectly by severely criticizing the current policy of persecution, which relied on external coercion to bring about a superficial uniformity over matters that were said to be 'indifferent' and that were, in fact, mere human invention. On closer examination it served only the interests of the current batch of parliamentarians. As if pointedly to underscore that fact, this is quite possibly the shortest paragraph Owen ever wrote: 'In the mean time, I am sure whoever gets by Persecution, the *King* looseth by it.'[55] Thus he encouraged Charles to pursue his stated intention of declaring an indulgence. In this sense the small tract was acutely tuned to current political circumstances and currents. Owen's *Peace-Offering, In an Apology and Humble Plea for Indulgence and Liberty of Conscience*, published in the same year, was less politically pointed; more obviously a plea for toleration; and – with its references to the Savoy Declaration of 1658 – written particularly on behalf of the Congregationalists.[56]

As well as advancing his agenda for toleration in print, Owen put his political skills into play at a time when politics 'was an intensely personal business at

---

[54]   Watts, *Dissenters*, 252; Spurr, 'Church of England', 928, 944.

[55]   This quote is the original paragraph, in Owen, *Indulgence and Toleration Considered* (1667), 23. See also Owen, *Indulgence and Toleration Considered* (1667): *Works*, xiii.535.

[56]   For the Savoy allusions, see Owen, *A Peace-Offering, in an Apology and Humble Plea for Indulgence and Liberty of Conscience* (1667): *Works*, xiii.546, 551.

every level ... Allies and information were indispensable, as were finely tuned political antennae'.[57] This posed no great challenge to Owen. In 1670 George Vernon attacked his political capacity in such conditions:

> Witness his fishing out the Kings Counsels, and enquiring whether things went well as to his great *Diana*, Liberty of Conscience? How his Majesty stood affected to it? ... Who were or could be made his Friends at Court? What Bills were like to be put up in *Parliament*? How that assembly was united or divided, &c. And according to the current and disposition of affairs, he did acquaint his *Under-Officers*, and they by their Letters each Post were to inform their Fraternity in each Corner of the Kingdom, how things were likely to go with them, how they should or[der] their business, and either for a time omit or continue their *Conventicles*, &c.[58]

Vernon's description – placing Owen at the very centre of the political operations of the Congregationalists – is entirely plausible. Clearly Owen's ability to cultivate patronage had not deserted him in hostile circumstances. John Asty marvelled at the breadth of Owen's connections. 'The Doctor had some friends also among the Bishops, particular Dr. [John] *Wilkins* Bishop of *Chester* who was very cordial in his respects to him, and Dr. [Thomas] *Barlow*, formerly his Tutor.'[59] Note that Barlow and Wilkins were two of the three Church representatives who met with Baxter, Manton and Bates in the negotiations of 1668,[60] suggesting the interlinking proximity of these networks. In addition, Owen 'drew the admiration and respects of several persons of honour and quality upon him, who very much delighted in his conversation; particularly the Earl of *Orrery*, the Earl of *Anglesea*, the Lord *Willoughby* of *Parham*, the Lord *Wharton*, the Lord *Berkley*, Sir *John Trevor*, one of the Principal Secretaries of State'.[61] Asty's list was hardly exhaustive. The second Duke of Buckingham was a notable omission; Owen allied with him to prepare a Bill for toleration. 'Buckingham is the great favourite', observed one contemporary, 'and his cabal are [the former Leveller] Major [John] Wildman, Dr. Owen and the rest of that fraternity, so that some say we are carried in Oliver's basket'.[62] Indeed, the

---

57   Spurr, *England in the 1670s*, 218.

58   Vernon, *Letter to a Friend*, 34.

59   Asty, 'Memoirs', xxx.

60   *Rel. Bax.*, iii.24–5; Goldie, *Entring Book of Roger Morrice*, i.239; Thomas, 'Comprehension and Indulgence', 198–9. Wilkins was, at that point, not yet a bishop. Spurr, 'Church of England', 934–5, 941.

61   Asty, 'Memoirs', xxix.

62   John Morland to Col. John Tempest, 18 February 1668: *Calendar of State Papers Domestic 1667–8*, 238.

terms of this Bill, almost wholly concerned with a freedom from restraint and penalty for those who adhered to the fundamentals of the faith, were very close to the related provisions in the 'Humble Petition and Advice'.[63] The similarity should be unsurprising; after all, the former had been published a mere 10 years earlier and both, it would seem, were penned by Owen. His Restoration efforts were continuous with those of the Interregnum. That makes the memory of the Interregnum only more relevant.

Owen's political connections reached to the very highest level. In 1670, as Charles worked quietly towards an indulgence, Owen met with the King's agents.[64] Two years earlier he had explained to Thomas Manton that 'Comprehension would neither doe the Kings businesse nor ours',[65] and he seems to have been remarkably in tune with Charles' own policy. To some degree he angled towards synchronizing the King's interests with his, with apparent success. After the Indulgence was revoked he continued to enjoy a welcome reception with Charles and with his brother James, the Duke of York. Asty, again:

> King *Charles* himself and the Duke of *York* paid a particular respect to him. When the Doctor was drinking the Waters at *Tunbridge*, the Duke of *York* being there, sent for him into his Tent, and several discourses pass'd between them about the Dissenters and Conventicles; and after he return'd to *London*, the King himself sent for him, and discoursed with him about two hours together, assuring him of his favour and respect, and telling him, he might have access to him, as he would.[66]

In a practical demonstration of goodwill Charles gave Owen 1,000 Guineas to distribute among the most afflicted nonconformists.

For all that Asty may have inflated Owen's proximity to power during the Restoration period, the man was clearly well positioned, and problematic. 'The determination of the Independents or Congregationalists, under the leadership of the redoubtable John Owen, to achieve toleration, repeatedly thwarted the delicate political negotiations for a comprehension.'[67] His interventions were significant enough to annoy Thomas Manton. His letter to Baxter, dated Saturday 26 September 1668, serves to illustrate not just Owen's centrality in

[63] Compare Gardiner, ed., *Constitutional Documents*, 454–5 with Haddon, *The Theological Works of Herbert Thorndike*, v.307–8.

[64] Thomas, 'Comprehension and Indulgence', 207.

[65] Th[omas] Manton to Baxter, 26 September [1668]: DWL MS *BC* ii.273r (*CCRB* #760).

[66] Asty, 'Memoirs', xxix.

[67] Spurr, *Post-Reformation*, 157. See also Lim, 'Trinity, *Adiaphora*, Ecclesiology, and Reformation', 291; and *Adiaphora*, Ecclesiology, and Reformation', 258.

broader events, but Baxter's as well. Manton had felt that the recent campaign for Comprehension 'endeavoured by our friends in Court was frustrated by Dr Owen's proposall of a toleration' in *Indulgence and Toleration Considered.* Hearing this, Owen had paid a visit to Manton to proclaim his innocence. Significantly, he brought Annesley along with him. During the course of the conversation Owen 'dropped a motion about a meeting where 8 persons only should be present and the matter debated to bee whether the Comprehension should bee propounded by us but expressly asserting that this should not bee handled as a difference betweene us and the Independents but between us and many of our Brethren'. It is possible that Owen's proposal and Annesley's presence recognized that comprehension was no longer the preferred option among all Presbyterians, nor was it solely a Congregationalist agenda. Manton's response is intriguing: 'I waved this question and agreed (I thinke unwarily) to a meeting upon these Conditions[:] that you should be present, and that the question should bee generall, What Course wee should take for the obtaining of our Common liberty without clashing with one another.'[68] He had managed to set the terms for the project but the apologetic tone in his letter conveys how carefully he had to step to avoid undue concessions, and also how important Baxter's approval and presence was. 'But meet I will not unlesse you [are] one.'[69] We do not know if the meeting, set down for the following Thursday, ever took place, but if Owen was attempting to win over the Dons, he failed.[70]

Baxter did not enjoy the same height of political patronage as Owen. In contrast to Owen's apparently warm reception from Charles and James, in September 1668 Manton had to defend Baxter to Charles's face. A Justice of the Peace, probably Thomas Ross, had complained that Baxter was teaching publicly in breach of the Conventicle Act. Manton was forced to explain that a number of people had gathered on one occasion to hear Baxter teach but that had never been his intention or expectation. Charles professed 'that hee had a great respect for [Baxter] and his worth and learning,'[71] but the episode reveals the relative positions of, in this case, Manton and Baxter. Manton was the one to represent the Presbyterians before Charles. He was, in Baxter's words, 'nearest the Court, and of great Name among the *Presbyterians*, and being heard by many of great Quality'.[72] But if negotiations were to take place – formal or informal, public or

---

68   Th[omas] Manton to Baxter, 26 September [1668]: DWL MS *BC* ii.273r–v (*CCRB* #760). The word 'waved' may be in the archaic sense of turning aside (waive).

69   Ibid., 273v.

70   Thomas, 'Parties in Nonconformity', 95–6.

71   T[homas] Manton to Baxter [c.September 1668]: *Rel. Bax.*, iii.37, §85. I include the extra detail because the page numbering is irregular.

72   *Rel. Bax.*, iii.36, §85.

private – Manton insisted that Baxter was included. And he was included, even if by 1670 he was resolving, from bad experience, to do so no more.[73] He was consistently a member of various sets of negotiations during the remainder of his life. More than that, his extensive correspondence with a wide range of political players is testament to his own not insignificant network of contacts.[74]

Therefore, Owen and Baxter were central figures; there could be no progress without them. This alone makes the strain between them significant, especially when Baxter was the go-between with the Congregationalists, and Owen their representative. Following the series of conferences involving Manton, Bates and Baxter in the wake of the aborted Atkyns Bill for comprehension, Baxter 'privately acquainted Dr. Owen with the substance of the business, and consulted him, that they might not say, we neglected them'.[75] This consultation may well have been as begrudging as it sounds. It would be fascinating to discover whether Baxter's colleagues commissioned him to make this approach or whether he took it upon himself; either way, he was the wrong man for the job, and the conversation would have done nothing to bring the two parties together. We know this because of what happened next.

Failed Rapprochement

In 1670, Baxter added another section to the steadily lengthening manuscript of his autobiography. He and Owen had just passed through the most sustained period of interaction in the course of their careers; it was both fraught and fruitless. While the exchange was amicable enough on the surface, his account discloses the way in which haunting memories continued to hinder.

Baxter had detected a rise in 'separating principles' in the late 1660s,[76] and as we have seen he was not far wrong. Comprehension was losing ground to toleration. And, as we have also seen, Owen was a leading figure in the push for toleration. Hearing of Owen's visit to Manton and that Owen 'talked very yieldingly of a Concord between the Independents and Presbyterians (which all seemed willing of)', Baxter 'resolved once more to try with Dr. *Owen*'.[77] He was aware that if the two streams of nonconformity were known to be

---

[73]   Baxter to Thomas Manton, 17 February [1670]: DWL MS *BC* iv.204r (*CCRB* #794). See also *Rel. Bax.*, iii.37, §85.

[74]   For examples, see J.T. Cliffe, *The Puritan Gentry Besieged 1650–1700* (London: Routledge, 1993), *passim*.

[75]   *Rel. Bax.*, iii.34, §67.

[76]   Ibid., iii.61.

[77]   Thomas, 'Parties in Nonconformity', 96–8; *Rel. Bax.*, iii.61.

negotiating then political pressure would be brought to bear to scuttle all hopes of reconciliation, so he and Owen agreed to keep their discussions private in the meantime. As always, Baxter put his proposals on paper for Owen to consider. Owen responded in a letter dated 25 January 1669, Baxter replied on 16 February – this is the only correspondence we know of between the two men. Then Owen did what it seems everyone else had ever done with Baxter's papers: he ignored them for months on end.

> And to be short, I thus waited on [Owen] time after time, till my Papers had been near a Year and quarter in his Hand, and then I desired him to return them to me, which he did, with these Words, 'I am still a well-wisher to those Mathematicks' without any other Words about them, or ever giving me any more Exception against them.[78]

Samuel Taylor Coleridge wondered at the 'very chilling want of open-heartedness on the part of Owen' at this point,[79] but it is not difficult to explain. The whole affair had presented yet another iteration of earlier frustrating tendencies in their relationship. The true cause of the failure lay in the past.

To begin with, Baxter chose to approach Owen even 'though all our business with each other had been contradiction'. This was hardly the most promising frame of mind in which to open up discussion. 'I thought it my Duty without any thoughts of former things, to go to him, and be a Seeker of Peace.' According to Baxter, Owen took this rather well, but Baxter's initial resolve not to drag up the past inevitably gave way.

> I told him, That I must deal freely with him, that when I thought of what he had done formerly, I was much afraid lest one that had been so great a breaker, would not be made an Instrument in healing: But in other Respects I thought him the fittest man in *England* for this Work; partly because he could understand the Case, and partly, because his Experience of the Humours of Men, and of the mischief of dividing Principles and Practices, had been so very great, that if Experience should make any man wise, and fit for an healing Work, it should be him.[80]

This is a fascinating recollection that demonstrates Baxter's inability to forget Owen's past wrongs even when he tried. He also

---

[78]   *Rel. Bax.*, iii.69.

[79]   Derwent Coleridge, ed., *Notes on English Divines by Samuel Taylor Coleridge* (London: Edward Moxon, 1853), ii.106.

[80]   *Rel. Bax.*, iii.61–2.

ventured to tell him what a difficulty I feared it would be to him to go openly and fully according to his own Judgment, when the Reputation of former Actions, and present Interest in many that would censure him, if he went not after their narrowed Judgment, did lye in his way, and that I feared these Temptations more than his Ability and Judgment.[81]

It is difficult to see how Baxter could have conveyed this without sounding patronizing: he doubted Owen's judgement and ability, he feared he would get pushed around by his stricter brethren, and he could not see past Owen's 'Reputation of former Actions'. So much for not bringing up the past.

Baxter also carried with him the weight of broader failures by returning to his previous logic: if godly union was possible it would have happened during the Interregnum. 'The great difficulty had always been to find out the Terms on which we must be United, if ever it be done: This was it which could not be done in the Assembly at *Westminster*, nor in all the Years of our Liberty and Difference ever since.'[82] This makes it all the more impressive that Baxter was still prepared to try, and the resulting failure on this occasion would only have affirmed the worrying conclusion that reconciliation was, in fact, impossible.

According to Baxter, Owen was open, receptive and agreeable throughout this conversation, but with one clear limit. While they agreed to proceed on the basis of written documents Owen had no interest in doing the writing. Baxter initially asked him to write up the agreement, but Owen refused. Baxter then suggested 'that each of us might bring in a Draught; but he would needs cast it on me alone'.[83] Baxter did this, but it was far too long for Owen's liking; he desired a shorter, more narrow document. 'I urged him again in vain to do it: but he cast it upon me.' Apparently Owen responded warmly to this second document: 'he told me, that it was the fairest Offer, and the likeliest means, that ever he yet saw'. Even so, that is the document that sat so long unattended until Baxter was forced to retrieve it. It is impossible to avoid the gulf between Owen's words and actions. He offered Baxter only a polite neglect. There is little in his actions to suggest any genuine intention on his part to deal with him.[84]

Owen's brief letter to Baxter sounded both genuine and passively noncommittal at the same time: 'Upon the whole Matter, I judge your Proposals worthy of great Consideration, and the most probable medium for attaining of the End aimed at, that I have yet perused.' He asked Baxter to amend some features of his paper, including the omission of some parts 'reflective of former

---

81   Ibid., iii.64.
82   Ibid., iii.62.
83   Ibid.
84   Powicke came to the same conclusion, in *Life of the Reverend Richard Baxter*, 275.

Actings, when there was no such Agreement among us, as is now aimed at'.
Surprisingly he assented to using the 'Creed, as expounded in the first Four
councils' as the means of excluding Socinians and Papists.[85] Baxter was delighted
to hear it but he still devoted several paragraphs to defending a stricter form of
Scripture sufficiency.[86] He also rehearsed his ancient objections against the way
of separation that 'tendeth to extirpate Godliness out of the Land; by taking
a very few that can talk more than the rest, and making them the Church'.
Furthermore, '(pardon my plainness) I knew scarce any of you that did not by
an *unjust espousing of your few*, do the People a double Injury, one by denying
them their Church-Rights, without any regular Church Justice, and the other
by lazily omitting most that should have been done for their Salvation'.[87] When
Baxter arrived at Kidderminster he might have chosen to take the 20 professors
and make them the church, leaving behind the rest; instead he transformed
the whole parish. It was a fair point, but by making it with such force and at
such length he was hardly likely to win Owen over. 'I speak this to shew you
(if Experience signifie anything with you,) that your separating way tendeth to
Laziness, and the grievous hinderance of that Godliness which you seemed to
me more zealous for than others.' Baxter then contrasted Owen with 'two of the
worthiest Person of your way (Mr. *Nye* and Mr. [Thomas] *Elford*) whose ability
and Piety were beyond all question'.[88] Finally, he brought Owen back around to
the past. He asked Owen to consider the disastrous effects of previous divisions
upon the church in England and he implied that Owen might 'not thirst to see
them healed'. And

> he, that considereth what it was to continue such Divisions unheal'd for 20 Years,
> under such Warnings and Calls to Unity; and to do what we have done against our
> selves and others, after such smart, and in such manner to the last, is most dreadfully
> impenitent, if Repentance do not now make him zealous for a Cure. And in particular,
> if *you*, and Mr. *Nye*, and I, be not extraordinarily *zealous* for this work, there are scare
> three Men to be found in the World, that will be more heinously guilty, and without
> excuse: (I need not tell you why.)[89]

---

[85]   John Owen to Baxter, 25 January 1668[/9]: DWL MS *BC* v.15r and *Rel. Bax.*, iii.63–4
(*CCRB* #769; and *CJO* #72).

[86]   Baxter to John Owen, 16 February 1668[/9]: *Rel. Bax.*, iii.65 (*CCRB* #771; and *CJO*
#73).

[87]   Ibid., 67.

[88]   Ibid., 68. Thomas Elford had been Nye's assistant at Acton. He succeeded Nye as Rector
in 1654, ministering there until his ejection at the Restoration.

[89]   Ibid.

Baxter's typically direct, tactless, heavy-handed and self-defeating approach does much to explain Owen's inaction. He told Baxter he resented this 'chiding letter' that seemed to doubt the authenticity of his desires towards peace. Baxter tried to say that he intended only to warn Owen of the various temptations sitting in his way; 'I meant that not as an Accusation'.[90] If so, it was a very ham-fisted attempt. Baxter's lack of political skill tripped him over again, but that was not the biggest problem. The main difficulty lay in Baxter's memory of the past. Owen had indeed continued 'in such manner to the last', in bringing down Richard Cromwell in 1659. Baxter simply could not see Owen's actions in any other light. And this, more than anything else, rendered his commendable attempt at rapprochement an utter failure in the end.

Needless to say, the affair did nothing to help their relationship. As time went on Baxter came to hear that Owen 'divulged his dissent from my Proposals for Concord, which I offered him, though he would say no more against them to my self'.[91] They were reduced to talking about each other, not to each other. Nor did it help the movement. Noting that the rival efforts towards comprehension and toleration failed, Roger Thomas concludes that it 'would have been better if more had been done to co-ordinate the two points of view beforehand'.[92] Indeed it would. But given the centrality of Owen and Baxter, the continuity of current issues with those of the past, and the unmistakeable presence of Baxter's own memories, the strain between them was bound to hinder agreement, especially when Baxter's memory was, far from fading and softening, growing even worse.

Owen Defends the Nonconformists

At the same time as Baxter was waiting for Owen's response to his papers, Samuel Parker published *A Discourse of Ecclesiastical Politie*.[93] At that stage he was rapidly moving up the ladder in a career that would see him installed as Bishop of Oxford in 1686. Parker set out to argue that 'Indulgence and Toleration is the most absolute sort of Anarchy, and that Princes may with less hazard give Liberty to mens Vices and Debaucheries, than to their Conciences'.[94] His book

---

[90] Ibid., 69.

[91] *Rel. Bax.*, iii.73.

[92] Thomas, 'Comprehension and Indulgence', 204.

[93] The book appeared in 1669, though the date on the title page is 1670. Jon Parkin, 'Parker, Samuel (1640–1688)', *Oxford Dictionary of National Biography*, Oxford University Press, 2004 [www.oxforddnb.com/view/article/21336, accessed 16 December 2009].

[94] Samuel Parker, *A Discourse of Ecclesiastical Politie Wherein...the Mischiefs and Inconveniences of Toleration are Represented* (1670), Preface to the Reader, xiv.

also belittled and caricatured the nonconformists to an extent that even he recognized 'the Vehemence and Severity of its Style'.[95] Certainly it begged for a reply.

According to Baxter, Owen asked him to write it 'by telling me and others that I was the fittest Man in England for that work (on what account I now inquire not)'. It was indeed an intriguing suggestion from Owen. It suggests either that he had confidence in Baxter's views on toleration or he felt that Baxter's lack of support for toleration made him an ideal defender of the nonconformists. Whatever the case, Baxter was not much interested. He had defended them in the past 'with so little thanks from the Independents ... that I resolved not to meddle with them any more'.[96] Owen was on his own and, indeed, he was the one to launch a reply in *Truth and Innocence Vindicated* (1670). But he was not the only one: several other anonymous writers as well as Andrew Marvell took Parker on. Owen's response – it opens with a sentence 151 words long – does not compare with the literary skill and brilliance of Marvell, but his cool logic and occasional sarcasm cheered his fellow nonconformists enormously; according to John Asty, 'this performance advanced the Doctor's reputation very much'.[97]

Baxter also could appreciate the incisiveness of Owen's counter-attack and he perceived that his 'esteem was much advanced with the Nonconformists', but he was not nearly so enamoured as everyone else. He felt that Owen had been helped by the delay in Parker's response, published in 1671 as *A Defence and Continuation of the Ecclesiastical Politie*. He also noticed what others had neglected to observe: *Defence and Continuation* was a scathing reply that directly attacked Owen, but Owen had offered no response at all. Parker was able to quote liberally from Owen's several sermons to Parliament to demonstrate his support for the wars and to establish his view of the gospel and toleration in a way that connected those views with civil upheaval and rebellion.[98] Baxter felt that Parker had won the day with this line of attack

> Because of all the Men in *England* Dr. *Owen* was the Chief that had Headed the Independents in the Army with the greatest height, and Confidence, and Aplause, and afterwards had been the greatest persuader of *Fleetwood*, *Desborough*, and the rest of the Officers of the Army, who were his *Gathered Church*, to compel *Rich. Cromwell* to dissolve his Parliament; which being done, he fell with it, and the King was brought in.

---

95   Ibid., iii.

96   *Rel. Bax.*, iii.42.

97   Asty, 'Memoirs of Owen', xxvi–vii. See also the prefatory note to *Truth and Innocence Vindicated* in *Works*, 13.344.

98   [Parker], *Defence and Continuation of the Ecclesiastical Politie*, 188ff.

Therefore, Owen could not answer Parker's accusations because he had no answer. So, 'being neither able to repent (hitherto) or to justify all this [he] must be silent, or only plead the [Act] of Oblivion: And so I fear his unfitness for this Work was a general injury to the Nonconformists'.[99]

It is clear from this account, written soon after Parker's attack, that Baxter's memory was continuing to slip. In that one sentence he skipped from the wars straight to the fall of Richard Cromwell and then, without any pause, directly to the return of the King. But this simplistic concatenation elided too much complexity with the result that Owen became much larger in Baxter's mind, not smaller. He was now the one 'of all the men' in England least able to answer Parker on this point, because he was the one most responsible for the rebellion not just against Charles but against Richard as well. Even though Owen had had next to no involvement in the army during the 1640s, he was now 'the Chief that had Headed the Independents in the Army with the greatest height, and Confidence, and Applause'. He was the 'greater Persuader' of Fleetwood and Desborough. By the early 1670s Baxter had repackaged the past in a way that distilled Owen's place and power beyond anything that was reasonably plausible. That intensification in memory invested this account with an undertone of petulance towards the Congregationalists who had been so ungrateful and towards Owen who had been given such applause. Baxter might have interpreted Owen's suggestion (that he might reply to Parker) as a compliment, but there was little chance of that. Instead, Baxter shrugged his indifference. And he departed from his fellow nonconformists when he concluded that Owen had lost the debate with Parker and done them no favours at all.

It is essential to recall that we have access to Baxter's mind during this period in a way that his contemporaries did not. He explicitly rehashed Owen's actions in 1659 only in private, in the steadily accumulating layers of what would become the *Reliquiae Baxterianae*. But there were some later published statements that served to convey Baxter's harsh view of Owen. Even though they came later, they help to illustrate Baxter's perspective in these years from 1667 to 1673. They further reveal just how Baxter's increasingly stripped-down memory of Owen was changing and simplifying. The point is, though, that these thoughts appeared in public only after Owen was dead.

---

[99] *Rel. Bax.*, iii.42.

Digging up the Dead

Owen's last years were marked by physical decline, even as he continued to write. He completed his massive four-volume study of the Epistle to the Hebrews (the first volume was published in 1668) as well as his *Meditations and Discourses on the Glory of Christ* (published posthumously in 1684). They were a fitting end to a life of writing, devotion and scholarship that had been marked by a consistent Christological concern, and they put that life in perspective. '[L]et pain, and sickness, and sorrows, and fears, and dangers, and death, say what they will ... ; ... they are all outward, transitory, and passing away, whereas our minds are fixed on those things which are eternal, and filled with incomprehensible glory.'[100] But there was no mistaking his pain and sickness. 'Some few years before he died he was often ill, and sometimes confined to his bed or chamber.'[101] Finally he died, at the age of 67, on 24 August 1683. He was buried at Bunhill Fields where his crypt still stands, attended 'by near a hundred Noblemens, Gentlemens, and Citizens Coaches with six Horse each, and a great number of Gentlemen in Mourning on Horseback'.[102]

Shortly after Owen's death a manuscript circulated in his name giving 12 arguments against communion with parish churches.[103] Just as it appeared Baxter had finished what would become the second part of *Catholick Communion Defended Against Both Extremes*, in which he had justified communion with parish churches. The effect of that would have been negated, he feared, if he left the manuscript unanswered, so he quickly wrote a reply.[104] It became the third part of *Catholick Communion Defended*, published in 1684 with its own title page and pagination as *An Account of the Reasons Why the Twelve Arguments Said to be Dr. John Owen's Change not my Judgment about Communion with Parish-Churches.*[105] This was the first time in nearly 30 years that Baxter directly attacked Owen in a work dedicated to that purpose. Eventually Baxter would gain a reputation as one who trampled on the memory of dead men,[106] and the

---

[100]   Owen, *Meditations and Discourses on the Glory of Christ* (1684): *Works*, i.279.

[101]   Asty, 'Memoirs', xxxi.

[102]   [Anon.], 'Life of Owen', xxxvii. Wood says that there were 67 coaches parked outside at his funeral. Wood, *Athenae Oxonienses*, ii.747.

[103]   For context and assessment, see Frederick J. Powicke, *The Reverend Richard Baxter Under the Cross (1662–1691)* (London: Jonathan Cape Ltd., 1927), 203–11.

[104]   *Rel. Bax.*, iii.198.

[105]   Baxter subsequently added two further elements to *Catholick Communion Defended*, so this second version was published in five parts. See the headnote to *CCRB* #1129.

[106]   Even in *Death of Christ and of Justification* (1655) Owen complained that Baxter 'will not pardon a man in his grave, but will take him up and cut him in a thousand pieces', in *Works*,

timing does him little credit. He had, of course, been storing up several critiques of Owen as the manuscript of the *Reliquiae Baxterianae* took shape. This fact and the publication of his *Account* suggest that he remained reluctant to provoke the provokable Owen only as long as Owen remained alive to be provoked. Once he was dead, Baxter's restraint appeared to give way. And once more the past did its work in the background. The result was not especially edifying.

Baxter's *Account* has four different elements written in successive stages; it is important to work through them in the order they were written. The first part was the body of the book, in which Baxter outlined no less than 42 errors in Owen's 12 arguments. There was some doubt about whether Owen was in fact the author,[107] but Baxter wrote as though he was. For example, one of the arguments was 'the strangest that I ever read from so learned a Man, and is a great mistake'.[108] For another, Baxter drew on what was very much a shared history. In defending set forms he revisited the 1654 sub-committee on the fundamentals in order to show that Owen himself had been instrumental in crafting a set form to be imposed on the nation. 'But Arch-bishop *Usher* being chosen for one [of the delegates], and refusing, and I being by his consent substituted in his room, broke that attempt.'[109] This is a curious revision of events, given that a confession was formulated and circulated to Members of Parliament; it was the dissolution of Parliament above all that got in the way. But it nicely captures Baxter's negative role in that episode. In making the point that every church has error he returned to the Savoy Confession and its two errors: that we are saved by faith alone, and by the imputation of Christ's righteousness alone. He had not mentioned these errors in the postscript he wrote immediately after seeing the Confession; now they were at the forefront of his mind. And when he asked some of the participants still living why they agreed to such obvious errors 'they said, That it was Dr *O*'s doing'.[110] Baxter even alluded to Owen's near-Antinomianism. '[Owen] hath heard those called *Arminians* on the one side, and *Antinomians* on the other, oft fluently express their Opinions in God's Worship: The former he took to be heinous Errors.'[111] No one who was familiar with Baxter's debates with Owen during the 1650s would have missed the punch when Baxter omitted to say that Owen had also viewed the Antinomians

xii.593.

[107] Richard Baxter, *An Account of the Reasons Why the Twelve Arguments Said to be Dr. John Owen's Change not my Judgment about Communion with Parish-Churches* (1684), Preface, sig. F1r. In *Catholick Communion Defended*.

[108] Baxter, *Account of the Reasons*, 13–14.

[109] Ibid., 4.

[110] Ibid., 8.

[111] Ibid., 21.

as heinous heretics. In Baxter's mind, Owen was still too close to them for that. All of this was reinforced by Baxter's deployment of Philip Nye in two places to show his essential agreement with Baxter, and by implication Owen's own singularity compared to this more reasonable Congregationalist.[112]

History, then, played a large part in Baxter's attack on Owen. The reason, he said, is that 'if I set not Experience against Experience, I shall leave abundance unto the danger of error, who can judg by little else than Experience, and that see and feel what's present, and forget what is long past and gone'.[113] Thus he took several pages to recount the history of the 1640s and 1650s to show that separation was responsible for all of England's troubles. In the beginning the separatists were few and insignificant. When the Dissenting Brethren took their stand at Westminster the 'great Breach' began. The complacent majority largely stood by while a determined minority worked their way. Cromwell's rise brought together the tolerable Independents, to use Baxter's labels, and the intolerable separatists. They cut off the King, cast out the Lords, and pared back the Commons. Through the 1650s they changed the constitution on a whim. Then, the consummation of their crimes: 'After the death of *Oliver*, his Son [was] set up, and his Parliament first pull'd down (in which the Reverend Author, now opposed, told me, he was an agent) and next himself.' Finally, 'by God's most remarkable hand, the conquering Army dissolved utterly without one drop of blood, and the King restored without opposition'.[114]

It was inevitable that Baxter would make his way around to Owen's part in the downfall of Richard Cromwell and this time he played a trump card: Owen had admitted the crime himself. This is an intriguing possibility. If Baxter did have the kind of conversation with Owen in late 1668 as he said, in which he reminded Owen of former things, it seems reasonable to expect that Owen would offer a defence. It also seems possible that what was in Owen's mind a defence, was heard and interpreted – and remembered – by Baxter as an admission. We cannot now know and Owen was no longer alive to deny it. Clearly, though, Baxter continued to pin most of the blame on Owen. He even made this most astonishing assertion:

> I will tell the Bishops, that they should not be too angry with the Learned Author
> of these twelve Arguments: For I know not three men alive, whom they are more
> beholden to for their restitution, by opening the door, and sweeping the way, and
> melting down or pulverizing all that was like to have resisted them. I speak not on the

---

[112]   Ibid., 6, 22.
[113]   Ibid., 24.
[114]   Ibid., 26–8.

> *Intentions*, but of the *Action*; by which the Separatists cut down the banks, and when
> they had let in Prelacy and Liturgy which they dislike, they write and talk against
> them.[115]

Owen's part in the affairs of the 1650s had done nothing but grow ever larger in Baxter's mind during the intervening decades. Now, it seemed, Owen had almost single-handedly opened the door for the oppressive prelacy they both had suffered under. The blame Baxter fastened on Owen showed no signs of ever reaching an end.

After the main body of the *Account* was completed, Baxter wrote the Preface. He conceded that Owen's authorship of the 12 arguments was debatable but claimed to be concerned with the issue itself, not the man. And he tried to forestall any criticism of his indulgence in past events. 'Some wise and good men will blame me for making our differences to be so much known, especially for remembering old miscarriages' but he was compelled by conscience to speak the truth.[116]

> And the Author, that I deal with, necessitateth me to recite the late fruits of Separation,
> in pulling down all Governments, casting out all the Ministers in *Wales*, and were near
> casting down those of *England*, with Tithes and Universities, persecuting and killing
> godly men, and fathering all on God, and now flying from the Bishops when they had
> opened them the door to return.[117]

This was a remarkably warped view of Owen, if Baxter did indeed mean to convey that he was one with the separatists and sectaries who sought to destroy both tithes and universities. John Owen – Dean of Christ Church and Vice-Chancellor of Oxford University – was no ally of theirs. But this was now how Baxter remembered the man. This was simply a recapitulation of his earlier connection between Owen and the sects.

The third element is a letter to an unknown correspondent dated 7 April 1684 and tacked on the end of the whole book.[118] Baxter never discovered the author's identity but we may assume it was Stephen Lobb, a Congregational Minister in London who had crossed swords with Baxter in 1678 over his views on justification.[119] Now he had heard that Baxter intended to reply against Owen. He begged Baxter to handle the matter in private and not to attack his

---

[115]   Ibid., 29.

[116]   Ibid., Preface, sig. F1r (*CCRB* #1130).

[117]   Ibid., sig. F1v.

[118]   For discussion of the recipient of this letter, see the headnote to *CCRB* #1132.

[119]   See *CCRB* #1024 and 1025

fellow sufferers again in public. He also offered to send Baxter a manuscript of Owen's larger thoughts on the matter that were 'preparing for the press'.[120] Baxter first replied to Lobb privately, indicating his willingness to hold on to the already-printed copies of his reply to Owen, though '2 or 3 are sold already'. He also hoped those papers would not be in Owen's handwriting as it seems even that displeased him: 'I know of old that it is the least legible that I have seen of any Learned mans.'[121] But Lobb's messenger never arrived to pick up the letter. A week later Baxter wrote the letter that appeared at the end of his *Account*. He expressed his willingness still to hold on to the book if Lobb would send Owen's papers. And he berated Lobb for doing Owen a grave injustice. Baxter had appreciated 'so much sound and excellent matter, and so many healing peaceable passages' in Owen's later writings, which served to 'hide this one great Mistake' on communion with parish churches. What Lobb had done was to dredge up that one mistake and expose it. Baxter preferred that it lay buried, but now that it had been excavated he had no choice but to attack it – so that he might preserve the memory of Owen better than Lobb had done. So there is in this letter a distinct change of tone towards Owen. Perhaps the copies that had been sold had provoked a reaction – he was 'chided' for answering Owen[122] – or Lobb's letter might have signalled the trouble Baxter bought for himself by attacking Owen so specifically. Immediately after the letter Baxter added a note. 'Reader, I have not had time to gather the Errata of the Press or Copy; only I entreat you to insert an omitted line ... because the sense is altered by the omission.' Baxter's new words came at the end of the sentence that so pointedly blamed Owen for inadvertently bringing in the prelates. The effect of inserting them was to shift the blame away from Owen and onto 'those of the Opinion which he pleads for'.[123] But it rendered the sentence meaningless, since it began by identifying Owen among 'the three men alive' who were most responsible – not a group. Clearly, this was a very last-minute attempt to blunt his attack on Owen at its sharpest point.

This new, conciliatory tone also crept into the fourth element of his *Account*, the Postscript. He wrote it after he had read through the body of the book 'to say somewhat of the *Matter* and *Manner* of this Writing' and 'to say more, lest I be

---

[120]   Stephen Lobb? to Baxter [c.late March 1684]: DWL MS *BC* vi.244r (*CCRB* #1132).

[121]   Baxter to Stephen Lobb?, 1 April 1684: DWL MS *BC* vi.241r (*CCRB* #1133).

[122]   Baxter, *Account of the Reasons*, Postscript, sig. M3v.

[123]   The sentence became, with the added words in italics: 'For I know not three men alive, whom they are more beholden to for their restitution, by opening the door, and sweeping the way, and melting down or pulverizing all that was like to have resisted them, *than those of the Opinion which he pleads for.*' See Baxter, *Account of the Reasons*, 29 and sig. O1v.

misunderstood'.[124] He was now very much on the defensive: all the parties in the Church 'revile and hate me'.[125] Much of it is taken up with explaining why it had been so necessary to rake over very old coals, but he also took the opportunity to throw in a few placatory compliments.

> But let the Reader know, That it is so far from my design to wrong the Name of Dr. Owen, by this Defence; that I do openly declare, That except in this point of his Mistake, (and who mistaketh not in more than one?) I doubt not he was a Man of rare Parts and Worth: and tho in the Tryals of the late Distractions in this Land, I mention some of his Concessions; it is to tell you that I had reason to hope that he repented for doing no more in his publick opportunities against the Spirit of Division, which dissolved us. And which of us need not repentence for our faults in those days of Tryal?[126]

This is rare praise of Owen, but it is very faint. In fact, what seems at first glance to be an affirmation is a series of veiled accusations. Owen was 'a Man of Rare Parts and Worth' but: he made a mistake in rejecting parish communion; he could have done more to bring unity among the godly; he had a hand in the dissolutions of the Interregnum; he really should have repented for his actions and he might have done. Baxter also observed that in his later years Owen was 'of more complying mildness, and sweetness, and peaceableness, than ever before'.[127] In other words, Owen used to be sharp and angry and divisive – all true to an extent – but he became less so as he grew older. Again, Owen was damned by faint praise. And while Baxter could happily concede that Owen was now with Christ in heaven he was sure that Owen felt only repentance for his mistake in denying the liturgy and parish communion. To underline the point Baxter wrote a long paragraph putting words in Owen's mouth: 'I was ... of too narrow mistaken Principles, and in the time of Temptation, I did not forsee to what Church-Confusion, and Dissolution, and Hatred, and Ruin, dividing Practices of some did tend.'[128] These extended reflections projected onto Owen are surely among the most bizarre and ironic that Baxter ever penned. His arrogance in presuming to speak not just for someone who was dead, but for someone whom he had attacked, opposed and misinterpreted for most of his career, is really quite stunning. 'No doubt but now this is D. O's mind.'[129] Baxter was so utterly

---

124 Baxter, *Account of the Reasons*, Postscript, sig. M1r.
125 Ibid., sig. M1v.
126 Ibid., sig. M3v.
127 Ibid., sig. M4r.
128 Ibid.
129 Ibid., sig. M4v.

convinced that he was right, and Owen wrong, that he would dare to constrain Owen's heavenly felicity. It is difficult to think of another occasion when he was so tactless and insensitive. And, as always, we might note that while Owen allegedly now repented of his error over the liturgy, his greatest crimes lay much further back 'in the time of Temptation'.

Baxter's attack on Owen created no little stir. An anonymous writer who knew both men wrote *A Vindication of the Late Reverend and Learned John Owen D.D.* in response. He expressed a sense of wounded disbelief – not so different from John Asty's a decade later – that Baxter would so needlessly attack Owen's memory after he was dead.[130] Baxter had acted like the hyenas when they 'feed on dead Carkases, when they have torn them out of their Graves'.[131] 'And had the Doctor, surviving you, trampled on your Grave, and taken such unequal advantages against your good Name, and Principles, as you have done of his' he would have written a similar defence of Baxter.[132] Most acutely, the writer could scarcely credit Baxter putting those words in Owen's mouth. No one he had talked to could reconcile such a move with Baxter's 'Learning, or Candour'; it was 'unwarrantable by the strictest Rules of Ecclesiastical Combating'.[133] By speculating on Owen's repentance in heaven Baxter had undone so much of the foundation of his own good reputation. Indeed, the writer spotted the obvious irony in 'this uncomfortable mistake of yours, that renders the Saints everlasting rest not such a rest'.[134] Some others, who apparently wanted to defend Baxter but found it impossible to do so, shrewdly deduced the fundamental cause of Baxter's unnecessarily personal and ill-timed assault: 'this is but the working of an old Spleen against the Doctor, and taking very ungentily this advantage'.[135] The writer himself thought it 'distastful and fruitless' for Baxter to ignore the Act of Oblivion and to spend so much time 'exposing old miscarriages'.[136] He could think of no one alive who was 'less fit' than Baxter to throw these accusations around.

> I speak it not in respect of your Abilities ... but in respect of the want of that good
> understanding betwixt you, while the Dr. lived; which was commonly noised: I say
> not where the fault lay, I should have been glad to have been the means to cure, or

---

130　[Anon.], *Vindication of Owen*, 3.
131　Ibid., 17.
132　Ibid., 2.
133　Ibid., 11, 10.
134　Ibid., 13.
135　Ibid., 9.
136　Ibid., 16, 17.

conceal it. But take things as they are, and it will be next a Miracle if this work of yours be not imputed to some ill Original.[137]

It seems the strain between Owen and Baxter was an open secret – so well known that it could only be cured or concealed – and people were bound to make the connection. The writer had pointed out the fundamental incongruity in Baxter's position. His stated target was an unwillingness to commune with parish churches. Strictly speaking, that was an issue for the Restoration period. But Baxter condemned that essentially separatist stance by showing its alleged effects during the Interregnum. He could not see the present except in terms of the increasingly distant past, so he should not have been surprised when his attack on Owen was read in that light.

Indeed, the anonymous vindicator was not alone in his sentiments. According to Baxter, 'a swarm of revilers in the City poured out their keenest Censures' on his actions.[138] Samuel Young says that Baxter's 'base Trick of thus abusing Dr. *Owen* and his people hath made him odious'.[139] In his autobiography Baxter conceded that 'it had been more prudent to have omitted [Owen's] Name'. In public, he responded to the furore in *Catholick Communion Doubly Defended* (1684) where he demonstrated a typically limited form of contrition for ever identifying Owen by name. In the end he admitted that the *Vindication* 'doth turn the Scales, and make me repent that I named the Doctor'.[140] But before he got to that point he further justified his reasons for doing so: he saw no reason for all dissenters to be accused of holding a position put forward by one man who was never nominated to represent them;[141] and a strong stand was required 'in so great a Cause, and at such a time, when they [the false arguments of Owen] tend to drive hundred thousands from all Church Worship and Communion'.[142] Baxter imagined a 'Ship of Passengers, whose Pilot hath cast them by Errour on the Sands or Rocks, and that some that pity them as they are sinking, tell them their Pilots mistake hath endangered them, and they must take better advice', but the passengers respond only with scorn.[143] This is so unconstructive as to be almost comical: instead of rescuing the survivors Baxter would criticize the errors of the pilot and tell the people they really should have found another. It

---

[137]   Ibid., 22.

[138]   *Rel. Bax.*, iii.198.

[139]   [Young], *Vindiciae Anti-Baxterianae*, 216.

[140]   Richard Baxter, *Catholick Communion Doubly Defended: By Dr. Owens Vindicator and Richard Baxter. And the State of that Communion Opened* (1684), 29.

[141]   Ibid., 6, 22.

[142]   Ibid., 7.

[143]   Ibid., 15.

serves to reveal exactly how Baxter saw himself in this situation: he was not the one in the wrong. He now regretted some of the words that the anonymous vindicator had quoted back at him, but he maintained he had done only his duty.[144] He restated his case in 35 principles; he defended his view of Owen's knowledge and repentance in heaven; and he justified his bringing up the past: the Act of Oblivion 'forbad reproaching, and troubling one another, but not remembering our sin, nor feeling when we suffer, nor asking what caused it, to stop the like again, if not for a cure'.[145] No legislation could stop Baxter from recalling past sins, especially Owen's. But he did claim to have forgiven him.

> As to your hints of suspicion of my sense of old differences, if I know my heart, I forgave, and fully put up all Personal Quarrel long ago: But the National Concerns made so deep a wound in my heart, as never will be fully healed in this world.[146]

Baxter was hardly going to admit to holding a grudge and he may have been able to convince himself that he had indeed forgiven Owen his past misdeeds. If so, he did not know his heart as well as he hoped. The many lingering accusations were too personal and too specific and too many to think that Baxter had successfully detached Owen from that irreparable inner wound. I suggest that sentiment tells it as it was – heartfelt, and with no exaggeration. Baxter carried the wounds of the 1650s with him and it proved impossible, whatever his best intentions, not to see Owen as the one who, above all others, had done so much to inflict them.

Fatal Memory

Baxter explicitly brought up the events of 1659 only after Owen had died, in this controversy and in the manuscript of his autobiography, which he knew would remain private until after his own death. This is one reason why John Asty was so unimpressed: Baxter had not taken the opportunity to confront Owen with his accusations directly while he was still alive to defend and explain himself.[147] Samuel Young was also affronted on Owen's behalf: 'I do not think he ever told the Doctor thus when alive, and often in his Company.'[148] Of course Owen and Baxter may have had a conversation along those lines in the late 1660s but, if so,

---

[144]   Ibid., 8, 9.

[145]   Ibid., 9–28, 31.

[146]   Ibid., 7.

[147]   University of Edinburgh Library: 'New College Comm 2', 152, 154 (these two pages are contiguous; the material on page 153 is out of place).

[148]   [Young], *Vindiciae Anti-Baxterianae*, 45.

Baxter did not hear Owen's defence or he chose to disbelieve or ignore it. Asty's point is generally true: Baxter made his accusations only when one or both of them were dead.

And yet, I suggest that the memory of Owen's part in the downfall of Richard Cromwell was apparent in much of Baxter's Restoration writings, but it operated in a very generalized way. To go further, it is possible that 1659 (which I will use as a shorthand for Owen's part in those events) vitiated Baxter's interpretation of the events of the 1640s and 1650s, and permanently jaundiced his view of the Congregationalists in general. In order to advance this hypothesis I will return to the context of 1667 to 1673 and I will contrast Baxter's interpretation in April or May 1659 with his perspective in 1670/1. For the former, I will take his words in the final chapter of his *Holy Commonwealth*, written in the days before he heard the news of Richard's fall. For the latter, Baxter stirred up renewed controversy and bitterness with the Congregationalists by publishing his *Cure of Church Divisions* in 1670. If ever we should expect him to call on the memory of 1659, it is there.

At the end of *A Holy Commonwealth* Baxter gave an account of why he had supported Parliament during the civil wars. He distinguished between 'the *Old Cause*' that he supported (defending the King and the ancient constitution) and its corruption in the later determination to destroy the monarchy, to locate sovereignty in the people alone, and to remove the magistrate's power in matters of religion.[149] He also placed blame on both sides. Among those on his own side some had been 'too impatient' under the Laudian impositions, with 'too peevish scrupling and quarrelling, where there was no cause, or not so much as was pretended. But who can be free from causeless scruples, that hath any Faith of his own, and is not careless of his soul'. So Baxter himself shared in the blame. 'I think that all of us did rush too eagerly into the heat of Divisions and War, and none of us did so much as we should have done to prevent it.'[150] Despite this genuine regret, and despite a strikingly honest admission of his own guilt 'that I spoke so much to blow the Coals',[151] at the end of it all Baxter vindicated the cause by its fruit.

> Nor can I be so unthankfull as to say, for all the sinnes and miscarriages of men since, that we have not received much mercy from the Lord: When Godlines[s] was

---

[149]   See Baxter, *Holy Commonwealth*, 482–3. The language of the 'good old cause' was wide open to interpretation. Henry Vane's influential understanding of what it comprised, for example, was precisely the opposite of Baxter's. See Henry Vane, *A Healing Question Propounded and Resolved* (1656); and Woolrych, 'The Good Old Cause and the Fall of the Protectorate', 134–5.

[150]   Baxter, *Holy Commonwealth*, 485.

[151]   Ibid.

the common scorn ... through the great mercy of God, many thousands have been converted to a holy, upright life, proportionately more than were before, since the reproach did cease, and the prejudice was removed, and faithfull preachers took the place of scandalous ones, or ignorant Readers. When I look upon the place where I live, and see that the Families of the ungodly, are here one, and there one in a Street, as the Families of the godly were heretofore ... it forceth me to set up the Stone of Remembrance, and to say, 'HITHERTO HATH THE LORD HELPED US'.[152]

His comments here capture him in the full radiance of his sunny optimism at the precise moment before the clouds closed in. It is also as close as he ever came to imitating anything like the positive message of Owen's 1646 sermon to Parliament. Sins had been committed along the way, no doubt, but England's spiritual settings in early 1659 were no bad thing.

We can contrast this with Baxter's interpretation of the same events in the early 1670s when he was strikingly heated towards the Congregationalists, who were now to blame for almost everything. At the risk of repetition, three examples will serve to illustrate his perspective. First, in the Preface to the *Cure of Church Divisions*, he explained how in

these same principles, which I here detect, I have seen how confidently the killing of the King, the rebellious demolishing of the Government of the Land, the killing of many thousands of their Brethren, the turnings and overturnings of all kinds of Rule, even that which they themselves set up, have been committed, and justified, and prophanely fathered upon God. These and much more such fruits of Love-killing principles, and divisions I have seen.[153]

Second, in his final reply to Edward Bagshaw, who had attacked him in print for publishing the *Cure*, Baxter recalled how he had seen

the spring, multiplication, growth, and fruits of Dividing Principles, Dispositions, and Practices in these Kingdomes, not being totally innocent therein myself, in my inexperienced youth; [I have] seen so much bloud shed, so many Governments overturned, and so many ministers openly reviled, abused ejected, silenced, and so many damnable heresies risen up; and all this done in the name of God ... and all this

---

[152]   Ibid., 487–8.

[153]   Richard Baxter, *The Cure of Church Divisions: Or, Directions for Weak Christians, to keep them from being Dividers, or Troublers of the Church. With Some Directions to the Pastors, How to Deal with Such Christians* (1670), Preface, sig. B1r–v.

as fruit of former Church-Divisions, obstinately continued twenty years, (to look no farther) and the effect of the same spirit still working in both extremes.[154]

Finally, in a letter to Henry Oasland, who had privately remonstrated with Baxter for seeming to attack his fellow nonconformists in their time of suffering and persecution, Baxter explained that he was bound to say something

> in that age and yeare when the same sin of separating principles, which corrupted Oliver's Army, which overturned all Governments, which have silenced 1800 ministers, and brought us all into this confusion and cast the greatest dishonour on Religion that ever was done in England, that hath bred Ranters, Quakers, Seekers, Infidels, when these same principles I say have the strongest temptation to increase, and do in City and Country multiply an hundredfold.[155]

This is far removed from Baxter's reluctance in early 1659 to go out of his way to attack the Congregationalists; it has much more in common with his bitterness and gloom in late 1659. Indeed, notwithstanding the dramatic change in political climate between 1659 and 1670 (and the drift towards effective Congregationalism among some of his Presbyterian colleagues), and given the power of Baxter's determined construction of Owen's role in the downfall of Richard Cromwell, it is certainly plausible that 1659 was the one major event sufficient to have brought about this critical posture and tone.

Baxter consistently claimed that in his *Cure* he was not attacking any particular group or party; his primary purpose was to 'disclaim ... *Love-killing* and *Church-dividing Principles*' in general,[156] and there is some truth to this. But there could be no avoiding the fact that the Congregationalists were the biggest target, especially when the most 'damnable' of the sects themselves were a distant memory and when Baxter himself revealingly wrote of 'the evils of Independency'.[157] More to the point, he defined '*Church-dividers*' as those 'who fly from the ancient simplicity and primitive terms of Church-communion, and adde (as the Papists do) their own little novelties as necessary things'.[158] Surely Owen was at the forefront of Baxter's mind as he wrote those words, making those '*Love-killing* and *Church-dividing Principles*' Owen's own principles. And that is the point. Baxter *was* attacking Owen in public, but he was doing so in a

---

[154]   Richard Baxter, *The Church told of Mr. Ed. Bagshaw's Scandals and Warned of the Dangerous Snares of Satan...in his Love-Killing Principles* (1672), 3–4.

[155]   Baxter to Henry Oasland, 29 June 1670: DWL MS *BC* i.22r (*CCRB* #804).

[156]   Baxter, *The Church told of Mr. Ed. Bagshaw's Scandals*, 8.

[157]   Baxter, *Cure of Church Divisions*, 232.

[158]   Ibid., 249.

way that was deeply coded. One can discern his accusations around 1659 in the three examples above: in his references to 'the turnings and overturnings of all kinds of Rule, even that which they themselves set up'; to 'so many Governments overturned'; and to 'the same sin of separating principles, which corrupted Oliver's Army, which overturned all Governments'. And Baxter's contention that these 'separating principles' had 'silenced 1800 ministers' is parallel to his later claim that Owen's actions had brought about the return of the Bishops.

More than that, 1659 now served as a distorting lens through which Baxter discerned all previous events. He saw them ever after in a new light quite distinctly at odds with his perspective in early 1659. Then, Baxter could regret the missteps, even share in the blame for them, but still rejoice in the evident fruit. But after 1659 and the dashing of all his hopes, and the subsequent dejection and ejection, he looked back on the 1640s and 1650s in a different way. In early 1659 he might have blamed himself and others for rushing too quickly into divisions; but now, he saw at work these '*Love-killing* and *Church-dividing Principles*', ruining everything they touched, responsible for every sin and failure, culpable for all England's recent woes – to blame, in fact, for all of Baxter's woes. And if this is true, then it made any sort of generous understanding towards the Congregationalists, and towards Owen, impossible. It is perhaps not going too far to say that the *Cure of Church Divisions* had its deepest roots not so much in the alarming increase in Congregational adherents in the late 1660s as in the dreadful events of 1659, although even that increase had its particular connection with Owen. The 1660s began with the good people of Kidderminster urging Baxter to return;[159] they ended with the news that Owen 'hugely riseth in the esteeme of this Country [county]',[160] a report that Baxter did not take well.[161] For all these reasons, we should not be surprised to hear that the one 'who behind my Back did most revile my Book, was Dr. *Owen*'.[162]

All of this raises the question of memory and how memory is formed and preserved. It would be foolhardy to try here to master such a vast and complex field of psychology and cognitive neuroscience, and on that basis to say anything definitive about how Baxter himself formed his memories. But perhaps some cursory observations lightly applied may be helpful in putting the nature of his recollections into better perspective. In 1932 Frederick Bartlett published *Remembering: A Study of Experimental and Social Psychology*. Though decades

---

[159]   From [The Parish of Kidderminster] to Baxter, 2 August 1660: DWL MS *BC* vi.71r (*CCRB* #652).

[160]   From [Henry Oasland] to Baxter [c.May 1670]: DWL MS *BC* iii.297v (*CCRB* #798). See also, *Rel. Bax.*, iii.73.

[161]   From Baxter to Henry Oasland, 29 June 1670: DWL MS *BC* i.25v (*CCRB* #804).

[162]   *Rel. Bax.*, iii.73.

old now, the book remains one of the most enduring influences on the study of memory.[163] In reporting the results of a series of experiments Bartlett rejects the view (typically associated with Sigmund Freud) 'that memory is primarily or literally reduplicative, or reproductive'. Instead, 'remembering appears to be far more decisively an affair of construction'.[164] That construction is marked by a dynamic called rationalization, the tendency to make sense of events by giving them 'a setting and an explanation'.[165] Events are given meaning by locating them within a 'schema', which Bartlett defines as 'an active organisation of past reactions, or of past experiences'.[166] That is, events are located and made sense of within pre-existing knowledge structures; they are placed within a larger story, and this shapes the construction of memory. Thus 'condensation, elaboration and invention are common features of ordinary remembering'.[167] Additional details may be brought in to reinforce the perceived meaning in the event, while incidental elements that are unnecessary or problematic may disappear, and all this without the person being aware of the selection that is going on. Once a reconstruction is established its outlines remain broadly stable over time. 'It now seems that attitudes, springing up upon a basis of some not very-well defined perceptual pattern, may strongly influence recall, and may tend in particular to produce stereotyped and conventional reproductions which adequately serve all normal needs, though they are very unfaithful to their originals.'[168] Bartlett did not go so far as to say that all memory is inaccurate,[169] but it is clearly the product of a process that is hardly objective, impartial or even fully conscious.

I think it is helpful to understand Baxter's memories of Owen in a similar fashion. He did not receive the news of Owen's involvement in Richard

[163]   See Daniel L. Schacter, 'Memory Distortion: History and Current Status', in *Memory Distortion: How Minds, Brains, and Societies Reconstruct the Past*, ed. Daniel L. Schacter (Cambridge, MA: Harvard University Press, 1995), 8; James L. McClelland, 'Constructive Memory and Memory Distortions: A Parallel-Distributed Processing Approach', also in Schacter, ed., *Memory Distortions*, 69; James Ost and Alan Costall, 'Misremembering Bartlett: A Study in Serial Reproduction', *British Journal of Psychology* 93 (2002): 243–6; and Daniel L. Schacter and Donna Rose Addis, 'The Cognitive Neuroscience of Constructive Memory: Remembering the Past and Imagining the Future', *Philosophical Transactions of the Royal Society B* 362 (2007): 773, 774.

[164]   Frederick C. Bartlett, *Remembering: A Study in Experimental and Social Psychology* (Cambridge: Cambridge University Press, 1932), 204, 205. I am grateful to Professor Lyn Tribble for pointing me towards Bartlett's work.

[165]   Ibid., 84.

[166]   Ibid., 201.

[167]   Ibid., 205.

[168]   Ibid., 55.

[169]   Ost and Costall, 'Misremembering Bartlett', 243–55

Cromwell's demise in an objective way. He fitted that information within the context of his previous dealings with Owen, and they had not gone well. He was predisposed to believe the worst of the man, not the best. It seemed entirely consistent and plausible to hear of Owen declaring that Richard 'must come down' and working hard to bring about that end. Baxter asserted that he could not command his intellect: 'Its only evidence of verity that can command it'.[170] He would believe only upon proof. But his handling of the evidence in the case of Owen is strikingly different from his handling of the evidence for the alleged Catholicism of King Charles I, for example. In that case – and in 1659, before the Restoration – Baxter bent over backwards to be generous and measured. While Charles certainly held a '*Grotian* design', he was no Papist.[171] But there was no such generosity towards Owen, since what he heard seemed to confirm – or could help to reinforce – his existing knowledge of Owen's personality and methods. Once Baxter accepted what he had been told, the element of Owen's engineering in 1659 would never be displaced from the overarching story that Baxter constructed to explain the bitter failure of the 1650s. The first evidence we have for the narrative arc of that story is in the pages of the *Reliquaie Baxterianae*, penned in 1664, where Baxter fleshed out at some length the connections between Owen, the army and the sects in a trajectory goes all the way back to the Dissenting Brethren.[172] As time went on, and as Baxter presented that story in briefer instalments, the memory condensed and simplified so that he could link up iconic events – the regicide, the fall of Richard, the return of the bishops – and blame the whole thing on only one man. While Owen was alive Baxter coded that blame under the generic 'spirit of separation', but it seems clear that Owen personified that spirit. Once Owen had died, he said as much. 'And the Author, that I deal with, necessitateth me to recite the late fruits of Separation, in pulling down all Governments ... and now flying from the Bishops when they had opened them the door to return.'[173]

This is Baxter's reconstruction. This is not to say whether the accusation against Owen was just or not, but the way Baxter framed it says as much about him as it does of Owen. For this reason, it is at least highly suspect. In Bartlett's words, it is a stereotyped and conventional reproduction, one that we should not take at face value. For the same reason we should also approach Baxter's post-Restoration posture towards the Congregationalists with caution. He placed on them a weight that was not entirely theirs to bear and it is time that historians saw his stance for what it was: the ongoing wound – only just bandaged, never

---

[170]   Baxter to Morgan Llwyd, 10 July 1656: DWL MS *BC* i.53r (*CCRB* #316).

[171]   Baxter, *Key for Catholicks*, 327.

[172]   *Rel. Bax.*, i.101–3.

[173]   Baxter, *Account of the Reasons*, Preface, sig. F1v (*CCRB* #1130).

healed – inflicted by the failure of all his hopes and dreams for England in the last years of the 1650s. What this goes to show is that 1659, not 1660, is the one year that marks off one half of his career from the other; and the one year that made the breach with Owen utterly irreparable.

Moving On

Richard Baxter died several hours before dawn on 8 December 1691,[174] eight years after Owen. Edward Harley, one of the executors of Baxter's will, remarked that London had never 'seen such vast numbers of people to attend any funeral. The streets and windows and balconies [were] all crowded, from Merchant Taylors Hall to Christ Church [Newgate] where he was interred [beside the grave of] his wife'.[175] Regrettably, the church was damaged by the war in 1941 and subsequently demolished, removing any physical testimony to their life and death.[176] But Baxter left enough other evidence to mark his passing, not least in bequeathing the manuscript of his autobiography to his young friend Matthew Sylvester – a far more enduring testament than any crypt or tomb. If only Owen had done the same.

On the Sunday after Baxter's death Matthew Sylvester preached a sermon in his memory, *Elisha's Cry After Elijah's God*. He concluded that sermon with a long and very human description of Baxter's demeanour and character. There, he offered this summation:

> He was no ways clandestinely rigid, or censorious as to others. When he told Men to their faces of their faults he would hear what they have to say, and then reprove them with as great pungency as he thought their fault deserv'd: but yet behind Mens backs he was always ready to believe the best; and whatever he could think on that might extenuate their Crime, if there was any likelyhood of truth therein, he would be sure to mention that.[177]

Sylvester's assessment is plausible enough, especially given his honesty about Baxter's 'pungency', but there was one notable exception to this pattern of

---

[174]   Matthew Sylvester, *Elisha's Cry After Elijah's God Consider'd and Apply'd With Reference to the Decease of the Late Reverend Mr. Richard Baxter* (1696), 16.

[175]   [Richard Ward, ed.], *The Manuscripts of His Grace The Duke of Portland Preserved at Welbeck Abbey* (London: Her Majesty's Stationery Office, 1894), iii.485. See also Nuttall. *Richard Baxter*, 112; Goldie, *Entring Book of Roger Morrice*, i.253.

[176]   Nuttall, *Richard Baxter*, 112.

[177]   Sylvester, *Elisha's Cry After Elijah's God*, 15.

generosity, one crime that could never be mitigated. Recall this comment of Calamy's: 'as to the main reflection upon [Owen], with regard to the affair of Wallingford House, and his concern in it, on which Baxter laid a considerable stress, (and which Mr. Sylvester had often heard Mr. Baxter discourse of with great freedom,) he would not by any means give his consent to have that out.'[178] Far from giving Owen the benefit of the doubt, Baxter had continued to criticize him in private, 'with great freedom'. Indeed, in the preface to the *Reliquiae Baxterianae*, written almost five years later, Sylvester had realized as much. There he made the same point about Baxter's 'acrimonious pungent Stile' but he changed the ending. Rather than thinking and speaking the best of others in private, Baxter was merely 'averse from blackening them more than there was reason for in his judgment: and from concluding Men graceless or hopeless from any particular Misdemeanours or Defects'.[179] Writing in 1696, in the preface to the *Reliquiae*, having just mentioned Owen's misdemeanours at Wallingford House, Sylvester could hardly claim that Baxter was generous in his private judgement. When it came to Owen, he clearly was not.

One important reason for this is that years after his death Owen's influence lived on. As he surveyed his career and Owen's at the close of 1691, Baxter might well have felt that – if the complexities of later seventeenth-century history were reduced to a simple battle between them – Owen had emerged the victor. Most obviously, Parliament had passed an Act of Toleration in 1689, not the Bill for comprehension. That particular push for comprehension was merely the most significant failure among many; at least eight Bills, most with Baxter involved in some fashion, had come to nothing.[180] By the time Baxter died comprehension was a dead thing. Looking back, the emergence of the 'Ducklings' and the semi-permanent effects of the temporary Declaration of Indulgence clearly betrayed the drift of things. 'By the 1680s [the Presbyterians] had come round to a dual ambition to achieve Comprehension for themselves and toleration for those who refused to be comprehended. Arguments for toleration were gaining ground.'[181] But for all that, the inevitability of toleration was not assured in the lead-up to 1689. In the face of King James II's overtly pro-Catholic agenda 'Baxter and his friends were able to bring about an extraordinary degree of unanimity among the Dissenters ... The Dons now came into their own'.[182] We might note that Baxter was finally able to achieve unity among the nonconformists only when

---

[178]   Rutt, ed., *Edmund Calamy: An Historical Account of My Own Life*, i.377.

[179]   *Rel. Bax.*, Preface to the Reader, §viii.

[180]   Goldie, *Entring Book of Roger Morrice*, i.234, 239, 244–5. For a brief summary of the eight failed Bills, see pp. 239–41.

[181]   Ibid., 236.

[182]   Thomas, 'Comprehension and Indulgence', 240.

Owen was no longer among those with whom he had to deal. But that unity was fleeting, as the dearest desire of 'the Dons' was set aside. The 1689 Toleration Act was in essence 'a deliberate act of exclusion, just as the Uniformity Act had been, and to that extent was its offspring rather than its reversal'.[183] In that light all of Baxter's labours had been for nothing. This did not stop him from publishing *Church Concord* in 1691 – a work entirely in concert with his earlier efforts in that the first part was written in 1655, the second in that promising year, 1667 – but his consistent prescription for unity among the godly, first presented in the *Saints' Everlasting Rest* all those years ago, went nowhere in the end. 'The [Glorious] Revolution thus marked the victory of the Independent conception of toleration over the Presbyterian hopes of comprehension.'[184] It was, in other words, a posthumous victory of Owen over Baxter.

Baxter fared better on the other main issue of dispute with Owen. 'In the first half of the century, Puritans had deplored the spread of Arminianism in England.' But by the time Baxter died it had become 'commonplace in England. It was an astonishing transformation, and in this respect at least Archbishop Laud had triumphed. Calvinist soteriology was dislodged, surviving only in pockets'.[185] Baxter was never an outright Arminian but he was certainly central to this drift away from Calvinist soteriology. Support had pretty well collapsed by 1691: a clear defeat for Owen, much more of a victory for Baxter. Yet that would not necessarily have been apparent at the time. In 1690 the complete works of the arch-Antinomian Tobias Crisp were republished by his son, Samuel.[186] In the preface, he attacked Baxter explicitly. And he included a certificate signed by 12 nonconformist ministers confirming the authenticity of Crisp's sermons. This was, to Baxter at least, a staggering reassertion of Antinomian doctrine seemingly condoned by his ministerial colleagues. Anti-Antinomianism had been a defining feature of his career, profoundly shaping his writings and his theology, and here it sprang to life again with cruel virulence.[187] He launched a vigorous counter-attack both in print and in the pulpit, and it would not have been at all clear by the time of his death that he had done enough to counteract the Antinomian disease. And while Crisp may have been the *provocateur* on this occasion, raised from the dead, Owen had also encouraged the Antinomian

[183] Goldie, *Entring Book of Roger Morrice*, i.244. Nicholas Tyacke is more positive, seeing it as a 'remarkable' achievement relative to the harsh political context of the time. See Tyacke, 'The "Rise of Puritanism" and the Legalising of Dissent', 41.

[184] Watts, *Dissenters*, 260.

[185] Goldie, *Entring Book of Roger Morrice*, i.256, 257.

[186] Tobias Crisp, *Christ Alone Exalted: Being the Compleat Works of Tobias Crisp D.D.* (1690).

[187] For more detail on this, see Cooper, *Fear and Polemic*, 170–177.

infection across the years. Indeed, in my earlier book I showed how it was the name of Owen, rather than Baxter, that was called on more often, even by anti-Antinomians, during the debate that continued to surge through the 1690s.[188] Antinomian or not, Owen's brand of Calvinism was on the way out, but Baxter had good reason to suspect that it was not dead yet.

Therefore, it is not surprising to find Baxter's familiar refrain repeated to the end. In the preface to *Church Concord*, finished on 11 April 1691, less than eight months before his death, Baxter reminded the Congregationalists among his audience

> that it was men of your Principles and Tempers that caused our former Confusions, and pull'd down after the King, the Parliaments of all sorts, the Protector and one another, till they set up their Quarters over the Gates, and pluckt up the Floodgates that have these Thirty years overwhelmed us, and hazarded all the Reformation.[189]

This same accusation had reappeared at various points during the Restoration period, all veiled hints at Owen's actions in 1659. It is true that, in the scheme of things, it took up precious few of Baxter's printed words; it was one more recurring theme among many. But it was an extremely important one to Baxter, a fact conveyed not just by the steady repetition but by the bitter tone of his explicit reflections on Owen in the *Reliquiae Baxterianae*. There the carefully coded message was finally deciphered.

All this is why Baxter chose to retain his comments on Owen's actions in the manuscript he handed on to Matthew Sylvester. It was more necessary than ever to advertise the consequences of Owen's 'separating principles' in order 'to stop the like again'.[190] The significance of what seemed to be at stake outweighed Baxter's usual impulse towards generosity in his private judgements. The events of 1659 revealed much about the course that England had, exactly three decades later, chosen for itself. The *Reliquiae Baxterianae* would be Baxter's last-ditch effort to stem Owen's apparent influence. And whatever the wounds to Owen's supporters, to his widow Dorothy and his friend John Asty, Sylvester could never in good conscience leave out Baxter's assessment of Owen's activities in 1659. It really would have been a betrayal of trust. For Baxter, 1659 was simply too important ever to be forgotten. The fact that we are still discussing it now is testament to his success.

---

188   Cooper, *Fear and Polemic*, 181–2.

189   *Church Concord*, Preface, sig.a2r.

190   Baxter, *Catholick Communion Doubly Defended*, 31.

Conclusion

The greatest discords and wars will be from the Love and Endeavour of Unity and Concord, and for the obtaining of them by impossible means.

Richard Baxter (1659)[1]

This book opened by asking two very precise questions: why did John Owen and Richard Baxter not like each other; and what effect did their strained relationship have on the development of English nonconformity? We are now in a position to answer these questions in a way that demonstrates just how closely interrelated they are. Understanding the breakdown in the relationship between these two men throws a great deal of light on the reasons why the Puritan movement more generally ended up permanently riven by conflict and disagreement.[2]

On the First Question

In 1645 Jeremiah Burroughes published his *Irenicum* in an effort to try to restore peace among the orthodox godly.[3] He was a Congregationalist minister and one of the Dissenting Brethren, but we might recall that Baxter pointedly contrasted his pacific 'spirit' with Owen's and called the *Irenicum* 'his excellent Book'.[4] In that work Burroughes addressed the fundamental question: 'how it comes to passe that godly men are divided, who above all men, one would think, should agree'.[5] It was clearly a question of obvious urgency within the whole community well before Owen or Baxter ever appeared on the scene, but they serve as an excellent illustration of its pressing importance. Indeed, the strange thing is that they agreed on so much. They were moulded in the Puritan tradition with similar concerns for the spread of the gospel, the centrality of

---

[1]   Baxter, *Key for Catholicks*, 392.

[2]   I would like to acknowledge some very fruitful conversations with John Coffey that have helped to shape this Conclusion.

[3]   Jeremiah Burroughes, *Irenicum, To the Lovers of Truth and Peace: Heart-Divisions Opened in the Causes and Evils of Them* (1645). Burroughes died in 1646 but his book was republished in 1653.

[4]   *Rel. Bax.*, i.103.

[5]   Burroughes, *Irenicum*, 226.

the Word of God, the reformation of society and the practical outworking of God's grace in righteous living. The logical corollary of this shared Puritan heritage was a common Calvinism. They both held that God predestined certain individuals for salvation and that these elect would be infallibly saved by the initiative, prevailing power and particular grace of God, while also maintaining a place for conditions and for human free will and responsibility. Both men earnestly sought church unity together with a generous degree of toleration for individual consciences. Both were seriously committed to pastoral ministry, to sound preaching and to catechizing among families as a matter of routine. And yet for all this impressive common ground the two men fell out with each other and were never able to reconcile. In this way they reflected that broader failure. How was it to be explained?

Their proximity lay at the very heart of the problem. Burroughes recognized how 'those that come nearest together, yet differing in some things, are many times at greater variance one with another, then those who differ in more things from them'.[6] Owen and Baxter should have been allies in the same cause but their minor differences made their alliance fragile and unstable. They wanted the same end but by different means, to the extent that each viewed the other not just as an impediment to those ends, but as actually facilitating those who opposed those ends. Thus Baxter accused Owen of doing the devil's work even as Owen was meeting with sincere, godly divines in the pursuit of Christian unity. Given their proximity, minor differences attracted a particular sense of aggravation. There is also an aspect of boundary maintenance in that each man was competing for support from the same broad audience. It required that each one's turf be delineated with some precision.

For this reason the issues that divided Owen and Baxter can seem trivial and small. They may have been small, but they were never trivial. As Burroughes also observed, 'the things that the Saints are conversant about, are great things, things of a high nature, about their last end, their eternall estates'. Working in the modern, secular discipline of History, we might need his warning: 'those who understand not the infinite consequence of those things, who have not had the feare of them fall upon their hearts, they wonder at the stiffness of mens spirits that they can be brought to yeeld no more in such things that they conceive they might yeeld in.' This certainly helps to explain why the Puritans, of all people, experienced their divisions:

> godly men give up themselves to the strictest rules of holinesse, they walk in the narrow
> way of Christ, it is broad enough to the spiritual part, but in regard of our corruptions,

---

[6]   Ibid., 240.

it is a narrow, pent way; they dare not give way to themselves to decline a haires bredth
from the rule, to gratifie others; they dare not bend to them, that they might sute more
with them, but must keep themselves to the straight rule ... hence there is clashing,
every one not having the same thoughts of the rule and way that others have.

Others who 'walk by loose rules, in ways that are broad' have no such trouble.
The fact is that 'godly men cannot yield for peace sake to such termes as other
men can'. This makes division inevitable, and we should hardly be surprised to
discover it.[7] The irony was most exquisite when the issue of disagreement was
the way towards peace itself. As Baxter pointed out from long experience: 'The
greatest discords and wars will be from the Love and Endeavour of Unity and
Concord, and for the obtaining of them by impossible means.'[8]

He and Owen illustrate the point. Each man saw the stakes as perilously
high and with good reason. Baxter had just endured the civil war trauma that
represented 'all the fruites of this Antinomian plant' – the Antinomians were
the ones to blame.[9] Yet Owen – deliberately or otherwise – gave succour to
the Antinomians with his doctrinal understanding that overly emphasized the
exactitude of the death of Christ in the place of the elect and at least gave credence
to the notion that they were justified from all eternity. And he did this from his
platform of Vice-Chancellor of Oxford University. No wonder it gave Baxter
chest pains; he felt there was little ground he could give. For his part, Owen
increasingly feared for the future of Trinitarian orthodoxy. What he witnessed
was indeed the beginning of a partial eclipse. Baxter's theology seemed to hasten
the slide with its emphasis on human responsibility in the process of salvation
and his adamant determination not to add even one word to the language of
Scripture in the effort to shore up the deity of the Holy Spirit. Given these
fears – especially within a polemical context that rendered any middle ground
untenable and that drove everyone to the extremes – it is no surprise that they
argued so bitterly.[10] In this light, the division itself makes perfect sense.

Joseph Caryl also helps us to understand the dynamics we have observed
in the relationship between Owen and Baxter – further proof that the strain
between them was far from unique. Caryl and Owen served with Cromwell
in Scotland, and Caryl turned down the post of Dean at Christ Church that

---

[7] For Burroughes' analysis here, see ibid., 237–9.

[8] Baxter, *Key for Catholicks*, 392.

[9] Baxter to [John Warren], 22 October 1651: DWL MS *BT* vi.116r, item #199 (*CCRB* #74). See also, Cooper, *Fear and Polemic*, 111.

[10] For the structure of seventeenth-century English polemic, see Cooper, *Fear and Polemic*, 4–7.

was subsequently offered to Owen.[11] Edmund Calamy later recalled him as a 'moderate independent',[12] but he also had close links with John Dury and his ecumenical endeavours.[13] In a similar vein to Burroughes, Caryl published *The Moderator* in 1652. His analysis offers a shrewd insight into how relationships among the godly became corroded. Problems began with a lack of trust and open communication. 'He that doth not confide in his neighbours, doth hinder them to confide in him, and hee that doth feare others, doth beget in them causes of feare against himselfe.'[14] In this fashion Baxter inadvertently strayed into dangerous territory by critiquing Owen's work in the Appendix to his *Aphorismes*. It was not an approach that was going to engender trust in Owen; instead it produced unease and uncertainty. In his turn Owen's response also did nothing to build trust and understanding. Even at that early point the opening breach may have been, in all practical terms, unbridgeable. 'For if I cannot bring my spirit to trust my neighbour, how can I expect that his spirit should be brought to trust mee? and if I thinke that hee doth not trust me, I will readily suspect him: if I suspect him, I will arme my selfe to oppose him, or weaken him lest hee oppose mee.' And so 'if I give way to these thoughts, I am at warre with him in my heart, and the affection of Christian love and ingenuitie, which onely can beget confidence, is lost between us.'[15]

In this way a crucial shift takes place early on in this process: the issue no longer resides merely in intellectual differences in certain points of belief, but in the strong feelings that are provoked by such differences. Those feelings are not an inevitable consequence; it is entirely possible for two people to disagree amicably. But this is far more difficult in a context in which trust has been lost. In its place, instincts of fear and opposition are aroused and all future actions are assessed through that filter of mistrust. We might recall Owen's initial response to the *Aphorismes of Justification*. The way he responded to Baxter's 'magisterial dictates' demonstrated that he had taken them extremely personally. This was an emotional response as much as anything. It set up a chain of similar responses in which new events are interpreted in the light of perceived hurts and aggravations in the past. This leads to the use of force (in words, if not weapons) in an effort

---

[11]   Toon, *God's Statesman*, 45–6, 48.

[12]   Parker, *Edmund Calamy: The Nonconformist's Memorial*, i.121.

[13]   P.S. Seaver, 'Caryl, Joseph (1602–1673)', *Oxford Dictionary of National Biography*, Oxford University Press, 2004; online edn, January 2008 [www.oxforddnb.com/view/article/4846, accessed 8 December 2010].

[14]   Joseph Caryl, *The Moderator: Endeavouring a Full Composure and Quiet Settlement of Those Many Differences Both in Doctrine and Discipline, Which Have So Long Disturbed the Peace and Welfare of This Common-Wealth* (1652), 3.

[15]   Ibid.

at self-protection against the foe. 'I cannot naturally rest secure as long as that which I count an enemy is not subdued, and whatever I doe not trust, I am apt to account an enemy.'[16] In sum:

> The first and original causes of disaffection and of breaches are for the most part not taken notice of, and hardly discerned by many, even then when they are discovered, because they lie very close to our nature, for they are commonly nothing else, but the neglect of charitable inclinations and duties; and the unadvised admitting of prejudices, and entertaining of evill surmises, which not being observed and cured, shelter in the mind, and first breed a shiness or warinesse of him, against whom they are conceived, then a distance from him, afterwards a strangeness to his ways; and lastly a breach of unitie with opposition.[17]

This analysis applies only to 'neighbours', those for whom trust is there to be lost. Thus this process of separation begins with positions of relative proximity in the same way that Owen and Baxter were proximate. Baxter allowed himself to develop a prejudice towards Owen, discerning in him a man who was proud and easily provoked. He had good cause to do so, but we can see how he allowed these hostile perceptions to 'shelter in the mind' reinforced by 'evil surmises'. All this hastened the progression: shyness, wariness, distance, strangeness 'and lastly a breach of unitie with opposition'. That is precisely where Owen and Baxter ended up. By the Restoration period they were reduced to talking behind each other's back. Owen was scathing about Baxter's plans for unity; Baxter 'often' and 'with great freedom' hammered Owen for his part in the fall of Richard Cromwell.[18] The fateful progression is clear: it serves to 'make our divisions by little and little irreconciliable'.[19] Minute differences and tiny steps led to gaping gulfs of mistrust, misunderstanding and permanent division.

Personality was an aggravating factor in all this.[20] Owen was easily exasperated; Baxter was simply exasperating. Owen was jealous for his reputation and did not take kindly to criticism or contradiction. While he could be remarkably even-handed in his polemical disputes, he did not suffer fools gladly. Thus Baxter's unwary reflections on Owen in the *Aphorismes* were never going to be well received. Furthermore, nothing in Baxter's authorial persona nor in his

---

[16]   Ibid.

[17]   Ibid., 67–8.

[18]   *Rel. Bax.*, iii.73; Parker, *Nonconformist's Memorial*, i.377.

[19]   Caryl, *Moderator*, 19.

[20]   See Alexandra Walsham, 'The Parochial Roots of Laudianism Revisited: Catholics, Anti-Calvinists and "Parish Anglicans" in Early Stuart England', *Journal of Ecclesiastical History* 49 (1998): 625; and Hughes, *Gangraena*, 409.

personal presence would cause Owen to revise his estimation. Baxter's behaviour among the 1654 assembly of divines was obstructive and unproductive. It grated unbearably on Owen. It proved what was already apparent: Baxter was fixed in his views and inclined to speak the truth as he saw it; he revealed an impaired capacity for tact and diplomacy. Owen was a master at the art of politics but Baxter came across as clumsy and inept, doing little to earn Owen's respect. Similarly, Owen came across as high-handed, proud, magisterial and conniving, also doing little to earn Baxter's respect. Their mutual prejudices only hardened.

As Caryl's progression played itself out, the memory of past hurts and perceived slights accumulated. Jonathan Scott considers the issue of memory in the context of Restoration politics: 'this political culture had suffered a traumatic collective experience with which it was necessary to come to terms.' It did this by framing, in contested ways, a story that made sense of that experience, one that provided salutary lessons in arbitrary government, anarchy and the dangers of popery. 'This situation remained in place until well into the eighteenth century, when successful restoration began to permit national forgetting.'[21] Memory could thus be a powerful shaping influence long after the initial events occurred. In the words of Mark Goldie, 'England lived with the memory, the open wound, of recent rebellion and strife'.[22] So did Baxter: 'the National Concerns made so deep a wound in my heart, as never will be fully healed in this world.'[23] The failure to reach accommodation during the 1650s was a traumatic blow. Owen's alleged role in 1659 was the hardest blow of all. Samuel Young was not wrong when he called Baxter's reconstruction 'the famous story, never to be forgiven, never to be forgotten'.[24] The wider blame for the failure of all Baxter's dreams just as they were at their brightest crystallized in Owen. The memory helped Baxter to simplify the messiness of 1659 by overlaying a story that resolved itself into one man's culpability. Once formed, the memory remained a permanent, unseen obstacle to any hope of reconciliation between the two men. The Act of Oblivion did nothing to touch Baxter's determination never to let the world forget what Owen had done. We might speculate that Owen also nursed his own regrets and disappointments. He had come just as close as Baxter to seeing his aspirations realized, only to be consistently disappointed. It is just possible that he too was dismayed by the demise of the Protectorate in 1659. He might also have harboured the memory of Baxter's irritations along the way, not least his obstinance in 1654.

---

[21]   Jonathan Scott, *England's Troubles: Seventeenth-Century English Political Instability in European Context* (Cambridge: Cambridge University Press, 2000), 162–6.

[22]   Goldie, *Entring Book*, i.152.

[23]   Baxter, *Catholick Communion Doubly Defended*, 7.

[24]   [Young], *Vindiciae Anti-Baxterianae*, 41.

Baxter had discerned the problem the year before. He urged his fellow ministers to 'forget all former injuries and differences so far, [and] presently to address themselves to seek Peace and Reconciliation'. He encouraged them to lay aside all blame and to cease 'vilifying their Brethren behind their backs'.[25] In the end he would prove incapable of following his own advice. Likewise, Burroughes offered a similar caution: 'Where we see there hath been mistakes and differences thorough humane frailty ... let all former unkindnesses be forgotten, so as to never rip up old things to charge them one upon another: let there be a line of forgetfulnesse drawn over them; let them be buried in oblivion.'[26] Again, this was good advice but too much to ask. This line of forgetfulness proved impossible to hold. The result could only be steadily deepening rifts and division not just between Owen and Baxter but within the whole movement to which they belonged.

On the Second Question

In the Introduction I suggested that the strain between Owen and Baxter mattered for two main reasons. The second of those reasons is that by understanding how they came to their differences we will better understand the development of the wider divisions among the orthodox godly. I hope the discussion so far has already helped to illuminate the ways in which that is the case. Authors like Burroughes and Caryl were describing broad patterns, not the isolated instance of Owen and Baxter, so accounting for their particular divergence also accounts for the general divergence going on around them. The first of those reasons why this mattered has to do with the stature of Owen and Baxter within the movement. They were influential, prolific and very visible authors and authorities; they were indispensable figures for any viable negotiations between the Presbyterians and the Congregationalists; they were increasingly senior statesmen among the orthodox godly. If they could not agree, what hope was there?

Perhaps the best way of illustrating the significance of that is to draw a contrast between the post-war setting in which Owen and Baxter came apart and the pre-war Puritan context that retained impressive mechanisms to preserve godly unity. The scholarship of Peter Lake is especially helpful here. Through several colourful case studies he shows that there was plenty of disagreement within the early Stuart Puritan community in London, but in general 'order and the appearance of consensus were restored through an essentially co-operative

---

25   Baxter, *Christian Concord*, Explication, 95, 101.
26   Burroughes, *Irenicum*, 286–7.

process of control, advice and censorship'.[27] In this process the godly laboured among themselves to restore agreement. Ecclesiastical authorities worked with the community to help moderate the effects of disagreement by encouraging communication and by negotiating what could or could not make its way into print.[28] These relationships demonstrated a 'capacity to control and contain a wide range of personal and doctrinal tensions and rivalries'.[29] A good example of this is the bitter conflict that broke out in 1611 between Anthony Wotton and George Walker.[30] Wotton was a senior Puritan minister in London; Walker was a new arrival with obvious ambition and a nose for sniffing out heresy. He accused Wotton of holding Socinian views on justification. To advance his case Walker tried to enlist the aid of another senior Puritan figure, Alexander Richardson, before preaching openly against Wotton in two sermons. Friends of Wotton then met with Walker to try to smooth things over, with no success. Walker challenged Wotton to have their case heard before a panel of eight Puritan divines, four to be chosen by each side, and after some initial reluctance from Wotton the proceedings took place. The panel concluded that while there were points of difference Wotton's views did not amount to heresy. Walker refused to accept the judgement, but neither he nor Wotton were allowed to state their case in print. That was left to William Bradshaw, whose *Treatise of Justification* 'struck an irenic, consensus-building pose' by conveying the outcome of the dispute to those in the know without naming names. Thus 'we can see godly opinion seeking to maintain unity, order and consensus ... by constructing room for disagreement and dispute; and doing so, moreover, in close collaboration with the ecclesiastical authorities'.[31]

Another similar example is that of John Cotton in New England, a story that is more well known. Cotton arrived in the new colony in 1633 to become a second minister within the church at Boston. His views on assurance led him into conflict with Thomas Shepard, another minister with a nose for heresy, who accused Cotton of Antinomianism. Other Antinomian figures in the resulting controversy (such as Anne Hutchinson and the minister John Wheelwright) would find themselves outside of the Puritan community, and the controversy was incredibly destabilizing while it lasted, but the whole affair was finally reined back in. Cotton managed to retain his place within the brotherhood, if only just, through 'a serious effort to mend fences' that involved 'extensive private

---

27   Lake, *Boxmaker's Revenge*, 244.
28   Ibid., 245.
29   Ibid.
30   Ibid., 221–32.
31   Ibid., 233.

conferences' and finally a synod to settle the remaining issues of dispute.[32] 'This outcome, unity of a sort through diversity, appears to have been the achievement of a moderate party' that included John Davenport and especially John Winthrop, who guided the synod with common sense and moderation.[33]

The point is that in both these instances effective self-regulating mechanisms worked to keep division in check and to maintain at least the appearance of unity and consensus. By the time Owen and Baxter came into contact those mechanisms had broken down. Even the Westminster Assembly had worked impressively hard to keep the debates and divisions hidden from public view. Some differences were obvious, of course, but the extent of their debates now being brought to light by the industry of Chad van Dixhoorn is surprising, and the Assembly managed to speak with one voice in the end. That seems the last time a common voice was possible. Any earlier, the differences between Owen and Baxter might have also been managed behind closed doors out of sight of the wider public. Now, their dispute was all too obvious and apparent.

With the collapse of licensing and censorship the earlier difficulty of making oneself heard in print had given way to a relative freedom to publish, which removed a crucial obstacle in the way of initial disagreements developing into something much worse. The story of Owen and Baxter fully illustrates what Peter Lake has indicated:

> by the early 1640s the formal structures of authority ('censorship' very broadly defined) with which the order- and orthodoxy-obsessed tendencies and tenets of mainstream Puritanism had co-operated to keep [differences] more or less under ground, had largely collapsed. So, too, under the mounting pressure of events and intra-puritan dispute, had the internalised reticencies, the self-censoring controls which the godly had previously brought to bear on their own internal bickering and disagreements.[34]

Appearing in print raised the stakes considerably. It served to harden divisions rather than to soften them; 'print brought with it a certain public authority, it attached a certain aura or charisma both to the author and his opinions'.[35] This is precisely true of Owen and Baxter. Here the Puritan community had a very visible split between two of its senior figures who from the beginning carried out their battles in print. By the Restoration period their mutual dislike was a

---

[32]   Michael Winship, *Making Heretics: Militant Protestantism and Free Grace in Massachusetts, 1636–1641* (Princeton, NJ: Princeton University Press, 2002), 149, 151, 155–63.

[33]   Ibid., 164.

[34]   Lake, *Boxmaker's Revenge*, 410.

[35]   Ibid., 411.

well-known, well-established fact. Many rightly interpreted Baxter's criticism of Owen after his death as the product 'of an old Spleen against the Doctor'.[36]

The difficulty of mitigating their differences was exacerbated because the grounds of their disagreements were so broad. They clashed over soteriology, over ecclesiology and over the best way to achieve a religious settlement within what was also a political context. Inasmuch as I have tried to measure their common ground and to point out their proximity, these were significant differences over more than just one issue. Baxter's geographical remoteness also did not help. It is not clear whether those earlier mechanisms would have coped with two authors living in different parts of the country, since both the Wotton/Cotton difficulties took place within relatively confined locales. Even so, Baxter's isolation made any potential means of achieving reconciliation very difficult indeed.

Not only that, Francis J. Bremer has shown how such a basic thing as friendship helped to hold the godly community together over time.[37] In particular, the strong bonds of friendship among the Congregationalists provided a necessary impulse towards unity and consensus within a system that lacked some of those institutional mechanisms that worked to similar effect.[38] Distance rendered these bonds much more fragile.[39] Again, Baxter's geographical isolation proved an impediment but so too did another aspect of his isolation, the lack of university training, since Bremer shows just how enduring and influential the friendships formed at university could be.[40] Baxter had no such rich experience. Owen did, of course, but we have observed in him a marked self-containment in which aims and agendas seem to have taken precedence over deep, warm, lasting friendships. He was seen more often ignoring the advice of his friends than following it. Therefore, such a simple thing as friendship helped to preserve godly unity, but that was entirely lacking in this relationship. Friendship never had a chance to form and, even if it had, the different postures of isolation in Owen and Baxter would have stunted its growth. Instead what we see is a tale of increasingly personal acrimony and dislike.

Therefore, the falling out between Owen and Baxter mattered. Owen's prodigious efforts at Oxford in service of the Protectorate along with his steady, weighty publications gave him a standing that no one could ignore. Baxter's pastoral labours at Kidderminster and his lengthy evangelistic and devotional works likewise rendered him a figure of considerable standing. It is

---

36   [Anon.], *Vindication of Owen*, 9.
37   Bremer, *Congregational Communion*, 5–6.
38   Ibid., 111.
39   Ibid., 113.
40   Ibid., 29–30.

not as if they were sectarian figures whose influence was small, whose differences could be brushed aside. Thus in terms of the long-term fragmentation within nonconformity this is a much more fruitful place to look for causes than the earlier historiographical emphasis on sectarianism. I am certainly willing to accept that the prominence of these two men may have been overstated in the historiography and that others have suffered in their shadows, but it is still the case that they stood at the very heart of the tradition and were increasingly important as key players in the process of its development. But there were no longer any mechanisms sufficient to bring them together. When they tried to find rapprochement in the late 1660s, working entirely by themselves, it proved impossible: the weight of the past was too great an anchor on their hopes for the future. Fatal memory did its work. Their permanent separation advertised the fact that the earlier quality of clerical communion was permanently impaired. The movement itself was irreparably damaged if these two leaders could not be brought to see eye to eye. Right to the end, it is true, there was much they held in common. But it was not nearly enough. The rupture between them proved to be permanent, and we cannot avoid its influence on the formation of English nonconformity.

Select Bibliography

Only works cited in the text are included in this bibliography, which is arranged as follows:

1. Manuscript Sources

2. Printed Primary Sources

A. Works by John Owen

*B. Works by Richard Baxte*r

i. Edited works
ii. Other works
iii. Posthumous works

C. Works by Other Authors

D. Modern Editions of Primary Material

3. Secondary Sources

A. Works on John Owen

i. Books
ii. Articles and chapters
iii. Unpublished theses

B. Works on Richard Baxter

i. Books
ii. Articles and chapters
iii. Unpublished theses

C. Other Works

i. Books
ii. Articles and chapters
iii. Unpublished theses

1. Manuscript Sources

Bodleian Library, Oxford

Papers Relating to the Time of Cromwell and the Visitation: OUA SP/E/4
Register of Convocation: Volume T

British Library, London

Manuscript portion of the *Reliquiae Baxterianae*: Egerton 2570
Letters to Henry Cromwell: Lansdowne Manuscripts 821 and 823

Dr Williams' Library, London

Baxter Correspondence[DWL MS *BC*]
Baxter Treatises[DWL MS *BT*][1]

National Archives, London

State Papers [SP]

University of Edinburgh Library, Edinburgh

New College Comm 2

---

[1]   I have consulted both the correspondence and the treatises on microfilm, which is available from World Microfilms, 2–6 Foscote Mews, London W9 2HH, England;   www. microworld.uk.com/microfilms.asp.

2. Printed Primary Sources

A. Works by John Owen

The Works of John Owen, ed. William H. Goold, 16 vols. Edinburgh: Banner of
     Truth reprint, 1983:
A Display of Arminianism (1643)
The Duty of Pastors and People Distinguished (1643)
Two Short Catechisms (1645)
A Short Defensative About Church Government (1646)
A Vision of Free Mercy (1646)
Ebenezer: A Memorial of the Deliverance of Essex County (1648)
The Death of Death in the Death of Christ (1648)
Righteous Zeal Encouraged by Divine Protection (1649)
The Shaking and Translating of Heaven and Earth (1649)
Branch of the Lord the Beauty of Zion (1650)
Of the Death of Christ (1650)
A Dissertation on Divine Justice (1653)
The Doctrine of the Saints' Perseverance (1654)
Of the Death of Christ and of Justification (1655)
Vindiciae Evangelicae: Or the Mystery of the Gospel Vindicated (1655)
God's Presence with a People the Spring of their Prosperity (1656)
God's Work in Founding Zion (1656)
A Review of the True Nature of Schism (1657)
Answer to a Late Treatise of Mr Cawdrey about the Nature of Schism (1657)
Of Schism: The True Nature of it Discovered and Considered (1657)
A Vindication of the Hebrew and Greek Texts (1659)
*Of the Divine Original, Authority, Self-Evidencing Light and Power of the
     Scriptures* (1659)
The Glory and Interest of Nations Professing the Gospel (1659)
A Vindication of the Animadversions on 'Fiat Lux' (1664)
*A Peace-Offering, in an Apology and Humble Plea for Indulgence and Liberty of
     Conscience* (1667)
Indulgence and Toleration Considered (1667)
Reflections on a Slanderous Libel (1670)
Meditations and Discourses on the Glory of Christ (1684)

Biblical Theology: The History of Theology from Adam to Christ, ed. Stephen P.
     Westcott. Grand Rapids, MI: Soli Deo Gloria Publications, 2009.

B. Works by Richard Baxter

i. Edited works

The Practical Works of Richard Baxter with a Preface Giving Some Account of the Author, and of this Edition of his Practical Works: An Essay on his Genius, Works and Times; and a Portrait. 4 vols. Ligonier, PA: Soli Deo Gloria reprint, 1990–1:
The Saints' Everlasting Rest (1650)
True Christianity (1654)
The Reformed Pastor (1656)
Confirmation and Restauration (1658)
A Treatise of Self Denial (1659)
A Christian Directory (1673)

ii. Other works

A Breviate of the Doctrine of Justification, Delivered in many Books, By Richard Baxter: In many Propositions, and the Solutions of 50 Controversies about it. 1690. In *Scripture Gospel Defended.*

A Breviate of the Life of Margaret...Wife of Richard Baxter. 1681.

A Defence of Christ, And Free Grace: Against the Subverters Commonly Called, Antinomians or Libertines. 1690. In *Scripture Gospel Defended.*

A Holy Commonwealth, Or, Political Aphorisms, Opening the True Principles of Government: For the Healing of the Mistakes, and Resolving the Doubts, that Most Endanger England at this Time. 1659.

A Key for Catholicks: To Open the Jugling of the Jesuits, and Satisfie All that are but Truly Willing to Understand, Whether the Cause of the Roman or Reformed Churches be of God. 1659.

A Treatise of Justifying Righteousness, In Two Books: I. A Treatise of Imputed Righteousness, Opening and Defending the True Sense, and Confuting the False... II. A Friendly Debate with the Learned and Worthy Mr. Christopher Cartwright. 1676.

An Account of the Reasons Why the Twelve Arguments Said to be Dr. John Owen's Change not my Judgment about Communion with Parish-Churches. 1684. In *Catholick Communion Defended.*

An Unsavoury Volume of Mr Jo. Crandon's Anatomized: Or a Nosegay of the Choicest Flowers in that Garden, Presented to Joseph Caryl by Rich. Baxter. 1654. In *Rich. Baxters Apology.*

Catholick Communion Defended Against Both Extreams and Unnecessary Division Confuted, by Reasons Against Both the Active and the Passive Ways of Separation. 1684.

Catholick Communion Doubly Defended: By Dr. Owens Vindicator and Richard Baxter. And the State of that Communion Opened. 1684.

Certain Disputations of Right to the Sacraments and the True Nature of Visible Christianity. 1657.

Christian Concord: Or the Agreement of the Associated Pastors and Churches of Worcestershire. With Richard Baxter's Explication and Defence of it, and his Exhortation to Unity. 1653.

Church Concord: Containing, I. A Disswasive from Unnecessary Division and ... II. The Terms Necessary for Concord Among All True Churches and Christians. 1691.

Five Disputations of Church-Government, and Worship. 1659.

Humble Advice: Or the Heads of Those Things Which Were Offered to Many Honourable Members of Parliament. 1655.

Of Justification: Four Disputations Clearing and Amicably Defending the Truth, Against the Unnecessary Oppositions of Divers Learned and Reverend Brethren. 1658.

Plain Scripture Proof of Infants Church-membership and Baptism Being the Arguments Prepared for (and Partly Managed in) the Publike Dispute with Mr. Tombes. 3rd edn. 1653.

Rich. Baxters Account Given to his Reverend Brother Mr T. Blake of the Reasons of his Dissent from the Doctrine of his Exceptions in his Late Treatise of the Covenants. 1654. In *Rich. Baxters Apology.*

Rich. Baxter's Admonition to William Eyre of Salisbury; Concerning his Miscarriages in a Book Lately Written for the Justification of Infidels, Against M. Benj. Woodbridge, M. James Cranford and the Author. 1654. In *Rich. Baxters Apology.*

Rich. Baxters Apology Against the Modest Exceptions of Mr T. Blake. And the Digression of Mr G. Kendall. Whereunto is Added Animadversions on a late Dissertation of Ludiomaeus Colvinus, alias, Ludovicus Molinaeus, M. Dr Oxon. And an Admonition of Mr W. Eyre of Salisbury. With Mr Crandon's Anatomy for Satisfaction of Mr Caryl. 1654.

Rich: Baxter's Confession of his Faith, Especially Concerning the Interest of Repentance and Sincere Obedience to Christ, in our Justification and Salvation. 1655.

Richard Baxter's Confutation of a Dissertation For the Justification of Infidels: Written by Ludomaeus Colvinus, Alias Ludovicus Molinaeus, Dr. of Physick and History-Professor in Oxford, Against his Brother Cyrus Molinaeus. 1654. In *Rich. Baxters Apology.*

The Church told of Mr. Ed. Bagshaw's Scandals and Warned of the Dangerous Snares of Satan...in his Love-Killing Principles. 1672.

The Cure of Church Divisions: Or, Directions for Weak Christians, to Keep them from being Dividers, or Troublers of the Church. With Some Directions to the Pastors, How to Deal with Such Christians. 1670.

The Grotian Religion Discovered, At the Invitation of Mr. Thomas Pierce in his Vindication, With a Preface Vindicating the Synod of Dort. 1658.

The Humble Petition of Many Thousands, Gentlemen, Free-holders, and Others, of the County of Worcester to the Parliament of the Commonwealth of England. 1652.

The Judgment and Advice of the Assembly of the Associated Ministers of Worcester-shire Concerning the Endeavours of Ecclesiasticall Peace, and the Waies and Meanes of Christian Unity, which Mr John Durey doth Present. 1658.

The Saints' Everlasting Rest: Or, a Treatise of the Blessed State of the Saints in their Enjoyment of God in Glory. 1650.

The Saints' Everlasting Rest: Or, a Treatise of the Blessed State of the Saints in their Enjoyment of God in Glory...The Second Edition Corrected and Enlarged. 1651.

The Scripture Gospel Defended, And Christ, Grace and Free Justification Vindicated Against the Libertines, Who Use the Names of Christ, Free Grace and Justification, to Subvert the Gospel, and Christianity...In Two Books. 1690.

The Substance of Mr. Cartwright's Exceptions Considered. 1675. In *Treatise of Justifying Righteousness.*

Universal Concord...Containing the Particular Terms of Reconciling the Severall Differing Parties that are Reconcileable. 1660.

iii. Posthumous works

Lamont, William, ed. *Baxter: A Holy Commonwealth.* Cambridge: Cambridge University Press, 1994.

Read, Joseph, ed. *Universal Redemption Of Mankind, By The Lord Jesus Christ: Stated and Cleared by the late Learned Mr. Richard Baxter. Whereunto is Added a Short Account of Special Redemption, by the Same Author.* 1694.

Sylvester, Matthew, ed. *Reliquiae Baxterianae, or, Mr. Richard Baxter's Narrative of the Most Memorable Passages of his Life and Times.* 1696.

C. Works by Other Authors

A Declaration of the Faith and Order Owned and Practised in the Congregational Churches in England. 1658.

[Anon.]. *A Vindication of the Late Reverend and Learned John Owen D.D.* 1684.

An Ordinance of the Lords and Commons Assembled in Parliament for the Calling of an Assembly of Learned, and Godly Divines. 1643.

Baker, Richard. *A Chronicle of the Kings of England*. 1682.

Bartlet, William. *A Model of the Primitive Congregational Way...Together with the Maine Points in Controversie, Touching the Right Visible Church-state Christ hath Instituted under the Gospel*. 1647.

Bastwick, John. *The Utter Routing of the Whole Army of all the Independents and Sectaries...Or, Independency Not God's Ordinance*. 1646.

Biddle, John. *A Brief Scripture Catechism for Children: Wherein, Notwithstanding the Brevity Thereof, All Things Necessary unto Life and Godliness are Contained*. 1654.

Burgess, Anthony. *The True Doctrine of Justification Asserted and Vindicated from the Errours of Many*. 1654.

Burroughes, Jeremiah. *Irenicum, To the Lovers of Truth and Peace: Heart-Divisions Opened in the Causes and Evils of Them*. 1645.

Calamy, Edmund. *An Abridgement of Mr. Baxter's History of His Life and Times*. London: Thomas Parkhurst, 1702.

Caryl, Joseph. *The Moderator: Endeavouring a Full Composure and Quiet Settlement of Those Many Differences Both in Doctrine and Discipline, Which Have So Long Disturbed the Peace and Welfare of This Common-Wealth*. 1652.

Cawdrey, Daniel. *Independencie a Great Schism Proved Against Dr. Owen his Apology in his Tract of Schism*. 1657.

_ . *Independency Further Proved To be a Schism: Or, A Survey of Dr Owen's Review of his Tract of Schism*. 1658.

Commissioners of the General Assembly of the Church of Scotland. *A Solemn Testimony Against Toleration and the Present Proceedings of Sectaries and their Abettors in England in Reference to Religion and Government*. Edinburgh, 1649.

Cotton, John. *The Doctrine of the Church, to which is Committed the Keyes of the Kingdom of Heaven*. 1643.

Crandon, John. *Mr Baxters Aphorisms Exorized and Anthorized: Or an Examination of and Answer to a Book Written by Mr. Ri: Baxter*. 1654.

Crisp, Tobias. *Christ Alone Exalted: Being the Compleat Works of Tobias Crisp D.D.* 1690.

Davenant, John. *Animadversions...Upon a Treatise Entitled God's Love to Mankind*. Cambridge, 1641.

Delaune, Thomas. *Truth Defended: Or, a Triple Answer to the Late Triumvirates Opposition on their Three Pamphlets, viz. Mr. Baxter's Review, Mr. Wills his Censure, Mr Whiston's Postscript to his Essay*. 1677.

Dury, John. *A Declaration of John Durie, a Minister of Jesus Christ to Witness the Gospell of Peace*. 1660.

Eyre, William. *Vindiciae Justificationis Gratuitae: Justification Without Conditions; Or, The Free Justification of the Sinner.* 1654.

Goodwin, John. *Anti-Cavalierisme, or, Truth Pleading as Well the Necessity, as the Lawfulness of this Present War.* 1642.

_____. *Redemption Redeemed: Wherein the Most Glorious Work of the Redemption of the World by Jesus Christ is...Vindicated and Asserted.* 1651.

Goodwin, Thomas, et al. *An Apologeticall Narration, Humbly Submitted to the Honourable Houses of Parliament.* 1644.

_____. *The Reasons of the Dissenting Brethren Against the Third Proposition Concerning Presbyteriall Government.* 1645.

_____. *The Independents Declaration Delivered in to the Assembly...Declaring their Grounds and Full Resolutions Concerning Church-Government.* 1647.

Hoard, Samuel. *Gods Love to Mankind Manifested, By Dis-prooving his Absolute Decree for their Damnation.* 1633.

Horn, John. *The Open Door for Mans Approach to God.* 1650.

Hotchkis, Thomas. *An Exercitation Concerning the Nature of Forgivenesse of Sin.* 1654.

Kendall, George. *Theokratia: Or, A Vindication of the Doctrine Commonly Received in the Reformed Churches.* 1653.

Moore, Thomas. *The Universallity of God's Free-Grace in Christ to Mankind Proclaimed and Displayed.* 1646.

Nedham, Marchamont. *A True State of the Case of the Common-Wealth of England, Scotland and Ireland.* 1654.

[Newcomen, Matthew.] *Irenicum, Or An Essay Towards a Brotherly Peace and Union Between those of the Congregational and Presbyterian Way.* 1659.

Overbury, Thomas. *An Expostulatory Letter to the Author of the Late Slanderous Libel against Dr. O.* 1671.

Owen, John, et al. *Proposals for the Furtherance and Propagation of the Gospell in this Nation: As...Also, Some Principles of Christian Religion, without the Beliefe of which, the Scriptures doe Plainly and Clearly Affirme, Salvation is not to be Obtained.* 1652.

Parker, Samuel. *A Discourse of Ecclesiastical Politie Wherein...the Mischiefs and Inconveniences of Toleration are Represented.* 1670.

_____. *A Defence and Continuation of the Ecclesiastical Politie: By Way of Letter to a Friend in London Together with a Letter from the Author of the Friendly Debate.* 1671.

Peter, Hugh. *Gods Doing and Mans Duty, Opened in a Sermon Preached Before Both Houses of Parliament.* 1646.

Pope, Walter. *The Life of the Right Reverend Father in God, Seth, Lord Bishop of Salisbury.* 1697.

Robertson, William. *An Admonitory Epistle unto Mr Rich. Baxter, and Mr Tho. Hotchkis*. 1655.

Stillingfleet, Edward. *The Unreasonableness of Separation: Or, an Impartial Account of the History, Nature, and the Pleas, of the Present Separation from the Communion of the Church of England*. 1681.

Sylvester, Matthew. *Elisha's Cry After Elijah's God Consider'd and Apply'd With Reference to the Decease of the Late Reverend Mr. Richard Baxter*. 1696.

The Confession of Faith and Catechisms, Agreed upon by the Assembly of Divines at Westminster. 1649.

Tombes, John. *True Old Light Exalted Above Pretended New Light*. 1660.

Twisse, William, et al., *Certaine Considerations to Dis-swade Men from Further Gathering of Churches in this Present Juncture of Times*. 1643.

Vane, Henry. *A Healing Question Propounded and Resolved*. 1656.

[Vernon, George]. *A Letter to a Friend Concerning some of Dr. Owen's Principles and Practices*. 1670.

[Young, Samuel]. *Vindiciae Anti-Baxterianae: Or, Some Animadversions on a Book, Intituled, Reliquiae Baxterianae; Or, the Life of Mr. Richard Baxter*. 1696.

D. Modern Editions of Primary Material

Birch, Thomas, ed. *A Collection of the State Papers of John Thurloe, Esq. Secretary, First, to the Council of State, and Afterwards to the Two Protectors, Oliver and Richard Cromwell*. 7 vols. London, 1742.

Burnet, Gilbert, ed. *Bishop Burnet's History of His Own Time*. Vol. 1. London: Thomas Ward, 1724.

Carlyle, Thomas, ed. *Oliver Cromwell's Letters and Speeches with Elucidations Complete in One Volume*. New York: William H. Colyer, 1846.

Clark, Andrew, ed. *The Life and Times of Anthony Wood, Antiquary, Of Oxford, 1632–1695, Described by Himself*. Vol. 1, *1632–1663*. Oxford: Clarendon Press, 1891.

Firth, C.H., ed. *The Memoirs of Edmund Ludlow Lieutenant-General of the Horse in the Army of the Commonwealth of England 1625–1672*. 2 vols. Oxford: Clarendon Press, 1894.

Firth, C.H. and R.S. Rait, eds. *Acts and Ordinances of the Interregnum 1642–1660*. Vol. II, *Acts and Ordinances from 9th February, 1649, to 16th March, 1660*. London: His Majesty's Stationery Office, 1911.

Gardiner, Samuel Rawson, ed. *The Constitutional Documents of the Puritan Revolution 1625–1660*. 3rd edn. Oxford: Clarendon Press, 1906.

Goldie, Mark, gen. ed. *The Entring Book of Roger Morrice 1677–1691*. 7 vols. Woodbridge: The Boydell Press, 2007.

Gutch, John, ed. *The History and Antiquities of the University of Oxford in Two Books: By Anthony á Wood, M.A. of Merton College: Now First Published in English from the Original Manuscript in the Bodleian Library*. 2 vols. Oxford: John Gutch, 1796.

Haddon, Arthur West, ed. *The Theological Works of Herbert Thorndike, Sometime Prebendary of the Collegiate Church of St. Peter, Westminster*. Vol. 5, *The True Principle of Comprehension*. Oxford: John Henry Parker, 1854.

Laing, David, ed. *The Letters and Journals of Robert Baillie, A.M. Principal of the University of Glasgow*. 3 vols. Edinburgh: Robert Ogle, 1842.

Lee, Matthew Henry, ed. *Diaries and Letters of Philip Henry, M.A., Of Broad Oak, Flintshire A.D. 1631–1696*. London: Kegan, Paul, Trench and Co., 1882.

MacFarlane, Alan, ed. *The Diary of Ralph Josselin 1616–1683*. London: Oxford University Press, 1976.

Magrath, John Richard, ed. *The Flemings in Oxford Being Documents Selected from the Rydal Papers in Illustration of the Lives and Ways of Oxford Men 1650–1700*. Oxford: Clarendon Press, 1904.

Matthews, A.G., ed. *The Savoy Declaration of Faith and Order 1658*. London: Independent Press Ltd, 1959.

Ogilvie, James D., ed. *Diary of Sir Archibald Johnston of Wariston: Volume III 1655–1660*. Edinburgh: T and A Constable Limited, 1940.

Parker, Samuel, ed. *Edmund Calamy: The Nonconformist's Memorial: Being an Account of the Ministers Who Were Ejected or Silenced After the Restoration... Now Abridged and Corrected by Samuel Parker*. 2 vols. London: W. Harris, 1775.

Paul, Robert S., ed. *An Apologeticall Narration*. Philadelphia, PA: United Church Press, 1963.

Rutt, John Towill, ed. *Diary of Thomas Burton, Esq. Member in the Parliaments of Oliver and Richard Cromwell, from 1656 to 1659...with an Introduction Containing an Account of the Parliament of 1654 from the Journal of Guibon Goddard, Esq, M.P.* 4 vols. London: Henry Colburn, 1828.

____ . *Edmund Calamy: An Historical Account of My Own Life With Some Reflections on the Times I Have Lived In (1671–1731)*. 2 vols. London: Henry Colburn and Richard Bentley, 1829.

Schlatter, Richard, ed., *Richard Baxter and Puritan Politics*. New Brunswick, NJ: Rutgers University Press, 1957.

Spalding, Ruth, ed. *The Diary of Bulstrode Whitelocke 1605–1675*. Oxford: Oxford University Press, 1990.

Stephen, William, ed. *Register of the Consultations of the Ministers of Edinburgh and Some Other Brethren of the Ministry.* 2 vols. Edinburgh: Scottish History Society, 1921.

Toon, Peter, ed. *The Correspondence of John Owen (1616–1683) With an Account of his Life and Work.* Cambridge: James Clarke and Co. Ltd, 1970.

_____ . *The Oxford Orations of Dr. John Owen.* Linkinhorne: Gospel Communication, 1971.

[Ward, Richard, ed.] *The Manuscripts of His Grace The Duke of Portland Preserved at Welbeck Abbey.* Vol. 3. London: Her Majesty's Stationery Office, 1894.

Wood, A. *Athenae Oxonienses: An Exact History of all the Writers and Bishops who have had their Education in the...University of Oxford from...1500 to the Author's Death in 1695.* 2nd edn. 2 vols. London: Knaplock, Midwinter and Tonson, 1721.

3. Secondary Sources

A. Works on John Owen

i. Books

Daniels, Richard. *The Christology of John Owen.* Grand Rapids, MI: Reformation Heritage Books, 2004.

Gleason, Randall C. *John Calvin and John Owen on Mortification: A Comparative Study in Reformed Spirituality.* New York: Peter Lang, 1995.

Kapic, Kelly. *Communion with God: The Divine and the Human in the Theology of John Owen.* Grand Rapids, MI: Baker Academic, 2007.

Kay, Brian. *Trinitarian Spirituality: John Owen and the Doctrine of God in Western Devotion.* Carlisle: Paternoster, 2007.

Moffatt, James. *The Golden Book of John Owen: Passages from the Writing of the Rev. John Owen, M.A., D.D., Sometime Vice-Chancellor of the University of Oxford and Dean of Christ Church: Chosen and Edited with a Study of his Life and Age.* London: Hodder and Stoughton, 1904.

Orme, William. *Memoirs of the Life, Writings and Religious Connexions of John Owen, D.D. Vice-Chancellor of Oxford and Dean of Christ Church, During the Commonwealth.* London: T. Hamilton, 1820.

Rehnman, Sebastian. *Divine Discourse: The Theological Methodology of John Owen.* Grand Rapids, MI: Baker Academic, 2002.

Spence, Alan. *Incarnation and Inspiration: John Owen and the Coherence of Christology.* London: T&T Clark, 2007.

Toon, Peter. *God's Statesman: The Life and Work of John Owen*. Grand Rapids, MI: Zondervan, 1971.

Trueman, Carl R. *The Claims of Truth: John Owen's Trinitarian Theology*. Carlisle: Paternoster Press, 1998.

_____ . *John Owen: Reformed Catholic, Renaissance Man*. Aldershot: Ashgate, 2007.

ii. Articles and chapters

[Anon.]. 'The Life of the Late Reverend and Learned John Owen'. In *Seventeen Sermons Preach'd by the Late Reverend and Learned John Owen*, iii–lvi. London: William and Joseph Marshall, 1720.

Asty, John. 'Memoirs of the Life of John Owen'. In *A Complete Collection of the Sermons of the Reverend and Learned John Owen…And to the Whole are Prefixed Memoirs of His Life*, ed. John Asty, i–xxxviii. London: John Clark, 1721.

Bates, Ely. 'Baxter and Owen'. *The National Review* 15 (1862): 95–120.

Cooper, Tim. 'John Owen Unleashed: Almost'. *Conversations in Religion and Theology* 6 (2008): 226–42.

_____ . 'Why Did Richard Baxter and John Owen Diverge? The Impact of the First Civil War'. *Journal of Ecclesiastical History* 61 (2010): 496–516.

Kapic, Kelly. 'John Owen Unleashed: Almost. Response to Tim Cooper'. *Conversations in Religion and Theology* 6 (2008): 250–257.

Lim, Paul Chang-Ha. 'The Trinity, *Adiaphora*, Ecclesiology, and Reformation: John Owen's Theory of Religious Toleration in Context'. *Westminster Theological Journal* 67 (2005): 281–300.

_____ . '*Adiaphora*, Ecclesiology and Reformation: John Owen's Theology of Religious Toleration in Context'. In *The Development of Pluralism in Modern Britain and France*, ed. Richard Bonney and D.J.B. Trim, vol. 2, 243–71. Oxford: Peter Lang, 2007.

Mason, Matthew W. 'John Owen's Doctrine of Union with Christ in Relation to His Contributions to Seventeenth Century Debates Concerning Eternal Justification'. *Ecclesia Reformanda* 1 (2009): 46–69.

Orme, William. 'Memoirs of the Life and Writings of Dr. Owen'. In *The Works of John Owen D.D.*, ed. Thomas Russell, vol. 1, 1–363. London: Richard Baynes, 1826.

Rehnman, Sebastian. 'John Owen: A Reformed Scholar at Oxford'. In *Reformation and Scholasticism: An Ecumenical Enterprise*, ed. Willem J. van Asselt and Eef Dekker, 181–203. Grand Rapids, MI: Baker Academic, 2001.

Trueman, Carl. 'John Owen Unleashed: Almost. Response to Tim Cooper'. *Conversations in Religion and Theology* 6 (2008): 242–4.

iii. Unpublished theses

Cook, Sarah Gibbard. 'A Political Biography of a Religious Independent: John Owen, 1616–1683'. PhD Thesis, Harvard University, 1972.

Leggett, Donald. 'John Owen as Religious Adviser to Oliver Cromwell 1649–1659'. MPhil Thesis, Cambridge University, 2006.

McGrath, Gavin. 'Puritans and the Human Will: Voluntarism Within Mid-Seventeenth Century English Puritanism as Seen in the Works of Richard Baxter and John Owen'. PhD Thesis, Durham, 1989.

Vose, Godfrey Noel. 'Profile of a Puritan: John Owen (1616–1683)'. PhD Thesis, State University of Iowa, 1963.

Williams, Lloyd Gwynn. '*Digitus Dei*: God and Nation in the Thought of John Owen: A Study in English Puritanism and Nonconformity, 1653–1683'. PhD Thesis, Drew University, NJ, 1981.

B. Works on Richard Baxter

i. Books

Beougher, Timothy. *Richard Baxter and Conversion: A Study of the Puritan Concept of Becoming a Christian*. Fearn: Mentor, 2007.

Black, J. William. *Reformation Pastors: Richard Baxter and the Ideal of the Reformed Pastor*. Bletchley: Paternoster, 2004.

Boersma, Hans. *A Hot Pepper Corn: Richard Baxter's Doctrine of Justification in Its Seventeenth-Century Context of Controversy*. Zoetmeer: Uitgeverij Boekencentrum, 1993.

Capill, Murray A. *Preaching With Spiritual Vigour: Including Lessons from the Life and Practice of Richard Baxter*. Fearn: Mentor, 2003.

Cooper, Tim. *Fear and Polemic in Seventeenth-Century England: Richard Baxter and Antinomianism*. Aldershot: Ashgate, 2001.

Keeble, N.H. *Richard Baxter: Puritan Man of Letters*. Oxford: Clarendon Press, 1982.

Lamont, William M. *Richard Baxter and the Millennium: Protestant Imperialism and the English Revolution*. London: Croom Helm, 1979.

Lim, Paul Chang-Ha. *In Pursuit of Purity, Unity, and Liberty: Richard Baxter's Ecclesiology in its Seventeenth-Century Context*. Leiden: Brill, 2004.

Nuttall, Geoffrey F. *Richard Baxter and Philip Doddridge: A Study in a Tradition*. London: Oxford University Press, 1951.

_____ . *Richard Baxter*. London: Thomas Nelson and Sons, 1965.

Orme, William. *The Life and Times of Richard Baxter With a Critical Examination of his Writings*. 2 vols. London: James Duncan, 1830.

Packer, J.I. *The Redemption and Restoration of Man in the Thought of Richard Baxter*. Carlisle: Paternoster Press, 2003.

Powicke, Frederick J. *A Life of the Reverend Richard Baxter 1615–1691*. London: Jonathan Cape Ltd., 1924.

_ . *The Reverend Richard Baxter Under the Cross (1662–1691)*. London: Jonathan Cape Ltd., 1927.

ii. Articles and chapters

[Anon.] 'Original Letters and Papers from Richard Baxter's MSS'. *Monthly Repository* 20 (1825): 287–9.

Bates, Ely. 'Baxter and Owen'. *The National Review* 15 (1862): 95–120.

Cooper, Tim. 'Richard Baxter and his Physicians'. *Social History of Medicine* 20 (March 2007): 1–19.

_____ . 'Why Did Richard Baxter and John Owen Diverge? The Impact of the First Civil War'. *Journal of Ecclesiastical History* 61 (2010): 496–516.

Derham, A. Morgan. 'Richard Baxter and the Oecumenical Movement'. *Evangelical Quarterly* 23 (1951): 96–115.

Fisher, George P. 'The Theology of Richard Baxter'. *Bibliotheca Sacra and American Biblical Repository* 9 (1852): 135–69.

Keeble, N.H. *'Loving & Free Converse': Richard Baxter in his Letters*. London: Dr Williams' Trust, 1991.

_____ . '"Take Heed of Being too Forward in Imposinge on Others": Orthodoxy and Heresy in the Baxterian Tradition'. In *Heresy, Literature and Politics in Early Modern English Culture*, ed. David Loewenstein and John Marshall, 282–305. Cambridge: Cambridge University Press, 2006.

Knox, R. Buick. 'Archbishop Ussher and Richard Baxter'. *Ecumenical Review* 12 (1959): 50–63.

Lamont, William M. 'False Witnesses? The English Civil War and English Ecumenism'. In *The Development of Pluralism in Modern Britain and France*, ed. Richard Bonney and D.J.B. Trim, vol. 1, 89–107. Oxford: Peter Lang, 2007.

Nuttall, Geoffrey F. 'The MS. of *Reliquiae Baxterianae* (1696)'. *Journal of Ecclesiastical History* 6 (1955): 73–9.

_____ . 'The Personality of Richard Baxter'. In *The Puritan Spirit: Essays and Addresses*, ed. Geoffrey F. Nuttall, 104–17. London: Epworth Press, 1967.

Trueman, Carl R. 'Richard Baxter on Christian Unity: A Chapter in the Enlightening of English Reformed Orthodoxy'. *Westminster Theological Journal* 61 (1999): 53–71.

_____ . 'Lewis Bayly (d.1631) and Richard Baxter (1615–1691)'. In *The Pietest Theologians: An Introduction to Theology in the Seventeenth and Eighteenth*

Centuries, ed. Carter Lindberg, 52–67. Malden, MA: Blackwell Publishing, 2005.

iii. Unpublished theses

Condie, Keith. 'The Theory, Practice, and Reception of Meditation in the Thought of Richard Baxter'. PhD Thesis, University of Sydney, 2010.

Douglas, Walter B.T. 'Richard Baxter and the Savoy Conference of 1661'. PhD Thesis, Manchester University, 1972.

McGrath, Gavin. 'Puritans and the Human Will: Voluntarism within Mid-Seventeenth Century English Puritanism as Seen in the Works of Richard Baxter and John Owen'. PhD Thesis, Durham, 1989.

C. Other Works

i. Books

Abernathy, George R. *The English Presbyterians and the Stuart Restoration, 1648–1663*. Transactions of the American Philosophical Society, New Series vol. 55, part 2. Philadelphia, PA: The American Philosophical Society, 1965.

Armstrong, Brian G. *Calvinism and the Amyraut Heresy: Protestant Scholasticism and Humanism in Seventeenth-Century France*. Madison, WI: University of Wisconsin Press, 1969.

Bartlett, Frederick C. *Remembering: A Study in Experimental and Social Psychology*. Cambridge: Cambridge University Press, 1932.

Benedict, Philip. *Christ's Churches Purely Reformed: A Social History of Calvinism*. New Haven, CT: Yale University Press, 2002.

Bosher, Robert S. *The Making of the Restoration Settlement: The Influence of the Laudians 1649–1662*. London: Dacre Press, 1951.

Brailsford, Mabel Richmond. *The Making of William Penn*. London: Longmans, Green and Co., 1933.

Bremer, Francis J. *Increase Mather's Friends: The Trans-Atlantic Congregational Network of the Seventeenth Century*. Worcester, MA: American Antiquarian Society, 1984.

_____ . *Congregational Communion: Clerical Friendship in the Anglo-American Puritan Community, 1610–1692*. Boston: Northeastern University Press, 1994.

Carlton, Charles. *Going to the Wars: The Experience of the British Civil Wars 1638–1651*. London: Routledge, 1992.

Clark, Henry W. *History of English Nonconformity: From Wyclif to the Close of the Nineteenth Century*. 2 vols. New York: Russell and Russell, 1965.

Cliffe, J.T. *Puritans in Conflict: The Puritan Gentry During and After the Civil Wars*. London: Routledge, 1988.

_____ . *The Puritan Gentry Besieged 1650–1700*. London: Routledge, 1993.

Clifford, Alan C. *Atonement and Justification: English Evangelical Theology 1640–1790 – An Evaluation*. Oxford: Clarendon Press, 1990.

_____ . *Amyraut Affirmed or 'Owenism, A Caricature of Calvinism': A Reply to Ian Hamilton's* Amyrauldianism – Is it a Modified Calvinism? Norwich: Charenton Reformed Publishing, 2004.

Coffey, John. *Politics, Religion and the British Revolutions: The Mind of Samuel Rutherford*. Cambridge: Cambridge University Press, 1997.

_____ . *Persecution and Toleration in Protestant England 1558–1689*. Harlow: Longman Pearson, 2000.

_____ . *John Goodwin and the Puritan Revolution: Religion and Intellectual Change in Seventeenth-Century England*. Woodbridge: Boydell Press, 2006.

Coleridge, Derwent, ed. *Notes on English Divines by Samuel Taylor Coleridge*. 2 vols. London: Edward Moxon, 1853.

Collins, Jeffrey R. *The Allegiance of Thomas Hobbes*. Oxford: Oxford University Press, 2005.

Como, David. *Blown by the Spirit: Puritanism and the Emergence of an Antinomian Underground in Pre-Civil-War England*. Stanford: Stanford University Press, 2004.

Cooper, James F. *Tenacious of Their Liberties*. Oxford: Oxford University Press, 1999.

Coward, Barry. *The Stuart Age: A History of England 1603–1714*. London: Longman, 1980.

_____ . *The Cromwellian Protectorate*. Manchester: Manchester University Press, 2002.

Dale, R.W. *History of English Congregationalism*. London: Hodder and Stoughton, 1907.

Davies, Godfrey. *The Restoration of Charles II 1658–1660*. San Marino, CA: Huntington Library, 1955.

Davies, Julian. *The Caroline Captivity of the Church: Charles I and the Remoulding of Anglicanism*. Oxford: Oxford University Press, 1992.

De Krey, Gary S. *London and the Restoration, 1659–1683*. Cambridge: Cambridge University Press, 2005.

de Sola Pinto, Vivian. *Peter Sterry: Platonist and Puritan*. Cambridge: Cambridge University Press, 1934.

Dixon, Philip. *Nice and Hot Disputes: The Doctrine of the Trinity in the Seventeenth Century*. London: T&T Clark, 2003.

Drysdale, A.H. *History of the Presbyterians in England: Their Rise, Decline, and Revival*. London: Publication Committee of the Presbyterian Church of England, 1889.

Field, David P. *Rigide Calvinism in a Softer Dresse: The Moderate Presbyterianism of John Howe, 1630–1705*. Edinburgh: Rutherford House, 2004.

Grainger, James. *A Biographical History of England*. London: T. Davies, 1769.

Greaves, Richard L. *Saints and Rebels: Seven Nonconformists in Stuart England*. Macon, GA: Mercer University Press, 1985.

Gribben, Crawford. *God's Irishmen: Theological Debates in Cromwellian Ireland*. Oxford: Oxford University Press, 2007.

Guthrie, William. *A General History of England from Edward the Sixth to the Restoration of King Charles the Second*. 4 vols. London: T. Waller, 1751.

Hardman Moore, Susan. *Pilgrims: New World Settlers and the Call of Home*. New Haven, CT: Yale University Press, 2007.

Helm, Paul. *Calvin and the Calvinists*. Edinburgh: Banner of Truth Trust, 1982.

Hetherington, W.M. *History of the Westminster Assembly of Divines*. Edinburgh: James Gemmell, 1890.

Hexter, J.H. *On Historians: Reappraisals of Some of the Makers of Modern History*. London: Collins, 1979.

Hill, Christopher. *The Experience of Defeat: Milton and Some Contemporaries*. London: Bookmarks, 1984.

Hughes, Ann. *Gangraena and the Struggle for the English Revolution*. Oxford: Oxford University Press, 2004.

Jones, R. Tudur. *Congregationalism in England 1662–1962*. London: Independent Press Ltd, 1962.

Jordan, W.K. *The Development of Religious Toleration in England*. Vol. 4, *From the Convention of the Long Parliament to the Restoration, 1640–1660: The Revolutionary Experiments and Dominant Religious Thought*. London: George Allen and Unwin Ltd, 1938.

Keeble, Neil. *The Literary Culture of Nonconformity in Later Seventeenth-Century England*. Athens, GA: University of Georgia Press, 1987.

Kendall, R.T. *Calvin and English Calvinism to 1649*. Oxford: Oxford University Press, 1979.

Lake, Peter. *The Boxmaker's Revenge: 'Orthodoxy', 'Heterodoxy', and the Politics of the Parish in Early Stuart London*. Stanford: Stanford University Press, 2001.

Lamont, William M. *Godly Rule: Politics and Religion 1603–60*. London: Macmillan and Co, 1969.

Little, Patrick and David L. Smith. *Parliaments and Politics*. Cambridge: Cambridge University Press, 2007.

Liu, Tai. *Puritan London: A Study of Religion and Society in the City Parishes.* Newark, DE: University of Delaware Press, 1986.

MacGillivray, Royce. *Restoration Historians and the English Civil War.* The Hague: Martinus Nijhoff, 1974.

MacLachlan, H. John. *Socinianism in Seventeenth-Century England.* Oxford: Oxford University Press, 1951.

Mallet, Charles Edward. *A History of the University of Oxford. Volume II. The Sixteenth and Seventeenth Centuries.* New York: Barnes and Noble, 1924.

Mayers, Ruth. *1659: The Crisis of the Commonwealth.* London: Royal Historical Society, 2004.

Mayfield, Noel Henning. *Puritans and Regicide: Presbyterian-Independent Differences over the Trial and Execution of Charles (I) Stuart.* Lanham, MD: University of America Press, 1988.

M'Crie, Thomas. *Annals of English Presbytery.* London: James Nisbet and Co, 1872.

Mortimer, Sarah. *Reason and Religion in the English Revolution: The Challenge of Socinianism.* Cambridge: Cambridge University Press, 2010.

Muller, Richard. *Post-Reformation Reformed Dogmatics: The Rise and Development of Reformed Orthodoxy, ca. 1520 to ca. 1725.* 4 vols. Grand Rapids, MI: Baker Academic, 2003.

Mulsow, Martin and Jan Rohls, eds. *Socinianism and Arminianism: Antitrinitarians, Calvinists and Cultural Exchange in Seventeenth-Century Europe.* Leiden: Brill, 2005.

Murphy, Andrew R. *Conscience and Community: Revisiting Toleration and Religious Dissent in Early Modern England and America.* University Park, PA: Pennsylvania State University Press, 2001.

Neal, Daniel. *The History of the Puritans, Or, Protestant Non-Conformists from the Death of King Charles I to the Act of Toleration by King William and Queen Mary, in the Year 1689.* 4 vols. Dublin: Brice Edmund, 1755.

Noll, Mark A. *America's God: From Jonathan Edwards to Abraham Lincoln.* Oxford: Oxford University Press, 2002.

Nuttall, Geoffrey F. *Visible Saints: The Congregational Way 1640–1660.* Oxford: Basil Blackwell, 1957.

Packer, J.I. *Among God's Giants: The Puritan Vision of the Christian Life.* Eastbourne: Kingsway Publications, 1991.

Paul, Robert S. *The Assembly of the Lord: Politics and Religion in the Westminster Assembly and the 'Grand Debate'.* Edinburgh: T&T Clark, 1985.

Piper, John. *Contending For Our All: Defending Truth and Treasuring Christ in the Lives of Athanasius, John Owen and J. Gresham Machen.* Wheaton, IL: Crossway Books, 2006.

Porter, Stephen. *Destruction in the English Civil Wars*. Gloucester: Allan Sutton Publishing, 1994.

Prior, Charles W.A. *Defining the Jacobean Church: The Politics of Religious Controversy, 1603–1625*. Cambridge: Cambridge University Press, 2005.

Royle, Trevor. *The British Civil War: The War of Three Kingdoms 1638–1660*. New York: Palgrave Macmillan, 2004.

Scott, David. *Politics and War in the Three Stuart Kingdoms, 1637–49*. Houndmills: Palgrave Macmillan, 2004.

Scott, Jonathan. *England's Troubles: Seventeenth-Century English Political Instability in European Context*. Cambridge: Cambridge University Press, 2000.

Shapiro, Barbara J. *John Wilkins 1614–1672*. Berkeley, CA: University of California Press, 1969.

Shaw, William A. *A History of the English Church During the Civil Wars and Under the Commonwealth 1640–1660*. London: Longmans, Green and Co., 1900.

Sherwood, Roy. *The Civil War in the Midlands 1642–1651*. Gloucester: Allan Sutton Publishing, 1992.

Spurr, John. *The Restoration Church of England, 1646–1689*. New Haven, CT: Yale University Press, 1991.

____. *English Puritanism 1603–1689*. Houndmills: Macmillan Press, 1998.

____. *England in the 1670s: 'This Masquerading Age'*. Malden, MA: Blackwell, 2000.

____. *The Post-Reformation: Religion, Politics and Society in Britain 1603–1714*. Harlow: Pearson Longman, 2006.

Sutherland, Martin. *Peace, Toleration and Decay: The Ecclesiology of Later Stuart Dissent*. Carlisle: Paternoster Press, 2003.

Toon, Peter. *The Emergence of Hyper-Calvinism in English Nonconformity 1689–1765*. London: The Olive Tree, 1967.

Tyacke, Nicholas. *Anti-Calvinists: The Rise of English Arminianism c.1590–1640*. Oxford: Oxford University Press, 1987.

Walsham, Alexandra. *Charitable Hatred: Tolerance and Intolerance in England, 1500–1700*. Manchester: Manchester University Press, 2006.

Watts, Michael R. *The Dissenters: From the Reformation to the French Revolution*. Oxford: Clarendon Press, 1978.

White, Peter. *Predestination, Policy and Polemic: Conflict and Consensus in the English Church from the Reformation to the Civil War*. Cambridge: Cambridge University Press, 1992.

Wilson, John F. *Pulpit in Parliament: Puritanism During the English Civil Wars 1640–1648*. Princeton, NJ: Princeton University Press, 1969.

Winship, Michael. *Making Heretics: Militant Protestantism and Free Grace in Massachusetts, 1636–1641*. Princeton, NJ: Princeton University Press, 2002.

Wood, A. Harold. *Church Unity Without Uniformity: A Study of Seventeenth-Century Church Movements and of Richard Baxter's Proposals for a Comprehensive Church*. London: Epworth Press, 1963.

Woolrych, Austin. *Commonwealth to Protectorate*. Oxford: Clarendon Press, 1982.

____ . *Britain in Revolution 1625–1660*. Oxford: Oxford University Press, 2002.

Worden, Blair. *The Rump Parliament 1648–1653*. Cambridge: Cambridge University Press, 1974.

Yule, George. *The Independents in the English Civil War*. Cambridge: Cambridge University Press, 1958.

____ . *Puritans in Politics: The Religious Legislation of the Long Parliament 1640–1647*. Appleford: Sutton Courtenay Press, 1981.

Zagorin, Perez. *How the Idea of Religious Toleration Came to the West*. Princeton, NJ: Princeton University Press, 2003.

ii. Articles and chapters

Beddard, R.A. 'Vincent Alsop and the Emancipation of Restoration Dissent'. *Journal of Ecclesiastical History* 14 (1973): 161–84.

_ . 'Restoration Oxford and the Remaking of the Protestant Establishment'. In *The History of the University of Oxford*, vol. 4, ed. Nicholas Tyacke, 802–62. Oxford: Clarendon Press, 1997.

Bolam, C.G. and Jeremy Goring. 'Presbyterians in Separation: The Cataclysm'. In *The English Presbyterians: From Elizabethan Puritanism to Modern Unitarianism*, ed. C. Gordon Bolam et al., 73–92. London: George Allen and Unwin Ltd, 1968.

Bradley, Rosemary. 'The Failure of Accommodation: Religious Conflicts between Presbyterians and Independents in the Westminster Assembly 1643–1646'. *Journal of Religious History* 12 (1982): 23–47.

Bremer, Francis J. 'The Puritan Experiment in New England, 1630–1660'. In *The Cambridge Companion to Puritanism*, ed. John Coffey and Paul C.H. Lim, 127–42. Cambridge: Cambridge University Press, 2008.

Capp, Bernard. 'Republican Reformation: Family, Community and the State in Interregnum Middlesex, 1649–60'. In *The Family in Early Modern England*, ed. Helen Berry and Elizabeth Foyster, 40–66. Cambridge: Cambridge University Press, 2007.

Clifford, Alan C. *Spotlight on Scholastics: Clarifying Calvinism: Responses to Carl Trueman, Richard Muller, Paul Helm*. Norwich: Charenton Reformed Publishing, 2005.

Coffey, John. 'Puritanism and Liberty Revisited: The Case for Toleration in the English Revolution'. *Historical Journal* 41 (1998): 961–85.

_____ . 'A Ticklish Business: Defining Heresy and Orthodoxy in the Puritan Revolution'. In *Heresy, Literature and Politics in Early Modern English Culture*, ed. David Loewenstein and John Marshall, 108–36. Cambridge: Cambridge University Press, 2006.

_____ . 'The Toleration Controversy During the English Revolution'. In *Religion in Revolutionary England*, ed. Christopher Durston and Judith Maltby, 42–68. Manchester: Manchester University Press, 2006.

Collins, Jeffrey R. 'The Church Settlement of Oliver Cromwell'. *History* 87 (2002): 18–40.

Collinson, Patrick. 'The Early Dissenting Tradition'. In *Godly People: Essays on English Protestantism and Puritanism*, ed. Patrick Collinson, 527–62. London: The Hambledon Press, 1983.

Cook, Sarah Gibbard. 'The Congregational Independents and the Cromwellian Constitutions'. *Church History* 46 (1977): 335–57.

Cragg, Gerald R. 'The Collapse of Militant Puritanism'. In *Essays in Modern English Church History in Memory of Norman Sykes*, ed. G.V. Bennett and J.D. Walsh, 76–103. London: Adam and Charles Black, 1966.

Cross, Claire. 'The Church in England 1646–1660'. In *The Interregnum: The Quest for Settlement 1646–1660*, ed. G.E. Aylmer, 99–120. London: Macmillan Press, 1972.

Davis, J.C. 'Cromwell's Religion'. In *Oliver Cromwell and the English Revolution*, ed. John Morrill, 181–208. London: Longman, 1990.

_____ . 'Religion and the Struggle for Freedom in the English Revolution'. *Historical Journal* 35 (1992): 507–30.

_____ . 'Living with the Living God: Radical Religion and the English Revolution'. In *Religion in Revolutionary England*, ed. Christopher Durston and Judith Maltby, 19–41. Manchester: Manchester University Press, 2006.

Donagan, Barbara. 'Did Ministers Matter? War and Religion in England, 1642–1649'. *Journal of British Studies* 33 (1994): 119–56.

Durston, Christopher. '"For the Better Humiliation of the People": Public Days of Fasting and Thanksgiving During the English Revolution'. *The Seventeenth Century* 7 (1992): 129–49.

_____ . 'Puritan Rule and the Failure of Cultural Revolution'. In *The Culture of English Puritanism, 1560–1700*, ed. Christopher Durston and Jacqueline Eales, 210–33. Houndmills: Macmillan Press, 1996.

Fincham, Kenneth. 'Oxford and the Early Stuart Polity'. In *The History of the University of Oxford*, vol. 4, ed. Nicholas Tyacke, 179–210. Oxford: Clarendon Press, 1997.

Fletcher, Anthony. 'Oliver Cromwell and the Godly Nation'. In *Oliver Cromwell and the English Revolution*, ed. John Morrill, 209–33. London: Longman, 1990.

Foster, Stephen. 'The Presbyterian Independents Exorcized: A Ghost Story for Historians'. *Past and Present* 44 (1969): 52–75.

Goldie, Mark. 'The Theory of Religious Intolerance in Restoration England'. In *From Persecution to Toleration: The Glorious Revolution and Religion in England*, ed. O.P. Grell, J.I. Israel and N. Tyacke, 331–68. Oxford: Clarendon Press, 1991.

Haller, William. 'The Word of God in the Westminster Assembly'. *Church History* 18 (1949): 199–219.

Harris, Tim. 'Introduction: Revising the Restoration'. In *The Politics of Religion in Restoration England*, ed. Tim Harris, Paul Seaward and Mark Goldie, 191–215. Oxford: Basil Blackwell, 1990.

Hexter, J.H. 'The Problem of the Presbyterian Independents'. *American Historical Review* 44 (1938): 29–49.

Hirst, Derek. 'The Failure of Godly Rule in the English Republic'. *Past and Present* 132 (1991): 33–66.

Hughes, Ann. 'The Frustrations of the Godly'. In *Revolution and Restoration: England in the 1650s*, ed. John Morrill, 70–90. London: Collins and Brown, 1992.

_____ . 'The Meanings of Religious Polemic'. In *Puritanism: Transatlantic Perspectives on Seventeenth-Century Anglo-American Faith*, ed. Francis J. Bremer, 201–29. Boston, MA: Massachusetts Historical Society, 1993.

_____ . '"Popular" Presbyterianism in the 1640s and 1650s: The Cases of Thomas Edwards and Thomas Hall'. In *England's Long Reformation 1500–1800*, ed. Nicholas Tyacke, 235–59. London: UCL Press, 1998.

_____ . '"The Public Profession of these Nations": The National Church in Interregnum England'. In *Religion in Revolutionary England*, ed. Christopher Durston and Judith Maltby, 93–114. Manchester: Manchester University Press, 2006.

Key, Newton E. 'Comprehension and the Breakdown of Consensus in Restoration Herefordshire'. In *The Politics of Religion in Restoration England*, ed. Tim Harris, Paul Seaward and Mark Goldie, 191–215. Oxford: Basil Blackwell, 1990.

Lamont, William. 'Authority and Liberty: Hobbes and the Sects'. In *Liberty, Authority, Formality: Political Ideas and Culture 1600–1900*, ed. John

Morrow and Jonathan Scott, 29–44. Charlottesville, VA: Imprint Academic, 2008.

Mahony, Michael. 'Presbyterianism in the City of London, 1645–1647'. *Historical Journal* 22 (1979).

Maltby, Judith. 'Suffering and Surviving: The Civil Wars, the Commonwealth and the Formation of "Anglicanism", 1642–60'. In *Religion in Revolutionary England*, ed. Christopher Durston and Judith Maltby, 158–80. Manchester: Manchester University Press, 2006.

McClelland, James L. 'Constructive Memory and Memory Distortions: A Parallel-Distributed Processing Approach'. In *Memory Distortion: How Minds, Brains, and Societies Reconstruct the Past*, ed. Daniel L. Schacter, 69–90. Cambridge, MA: Harvard University Press, 1995.

Morrill, John. 'The Church in England 1642–1649'. In *Reactions to the English Civil War 1642–1649*, ed. John Morrill, 89–114. London: Macmillan Press Ltd, 1982.

_____ . 'The Puritan Revolution'. In *The Cambridge Companion to Puritanism*, ed. John Coffey and Paul C.H. Lim, 67–88. Cambridge: Cambridge University Press, 2008.

Muller, Richard A. 'Calvin and the "Calvinists": Assessing the Continuities and Discontinuities Between the Reformation and Orthodoxy. Part One'. *Calvin Theological Journal* 30 (1995): 345–75.

_____ . 'Calvin and the "Calvinists": Assessing the Continuities and Discontinuities Between the Reformation and Orthodoxy. Part Two'. *Calvin Theological Journal* 31 (1996): 125–60.

Nobbs, D. 'Philip Nye on Church and State'. *Cambridge Historical Journal* 5 (1935): 41–59.

Nuttall, Geoffrey F. 'Presbyterians and Independents: Some Movements for Unity 300 Years Ago'. *Journal of the Presbyterian Historical Society* 10 (1952): 4–15.

_____ . 'The First Nonconformists'. In *From Uniformity to Unity 1662–1962*, ed. Geoffrey F. Nuttall and Owen Chadwick, 149–87. London: SPCK, 1962.

_____ . 'Richard Baxter and the Grotian Religion'. In *Reform and Reformation: England and the Continent c1500–c1750*, ed. Derek Baker, 245–50. Oxford: Ecclesiastical History Society, 1979.

Ost, James and Alan Costall. 'Misremembering Bartlett: A Study in Serial Reproduction'. *British Journal of Psychology* 93 (2002): 243–55.

Polizzotto, Carolyn. 'The Campaign against *The Humble Proposals* of 1652'. *Journal of Ecclesiastical History* 38 (1987): 569–81.

Ratcliff, E.C. 'The Savoy Conference and the Revision of the Book of Common Prayer'. In *From Uniformity to Unity 1662–1962*, ed. Geoffrey F. Nuttall and Owen Chadwick, 89–148. London: SPCK, 1962.

Schacter, Daniel L. 'Memory Distortion: History and Current Status'. In *Memory Distortion: How Minds, Brains, and Societies Reconstruct the Past*, ed. Daniel L. Schacter, 1–43. Cambridge, MA: Harvard University Press, 1995.

Schacter, Daniel L. and Donna Rose Addis. 'The Cognitive Neuroscience of Constructive Memory: Remembering the Past and Imagining the Future'. *Philosophical Transactions of the Royal Society B* 362 (2007): 773–86.

Sharpe, Kevin. 'Religion, Rhetoric, and Revolution in Seventeenth-Century England'. *Huntingdon Library Quarterly* 57 (1994): 255–65.

Simon, Walter. 'Comprehension in the Age of Charles II'. *Church History* 31 (1962): 440–448.

Smith, David L. 'Oliver Cromwell, the First Protectorate Parliament and Religious Reform'. *Parliamentary History* 19 (2000): 38–49.

Smith, Nigel. '"And if God was One of Us": Paul Best, John Biddle, and Anti-Trinitarian Heresy in Seventeenth-Century England'. In *Heresy, Literature and Politics in Early Modern English Culture*, ed. David Loewenstein and John Marshall, 160–184. Cambridge: Cambridge University Press, 2006.

Spurr, John. 'The Church of England, Comprehension and the Toleration Act of 1689'. *English Historical Review* 104 (1989): 927–46.

_____ . 'From Puritanism to Dissent'. In *The Culture of English Puritanism, 1560–1700*, ed. Christopher Durston and Jacqueline Eales, 234–65. Houndmills: Macmillan Press, 1996.

_____ . 'Religion in Restoration England'. In *A Companion to Stuart Britain*, ed. Barry Coward, 415–35. Malden, MA: Blackwell Publishing, 2003.

Thomas, Roger. 'Comprehension and Indulgence'. In *From Uniformity to Unity 1662–1962*, ed. Geoffrey F. Nuttall and Owen Chadwick, 189–253. London: SPCK, 1962.

_____ . 'The Break-Up of Nonconformity'. In *The Beginnings of Nonconformity*, ed. Geoffrey F. Nuttall et al., 33–60. London: James Clarke and Co, 1964.

_____ . 'Parties in Nonconformity'. In *The English Presbyterians: From Elizabethan Puritanism to Modern Unitarianism*, ed. C. Gordon Bolam et al., 93–112. London: George Allen and Unwin Ltd, 1968.

_____ . 'The Rise of the Reconcilers'. In *The English Presbyterians: From Elizabethan Puritanism to Modern Unitarianism*, ed. C. Gordon Bolam et al., 46–72. London: George Allen and Unwin Ltd, 1968.

Trevor-Roper, H.R. 'The Fast Sermons of the Long Parliament'. In *Religion, the Reformation and Social Change and Other Essays*, ed. H.R. Trevor-Roper, 294–344. London: Macmillan, 1967.

_____ . 'Three Foreigners: The Philosophers of the Puritan Revolution'. In *Religion, the Reformation and Social Change and Other Essays*, ed. H.R. Trevor-Roper, 237–93. London: Macmillan, 1967.

Trueman, Carl. 'Puritan Theology as Historical Event: A Linguistic Approach to the Ecumenical Context'. In *Reformation and Scholasticism: An Ecumenical Enterprise*, ed. Willem J. van Asselt and Eef Dekker, 253–75. Grand Rapids, MI: Baker Academic, 2001.

Tyacke, Nicholas. 'The Rise of Arminianism Reconsidered', *Past and Present* 115 (1987): 201–16.

_____ . 'The "Rise of Puritanism" and the Legalising of Dissent'. In *From Persecution to Toleration: The Glorious Revolution and Religion in England*, ed. O.P. Grell, J.I. Israel and N. Tyacke, 17–49. Oxford: Clarendon Press, 1991.

_____ . 'Religious Controversy'. In *The History of the University of Oxford*, vol. 4, ed. Nicholas Tyacke, 569–619. Oxford: Clarendon Press, 1997.

van Dixhoorn, Chad B. 'New Taxonomies of the Westminster Assembly (1643–52): The Creedal Controversy as Case Study'. *Reformation and Renaissance Review* 6 (2004): 82–106.

_____ . 'The Strange Silence of Prolocutor Twisse: Predestination and Politics in the Westminster Assembly's Debate over Justification', *Sixteenth Century Journal* 40 (2009): 395–418.

Vernon, Elliot. 'A Ministry of the Gospel: The Presbyterians During the English Revolution'. In *Religion in Revolutionary England*, ed. Christopher Durston and Judith Maltby, 115–36. Manchester: Manchester University Press, 2006.

Walsham, Alexandra. 'The Parochial Roots of Laudianism Revisited: Catholics, Anti-Calvinists and "Parish Anglicans" in Early Stuart England'. *Journal of Ecclesiastical History* 49 (1998): 620–51.

White, Peter. 'The Rise of Arminianism Reconsidered'. *Past and Present* 101 (1983): 34–54.

_____ . 'A Rejoinder'. *Past and Present* 115 (1987): 217–29.

Whiteman, Anne. 'The Restoration of the Church of England'. In *From Uniformity to Unity 1662–1962*, ed. Geoffrey F. Nuttall and Owen Chadwick, 19–88. London: SPCK, 1962.

Woolrych, A.H. 'The Good Old Cause and the Fall of the Protectorate'. *Cambridge Historical Journal* 13 (1957): 133–61.

Worden, Blair. 'Toleration and the Cromwellian Protectorate'. In *Persecution and Toleration: Papers Read at the Twenty-Second Summer Meeting and the*

Twenty-Third Winter Meeting of the Ecclesiastical Historical Society, ed. W.J. Sheils, 199–233. Studies in Church History Series, vol. 21. Oxford: Basil Blackwell, 1984.

_____ . 'Cromwellian Oxford'. In *The History of the University of Oxford*, vol. 4, ed. Nicholas Tyacke, 733–72. Oxford: Clarendon Press, 1997.

_____ . 'John Milton and Oliver Cromwell'. In *Soldiers, Writers and Statesmen of the English Revolution*, ed. Ian Gentles, John Morrill and Blair Worden, 243–64. Cambridge: Cambridge University Press, 1998.

Zakai, Avihu. 'Religious Toleration and Its Enemies: The Independent Divines and the Issue of Toleration During the English Civil War'. *Albion* 21 (1989): 1–33.

iii. Unpublished theses

Halcomb, Joel. 'A Social History of Congregational Religious Practice During the Puritan Revolution'. PhD Thesis, Cambridge University, 2009.

Lawrence, Thomas Michael. 'Transmission and Transformation: Thomas Goodwin and the Puritan Project 1600–1704'. PhD Thesis, Cambridge University, 2002.

Powell, Hunter. 'The Savoy Declaration'. MPhil Thesis, Cambridge University, 2008.

Index